ENCYCLOPAEDIA OF
CYBER LAWS AND CRIME

ENCYCLOPAEDIA
OF
CYBER LAWS AND CRIME

Vol. 3

Laws on E-Commerce

Edited by

S.R. Sharma

ANMOL PUBLICATIONS PVT. LTD.
NEW DELHI - 110 002 (INDIA)

ANMOL PUBLICATIONS PVT. LTD.
4374/4B, Ansari Road, Daryaganj
New Delhi - 110 002
Ph.: 23261597, 23278000
Visit us at: www.anmolpublications.com

Encyclopaedia of Cyber Laws and Crime

First Edition, 2003

ISBN 81-261-1432-0 (Set)

PRINTED IN INDIA

Published by J.L. Kumar for Anmol Publications Pvt. Ltd., New Delhi - 110 002 and Printed at Mehra Offset Press, Delhi.

CONTENTS

PREFACE

In the last years of the twentieth century a phenomenon has been witnessed which is likely to change the shape of human civilization. This is the explosion which has taken place in electronics and as a result of which there has been infinite expansion of knowledge that is commonly described as information explosion. The most astounding development in this area has been the geometric expansion of trade commerce entertainment and information jointly known as the internet or the web. The web accepts no restrictions of the country, race religion or country and has been totally responsible as a decisive factor in taking the world into what is now known as globalisation.

It is generally believed that a website is created every minute and along with its positive aspect it also brings about a new sense of responsibility. The free trade and commerce available through website in what is known as cyber space has also given birth to a mobile population where intent may be basically criminal. Thus we have hachers, virus carriers, sleepers and moles, who may constitute a real threat to the creativity of the web. There is, therefore, the eternal question of intellectual copyright and the policing of vast cyber space to protect and maintain what manhood can truly achieve.

Consequently the TRAI Act 1997 has been enacted by the Indian parliament in the 48th year of Republic of India on 28th March 1997 to provide for the establishment of the Telecom Regulatory Authority of India (TRAI) to regulate the telecommunication services and for matters connected therewith are incidental thereto.

As per Section 11 (2) of the TRAI Act TRAI is empowered to fix/revise tariff for various telecom services provided in India and service providers including the Department service provisions have to implement the tariffs, notified by the TRAI as per provisions of law.

The TRAI has been mandated to fix/revise tariff for various telecom services by virtue of section 11 (2) of TRAI Act.

The Encyclopaedia tries to cover as many laws as possible, promulgated by various countries and unions of countries like the European Union in this area to give a comprehensive and comparative view of CYBER Law.

The editor has no claims to originality and has simply compiled and edited the material collected from various sources. In view of the English language being the medium most of the material has been collected from American, British and Indian sources.

The editor is grateful to the Librarians of the library of the Supreme Court, the Indian Law Institute and the Ministry of Law, Justice and Company Affairs, for their kind assistance in locating the material from various sources.

The editor is specifically grateful to Shri Jawahar Lal Kumar, Managing Director, Anmol Publications Pvt. Ltd., New Delhi for venturing to publish the Encyclopaedia on Cyber Laws.

—Dr. S.R. Sharma

1 THE INTERNET: AN INTRODUCTION

WHAT IS THE INTERNET?

Using the Internet for the first time can be like travelling in a foreign country - the language, the symbols, the culture and customs are all quite different from any previously encountered. It can be quite intimidating at first but eventually the language and customs will become familiar, everyday and even enjoyable. This chapter is designed to introduce the new user to some of the terms that they will encounter when using the Internet for the first time. We look at the World Wide Web (WWW) and email and we also attempt to demystify some of the jargon and three-letter acronyms that new users will encounter in their ventures on-line.

The hype that surrounds the Internet today is not due to the underlying technology, important though it may be. A key reason is its ease of use. Compared with most other computer applications, using the Internet is incredibly easy. Any computer user who is reasonably familiar with how a personal computer (PC) is operated, can quickly get started given an Internet connection and the appropriate software. For most users, 10 minutes of training is all that is required. Another key reason is the wealth of information available over the Internet. Indeed, it would be hard to think of a topic that is not represented. What is more, new sources of information appear every day.

A Definition of the Internet

Although there is no official definition of the Internet, most industry commentators would agree upon a description such as a public international 'network of networks' (see Figure 1.1). Information technologists will quickly introduce the notion of networks into any conversation. It sounds complicated but need not be. On a conceptual level it is simply a group of computers that are physically linked together with cabling. In addition, all of these computers must be running software that allows them to recognise that they are all part of the same network. It is unclear exactly how many networks are attached to the Internet but current estimates (or rather, educated guesswork) suggest that over 150 million people have access either from home or work and this number is growing exponentially all the time.[1]

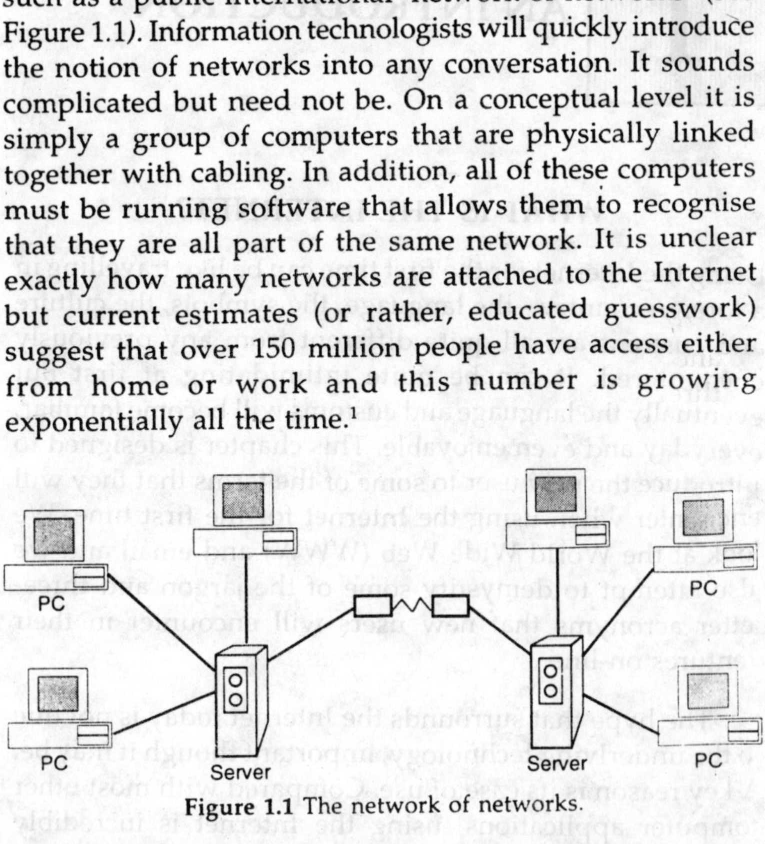

Figure 1.1 The network of networks.

The definition of the Internet as a network of networks has been further complicated by the recent development of 'intranets' and so-called 'extranets'. Intranets are internal company networks which use the same software as one would use to access the World Wide Web but are configured to prohibit public access. Instead, the Internet technology is used *within* the organisation. Intranets may or may not be connected to the Internet; they do not need to be connected in order to function. To make matters even more complicated, the term 'extranet' has also been introduced. Extranets, like intranets, use the same technology as the Internet but are set up so that corporations can securely share data with trusted outside users such as business partners, resellers or, in the case of law firms, with counsel or clients. Perhaps the most famous early example of an extranet is the Federal Express web site that allows customers to track the progress of their shipments. Both intranets and extranets are as important to the average lawyer as the public Internet. Thus, although not strictly related to the title, this book considers the business and technical implications of all three Internet-based applications: public web sites, intranets and extranets. After all, the only difference between the three different systems is the audience.

A 'Network of Networks'?

It is impossible to depict accurately what the Internet looks like topographically. Any map would be indecipherable as there are so many networks involved.[2] And any map would be immediately out of date. Thus the Internet is usually represented diagramatically as a cloud with the hypothetical user on one side and an information source on the other (see Figure 1.2).

Not surprisingly, the reality is more complicated than this. If we consider the network of a hypothetical corporation, each department may have its own network that allows its users to share files and perhaps to share the use of printers. Such departmental networks may be connected together to form a so-called 'Wide Area Network' (or WAN) across departments or between geographically disparate offices (see Figure 1.3). These Wide Area Networks may, in turn, be linked to form a global private network of networks. This matrix-type arrangement is a microcosm of the physical skeleton of the Internet, (the term 'Internet' being an abbreviation of the word 'internetworking').

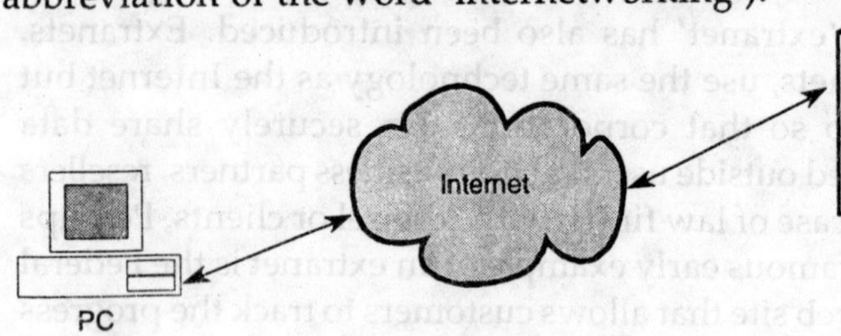

Figure 1.2 The Internet cloud diagram.

Who Owns the Internet?

The most straightforward answer to the question of who owns the Internet is that no one does. There is no single body that controls Internet activities. It is simply out there and is virtually impossible to 'switch off'. The Internet is the first global institution that has no government. Networks within different countries are funded and managed according to local policies and laws. This is both one of the Internet's greatest strengths and one of its main weaknesses. Ownership is distributed between countries

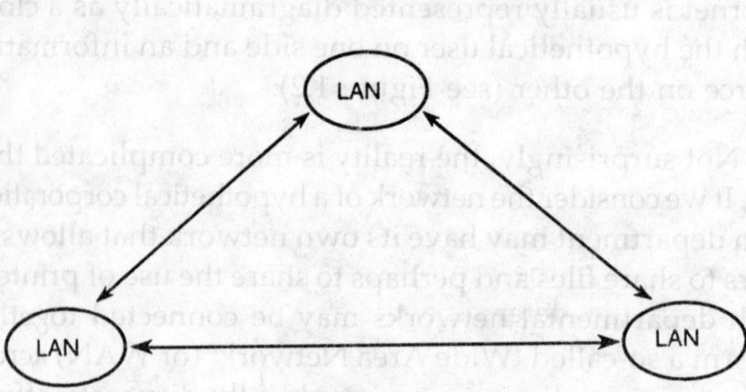

Figure 1.3 A WAN consists of linked LANs.

and their own governments, corporations, universities and the major telecommunications (telecoms) utilities. Each individual computer attached to the Internet will be owned by a corporation, firm or individual. Telecoms utilities own the physical wires over which dala is transferred. Internet Service Providers (so-called ISPs), telecoms utilities or universities will own the data-routing equipment. Thus a wide variety of organisations each play a part in 'owning' the Internet.

How is the Internet Managed?

Each network that is attached to the Internet, whether commercial, academic, military or government will have its own user policies and procedures. Thus there is some measure of localised regulation but such policies and procedures cannot be enforced upon other areas of the Internet beyond the control of an individual organisation.

In addition, there are a large number of official and unofficial interest and pressure groups competing to control the way in which the Internet is used. These include ISPs, software developers, Internet users, governments, think-tanks, free speech advocates, pressure groups advocating censorship, information scientists, information providers (both commercial and noncommercial), network administrators and corporations interested in the commercial potential but concerned about the legal liabilities. Over the past-six years, the Internet has become the focus, not only for computer programmers but all manner of interest groups. In particular, the major software manufacturers such as Microsoft, Oracle, Sun and Netscape now have significant influence over the future direction of the Internet partly because they determine the functionality of the access tools.

Furthermore, the Internet benefits from the existence

of a number of organisational bodies for technical and engineering aspects. One of the most important is the Internet Society: 'a professional membership society with more than 150 organisational and 6,000 individual members in over 100 countries... The Society's individual and organisational members are bound by a common stake in maintaining the viability and global scaling of the Internet. They comprise the companies, government agencies, and foundations that have created the Internet and its technologies as well as innovative new entrepreneurial organisations contributing to maintain that dynamic'.[3] The Internet Society incorporates the Internet Engineering Task Force (IETF): 'a large open international community of network designers, operators, vendors, and researchers concerned with the evolution of the Internet architecture and the smooth operation of the Internet'.[4] In addition there is the World Wide Web Consortium[5] (W3C) based in Geneva which is an international industry consortium founded to develop common protocols for the evolution of the World Wide Web. These bodies are the closest the Internet has to an executive. However, most users will have virtually nothing to do with them on a day-to-day basis. Instead, as individual users, management of the Internet will be governed by the rules and regulations laid down by their ISP. For more information on the practicalities of getting on-line.

What the Internet is Not

Information providers such as CompuServe, America On-Line (marketed as AOL in Europe) and until quite recently the Microsoft Network (MSN), offer users access to electronically 'ring-fenced' information resources in return for a monthly fee. Many people mistakenly believe that such services *are* the Internet - they are not. Although these information providers now offer users *access* to the

Internet (indeed, AOL is the largest world-wide access provider) they use proprietary software. There are also a large number of commercial databases accessible over the Internet such as Dow Jones, Westlaw and perhaps best known within the UK legal context, LEXIS-NEXIS. However, the Internet only serves as an access point for such services and, unlike much of the content one finds on the Internet, these services continue to be fee-based.

THE TWO KEY INTERNET SERVICES

Although there are a large number of different services available, by far the most important to most Internet users are the World Wide Web and email. Amongst the also-rans, there are services such as FTP, Usenet, Telnet, MUDs, Talk and Internet Relay Chat (IRC). These services are of minor importance to most users and are not addressed in this chapter. Most lawyers can manage quite happily with a basic understanding of just the World Wide Web and email.

1. The World Wide Web

Arguably the most important Internet service, the World Wide Web (known as 'WWW' or 'the Web') can be simply defined as a system of linking together millions of electronic documents ('web pages') on millions of computers ('web sites') across the Internet using highlighted links. Thus a web site is simply a collection of web pages. Although the World Wide Web and the Internet are terms that are used almost interchangeably, the Web is actually a subset of the Internet. However, like the Internet, no one body owns the Web. Individuals, organisations and corporations are each responsible for the documents they author and publish on the Web. Five million web sites were counted as at April 1999 (see the Netcraft Web Server Survey at http://www.netcraft.co.uk/survey/).

Origins of the Web

Since the end of the Second World War, scientists have imagined a seamless library where they could interact with the sum of human knowledge. An article by Vannevar Bush, published in 1945, offered a startlingly relevant vision of the World Wide Web, at that time still some 40 years away. Bush envisaged a machine called the 'Memex', a 'device in which an individual stores all his books, records, and communications, und which is mechanised so that it may be consulted with exceeding speed and flexibility' (Bush, 1945), and in addition would allow the user to follow his or her own associative trail of thought. This is very much the model of the Web except that in addition, the user is also able to look at electronic documents provided by others. The Memex concept was developed further 30 years later by Dr Theodore (Ted) Nelson who coined the term 'hypertext' to describe 'a body of written or pictorial material interconnected in a complex way that it could not be conveniently represented on paper. It may contain summaries or maps of its contents and their interrelations; it may contain annotations, additions and footnotes from scholars who have examined it' (Nelson, 1965).

In the 1980s, hypertext became a small branch of computing and was used in various different applications. Many readers will probably have already come across hypertext even if they have not used the Web. It is heavily used in the Help files that form part of Microsoft's Office applications such as Word and Excel. The next significant step towards Bush's vision came in 1989 with the development of a prototype World Wide Web by Tim Berbers-Lee and colleagues who, at the time, were working at CERN (the European Particle Physics Laboratory) in Geneva. Berners-Lee was interested in finding an easier method of sharing information between academic researchers. The elegant solution that he and his colleagues developed was not to impose standards on hardware or software (which is impossible given the number of different machine types and operating systems currently available), but on the data itself. The standard that was developed is called Hypertext Mark Up Language (or HTML) and is the 'glue' of the World Wide Web.

Why has the Web become so important? Partly it is because it is not owned by anyone. The technology is 'open' - users are not locked into one supplier, whether IBM, Microsoft or any of the other large IT suppliers. Web software is low cost. Much of it is free. Users require little training and applications can be built very quickly. Perhaps most importantly, it is because the software is simple to install and run. However, this is looking at the Web from a purely technical perspective.

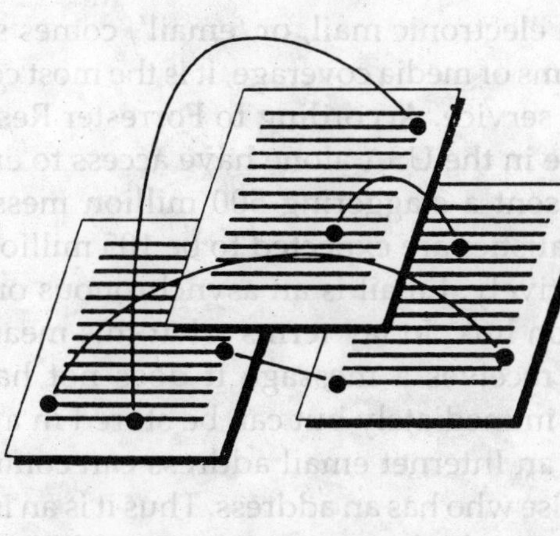

Figure 1.4 Hypertext linking.

From a user's point of view, the way in which the Web works is intuitive. Authors of web documents are able to create links between concepts and create trails of associations between ideas, whether within the same document or between different documents. These documents can be owned by the same author or they can be owned by any other web document author. The Web protects the user from the need to know where information is stored. Using the Web, the author can offer the user electronic versions of features more usually found in paper documents - footnotes, cross-references, citations, definitions, and so forth. The Web should be of particular value to lawyers because it mimics the way in which lawyers perform their research. For example, in the common law system, a decision of the Court does not exist in isolation. Instead, it is part of a matrix of other cases each referring to another, e.g. case A refers to case B which in turn refers to case C. In many ways the Web is like a giant series of electronic footnotes. The Web is a technology that should appeal to the way in which lawyers think about information.

2. *Electronic Mail*

Although electronic mail, or 'email', comes second to the Web in terms of media coverage, it is the most commonly used Internet service. According to Forrester Research, 47 million people in the USA alone have access to email, and in 1998 they sent a staggering 500 million messages. By 2002, these statistics are expected to be 105 million and 1.5 billion respectively. Email is an asynchronous one-to-one communication link. In lay terms what this means is that when a user receives a message it does not have to be responded to immediately but can be stored in a mailbox. Anyone with an Internet email address can communicate with anyone else who has an address. Thus it is an incredibly convenient method of communicating with friends and work colleagues whether in the next office or thousands of miles away.

Email can also be used for one-to-many communication with groups of like-minded people. By submitting their email address to electronic discussion groups, users can receive messages daily on topics of interest from like-minded individuals. They can also reply to messages which are, in turn, delivered to the mailboxes of all other individuals who have also subscribed to the discussion list. Although these are not particularly popular in legal practice, they are very popular in academia. For example, the UK Higher Education community enjoys the benefit of a service called Mailbase[6] which offers academics and students access to many hundreds, if not thousands, of discussion lists on a wide variety of discipline-specific issues. In the UK there are about 10 academic law-related discussion lists while in the USA there are many hundreds.[7]

Understanding Pull and Push

As communication methods, the Web and email work in fundamentally different ways. Nicholas Negroponte, Head of thc Media Labs at Massachusetts Institute of Technology (MIT), defined these different forms of interaction by coining the terms 'pull' and 'push'. The Web is a 'pull' technology whereas email is a 'push' technology (Negroponte, 1995).

Pull is an *active* use of Internet technology controlled by the user. For example, web users browse web sites by pulling pages from a site and then make decisions about what they would like to read next by clicking on hypertext links and pulling yet further pages from web sites. Once a web site is built, web visitors simply read what they want to read on the site.

Push is a *passive* activity. It is effectively browsing in reverse; other Internet users have to initiate the communication. When a user *sends* email information is pushed.'The user cannot demand to *receive* or 'pull' email.

In 1996, there was much discussion in the Internet press about using push-type technology more effectively.

Products such as PointCast and BackWeb came to symbolise the potential revolution in the delivery of information. It was claimed that these and other products like them would bring order to the chaos of the Web by allowing the user to specify in advance what web pages they wanted to view and have them delivered automatically. Delivery would occur either as specified by the user or as and when changes were made to the content. *Wired,* the self-proclaimed magazine for the new media 'digirati', told its audience to 'kiss your browser goodbye' as 'broader and deeper new interfaces for electronic media are being born' (Kelly and Wolf, 1997). However, these babies were stillborn -push technology failed to take off and the push bubble had burst by the end of 1997. As is so often the case with new technologies, the software failed to live up to increasingly unrealistic expectations. Nevertheless, the concepts of push and pull are still with us and they are useful terms to define services on the Internet.

WHERE IS THE INTERNET GOING?

The answer to this depends on to whom one speaks. For the IT industry, the Internet and in particular the Web, is the future of computing: any software that does not or cannot be made to interact with the Internet has no long-term future. For the traditional media industries such as television and radio, the Internet is a new business medium: an opportunity to extend the brand name and sell existing and future products. For many retail organisations, the Web is a new marketplace, the virtual High Street. For the individual, the Internet is a source of entertainment, education and increasingly valuable information on any topic one can imagine.

The Web is becoming a two-way medium; at its lowest level, users can now input information through the use of on-line forms using specially written scripts. It is now quite common for web sites to invite users to fill in forms in order to take part in surveys or register preferences. But these are only the first steps. Web developers are no longer interested in developing web pages. Instead, they want to develop web applications: applications that have all the functionality of traditional computer programs, but that run across the Internet. The Web can then be used for banking, for buying books, airline tickets, or even for the delivery of legal services. The Web is going to be everywhere. Personal computers are becoming increasingly cheaper and in some cases are available free of charge - see http://www.free-pc.com, an organisation that will provide a free sub-$ 1,000 near state-of-the-art computer and Internet access in exchange for permission to target advertising messages to machines even when they are not on-line. At the same time, forward-thinking manufacturers of digital personal assistants, watches, and even fridges and microwave ovens are all rushing to embed the Web into their products. An article in *PC Week* in September 1998 highlighted a Japanese company that is building 'intelligence' into their latest microwave ovens so that users can check their email, access the Web and perform basic banking operations. Over the next few years, technology will become pervasive. All manner of consumer products will be connected to the Internet.

The Internet is a heaving mass of technology, being driven at a frightening pace by a combination of forces. The real innovators are a relatively small number of technology companies, all hoping to 'do a Netscape' (or a Yahoo!) - to see their companies floated on NASDAQ.[8] The giants of the computing industry, such as Microsoft, Oracle, Sun and IBM, each with differing views and strong product portfolios, are all lining up in partnership and in competition with one another. The Internet is the new technology battleground. Cynics say that Microsoft would like the Internet to be merely an extension of their Windows environment. Oracle, Sun and IBM would like to use the Internet to wrest control of desktop computing out of the hands of Microsoft. For many of these companies, the Internet is the single biggest business opportunity since the development of the PC. It is very difficult to see where and when the momentum will finally stop. However, only when technical standards on information encryption, electronic commerce, credit card validation, etc., are decided, will the Internet evolve into the much-trumpeted and over-hyped information superhighway. Although maturing at an incredible speed, the current shape of the Internet is still quite immature. To use another scientific analogy, it is as though we have landed on the moon for the first time but have only explored one crater. There is so much more exploration to be done.

Some of the Problems to be Overcome

Standards

Part of the problem is that a small number of truly global IT companies have everything to gain by having their standards embedded into every piece of software used to access and navigate the Internet. They have often spent millions of dollars in research and therefore, quite naturally, they are loath to see their investment wasted. Thus it will probably be several years before we see the Internet as a fully mature institution.

Information Overload

Another major problem is information overload. In the words of Mitch Kapor, the founder of Lotus Corporation, 'trying to get information off of the Internet is like trying to get a drink from a firehose'. Reading one's email, belonging to a few discussion lists and exploring web sites of interest can be a full-time job in itself. There is also a desperate need for *quality* rather than quantity of information.

Tim Berners-Lee believes that the next task is to create order out of the chaos:

> Whereas phase one of the Web put all the accessible information into one huge book, if you like, in phase two we will turn all the accessible data into one huge database. This will have a tremendous effect on e-commerce. You could say, 'Find me a company selling a half-inch bulb to these specifications,' and a program will go through all the catalogs - which may be presented in very different formats - and figure out which fields are equivalent and then build a database and do a comparison very quickly. Then it will just go ahead and order it. It would be a real mistake for anyone to think the Internet is done or the World Wide Web is done. We're just at the start of these technologies, and there's a huge amount of research to be done.
>
> *Berners-Lee, 1998*

Political and Legal Issues

The Internet has also become a political football - the US Government and the European Union both have strong views on how the Internet should develop and be managed. There are also a significant number of legal issues that need to be resolved. These issues are not addressed in this book. However, it is important that the average Internet user is aware that they exist.

Summary

From being a quirky communications backwater for academic researchers and US government organisations, the Internet has become a global mainstream business and entertainment tool. The development of the first commercially available web browser (Mosaic) in 1993, has made the Internet relevant to anyone and everyone who wants to access information. Even Microsoft, an organisation acclaimed for its supposed foresight on what consumers want from technology, seriously misjudged the importance of the Web. But with popularity has come commercialisation and privatisation. Commercial organisations of all descriptions, from the smallest two-man start-up to the largest telecommunications groups have poured resources into their own Internet ventures. This has significantly changed the culture of the Internet.

We have come a long way in a short space of time but we are still some way from the much-hyped information superhighway, where every house, school, library, shop and office will have high-speed connections to the vast resources of the Internet as well as 'access to video-on-demand, on-line shopping for everything from the holiday of a lifetime to a loaf of bread and interactive virtual reality games. Indeed, the hype surrounding the Internet has made the term 'information superhighway' one of the most woeful cliches of the 1990s. Yet, given the rate of change on the Internet in the past five years, the deregulation of telecommunications world-wide, the establishment of global satellite networks[9] to carry Internet data traffic, and the enormously attractive commercial potential, such a scenario is likely to be with us much sooner than we expect.

FURTHER READING

Kennedy, AJ. (1999). *The Rough Guide to the Internet 1999*. Rough Guides, London.

Up-to-date, opinionated and written in plain English. Essential reading.

Krol, E. and P. Ferguson (1995). *The Whole Internet for Windows 95: User's Guide & Catalog*. O'Reilly and Associates, Cambridge,

Mass. *A very good starter book on the Internet although getting a little dated.*

NOTES

1. See http://www.nua.ie/surveys/. See also surveys by the Georgia Institute of Technology http://www.gvu.gatech.edu/usersurveys/ which are widely quoted in the media.
2. For maps of networks that make up the Internet, readers are referred to *An Atlas of Cyberspaces* at: http://www.geog.ucl.ac.uk/casa/martin/atlas/isp_maps.html
3. Quotation from the Internet Society web site - http://www.isoc.org/isoc/
4. http://www.ietf.org/overview.html
5. http://www.w3c.org
6. http://www.mailbase.ac.uk
7. A full list of US law-related discussion lists can be found at http://www.lib.uchicago.edu/~llou/lawlists/lawlists.txt
8. The stock market favoured by many new technology start-up companies. Based in New York and available on the Web at http://www.nasdaq.com
9. In 1998, the Iridium global phone network was completed. See http://www.iridium.com for more information. In 2002, the Teledesic global Internet network will be operational. See http://www.teledesic.com for more information.

BIBLIOGRAPHY

Berners-Lee, Tim (1998). An Interview with Tim Berners-Lee', *Los Angeles Times,* 8 June.

Bush, Vannevar (1945). 'As We May Think', The Atlantic Monthly, July. An electronic copy can be found at http://www.press.umich edu/jep/works/vbush/vbush.shtml *The Economist* (1998). The future of computing after the PC', 12-18 September p.93.

Kelly, Kevin and Wolf, Gary (1997). 'PUSH!. Kiss your browser goodbye: The radical future of media beyond the Web'. *Wired.* Issue 5.03, March. Conde Nast Publications.

Negroponte, Nicholas (1995). *Being Digital.* Hodder & Stoughton, London.

Nelson, T. (I965). *A File Structure for the Complex, The Changing and The Indeterminate.* ACM 20th National Conference.

2 ON-LINE MARKETING

A Law Firm Web Site—Not if But When!

Some lawyers may take the view that since their potential viewing audience might not have access to the Internet, the establishment of a web site would be a colossal waste of time and resources. That said, whether we like it or not,' according to some informed estimates, 33 per cent of the UK population and 10 per cent of the world's population will have their own Internet connection by the year 2000.[1] There will be the equivalent of an Internet connection for every man, woman and child on the planet by 2003 - through our PCs at work, our televisions at home, even the microwave and the fridge. The Internet, the Web and electronic commerce will become ubiquitous within a few short years, as common as the telephone or television. Moreover, despite the apparent absence of agreed security standards, US media reports suggest that e-commerce is already beginning to take off, at least in the USA. As the Internet becomes the global marketplace, law firms simply cannot afford not to have their own presence. Indefinite delay is not an option.

If, on the other hand, a web site is going to be used to demonstrate a breadth of services, to offer new ways of communicating with clients and contacts and to create a virtual community of shared interests (which may in turn lead to new clients and new instructions) then it will immediately prove a very worthwhile and cost-effective venture. A web site of this nature should also be seen as a stepping stone towards delivering full legal services over the Internet.

Merits of Different Media

A web site is not the only means by which a law firm can market its services. A web site should complement and work in tandem with existing marketing methods. Traditionally, law firms have tended towards glossy paper-based brochures. Paper-based products should not be abandoned: paper is a very good technology - it requires no specific hardware or software, it is flexible and portable (you can read it in the bath), it is more durable than digital media and, most importantly, everyone knows how to use it. However, glossy brochures are often immediately out of date, and paper cannot incorporate multimedia - sound or video clips. It only has one (linear) navigation option and it has no search mechanisms (other than the index one finds al the back of a book, and the average law firm marketing brochure does not include an index). CD-ROMs can incorporate all of the above. But CD-ROMs also have their own limitations: while replication is cheap, distribution is costly, errors are expensive to rectify, inclusion of new information involves a reprinting and replication of a new batch and the production cycle is fairly long. That said, in terms of integrating complex multimedia capabilities such as video clips, CD-ROMs are still a far better medium than a web site (at least, for the time being). The advantage is that CD-ROMs are usually run locally (i.e. from the user's PC). This means that access is faster than using the Internet. In addition, video clips require a constant connection level with the user's PC. This cannot be guaranteed on the Internet, with the result that video via the Web is usually jerky and difficult to watch. Distribution of information via a web site is cheap, errors can be rectified and new information added very quickly and the production cycle (from creation of text to publication) is swift. Unlike paper and CD-ROM, there is no marginal cost as the audience for the web site increases. If sufficient resources are made available, a high-quality web site can be put together in a couple of weeks. Another benefit of having a web site is the ability to link sites together. If a particular law firm has a site, other sites can link to it and vice versa. Linking up sites increases the likelihood of visitors to the site.

Perhaps the biggest selling point is distribution. The Web has a global reach. It doesn't matter where the web user or where the web site is. Many firms would gladly accept instructions from all areas of a country if they only had the resources to make their services known. Normally this involves the establishment of new offices and the development of a new client base over a number of years. This is an expensive and time-consuming operation. The cost of setting up profitable new offices in every major conurbation in the country is so prohibitive that few firms even dream of such a vision. By contrast, through the establishment of a web site, a firm has the potential to reach a global Internet audience of over 100 million people. No conference, seminar, or brochure will ever have this incredible potential reach. The ability to reach a geographically dispersed audience may be particularly useful if the firm in question has a niche practice. By setting up a web site, a two-partner firm in Carlisle can promote its services everywhere from Cornwall to Kent and northwards, and for that matter, to potential clients from Arizona to Zimbabwe. Admittedly, there are a number of legal services where there is a clear benefit for the client in having a legal advisor nearby - for example where attendance at local courts will be required or where the client might wish to speak with their legal advisor face to face on a regular basis. However, there is an equally large number of legal services (from residential conveyancing and probate law through to some of the most complex commercial arrangements) where the client simply does not care where their legal advisors are based—all they care about is getting the highest quality service at a reasonable price. The Web offers law firms this business opportunity.

THE '3 CS': CONTENT, COMMUNICATION AND COMMUNITY

This chapter offers a different view on how law firms might use the medium of the Web more effectively, without necessarily selling legal services explicitly over the Web. There are three essential elements of an effective information-based web site: content, communication and community. It is hoped that readers will recognise these elements underpinning all of the examples in this chapter. Good design allowing for easy navigation is also an essential ingredient. A poorly designed web site creates inconvenience and frustration for the user. A 'site should strive for simplicity and easy navigation. Jakob Nielsen, the web design guru, explains:

> If you have a bad user interface or if it's slow to download, that's the same as saying, 'No we have a store but it's not on the ground floor. It's on the 25th floor of a skyscraper. So only people who happen to go there will see it, it's open but only on Thursdays from three to four, and the salespeople don't want to talk to customers.'[2]

Since the focus here is on information-based web sites in the legal context, web site design is not addressed in this book.

Content

On the Internet, to borrow the sound bite, 'content is

king'. A quality, information-based web site starts with good content: that is, material focused on the needs of its audience. If there is nothing of substance on a site, no amount of clever programming gimmicks will disguise this fact. On the Web, there is a scarcity of *quality* information resources not information resources *per se.* The fundamental principle that all web developers should remember is that the main commodity now in limited supply is the user's attention span. Thus the overriding need to is put valuable information onto the user's screen as quickly as possible.

Communication

Publishing high-quality content on a web site is an essential ingredient for success but it does not automatically create an award-winning site. In addition to content there must be elements of communication, that is, dialogue or interactivity. The most successful information-based web sites encourage communication. This may be via subscriptions to email newsletters or via discussion forums. Such sites may also permit users to discover something new by asking questions or filling in forms on the site or by interacting with the site. They may also integrate email news facilities so that information is delivered directly to the user rather than making the user seek out information on the site.

Community

If the two concepts of content and communication are intelligently combined and nurtured, the site will develop as a virtual community and it is this sense of community that will sustain the web site over the longer term. Of course, this is easier said than done.

BUILDING AN OFFICE IN CYBERSPACE

While indefinite delay is not an option, the creation of a web site should not be rushed. It is better to have no web site at all than have a bad web site. The decision should have sound business justifications and be based on a sound vision of what the firm intends to achieve from its establishment. Just as using the Internet for the first time can be likened to travelling in a foreign land, the decision to establish a web site should be akin to establishing an office in a foreign country. There are clear parallels in terms of what is required; there should be people within the firm who understand what can and, importantly, what cannot be achieved from establishing a presence. Also, there should be clear and precise business targets with time scales attached.

Thus the first question should be: what is the purpose of the web site, what does the firm wish to achieve with it? Even non-transactional web sites (that is, sites that offer information as opposed to legal services) can be used in a variety of different ways: to gain new contacts, to develop new audiences for services, to gain information and understanding about both existing and potential customers/clients or to obtain new instructions that can be dealt with in the traditional way. Unfortunately, experience is showing that strategies are rarely so well thought out. Instead, most law firm web sites appear to exist simply because someone in a law firm decided that since every other law firm was putting one together, they should have one too. This 'me too' attitude has replaced any semblance of strategic thinking. Quite simply, this is not a sufficient justification for what will become yet another ongoing IT cost. If a law firm web site does none of the things described, but instead simply creates a library of electronic brochures it may serve little purpose other than to entertain and edify the Managing Partners. Such sites should not be built. Pleasing the senior Partnership may be a desirable goal in theory, but it is hardly an adequate business justification. Such web sites should never see the light.of day.

Understanding the Medium

The Web is not a mass medium like television; it is a medium for niche audiences. What does this mean? To use myself as an example, I am interested in law firm technology but I also enjoy hiking in the Yorkshire Dales and Ireland, skiing holidays, motorbikes of all descriptions, jazz and classical music, and (at the time of writing) my wife and I are expecting our first child. Consequently I have disparate and varied information needs. However, all of these interests can be catered for on the Internet. Similarly, each individual Internet user will have a unique combination of interests and needs.

Each law firm that is contemplating the establishment of a web site should recognise that it will be catering to a niche audience. That audience may be people who have had accidents, are threatened with eviction, are in business disputes, or they may be companies that want to outsource services, get planning permission, merge or acquire other companies, protect their intellectual property, and so on. Every law firm caters to a niche audience. Thus every law firm web site should do likewise.

This new medium should also be viewed as an opportunity to rethink a firm's corporate presentation from first principles. A simple electronic re-hash of existing corporate marketing and recruitment literature is simple and quick to achieve but it totally fails to take advantage of what the Web has to offer. One would never serve one's guests a meal consisting of yesterday's leftovers. Yet this is exactly how most law firms treat the Web. Good quality web content cannot be created from material designed for different media. Realistically, most law firms will not want to rethink their entire corporate branding and also start producing two versions of all publications. They may even have struggled to agree their existing logo and letterhead.

To rethink everything from first principles because of a new technology is clearly asking too much. But that is not what is being suggested here. Instead, the law firm 'brand' needs to be refocused to a particular audience or audiences.

Understanding Branding on the Internet

Quality web sites develop their reputation very quickly. But what makes or breaks the reputation of a web site? Many companies selling well-known products initially made the mistake of confusing the Internet with television, they attempted to transpose the 30-second commercial slot aimed at a mass audience, into a permanent web presence for a much more fragmented web-surfing audience. In a world where the competition is only a hyperlink away, one can easily 'change channels'. Consequently, it is much more difficult to extend existing brand names to the on-line medium and to secure the same loyalty that has been achieved in the non-digital world.

So what are the biggest brands on the Web? Yahoo!, AOL and Netscape are three of the biggest yet none of these existed 10 years ago. Brand promotion via traditional media outlets such as television and radio is now well understood. Corporate organisations understand the demographics of their television, newspaper and magazine audiences. They know thai a 15-second commercial for Coca-Cola in the middle of a soccer match will reach their intended audience of potential purchasers. On the Web, they reach an audience about which they know relatively little: surfers can come from anywhere. After an initial foray onto the Web, some well-known makers of fast-moving consumer goods admitted that they could not gain much from the medium and effectively withdrew from the digital marketplace. What they really meant was that they could not gain much by applying their traditional tried and trusted marketing strategies in a new medium.

This withdrawal gave them time to reconsider their product placement on the Web. They have now returned to the Internet older and wiser and the lessons they have learnt are likely to be equally applicable to the multi-channel digital television environment of the future.

So how does one sell fast-moving consumer goods over the Internet? One approach is to develop a site which offers information relevant to the product or brand in question. For example, the makers of a leading brand of toothpaste are not simply trying to sell more toothpaste, they are trying to market the benefits of effective oral hygiene (which incidentally might involve the use of related products such as mouthwash, dental floss and a new toothbrush). They recognise that their consumers are not interested in toothpaste *per se*, they are interested in having healthy teeth and gums. Thus the web site developer for the brand owner has two choices. The first is to develop a site based around the traditional old media electronic billboard approach where the principle message is 'Buy more of our toothpaste'. This approach is simple but is highly unlikely to be effective. Web surfers have over 2 million other 'channels' from which to choose; unlike television, they don't have to accept such blatant advertising as the price of viewing. An alternative and apparently more successful approach is to establish a site containing all manner of useful information about dental hygiene, including independent research papers (i.e. content) together with electronic forums for questions and answers about problems people may be having with their teeth and gums (i.e. communication), and special offers where visitors can receive samples of products in return for some information about themselves. By combining content with communication, the brand owner can effectively create a virtual community - an environment where people share common interests or concerns either over a period of years or for five minutes. Procter and Gamble have taken exactly this approach with their Pampers Parenting Institute site and there are many others examples in the fast-moving consumer goods marketplace.

First-Generation Law Firm Web Sites

By contrast, the web sites of the vast majority of UK law firms are a variation on a theme: the web site as the corporate electronic brochure. Few firms have got beyond the 'billboard' stage. Very few firms appear to have thought through how the electronic medium differs from the paper-based medium. Nor are these sites targeted at a particular audience. Most are a fairly unimaginative expansion of the corporate brochure - information about the firm, types of work undertaken, pictures of the partners, a recruitment brochure and perhaps maps of the area in which the office or offices are located. This is the path of least resistance, easily justified to the Partnership and quite cost effective because it requires so little forethought. The path of least resistance is also reflected in the site design. The compromise solution that is often adopted is a site that reflects the internal structure of the firm in terms of practice areas or offices. Inevitably, some Partners will complain that there is no direct link to their own department.

In a large firm, every department cannot have representation. Moreover, Partners need to recognise that the web site is not there in order to massage their egos. It should exist to serve clients and potential clients. Such an audience will rarely care about how the firm is structured, nor whether the firm has an office in Tokyo, Bradford or anywhere else. Instead they want a site that provides answers (or if not answers, at the very least, leads to where they might find the answers) to their business problems. Of those law firms that have web sites, how many of them actually talked to their clients and asked them what they wanted? A recent study[3] revealed that 90 per cent of all first-generation web sites were built without asking the potential user community what they wanted! This is a mistake that few organisations can afford to make twice. Developers of web sites for law firms might argue that the general lack of imagination so prevalent on their sites can be justified, at least in part, by the subject matter - the law is text-based and highly technical. It doesn't lend itself to a visual medium, they would say. Furthermore, it is not easy to turn pictures of lawyers and offices together with the latest news on a new Act of Parliament or EU Directive into exciting and visually compelling content. While the law does not lend itself to the creation of exciting web sites and no law firm is ever going to compete with the likes of Virgin or the BBC in the production of compelling and highly animated or technically sophisticated sites, this is missing the point entirely. Just as a site should not exist simply for the general entertainment and edification of the senior Partners, neither should it exist for the general entertainment of the web-surfing public. It should be designed for its niche market: to meet the needs of a specific audience.

SO WHO IS THE AUDIENCE?

There are likely to be three types of visitors to a law firm web site, the first two of which should be explicitly catered for. In order of importance, they are: clients or potential clients (i.e. those visitors with a business problem and presumably looking for a business solution); potential employees and new recruits; and finally casual visitors, those who may have come across the site by accident or may just be looking up the site because they have heard about it. By their very nature, casual visitors cannot be explicitly catered for.

Law firms should consider asking their web users about themselves at the first point of entry and establishing different styles of site according to the type of visitor. A by-product of this approach would be that the statistics gathered as a result would give the firm a good indication of the demographics of their current web site audience.

Clients

Looking at the first audience category, clients or potential clients will want to visit a site that is focused on their business needs. Why do people visit lawyers? Because they have a business need or a business problem. The same rule will apply to a lawyer's web site. Therefore the site should address business problems first and foremost. Yet, how many law firm web sites explicitly ask the client or potential client to attempt to define their business problem or even give their visitors an opportunity to narrow down the business or legal issues? Very few indeed. The lawyer will argue here that many clients don't know what their business problems are. This is a fair point but firms could and should be proactive in their control of where and how the visitor is directed through the site. All too often, law firm web sites allow users to meander without any guidance whatsoever, until (presumably) they get bored and wander off to other areas of Cyberspace. As far as the law firm is concerned, each web site visitor who fails to progress beyond the simple browsing of a few web pages is a business opportunity lost. Of course, the web site visitor always has the upper hand; he or she can simply type in a new web address and disappear into Cyberspace never to return. But law firms could attempt to manage the user experience by providing search facilities or drop-down lists of legal services available, so that visitors can be more easily directed to the information that interests them.

Lawyers are always very keen to profess that they are client-focused, yet when given a new medium in which to demonstrate this client focus most of them fail miserably by using traditional marketing tools and materials with which they feel comfortable.

Potential Employees

Potential trainees and new recruits are the second audience category. Their needs will be addressed by an entirely different type of site. They will want information that gives them a flavour of the firm, indicates that the people who work there are reasonable human beings, who enjoy their work, who work hard and play hard and that the firm will provide a thorough training while providing a genuine career path. They will want some brief information about the Partners and fee-earners, the offices, the history of the firm and an indication of where the firm sees itself in five years' time. It can be very helpful to include a few details about some recent legal matters that the firm has been involved in and (with the permission of clients) even to name a few higher-profile clients or matters where the firm has been involved. Most importantly, they will want to have the electronic facility to submit a c.v. or to submit a completed application form. As time goes on, potential trainee solicitors will become more technology-literate. They will expect to be able to submit a c.v. or to apply on-line; a law firm without this type of facility will be seen as slightly backward. Given that some UK law firms have to deal with many thousands of applications for only a few traineeships each year, using the Web as the first method of contact with the applicant is not only good marketing, it is also cost effective compared with mailing expensive brochures and forms. A web site of this nature will not only impress potential employees, it will also significantly reduce administrative overheads.

Of course, all groups whether clients, future employees or casual visitors will want to be reassured that the firm cares about its image. This will be demonstrated by a web site that is up to date, is easily navigable and makes best use of current web technology. But these aspects should be expected of *every* web site. At the moment, designers of law firm web sites try to please all of the people (the Partners, the general web-surfing public, clients, potential clients, employees, potential trainees) all of the time and manage to please no one.

Applying The '3 CS'

So what lessons are to be learnt in a law firm context where there is no discernible product other than the lawyers themselves, their experience and the expertise that they claim to offer? Some readers may feel that it is almost flippant to compare the marketing of consumer products such as toothpaste with the marketing of a far more cerebrally-based service such as legal advice. However, the lessons to be learnt in terms of on-line marketing are precisely the same. Law firms should establish web sites not about the 'brand' *per se* but about the problems likely to be encountered in particular legal situations and the solutions provided by the brand. In order to attract new visitors and then keep them as regular visitors a site should be seen to provide a service. It is important to create a sense of web site visitor loyalty by providing timely and updated information. It is also important to offer web site visitors the opportunity to communicate electronically with the firm. A web site should offer the user as many opportunities as possible to contact a human being. After all, only the human being can initiate a business relationship - a machine cannot.

CASE STUDY: A LAWFIRM & CO.

How would this type of Internet branding work in practice? Let us examine a mythical firm, called A, LawFirm& Co. which is very well known in the legal Industry for its employment law work. One of its main business objectives is to become the dominant player in this marketplace. How can a web site help? Instead of creating a generic site that says 'Welcome to A. LawFirm & Co. This is who we are and this is what we do: we are a law firm that does employment law', the firm could, instead, register a domain name such as employment-law.co.uk, or employmentlaw-resources.co.uk, and provide a service that contains useful information about the problems and pitfalls related to unfair dismissal, redundancy, fairness at work, and so forth. This might include such things as information about new and forthcoming legislation or EU Directives, or problems and pitfalls faced by employers, news on the latest Government statements regarding employment law, or new and forthcoming regulatory policies and papers. Naturally, the fact that such a service is provided by A. LawFirm & Co. would be prominent throughout the site and there could be links to information about recent matters that A. LawFirm has been involved in. The primary focus, however, would be a particular area of commerce, the legal problems likely to be faced and the possible solutions available, not the make-up of the firm itself. If such a service was well advertised, kept up to date and genuinely supported by the firm, it could quickly become a constant source of reference for human resource personnel and in-house lawyers and it is quite likely that a reasonable amount of referral work would result - the name of A. LawFirm & Co. having become synonymous with employment law information. In reality, the content would not be dissimilar from the various newsflashes and newsletters that most medium to large law firms already produce or distribute around the firm in the form of internal bulletins produced by librarians or information professionals. It is simply a matter of rechannelling existing expertise and information. The material already in existence would need to be refocused for a particular client audience.

The concept could be extended further to involve university research departments and think-tanks so the web site could be a forum for the sharing of ideas and business information within the user community. The limitations of such a site are few. Here, the law firm web site is not so much an extended corporate brochure as a general store, with users free to pick and choose what they wish from a range of informational 'goodies'. The Web can potentially turn every business and every law firm into an information provider, a publisher and facilitator for the development of a niche virtual community.

Of course, competitors would quickly catch on to such a venture and, no doubt, would take copious notes on the project. They might even contemplate their own similar venture. However, experience shows that being first to develop a new idea on the Internet is critical. It gives an organisation a competitive advantage of a significant magnitude, often sufficient to ensure that competitors are unable to compete even if they produce comparable products or services. On the Internet, being second can be as good as last. In order to secure its investment, the firm would have to establish a registration mechanism to discourage the competition from 'listening in' to the discussions. Eventually it could even start charging a fee to cover its own administrative costs, although the web site service would have to be very well established, almost woven into the fabric of the human resources community, before such steps could be taken.

There is no reason why A. LawFirrn & Co. could not set up other web sites which demonstrate its expertise in other areas of legal practice. Would this be compelling? Perhaps not for the average web surfer (but then law firm web sites should not be designed for the average web surfer). To those employees involved in human resource issues, over time it could become an invaluable service and one well worth paying for. Of course, such ideas are more easily elaborated on paper than actually implemented. There are significant hurdles to be overcome, e.g. such a concept must be successfully 'sold' to the Partnership. It would also require significant support from fee-earning lawyers to keep the content up to date. The web site developer would need to engender a sense of ownership in the project from the lawyers who will provide the content so that their site is foremost in their thoughts in terms of marketing initiatives. This would be no easy task and it is not surprising that most law firms favour the easier option of the bland 'corporate brochure' web site. But on the Internet, all marketplaces are new and the rewards are there in abundance for those who are prepared to take the risks - fortune favours the brave!

(It is not strictly necessary to register a distinct web site domain name. A firm can be simply assigned a name. Thus if the hosting ISP is called Connect and the law firm is called A. LawFirm & Co., then the web address might be http: / / www.connect.co.uk / lawfirmco / or alternatively http: / /www.lawfirmco.connect.co. uk. However, it is far more professional to have one's own domain name. It also reduces the likelihood of visitors not finding your site; a complex web address increases the chances of users typing it incorrectly. Even if a firm decides to register a domain name such as employment-law.co.uk, it is probably wise also to register the name of the firm at the same time in case it is needed in future. It is also possible to make any and all domain names point to the same site.)

The Next Level: Interaction

Whether the site is information based or transaction based, interaction is becoming an increasingly important aspect of on-line communication. For a web site to be considered truly outstanding, interaction is crucial.

If the award-winning web sites of the past few years are examined, there is a clear trend running through them; that is, allowing the user to do something via the site that could not be done in any other way. A few examples are necessary here.

Railtrack

This company is responsible for the UK's railway infrastructure. They commissioned and established an excellent web site which includes one interactive element, namely on-line timetables. Just type in your starting station, your destination, the date and the time you want to travel and watch as a customised timetable is delivered right to your desktop. Incidentally this service saves Railtrack money because the cost of establishing and running a web site is far less than paying people to answer the phone. It also reflects extremely well on the company because they are seen as providing some very useful practical information for five in other words giving something back to the user community.

The British Army

The British Army commissioned what has proved to be an outstanding and award-winning web site based on its advertising campaign 'Be the Best' (http://www.army.gov.uk). Potential recruits are invited to take an interactive challenge in one of many military hot-spots around the world, by working through a scenario in which they have to make decisions based on limited information. Users are presented with multiple-choice questions all of which require intelligent and lateral thinking. These scenarios engage the participant and also link well with the ongoing campaign in other media outlets to attract new recruits to the Army.

Couriers

Other highly successful web sites such as DHL Worldwide Express (http:// www.dhl.com) or Federal Express (http://www.fedex.com) allow the user to track the location of their parcels in real time. In other words, the user can see where their parcel is at any given time by using the site.

These web sites offer the user a clear benefit; namely, they make doing business with these companies easier.

While no law firm is going to be able to compete with the above organisations in creating visually compelling web sites, there is a clear role for interaction and it is surprising that so few law firms have experimented in this area.

Applying Interaction to the Case Study

Imagine a web site where users could find out how much their statutory redundancy payment might be if they were sacked; whether they are eligible for unfair dismissal, and so on. Ask any employment lawyer worth their salt and they would be able to draw up a rule matrix that reflects the way in which compensatory awards are calculated. Technically, it is quite feasible to develop that rule matrix into a computer program that runs on a web site using one of many Internet languages such as Java or Javascript, or a combination of VBScript and ActiveX. This program would ask most of the questions that a lawyer might ask of a new client regarding their employment dispute and would allow the web site visitor to come to some sort of conclusion about whether he or she is eligible for a particular award and if so, for how much.

To some this may be a frightening prospect. The experienced employment lawyer might immediately leap into the air in horror at such a proposal and argue that employment law is far too complex for a mere computer program and that there are all sorts of additional factors dependent on the circumstances of the case that could not be included in such a program. There are too many variables, and so forth. Besides, the lawyer might argue, didn't we try this in the 1980s with expert systems - and look where that got us? Again, all of this is fair comment, but also reflects the irrational and totally groundless fears of an experienced practitioner who fears that he or she is about to be replaced by a machine. There is a point at which such a program would cease to have any value and at this point the program should stop and the user should be told 'On the basis of the information that you have provided, we believe that you do/do not have a claim. You should now seek further advice from an experienced employment lawyer. Call (phone number) and ask for (name of employment lawyer). Your details have been saved and forwarded by email to this lawyer'. The web site should also state that it can only provide an estimate of the likely settlement and that there are other factors that would have to be considered based on the circumstances of the case, and that the information provided is only intended to be used as an estimate.

However, on the positive side, such a web site mechanism would save the lawyer a lot of time in the initial interview in establishing whether the client is eligible for a particular claim. It might also screen out potentially vexatious litigants. After working through the program, presumably only potential clients who thought that they would have a remote chance of success with a claim would go so far as to instruct a solicitor, It would also save the client a great deal of worry and anxiety far loo many people in the UK are unable to claim their rights under the law because they are too afraid to visit a lawyer for fear of the resultant bill. Using this mechanism, the client has learnt that they are eligible for some form of compensation, and learning this has cost them nothing. Meanwhile, the lawyer has gained a new client and may have also saved some time per instruction. Admittedly, employment law is an easy example of where such a service could work through the development of a relatively simple computer program. But there are other areas such as taxation, immigration, and so forth where similar rule matrixes could be applied.

There are other exciting and innovative ways in which

a law firm can offer services to potential clients. This is not rocket science. It is simply leveraging an existing investment in a particular area of law or legal practice technology. Some lawyers may be concerned that these measures may radically affect their own profitability in a negative way. In fact, the reverse is likely to be true.

On-Line Document Assembly

Law firms can now offer visitors to their web site access to document assembly tools over the Internet. Thus visitors can create their own legally valid documentation for simple transactions or executions such as wills, tax returns and Companies House documentation. The attraction here to the web site visitor would be that these standard form documents could be used in the knowledge that they are quality-assured by that firm. These are small gestures that have little impact on the 'bottom line' profitability of the firm, but they are likely to enhance its reputation, attract new business and also neatly demonstrate the firm's technical prowess. Here the law firm has begun to move from being a traditional provider of legal advice that happens to have a web site to being an on-line provider of practical useful legal information. We are slowly encroaching on the area of on-line legal services. Some law firms may feel that they are not in the position to offer complex password-protected sites offering online legal services. Arguably, however, all law firms are in the position to offer users valuable legal and business information partly as a 'loss leader' and partly as a marketing mechanism by which to obtain new work. In other words, by giving away a certain amount of legal advice without charge, the firm is likely to gain a great deal more from the site.

In addition, any firm using existing case management systems should seriously consider opening up such systems to the Web to allow clients to interrogate what is happening on their own matter. Just as banks are now offering consumer banking via the PC, allowing customers to see the balance on their accounts, law firms should give clients the facility to find out the latest action on their case or deal.

Summary

The days of random web surfing are probably at an end. With millions of web sites already available and new sites appearing on an average of one a minute, the attention span of the average web user has diminished dramatically. The appeal of electronic brochures is fading by the day and cannot be a sustainable basis upon which to fuel ongoing web site development. Those law firms that already have a 'brochureware' web presence should radically rethink their approach to the medium. Those law firms that do not have any web site at all, should learn from the mistakes of those that do. All law firms should be focusing their web sites on the needs of their prospective users.

The key to a successful information-based web site is content, but content that is focused, that addresses the needs of the target audience, augmented by the ability for users to communicate with the owners of the site and with other users. Web-based interactions will form an increasingly important aspect of the communication process where users will be able to learn something new. These two aspects properly nurtured will create a virtual community. Information sites that provide a home for people with shared interests and concerns will attract and retain an audience and consequently, are far more likely to succeed than the typical corporate billboard. However, the establishment of a web presence, rather than being an isolated on-line venture, should be the first point on what is likely to be a continuum of Internet-based legal services. In other words, it should be the first step towards delivering full legal services over the Internet.

WEB SITE DEVELOPMENT STRATEGIES

In this chapter we look at the practical aspects of developing a web site. In particular, we look at the tools to be used, whether to outsource development or hosting, the human resources issues and how to promote the site.

Many non-technical readers may wonder whether the subject of web site development is relevant to them. This chapter is important because lawyers need to understand what is involved in the development of a web site so that they can understand what can and, equally importantly, what cannot be achieved with a site. If lawyers do not understand these issues, they will be ill equipped either to commission or to manage their own sites. Thus we will cover issues such as the technical infrastructure of the site (whether to use a database and/or personalisation technologies); whether to outsource the site development and hosting; the possible tools that can be used; the human resource issues if developing a site in-house; and the problems of promoting the site through search engines, email and Usenet groups. Many of the issues addressed here are relevant to all types of web sites, whether used for marketing, sharing information and know-how or for the delivery of legal services. In terms of the final product, the technology used is the same. The difference is the audience. However, in terms of the development issues, intranet sites are different animals altogether. Thus the practical implications of developing intranet sites will be dealt with in the following chapter.

A Static or Dynamic Site?

The amateur web developer can easily create a web site consisting of a group of static web pages. The production of such sites is very simple but it creates a number of problems in terms of future administration and redesign, particularly when the site grows. If the content and design are all contained within the same files then whenever the Webmaster (see the Glossary for a definition) of the site needs to update or change any of the pages, he or she must access each individual page and make the changes manually. 'Static' here means that in order for the contents of a web page to change, the web developer must make those changes manually. While this is not a problem on a small site consisting of say, 50 pages or less, it becomes a major administrative headache when the site consists of several hundreds or thousands of pages. Instead of performing important administrative tasks such as checking the site for dead links (countering so-called link rot') and making sure that the site is registered with search engines so that it can be found easily by Internet users, the Webmaster will spend considerable time simply adding editing und removing content. Instead of being a facilitator and manager of a well-ordered site, the Webmaster becomes the bottleneck in the publication process. The problems of developing static HTML pages rather than using a database become even more apparent when the site designer decides that the original design has outlived its usefulness and that the site must be redesigned. All of the content, the text and graphics have to be manually extracted from the site. This is such a frightening prospect that most web site designers simply do not attempt it but instead begin again from scratch.

The alternative is a so-called dynamic or database-driven site. 'Dynamic' means that the content changes based on how the user interacts with the site and, at its simplest level, a database is a store of structured electronic information. Databases are particularly important for catalogue-type web sites. The database is used to store the content of text and graphics. In addition, different HTML templates are created to present that content. Using some clever programming tools, the various web pages that make up the site can be created dynamically; thus when a visitor visits a web page he or she actually fires off a request to the database. The required information is then extracted from the database and passed to a template. All of this happens seamlessly each time a web site visitor clicks on a different link. The site behaves like any other but it is far easier to administer. If the content or the design of the site is going to be frequently changed or updated, then a database-driven system is easier to administer and redesign. In addition, because the content is separate from the design, non-technical employees can be permitted to update information for themselves. In other words, there is no information bottleneck. Firms can create their own customised solutions or purchase so-called 'content management systems'.[4] Unless the site is very simple, most developers of new web sites would prefer to manage their sites using a database of some description.

Evolution or Big Bang?

In developing a web site, the firm has two choices: the 'big bang' approach develop and deliver a completed web site in one attempt; or the staged approach - develop a site in different modules each of which is added over time. The chosen approach will depend on the purpose of the site. For example, if the web site in question is designed to provide a legal service which charges a fee in return for specific information, it must be comprehensive. The site will soon lose credibility if users discover pages which contain nothing more than the 'This page is currently under construction' statement. Where the site is sizable, the big-bang approach can result in excessive delay in releasing a first version. If a law firm is determined to publish all of its external marketing materials, such as brochures, newsletters, recruitment brochures and so forth, then turning all these documents into a web-readable format can be a very time-consuming task, unless it can be automated. The staged approach gives all participants an opportunity to comment and the web developer can alter the content based on the feedback received. Given the low attention threshold of the average web surfer, it is better to provide users with a small amount of truly useful information than to provide them with links to more materials than they could ever wish to read.

Choosing the Right Tools

Earliest web site developers had to use the most basic of word-processing tools in order to create their web pages. There are hundreds of different web development tools available and the decision regarding which tools to choose may seem impossible. They vary in price from free of charge to tens of thousands of pounds. Some tools are simple HTML editors. This means that the web site developer must know and enjoy working with HTML. Indeed, many web site designers who come from a programming background will only use HTML editors because they want to work directly with the code and feel the need to have complete control over what is being created. These concerns are understandable but can retard the development process considerably if the site is large. Others tools are so-called WYSIWYG tools - 'what you see is what you get'. In other words, whatever is created on the screen is exactly what the web site visitor will see. Here the coding is all hidden from the designer. Some tools also come with design templates already built into them, which means that the services of a graphic designer may not be required, thus reducing costs. Other tools allow developers to integrate programming code that extends the abilities of the web page to allow for animation, movement and the integration of sound and video.

The decision regarding which tool or tools to choose should be driven by the purpose of the site. Where firms choose to outsource their web development, the decision is usually made for them. However, a good web design agency will recognise the ultimate purpose of the site and choose its tools accordingly. If it is decided that the site should include a database because it is going to change regularly, it will have many information contributors. If it is going to include an element of personalisation, then the tools chosen should integrate databases easily. But the decision will also be affected by the skills sets available. For example, if the web designer comes from a design background, then he or she will not be interested in working at code level. Similarly, if the web designer comes from a programming background, then he or she will prefer to work with the code and avoid many of the design issues.

Thankfully the decision regarding which web tools to choose will eventually disappear: any software package capable of creating a printed page will also be capable of creating a web page. In order to survive, the likes of Microsoft, Corel and Adobe will all have to build this web functionality into their software. (Microsoft are doing exactly this with their Office 2000 suite; HTML and XML are native formats in that package.) Thus instead of having to learn specific web development tools, employees can simply use their existing skills and with the click of one button, publish to their web site whether external or internal. However we are still some way from this happy scenario.

MARKETING TO AN AUDIENCE OF ONE

In order to ensure that the information being provided on the web site is always relevant, the web developer needs to learn about the interests, concerns and aspirations of the web site audience.

Early attempts to achieve this aim were through the establishment of an electronic guest book on the web site. However, within weeks all web sites seemed to have such guest books and users quickly lost interest in filling out details about themselves for no good reason. The next ploy by web site developers was to password-protect certain sections of the site which could be unlocked in return for some personal information. This is, of course, simply another variation on a well-used marketing technique - who hasn't filled in a form in order to claim a discount or a free offer? This appears to be a more effective approach. Users are willing to trade some information about themselves in return for useful information. This technique is widely deployed. However, insisting on user registration before entering a web site is likely to turn many users away, particularly if they have no idea what is on the other side of the virtual door. In addition, it is becoming clear that passwords and electronic forms interrupt the information search flow of the user. What is more, some web users are even given to lying on forms and there is nothing that the web site owner can do to prevent such behaviour. Passwords are also difficult to remember. Instead, web sites need to offer users a 'taster' of what they will find on the other side of the entry form in the hope that they will feel sufficiently enticed to take the trouble to fill in the form.

A more subtle approach to the collection of personal information is to personalise the user experience of the web site, by effectively creating a unique home page for each visitor. Personalisation is a major transformation of a web site and carries a significant cost with it. But it also encourages users to return because they feel that they have found a service that understands their needs. The easiest method is to persuade visitors to provide the web site with information about themselves, their habits, their interests and their needs. This information would then be fed into a database and saved. The visitor would also have to be given some unique form of identification so that when they revisit the web site, the site recognises them and presents relevant information based on what the site 'knows' about that visitor.

An Example of Personalisation

How would this system of personalisation work in practice? Imagine a travel agency web site offering a range of last minute deals for visitors to peruse and purchase.

A user who visits the site might be invited to identify specific interests by clicking on various categories in response to a series of a questions 'I want a beach holiday', 'I want to go to the Caribbean', 'I want a beach-front villa', and so forth. If a user decides that he or she is interested in going on a beach holiday somewhere hot, the site presents various holiday destinations and by clicking through pages, the user picks a holiday. Choices would be determined through the use of pre-existing keywords picked from lists. The information gathered about this user's preferences would be saved in a database. The web site would also send a small piece of code containing a unique value to the user's machine. When the visitor revisits the web site, the site would look for that unique value and, if found, would present information based on known preferences. This might be similar beach holidays or it might be advertisements selling related products such as sun-tan lotion, camera film, holiday insurance, and so forth.

In addition, after the user returns from the holiday, he or she might automatically receive an email from the web site offering cheap photo development. The following year at around the same time, the web site might automatically dispatch an email announcing similar deals to the same or complementary destinations. All of the above is technically feasible but requires much more complex programming than the traditional 'flat' site and consequently is not commonplace on the Web. However, a number of web sites already employ this type of customised mechanism, for example CNN with their custom news service.

Collaborative Filtering

An alternative to the keyword-based approach is to compare the inputs of a given user with the input profiles of other users in order to present users with relevant products or services. This system is called collaborative filtering. These services can be quite expensive and also tend to require a large amount of data. One site where this type of mechanism has proved worthwhile is the Movie Critic web site[5] which claims to find users a movie that they would enjoy, based on what they tell the site about their own preferences. Users have to provide a personal rating on at least 12 different films. Based on the information provides the web site then interrogates its own database to present the user with a list of possible movies in various categories that might interest them. This site uses a product called Likeminds which is made by Andromedia.[6] There are also a number of competing products on the market such as NetPerceptions[7] and Firefly.[8] These systems are impressive, but are complex to establish and are unlikely to have an immediate appeal to law firms.

Rule-Based and Case-Based Personalisation

There are also so-called rule-based and case-based personalisation systems available. Using rule-based systems, the web site developer must define the rules based on their own assumptions. For example, a rule on a law firm web site might be: a visitor looking for information about trademarks is not likely to be interested in insolvency. Similarly, visitors looking for information about the firm's offices in Birmingham are also likely to be interested in the latest newsletter produced by the Birmingham office. Based on a complex rule-matrix, the web developer can present users only with information deemed relevant to them. Because of the complexity involved in setting up the rule-matrix, case-based personalisation is considered to be a more favourable option. Here, users can define for themselves what they are interested in by clicking on buttons marked 'Find me more items like this'. The web site software will then go away and examine the contents of the site looking for patterns in the language or instances of keywords.

Personalisation is an important trend for the future of larger informational web sites in terms of delivering information that is directly relevant to the needs of users. However, it is an expensive solution both in terms of the initial outlay for the software and the time required to establish and customise it. Issues that should be thought about before any tools are considered are: how big is the site? How much traffic does it attract? What is the purpose of the site? Most of the time, on law firm web sites, personalisation oilier than via user-driven keywords will be an expensive outlay and is unlikely to be justified for pure marketing-based sites.

OUTSOURCE OR DESIGN IN-HOUSE?

Developing HTML pages, the language of the Web, is relatively easy. Therefore it is also easy to do badly. The answer to the question of whether to outsource or to design in-house depends on the purpose of the site and the skills available. Even if a firm possesses the necessary skills, the amount of time required to produce a quality web site should not be underestimated; quality web sites cannot appear overnight.

Choosing a Web Design Studio

Although web design is such a new area, there are a large number of start-up companies all wanting web site development business. Finding a quality design studio can be akin to a lottery because it is very difficult at the outset to distinguish the good from the indifferent. As the relationship between client and design studio develops, however, this becomes a lot easier to discern. Like estate agency, it is a profession which anyone can join. There is no professional body and there are no examinations. As with any new product, it is easy to be duped into purchasing add-ons that are not required. Therefore, in choosing a web design studio, there are a number of questions that should be asked.

QUESTIONS TO ASK BEFORE CHOOSING A WEB DESIGN STUDIO

1. What is the design studio's track record? Has the studio won any awards? Can they provide references from existing clients or from organisations that have used them in the past?
2. What does their balance sheet look like? Are they in sound financial health? In other words, will they still be in business in two years' time? All clients will be looking for cast-iron financial guarantees. Unfortunately, in a business that is so new, there can be no guarantees. Studios expand, contract and merge. However, a strong track record will give some comfort.
3. Can the agency explain their ideas in plain English? It is very easy to get caught up in the technology of the Internet. Can they explain their use of the technology in simple terms? All web design studios will want to impress their prospective clients with their knowledge and their abilities to apply the latest technologies. However, technology on the Web is moving so quickly that it can be quite difficult to determine what is a significant development and what is simply well-honed marketing. It is advisable to take much of their advice about new technologies with a pinch of salt. What is more, by the time the studio actually implements the web site, that piece of wizardry may well be redundant.

4. If the design studio outsources particular aspects of site development, to whom do they outsource? It has been known for some agencies to outsource their development to more than one design studio. This is a major mistake. Each studio will want to put their own design stamp on the site. The result would be a site that lacks consistency and uses disparate technologies. Agencies with such practices should be avoided.
5. Can the design studio provide longer-term support for all sections of the web site whether built by themselves or by others?
6. Do they listen? In all likelihood, the agency will probably not have done any work for a law firm in the past. Despite claims to the contrary they are unlikely to understand the needs of the practice. Are they willing to learn or do they have very fixed ideas about what is required?
7. Do they provide a single point of contact who will coordinate all aspects of the project and liaise with the firm as the project develops?
8. Can they be flexible? Can they develop a modular web site - one that can be easily expanded later as budgets allow - or will they only consider developing a single technological edifice? Sites should be scalable. Firms will not wish to tear the site down and start again in 18 months' time because of a lack of forethought.
9. Are they interested in a long-term relationship or in a one-off web development job?

As is the case with good lawyers, the very best are always swamped with work. Indeed, some web design companies are so overwhelmed with work that, occasionally they have to implement a moratorium on new instructions. That in itself speaks volumes about their reputation and quality. Costs can vary enormously and, as with most products and services, you get what you pay for. At the lower end of the market it is possible to have a site created, consisting of between 20 and 30 pages, with an investment of as little as £1,000. The problem with this is that the firm risks owning a web site that looks like it cost £1,000. In some ways this is worse than no web site at all. No law firm would produce a new brochure with shoddy graphics, photos with fuzzy edges on a piece of recycled photocopying paper. Why should a web site be any different? The firm should apply the same rigorous standards of quality that they would apply to any other piece of marketing literature. Arguably, they should be more stringent. After all, what paper-based marketing brochure for a law firm could possibly reach a potential audience of millions?

At the top end of the web site development market, major High Street retailers are said to have paid between £50,000 and £100,000 or more for their web sites. For this fee, the design consultancy would analyse the supposed needs of the firm, develop prototype designs and deliver the first version of the site. This fee may not even cover major ongoing maintenance expenses. However, if a firm is adamant about creating a web site in-house, then some web design companies are willing to work with clients on the business needs stage and to develop appropriate proposals for visual design and site navigation for a few thousand pounds. This can often be money well spent as they have a much better view of the trends in web design and will be able to steer a firm away from an idea that might otherwise appear worthwhile.

Outsource or In-House Hosting?

Once the web site is completed, it has to live somewhere on the Internet so that users can access it. In other words, the site has to be 'hosted' on an Internet-enabled machine. Hosting can be either in-house or external. There are a number of factors to consider here: security, speed, service levels and technical know-how.

In terms of security, ideally the site should be behind a firewall (see the Glossary for a definition). Firewalls are the first line of defence against hackers. Although it is feasible to hack through a firewall, this requires significant technical abilities and a great deal of determination. Firewalls also have warning systems built into them and thereby discourage the casual hacker. However, firewalls are an additional expense; to protect just one small web site the cost may not be justified.

In terms of speed, unless the firm has the benefit of a high-speed direct connection via a leased line, an ISP's service is likely to be superior. The firm should establish how the host is attached to the Internet. What are the response times like? These should be independently verified. An ISP will offer a '24/7/365' service (that is, 24 hours a day, 7 days a week, 365 days a year). Law firms are unlikely to be prepared to employ someone just to keep an eye on their web site at weekends.

Finally, there is the argument used to justify any form of IT outsourcing: ISPs specialise in the hosting of web sites; law firms do not. In choosing a host, the following issues should be considered: what guarantee is provided regarding the service level? All ISPs should be able to guarantee 95 per cent+ 'uptime'. Do they provide refunds if the service level is not achieved? Can the host run basic Common Gateway Interface (CGI) scripts (see Glossary for a definition) or other services that allow for interaction? Can the host provide a secure on-line service? While the firm may not require this at present, if they are intending to offer legal services in due course it is wiser to choose a host that has such capabilities.

Budgeting for Maintenance

Where the web site hosting is outsourced, responsibility for keeping the site current will probably lie with the host organisation. If the site is to be managed in-house, responsibility for maintaining the site will rest with a single individual, usually known as the Webmaster. Where the site is large, it may be the responsibility of a number of employees. The maintenance budget is a major expense but is easily overlooked. Evidence is emerging that the cost of maintaining a site can be as much us the cost of developing it in the first place. It is hoped that the cost of updating materials, reorganising and revising old pages will be covered either through the employment of a Webmaster or a fee to a company that hosts the web site if it is outsourced. However, there are likely to be additional expenses for technical features that were not envisaged in the first version of the site. Furthermore, the site will need to be redesigned after no more than two years, in order to accommodate the raised expectations of both the firm and visitors and also to avoid an outdated 'look and feel'.

The Publication Process

Most law firms that produce regular newsletters or similar marketing materials do so as follows. A group of lawyers will write some material on the current legal issues of the day and will send it for desktop processing (DTP) either internally or externally (this will give a 'look and feel' that is the firm's house style). They may then amend the proof, agree the changes and send the final proof back to the DTP team from where it will go to an external printers for printing. Copies are then returned and distributed to clients. Unfortunately, the introduction of a web site does not interrupt this seemingly smooth process. Instead, the web site developer is treated in the same way as any other person - they are at the end of this information chain. The Webmaster will receive an electronic version of the newsletter from DTP or from the printers, remove all of the carefully added formatting and replace it with the necessary web formatting. This is an unnecessary, time-consuming and wasteful process. Instead, as the Web becomes increasingly important, it should eventually *drive* the marketing and publication process. Over time it should become the primary form of publication from which all other hard-copy publications are generated. How can this be achieved? The major hurdle here is not technology but cultural change. There must be a willingness on the part of the Partnership to tear up the rule book on how things have been done in the past and start from first principles. This is a major change in the way in which the firm presents its services.

THE HUMAN RESOURCES ISSUES

If the web site development work is to be performed in-house, then there will be a number of human resources issues that require some forethought. First, law firms should recognise that there is a fundamental cultural mismatch between employer and employee. Law firms are generally conservative organisations, based on the partnership model of management, with traditions of formal business dress, strict hours, rigid hierarchies, clear career progression (for lawyers) and, it must be said, a general dearth of design creativity. As advisors on risk avoidance and risk management, lawyers are not natural entrepreneurs or risk-takers. They will be less inclined to innovate with their web site, whether it is developed internally or externally.

By contrast, those working in the new-media industries possess characteristics which are the very antithesis of the above. They will be graphics designers and programmers attracted by the new challenges that the Web presents. These potential employees will probably prefer informal and non-hierarchical work environments where standards of dress are more relaxed, hours of attendance are flexible and ability in front of a computer screen is everything. The average law firm currently offers few attractions and incentives to such people. Law firms need to consider methods by which these impediments may be overcome.

Whether the firm is building a simple ('plain vanilla') web site, an intranet, or an extranet offering legal services, the process will involve people. Because the web industry is so new, there are all sorts of people claiming to have relevant web experience, possessing job titles that are largely meaningless to outsiders such as Webmaster, Production Manager, Web Consultant, Web Technologist, Web Guru, and so on. The Partners in an average law firm may not even understand what they want to achieve from this new medium, let alone what skills are required or who to employ.

What Skills are Needed?

Depending on the size of the site, an ideal internal web site development team might consist of:

* **A Webmaster.** Ideally this would be someone who has experience with installing and maintaining web servers, system administration and an understanding of the Internet generally. Their role would be to coordinate the addition of new content, verify content (i.e. make sure that everything works), register the site with search engines (if it is an Internet web site) and drive new developments. The Webmaster may also be responsible for selling the merits of the project to the firm. Whether this can be achieved will depend on the character and interests of the individual in question.
* **A programmer.** This might be someone who knows about HTML but in addition comes from a programming background and may have experience with any of the following languages: Perl, C/C++, Java, Javascript, VBScript and database development and connectivity (see Appendix A, Other significant Internet technologies).

* **A graphics designer.** This person would be responsible for the creation and maintenance of graphics and would design the overall look and feel of the site. He or she is crucial in developing a consistent look and feel of a site that is both captivating and professional.

This is the ideal group for a small web site. A smaller in-house web site development team might simply consist of an HTML coder who would also perform programming tasks together with a graphics designer. These roles might be full or part time. Indeed, if the right person can be found, he or she could take responsibility for all of those rules but this is a heavy workload and such candidates are rare.

Hiring the Right Candidate

Those who call themselves Webmasters will have a wide range of experience. However, the candidate with the most experience or qualifications may not be the most appropriate person for the job. Employees who know everything about building web sites are unlikely to be working for a law firm two years later; for them the grass will always be greener elsewhere. Instead, law firms should be looking for candidates who have an understanding of the main concepts of web site building, an aptitude for learning new tools and/or programming languages and the ability to communicate new ideas. This last point is a major factor, arguably the deciding factor. Not only is the Webmaster going to have to build a web site, but having built it, he or she will need to 'evangelise' - sell the benefits internally to his fee-earning colleagues in a non-technical way. Arguably, aptitude rather than knowledge could be the defining factor in the hiring process. The experience of most early corporate web site developers, both legal and non-legal, appears to be that they hired people who were too technical, interested in technology but not in the content, and who understood how the Web worked but were unable to communicate the potential benefits.

The ideal Webmaster in the law firm context is an intermediary as opposed to a specialist. He or she should have an ability to stand between the firm and the programmers and designers (whether internal or external), with an appreciation of the overall picture. The web development team should be able to appreciate what their programming and design counterparts can and, equally importantly, cannot do. They should also have an awareness of the latest technologies, but with the ability to look beyond the hype and explain to the firm why they might or (more probably) might not need the latest piece of wizardry. They should also have an appreciation of how the Internet works from a technical perspective, with the ability to ask the right questions of their service providers if required. The Webmaster will also need to be able to project manage, to interact with the Partners of the firm, to manage the programming and development, to manage the budget and deliver the finished project on time (and ideally under budget). If this sounds like a big undertaking, it should do. It is therefore important that the Webmaster should be paid appropriately.

What are Web Managers Worth?

While law firms may pay higher salaries than web design consultancies, they do not generally pay as much as financial institutions for IT skills, and until the year 2000 issue is resolved, overall salaries for IT professionals will remain high. As stated above, in the web development business there are so many job titles that it can be quite difficult to know whether one is comparing like wild like. Thus the question of salaries is difficult to answer with any degree of accuracy. One organisation's production manager is another organisation's design manager. However, law firms should attempt to make themselves aware of what web developers are paid elsewhere (because one can be quite sure that the developers themselves will know!). As a rough guide, in 1999 in the UK Webmasters were being paid somewhere between £20,000 and £35,000 per annum, but these figures will change over time. There are a number of IT job-related web sites and these can give a useful indication of what the market will currently support.[9] Most web designers are realistic. They recognise that innovative projects and higher salaries are rarely found in the same place.

Keeping a Webmaster Long Term

The key here is creating the right environment. People do not come to work just for the money. This is particularly true of IT professionals. First, there needs to be a demonstration from the Partnership that they believe that the Web is a worthwhile investment. As has been demonstrated in earlier chapters, quality web sites, whether internal or external, can be expensive undertakings. The firm needs to demonstrate, or have already demonstrated, its willingness to invest. Second, web developers should be given the freedom to develop new ideas for their creation, whether web site, intranet or extranet and be able to act upon them. This requires two things: first, encouragement to innovate, to explore and experiment with new ways of doing things, by spending time researching on the Web, and second, a budget to fund any.new innovations, whether through the purchase of external training courses, books or occasionally external consultancy. In addition, funding should stretch to conference and/or seminar attendance. Webmasters, like all other IT staff, should also be encouraged to share their experiences internally with other IT staff through presentations and in-house IT seminars, in order to grow their careers. An innovative environment (or at least one that does not actively discourage innovation) will reflect well on the firm, improving its ability to attract and keep IT talent. In such a fast moving area as web development, ongoing training is essential. Indeed, a firm that does not provide opportunities for life-long IT learning will be considered fairly backward. Of course the issues above apply as much to any IT project as to a web-based project.

Engendering a Firm-Wide Sense of Ownership

While having the right project manager in place is important, it is also important that the firm recognises that, although information technology is the enabler, the web site is part of the overall client *service* and client service is the responsibility of all fee-earners. The web site is not to be viewed as an isolated IT project.

What does this mean in practice? Web sites have an overriding need to be up to date—there is nothing more irritating for the user than finding web pages that have clearly not been updated for months. Currency of web pages is essential to the credibility of the firm's Internet presence. What is more, it makes little commercial sense to spend substantial time and resources in establishing a web site only to neglect it once it is established. Law firm web sites tend to be viewed by lawyers as an isolated technology venture, rather than a project that can be integrated with other projects and one in which all staff can participate. However (particularly in larger firms spread across many offices), it will be almost impossible for one person to know about every newsworthy item, publication and event that may merit on-line publication. Content management policies and lines of communication must be established between the individual or group responsible for the site and the different departments.

A sense of ownership needs to be engendered in every solicitor and member of the support staff so that the Webmaster does not carry the responsibility for updating what may become several hundred or thousand pages of text. Groups of lawyers should be invited to 'own' sections of the site so that they, not the Webmaster, assume responsibility for the content in different parts of the site. In addition, lawyers need to be web-aware. For example, when writing articles for professional publications, every solicitor in the firm should be thinking about whether a copy could go on the web site and if necessary negotiate copyright clearance so that the article can be published in parallel - both on paper and on-line. Publishers are usually quite happy to allow this as long as there is an appropriate acknowledgement on the web site. The firm also needs to involve librarians and information professionals because, traditionally, it is they who have access to some of the best and most 'web-worthy' information.

MEASURING SUCCESS: USER LOGS

Once the site is up and running (whether in-house or outsourced), the firm should have access to its web site statistics. This should consist of a daily information log file that, when analysed by web site analysis software shows the number of 'hits' or 'impressions' (pages of HTML and graphics) 'served' or transferred to end users; the number of pages of HTML served; the hourly, daily, weekly and monthly peaks and troughs in demand; and the most popular pages types of browsers used, top referring sites, and so forth. All of this information can be quite revealing. For example, if Saturday or Sunday afternoons show major peaks in activity, then it suggests that visitors are simply wandering around the Web and happened to have stumbled across the site. If, by contrast, more of the hits occur during office hours, this suggests that visitors are using the site for work-related purposes.

Most importantly, the logs may also reveal at least some information on who is visiting. For example, if someone is working for a corporation such as AT&T, their Internet domain name might be 'att.com.' This domain name will be registered in the log file. However, the files cannot identify individual names of visitors and will not do so for the foreseeable future; the person browsing the site could be the Head of the Legal Services Department or the mail-room clerk! Until this is achieved, the value of such information is somewhat limited. A further complication is that when users access a web site via major on-line service providers such as CompuServe or AOL (see Appendix A, Search engines), it is impossible to identify the user other than to observe that they used CompuServe or AOL to access the site. If users are required to log in and are authenticated, then actual users' names will be held on an internal database. However, this mechanism brings with it an administrative overhead and certain legal obligations arising from the data protection legislation. It is also feasible to monitor web site hits as they happen but the software required is expensive and usually unnecessary for the level of traffic that a law firm web site will attract.[10]

A high rate of hits on a law firm web site may please both the Webmaster and the Managing Partner but in reality, the overall numbers of hits proves little. The statistics may tell the firm which are the most visited pages and this in turn may suggest a need to reorganise the site so that certain less-used pages are made more visible. But even if a legal web site has a massively high hit rate, unless these hits are converted into new instructions the site is adding nothing to the firm's profitability or growth and therefore serves little purpose other than to raise awareness of the firm's brand in cyberspace. While total audience viewing figures are significant in the television industry, they prove little in this medium. John MacKensie, a Scottish solicitor, writes about his experiences in setting up his law firm's web site:

> At present around 150-170 remote hosts (let's call them people) access Carlton's web pages each week, which is a more satisfactory figure for a small legal firm outwith the central belt in Scotland. Compare this activity to our property shop. We would be delighted if there were 150 people coming into our property shop each week!
>
> *Edwards and Waelde, 1997*

This may be true, but few solicitors would be pleased if, of those 150 people, not one of them stopped to talk to one of their representatives but instead simply picked up some sales literature and walked straight out of the shop. An estate agent, for example, will always want customers to stop and chat with a representative and having established a business relationship, will want to put that customer on a mailing list to keep them informed of relevant properties which might lead to a new instruction.

WEB SITE PROMOTION

In the film *Field of Dreams*, the main character, played by Kevin Costner, is driven to create a baseball pitch in the middle of corn-fields, somewhere in the mid-western United States, in the belief that the ghosts of great baseball players from the past would appear. His character was driven by the belief that 'If you build it, they will come'. While the idea made a good concept for a film, unfortunately it does not apply to the average web site. There are, after all, literally millions of other sites that could be visited. The fact is that the top 10 web sites (the big brand names on the Web such as Yahoo!, AOL and Netscape) attract in excess of 75 per cent of all web site traffic. (Of course, web surfers do not necessarily stay at these top ten sites for very long; instead they use them as jumping-off points to access other parts of the Internet.) But those top 10 sites have the first contact with the user. Thus advertising on such services is astronomically expensive. The remaining 99 per cent of web sites are left to fight amongst themselves for the viewing interests of the remaining 25 per cent of web traffic. As the number of web sites increases, the likelihood of a visitor simply stumbling across a site and finding it useful will reduce even further. Web site promotion is therefore essential. It is also a time-consuming, ongoing and thankless task; no one will congratulate the Webmaster if thousands of people visit the firm's web site - somehow that will be expected - but the firm's management will want explanations if the expected flood turns out to be only a trickle. Web site promotion ultimately costs money. While a great deal can be achieved for nothing, buying people's attention costs.

The first action that the firm must take is to agree amongst themselves what it is that they are attempting to promote. What is the 'Unique Selling Point' of the site? The web site itself is *not* the unique selling point. The web site is a medium by which to communicate certain messages. What are those messages? In the case of a company selling antique furniture over the Internet, the unique selling point is probably self-evident: the company will want to tell its audience that they have an on-line catalogue of furniture through which customers can browse and order from the comfort of their own homes. Another message will be that customers can obtain a high quality of service throughout and beyond the purchase and be assured that they are getting a good price on the item in question. If the firm is already in the happy position of selling legal services over the Internet (and only a few currently are), then the unique selling point is simple to discern: legal advice 'on tap'. In the case of a law firm that is offering information about itself and its services, the unique selling point will be harder to fathom. Whatever the nature of the site, there must be a clear agreement about what the firm is 'selling', otherwise any advertising strategy is doomed from the outset. (Some lawyers may resent the use of the word 'selling' to describe the marketing of legal services. However, this author is firmly of the belief that legal services have always been sold. What is different today, as opposed to 10 years ago, is that the word is actually being used. The Internet is only going to increase this trend.)

The first so-called sales pitch must take place internally. Every member of staff should be made aware that the firm actually has a web site and they should all know its address. This is particularly important with switchboard operators; they should have such basic information memorised. The web site address should also be included on all letter-headed paper, business cards and signatures at the foot of email messages. In addition, press releases and articles written for the legal or trade press should make reference to the firm's web site with the inclusion of the words 'Further copies of this press release or article can be found on the firm's web site' followed by the web address. The referencing process between paper and non-paper publications should be two-way and should be systematic.

Publicity

Writing and distributing press releases is usually considered to be the best and easiest method by which to get press attention. However, given the amount of attention that is already given to the Internet by traditional media outlets, any message about yet another web site which is conveyed via a press release is likely to be lost in the media whirlwind. Also, unless the law firm web site itself is a radical departure from the accepted norm and the first to try such a venture, it is unlikely to garner much interest outside of the legal press. When the site is launched, it may be valuable to draft a press release and send it to relevant legal and commercial journals, particularly those known to be read by the firm's clients. Again, niche marketing is needed for a niche audience. Where press releases may prove useful is in giving journalists accurate background information. However, there are other ways in which to draw attention to the existence of the web site. Articles that reference the web site are a much more effective way of enticing an audience. For example, if a lawyer is interviewed in the mainstream press on an important and topical legal issue, or has written an article for a trade or industry journal, a reference to the web site in that article together with the web address is likely to deliver a high number of hits to the site.

Search Engines

It is estimated that in excess of 80 per cent of all web users find sites via search engines. Externally, the site will need to be registered and have its registration maintained with all of the major search engines such as Yahoo!, AltaVista, Netscape, Lycos, HotBot, Infoseek, etc.

There are generally two ways to register a site. First, the Webmaster can visit the search engine site and register it directly. But not all search engines allow direct registration. Second, the Webmaster can use a web site such as Submit It, Register-It or Exploit[11] to register the site. Webmasters have less control using this second method and in order to have a site registered on every search engine they may have to pay a small fee. However, in terms of the time taken to register a site with each individual search engine, using one of the above services is very cost effective. Registrations with a dozen or so search engine sites can normally be obtained through these services without charge. There are also many dozens of companies (mostly in the USA) that claim they can deliver thousands of people to a web site. (Anyone who has ever run a web site for more than a couple of weeks will have received junk email or 'spam' from such companies.) The value that these companies provide is dubious at best. If time is of the essence, then they may be useful, but generally they appear to provide a service which can be performed by Webmasters themselves. All that is required is time.

Email and Newsgroups

Email is the natural counterpart technology to accompany the web site. After all, if visitors to the firm's web site want to contact someone from within the firm, they will, in all likelihood, use email. However, what looks like email to the sender may look like 'spam' to the recipient (see Glossary). Unless there is something specific that a firm wishes to draw to the attention of a particular individual and email is the best way of doing it, promoting a web site via email should be avoided. Email should be used with caution when promoting a web site.

The same rule applies to newsgroups. Newsgroups are the 'Wild West' of the Internet, where beginners should rightly fear to tread. They are small online communities for like-minded individuals eager to discuss or explore particular areas, issues or products. Generally, blatant advertising for web sites or any other service or product is not accepted in newsgroups unless it is explicitly agreed. Otherwise, such actions would be a clear breach of 'netiquette' (see Appendix D in this book, p.208). Newsgroups are set up for discussion of specific topics whatever they may be, ranging from discussion about a new piece of software, the news, from 'Barney The Purple Dinosaur' through to how to become an urban terrorist.

The key point about newsgroups is that they are usually about one particular topic and no other. Most newsgroup users would say that if a user wants to discuss something different, then that user should start his or her own newsgroup. Unfortunately, it was a firm of US lawyers that decided to break the accepted netiquette of newsgroups. Two Arizona lawyers posted a message about how immigrants might obtain a Green Card which would allow them to work in the USA, by using the services of their firm. The fact that they posted it at all was bad enough. The fact that they posted it to every single newsgroup managed to infuriate almost every other Usenet user. Not only was the advert irrelevant to almost every newsgroup, it was also advertising a commercial service. The Green Card incident is now quite well known in Internet folklore as one of the most blatant breaches of Internet etiquette. While they were not the first individuals to deviate from the accepted norms of newsgroup behaviour, the firm was the first to show no remorse over the incident. Needless to say, retribution by certain elements of the newsgroup community was swift and relentless; these two lawyers could not use their email for weeks as irate programmers devised new and cunning ways to keep sending them abusive emails. It is hard to have a great deal of sympathy for the lawyers in question. They argued that they had broken no laws and from their point of view, if they got one new piece of work and could cope with the electronic abuse, they were happy. However, in the process they managed to reduce the reputation of US lawyers still further.

Web site promotion via newsgroups should be performed very carefully. Groups should be selected to match exactly the interests of the participants. Before posting to the newsgroup, the contents of the ongoing discussion should be examined; appearances can be deceiving. When posting to the newsgroups in question, the message should be focused on a particular aspect of the discussion which has direct relevance to a particular section of the firm's web site. No matter what the subject, blatant product 'pitches' are unlikely to be warmly received.

Advertising on the Internet

At present, advertising on the Internet would appear to have little to offer the law firm. Some large commercial sites make a percentage of their revenue though so-called 'banner advertising' - they display adverts for products or services which the user can click on and link to a given site to obtain more information or perhaps make a purchase. Banners first appeared on web sites in about 1994. Since that time, they have become animated so that the advertiser can pose a question such as 'Looking for cheap flights to Miami. . .' and then have the advert refresh with the words 'London to Miami for $299 -American Airlines', or whatever the offer happens to be. The larger search engine web sites have been particularly effective at utilising banner advertising and many obtain a high percentage of their income by such means. Through some clever programming, they are able to personalise the advert the user sees. Thus, if a user visits one of the popular search engines such as AltaVista (http://www.altavista.com) wanting to search for tennis clubs, when they are presented with the results of their search, they might also see an advert from a ticketing agent offering tickets for the forthcoming Wimbledon championships. The ticketing agent may pay either a flat fee or so many pence or cents 'per click-through' for such an advert. Banner advertising is an important new area in Internet marketing because adverts can micro-target advertising at any type of consumer, based on his or her interests. At present, adverts can be changed according to user's browser, operating system, and domain (.com, .edu, and so on). The web-browsing audience is also relatively wealthy; according to a 1998

Business Week report in the USA, 40 per cent of the web audience earn over $50,000 per annum. Web-based advertising also allows the advertiser to see which adverts are getting the highest number of click-throughs making for more evenly targeted and effective advertising.

How could banner advertising be relevant to the on-line services of a law firm (whether informational or transactional)? Banner advertising could be very effective where there are particular legal deadlines to be met, for example in relation to compliance with a European Directive, a new Act of Parliament, year 2000 compliance, Euro compliance, and so forth. There is no reason why a law firm could not run a brief banner-advert campaign to highlight the legal risks associated with these events, allowing web surfers to click-through to the web site, where they would be offered a brief summary of the problems that they might face together with the name and phone number of who to contact if they need further information. So far as this author is aware, no law firm has yet taken such a step.

ACTION POINTS

1. Get a web site, not as a 'me too' reaction but with sound business justifications. View it as opening an office in Cyberspace and prepare accordingly. Recognise that a marketing web site is not so much an isolated IT project but a client service and must be treated as such. IT is only the enabler.
2. Learn the lessons from the first generation of law firm and fast-moving consumer goods web sites: 'brochureware' doesn't work!
3. Recognise that the Web is a niche medium. Cater to your niche: clients, potential clients and potential employees.

4. Content is king but it must be focused content addressing the needs of your audience - business problems first, profiles, offices and firm structure second.
5. Communication is two way. Give your visitors an opportunity to communicate. Dialogue creates business relations. PR doesn't.
6. Give your visitors a reason to return. Build a virtual community for visitors with shared interests.
7. Give visitors something they cannot get any other way build an interactive site.
8. Give visitors access to documents. They will recognise und appreciate the value of such actions and having used such documents successfully, will trust your firm. You have made a prospective client.
9. If you have existing case management systems, 'web-enable' them. Make it easier for your clients to do business with you.
10. How much time, money and resources does your firm have to give to this project? This will determine the answer to all other questions.
11. How complex is the site? If it is complex and/or to be updated frequently - look at using databases or 'content management systems'.
12. Do you want to 'personalisc' the user experience? If so, examine the soft-ware options here. Can you afford it?
13. Can you develop in-house or do you want to outsource development? There are benefits and problems with both approaches.
14. Hosting—in-house or externally? Again, there are benefits and problems with both.

15. Examine your own publishing processes and re-engineer them if necessary.
16. Advertise - use a variety of different mechanisms.
17. Keep an eye on your web site statistics - they can offer useful information on what is working and what isn't.

FURTHER READING

Hagel, J. and Armstrong, A.G. (1997). *A Net Gain - Expanding Markets through Virtual Communities.* Harvard Business School Press.

Sterne, Jim (1996). *World Wide Web Marketing: Integrating the Internet into Your Marketing Strategy.* John Wiley and Sons, Chichester.

Unfortunately it is very difficult to get hold of a generic guide to developing web sites as almost all books focus on one technology for developing sites at the expense of all the others. Generally, you have to choose your technology first, then read about it rather than do the reading first and then choose your technology from a position of knowledge. One useful read is

Cintron, D. (1999). *Fast Track Web Programming: A Web Programmer's Guide to Mastering Web Technologies.* John Wiley and Sons, New York.

NOTES

1. The Global Internet Survey 1998 Special Report, produced by Information Strategy in association with INSEAD and Novell-. And, BT in their booklet, *E-commerce.*
2. Jakob Nielsen on Dinosaurs, 1 February 1999 issue of *CIO Web Business Magazine* at http://www.cio.com/archive/webbusiness/
3. *The Net and Small Business,* Michalski, Jerry, July 1998, Gartner Group Report. See http://www.gartner.com.
4. Examples include Vignette's Storyserver, Webdevelopment's Mediasurface or Cromwell Media's Bladerunner.
5. http://www.moviecritic.com
6. http://www.andromedia.com
7. http://www.netperceptions.com
8. http://www.firefly.com

9. See for example, Jobserve (http://www.jobserve.com), Jobsite (http://www.jobsite. co.uk), Jobworld (http://www.jobworld. com)
10. Aria by Andromedia collects data and reports in real time. 'Intelligent' tools such as this are focused at the top end of the market. A complete Aria installation may cost from $10,000 to $100,000.
11. http://www.register-it.com and http://www.exploit.com

BIBLIOGRAPHY

Edwards, L. and Waelde, C. (eds) (1997). *Law and the Internet*. Hart Publishing, Oxford. See John MacKensie's paper 'Setting up a legal web site: pitfalls and promises', p. 33.

3 THE LAW FIRM INTRANET

WHY DOES MY FIRM NEED AN INTRANET?

Intranets are an exciting, new and significant yet entirely accidental technology that have emerged from the development of the Web in the early 1990s. They are already delivering clear benefits across.disparate industries. They make access to information quicker and easier for employees, allowing them to act more quickly. They are cheaper and easier to support than most previous technologies. They facilitate the sharing of knowledge and can potentially give organisations a significant competitive advantage. While the concept of the intranet has been around for several years, UK corporations and law firms have come relatively lately to this particular party. In most organisations, the argument in favour of intranet development is overwhelming. This chapter looks at the particular problems and practicalities of developing intranets in the law firm context.

Intranets: A Definition

The term 'intranet' is somewhat confusing. When it first appeared in mid-1995, many people assumed that it was just a mistaken way of spelling 'Internet'. Strictly speaking, it means the 'network within'. What it actually means is the use of Internet technologies, and in particular the development of web sites, in a private (but not necessarily local) context. Another way of defining an intranet is the deployment of Internet technology inside the organisation. Intranets should be distinguished from Internet web sites and extranet web sites. Intranets are used to provide information to a private internal audience, whereas Internet web sites are used to provide information to a public audience. The third type of web site, extranets, provide information to a distinct group of users, such as clients or counsel. It is hoped that many lawyers will now be familiar with the terminology Indeed many UK lawyers will already have access to their own firm's internet. However, the similarities between the various systems are few: while the Internet, intranet and extranet all use common technology, they are quite different animals in terms of management and development issues.

Justifying the Investment

Some lawyers still remain sceptical about the benefits to be found from implementing an intranet, viewing any intranet initiative simply as 'the emperor's new clothes': an excuse to spend money on a new IT project without any real demonstration of the benefits. This view is particularly prevalent where the firm in question already has a document management system[1] in place. Other lawyers may believe that Intranets are only relevant to the very largest of law firms. Both assumptions are incorrect. Intranets offer access to materials that might not be found in the document management system. Intranets can also be usefully implemented in law firms with as few as 10 employees.

Benefits to the End-Users

There are four benefits that can be used to justify an intranet investment to the user:

- **Access to the firm's corporate memory.** An intranet can be the home for all manner of information and is an extremely effective and efficient way of getting the right information into the hands of those that need it. Employee handbooks and the like are the most obvious types of content for the intranet. However, not all information is held in the form of documents; databases, large and small tend to proliferate across law firms. Intranets can be used to provide all users with access to these data sources.

- **Ease of use.** From a user's point of view, the web browser is very easy to use. Most web browsers have a few essential features - the back button, the forward button, the home button, a list of 'favourites' or most popular sites, an Address box or similar feature that allows users to enter the address (or URL - universal resource locator) of the site they wish to visit. Many employees will already have used web browsers to access the Internet as part of their work. Thus the training required to use an intranet is minimal, often non-existent.
- **A common presentation layer.** By developing an internal web site, a law firm can provide its employees with a breadth of information about all aspects of the firm, from something as everyday and mundane as the average interdepartmental memo to the most obscure information that can never be found when needed. In addition, the firm can incorporate its know-how. The intranet site can offer a common presentation layer to all of this information, meaning that all information can be located far more quickly and efficiently. The Internet is also becoming the presentation system of choice for commercial legal publishers. Therefore, it makes

sense to use the same web-based presentation system for all information whether created internally or externally. Giving users access to all of this information via one simple interface is a sensible and cost-efficient step.

- **Remote access.** Increasingly, lawyers need to be flexible about where they can work. With a little additional forethought, law firms can allow their employees to access the intranet from their computer at home, from their clients' offices, and even from their hotel rooms thousands of miles away from their base. What is more, the Web is becoming ubiquitous. Thus even if a lawyer doesn't have access to his or her own computer, they can still gain access to essential *internal* information via the Internet from web-based kiosks or terminals or from other remote locations. This means that lawyers will be able to function from any remote location as easily as if they were seated at their desks.

Benefits to the Firm

From the firm's point of view there are at least six key benefits. Perhaps the last of these is the most important.

- **Cost.** This has two aspects: first, there is the cost of building the intranet itself. Compared with most other technologies, developing a basic intranet is exceptionally cheap. It is entirely possible to create a stable, robust intranet site without spending any money on software. The web browser software used to access the intranet site is available free of charge. Similarly, many software packages used to host the web pages are also available without cost. However, intranets have a tendency to grow in terms of both overall content and in terms of users' expectations. Thus while they may begin life as relatively cheap projects, costs do tend to grow and should be budgeted for accordingly. Second, there are cost savings to be gained from using the intranet as opposed to the distribution of paper. Compared with sending paper around an organisation in order to communicate, the cost arguments are overwhelming. The most obvious short-term benefit is the saving in terms of printing materials. Instead of every employee receiving a copy of a document, whether they need it or not, all users can have access to a given document and only those who decide that they need a printed copy need print it off. It can be updated instantly, i.e. no costly printing re-runs.

- **Ease of development.** It is possible for anyone with even a modicum of technological aptitude to develop a static web site. What is more, the majority of web-development tools provide developers with design templates so that they can impose a corporate image and a standard 'look and feel' on all of the web pages that they create. To develop a basic law firm intranet can take as little as a few weeks. Compared with most other technological development projects few technical abilities are required to build a basic intranet site; the tools are becoming easier and easier to use; basic intranet development is not rocket science. However, most firms will quickly realise that their requirements are both more complex and more costly than those anticipated by developers of off-the-shelf solutions.
- **Use of existing networks.** Intranets also take

advantage of any existing PC networks within the law firm, although some upgrading may be required as the demand for information on the intranet increases. If the firm is not already using the TCP/IP protocol to give users access to the Internet, then it must be introduced. (All that is involved here is the installation of a small piece of software on each PC. This is likely to be the future computing protocol of choice in any event, and is therefore a wise investment for the future.)

- **Linkage to other IT systems.** The intranet can also link into so-called 'legacy systems' whether Practice Management Systems (used for accounting and billing purposes), Case Management Systems (most often used for managing large numbers of routine transactions such as residential conveyancing or debt collection matters), Document Management Systems (used for managing the massive amounts of documentation that law firms produce), Litigation Support Systems (used for managing all of the documentation that complex litigation produces), messaging, timesheets, researching. Potentially, all legal IT functions can be integrated into the intranet.
- **Reduced IT support.** An intranet can potentially reduce the workload on those responsible for PC support within the firm. For example, spreadsheets and small database packages are commonly used for one-off projects. Very often, more than one person will want to have access to the data contained there. To give more than one person access to such information will involve the installation of separate copies of the relevant software. However, if these applications are web-enabled, no new software is required. Instead,

everyone can use their web browser. (In case it is not already apparent, the Web is becoming the presentation layer of choice for most software packages and this is what is meant by 'web-enabled'.)

- **Empowerment.** Within every organisation there will be a group of employees for whom 'knowledge is power'. Given the opportunity, these employees will control access to even the most non-sensitive of information rigidly. Intranets are, potentially, an exercise in corporate democratisation. They have the power to make information available to all instead of a select few. With a decentralised approach to intranet content management, individuals can choose to make non-sensitive information available to all employees via the intranet, at no extra cost or even at less cost. Properly implemented, Intranets can radically alter the information culture of the firm. Where in the past information might be distributed on a need-to-know basis, intranets can shift the burden; they allow employees to ask themselves 'is there any reason why other people should not know about this? and assuming the answer is 'no' they will then publish that information. The importance of this cultural change should not be underestimated.

PATTERNS OF INTRANET DEVELOPMENT

Intranets can be likened to corporate information systems in the widest sense of the word, systems that can potentially provide employees with access to every form of information they would require in the course of their work. (The word 'potentially' should be noted here.) It is disappointing to note that most UK corporations do not share such high expectations about the ways in which intranets can be utilised. Just as most have taken the line of least resistance with their external web sites by publishing existing paper-based materials on the Web, most intranet usage is still limited to publishing existing information for internal consumption. For example, most corporate intranet sites will offer users access to Human Resources information, policy procedures and guidelines, information about various departments, what they can do for users and so forth. While providing access to the firm's knowledge base of corporate information is worthy in itself, this should only be a stepping stone to greater things.

Phases of Intranet Development

Ovum, the London-based IT research company predicts a four-phased wave of development in intranet applications (Pal, 1996):

- **Phase 1.** Information publishing applications - this is the simplest use of the technology and is what most UK corporations and law firms are doing at present. From the point of view of the intranet user, this process is likely to be quite beneficial; it means that employee handbooks and so forth are always available and always up to date. From the point of view of the web developer, this type of usage is worthy but dull. In addition, this is hardly using the technology strategically; it is simply doing what is most obvious. But it is a necessary first step which can prove the value of the intranet investment to a sceptical audience and paves the way for further phases of development. In the law firm context, it demonstrates to fee-earners how they could use this particular tool for higher-level tasks such as harnessing know-how.

- **Phase 2.** Informal collaboration applications - including web-enabled Groupware, such as bulletin boards, informal workflow and calendaring applications.
- **Phase 3.** Transaction-based applications - which integrate intranets with the core transaction systems. Transaction-based applications may be taken to include cxtranet-type applications where law firms provide legal services via the Web. This area is sufficiently important to be addressed separately.
- **Phase 4.** Formal collaboration applications - web-based workflow. In the law firm context, this would mean using the Web as a means of drafting documents collaboratively, working in conjunction with other lawyers and clients electronically.

This model of intranet development is useful to law firms up to a point. What it does not address is the significance of legal know-how in the law firm context. Precedents, research notes, conference papers and so forth are all considered to be know-how. Some lawyers consider these documents together with lists of clients' names and addresses to be the key intellectual assets, the crown jewels of the firm. A large percentage of a firm's know-how will exist on hard disk, in network directories and most importantly, in the minds of its Partners and employees. Transferring this knowledge onto a corporate information system such as an intranet is a major issue for law firms and of key significance if the firm wishes to leverage its own intellectual assets. This involves the application of so-called 'knowledge management' techniques, an area that is currently popular in management consultancy circles. The ideas and themes of knowledge management are addressed in the next chapter.

If the Ovum model is only of limited use, what are the alternatives? One method is to divide intranet development into two parts: firm-wide general information and know-how. An alternative method is the re-application of the 3 Cs model of content, communication and community. The intranet development process begins with content, i.e. simple information publishing. The second (communication) phase is achieved through the establishment of team-based applications, allowing intranet users to participate in the collaborative drafting of documents. The third phase is the development of virtual communities so that lawyers share their ideas and possible solutions to particular legal problems.

PRACTICAL DEVELOPMENT ISSUES

There are a number of considerable hurdles to be overcome between the conception of the idea and actually rolling out an intranet into a law firm. First, law firms should consider whether they should build their own customised solution or whether they should buy a solution off the shelf. Some smaller firms may wish to adopt the latter option. There are an increasing number of modularised intranet tools containing suites of applications. The applications available might include such things as tools to sort employee lists and photos, track contacts, create organisational charts, provide users with an electronic employee handbook, improve internal communication via a corporate calendaring application, and so forth. All that is required of the firm is simply to add content, that is information specific to the individual firm. For smaller firms, these tools can be very cost effective: software costing in the region of $5,000 is available for an unlimited number of users. However, whether right or not, most medium to large firms shun such an approach and instead choose to develop their own bespoke 'solutions'.

Project Management Issues

Many of the project management issues relating to intranets are relevant to any form of IT development. However, there are some subtle differences. For example, unlike traditional software that must be rewritten, recompiled and reinstalled, since an intranet is no more than a web site, it can be quickly altered to satisfy users' changing information requirements. Unlike most other IT projects, it can also be launched incomplete. Arguably, intranets can never be complete because they should be constantly changing.

IT project management literature usually recommends the adoption and implementation of formal project management methodologies[2] in all IT projects. While budgets, Gantt charts, deadlines, Partnership sponsorship and all the other tools of IT project management are important to intranet projects, there is no need to spend years determining user requirements and producing complex business specifications. Prototype intranet sites can be developed within weeks, even days. Indeed, a small prototype demonstrator intranet web site is likely to be sufficient as a proof of the concept. However, it is one thing to create an intranet site. It is quite another to embed its use into the fabric of the firm. a key issue is integration - moving the concept of an intranet from another isolated IT project ('out there') to an integrated service ('in here'). Thus, the most critical issue for the development and ongoing success of an intranet in a law firm context is the culture of the firm. First, there needs to be an understanding of the existing culture of the firm and second, there needs to be an appreciation of the implications of the intranet project/service for cultural change. In short, law firm intranet development is probably 25 per cent technology and 75 per cent cultural change.

Intranets and Corporate Culture

Understanding the culture of the firm in this context is important for two reasons. First, the culture of the firm may provide some clues as to the potential problems faced by the intranet developer and may affect the tactics employed in developing and promoting the intranet. Second, and more important, intranets have the potential to radically alter and enhance the legal information environment; this technology is not neutral. While the development of the technology is swift and, compared with most other technology projects, straightforward, the implications of its introduction are complex. An intranet is an extremely powerful tool by which to promote the democratisation of corporate information. Intranets are designed to act as corporate information repositories. In doing so, they tend to mirror the organisational structure of the firm and this can reveal the inadequacies of current systems, processes and structures. The intranet may reveal a view of the law firm that the Partnership does not wish to see. Revealing and resolving internal problems is a painful but necessary process in creating a more effective organisation, which in retrospect will be seen as a good thing. The intranet developer should acknowledge that in democratising the publication and consumption of information, he or she is 'letting a genie out of the bottle'. In most cases, this is probably beneficial and may well be an explicit goal of the intranet project, i.e. to replace bureaucracy and departmentalisation with cross-practice synergies and stimulation. But before embarking on a journey, one should know what to expect at the destination.

Understanding the Firm's 'Gods of Management'

Charles Handy, economist, philosopher, writer and business strategist, classifies organisations and individuals into four types, his so-called four Gods of Management. The Gods are those of ancient Greece. What is the relevance of ancient Greece to modern management? Handy explains:

> To the Greeks, religion was more a matter of custom than a formal theology. Their gods stood for certain things and, to a degree, you chose your god because you shared the values and interests which they represented.
>
> *Handy, 1995*

As individuals within the workplace, we each have our gods. Mandy's Gods of Management are defined as follows:

- **Zeus.** The supreme God in Greek mythology. 'He was feared, respected and occasionally loved. He represented the patriarchal tradition, irrational but often benevolent power, impulsiveness and charisma' (Handy, 1995). This is used to describe an organisation usually based around a single leader. This culture is often the norm in smaller professional services firms, demonstrated by high levels of trust, personal commitment, quick decision making, an absence of bureaucracy and office politics. A Zeus culture is also symbolised by a power structure with one or more charismatic leaders, a club culture. Individuals are inclined to think 'now what would the boss do in this situation?'.
- **Apollo.** The God of order and rules. This represents a role culture, where everyone in the organisation understands their own purpose and mission. Good examples of role cultures are the Civil Service, monopolies and state industries, although such cultures can also be found in larger financial and insurance organisations. In terms of running the actual intranet project,

everything must be done by the rules, and corners cannot be cut. This type of organisational culture is not usually found in professional services firms where the focus is upon getting results for clients no matter what the internal structure of the firm.

- **Athena.** A young warrior goddess. This represents a task-oriented and problem-solving culture. Such organisations are non-hierarchical, encourage creativity, imagination and a team-based approach to problems. Many law firms aspire to be Athena-like in their approach to their work and intranets can play a key role in facilitating this. In terms of actually running the intranet project, it is probably the easiest culture in which to develop an intranet.
- **Dionysus.** In Greek mythology, strictly the God of the vine but also the God of wine and song. This model is used to refer to individuals who are unorthodox, individualistic and even anarchic in their approach to their work. In an organisational context, it is used to describe companies or firms that are characterised by informality, a decentralised power structure, and in some cases, incompetence. In a law firm context, it will be illustrated by lawyers who use the vocabulary of 'their own practice' without reference to the firm's practice or to its development. Dionysians as individuals are very difficult to manage, usually highly self-motivated (rarely motivated by others). They are the very antithesis of the team player. Dionysians proliferate in research institutions and universities, and unfortunately, in law firms as well. From an IT perspective, it is the most challenging of all environments.

Many, perhaps most, law, firms are a combination of three of these four models. There are other characteristics of an organisation that are not addressed by this analysis, such as a forward-looking culture as opposed to a 'dinosaur'; a traditional or clubby environment as opposed to a professional one; a 'learning' organisation as opposed to a 'know-it-all' organisation; an organisation that is 'believed in' or not 'believed in'. There are many others. Usually, the culture of the firm in terms of its strengths and weaknesses will be understood by its Partners or longer-serving employees. (It may be no surprise if they are either unwilling or unable to verbalise their understanding.)

It should be recognised that corporate cultures change of themselves. A small law firm might start out as a Zeus culture. As it grows there might be an attempt to impose some order onto the chaos that can accompany growth - the imposition of an Apollo culture. Athenian or task-based groups may appear as the firm attempts to branch out into new forms of legal work and the firm may, of course, attract Dionysian individuals. The particular balance of gods will vary from firm to firm. What is likely is that all firms will have some combination; the intranet developer will come across every type in due course.

Dealing with Individual Resistance to Change

Being right about the likely benefits of an intranet is insufficient. The business case for an intranet in terms of user benefits, empowerment and cost savings may be overwhelming, but all of this is as nothing if those resistant to change cannot be effectively managed or their opposition neutralised. The introduction of an intranet, like any other form of technology, will mean a change in working practices. Change for most people is unsettling, perhaps threatening and even disruptive; the intranet project manager needs to recognise this and manage this change effectively. Resistance will usually take one of two forms - active and passive. The active resister is more easily managed; they can be more easily identified, perhaps given further retraining and ultimately disciplinary proceedings can be invoked by the firm if active resistance is actually undermining the project. The passive resister is more tricky to deal with, but is no less of a threat to the success of the project. Passive resistance can take a number of forms: the passive resister can attend meetings, agree to perform certain tasks then do nothing; they can undermine the project by talking down the benefits to anyone who will listen; they can seek the ear of senior management and feed misleading or even factually incorrect information. In other words, they use the classic negative marketing techniques of engendering fear, uncertainty and doubt.

Handy's Gods of Management can also be applied to individuals as well as corporations, although most employees are too complex to be described as subscribers to a single god - they will possess a combination of traits. Understanding the type of individual is important for developing the appropriate techniques to deal with their concerns. When confronted with change most individuals go through a four-phased cycle of denial, resistance, exploration and confidence (Yeates and Cadle, 1996). Depending on the individual and measure of the changes involved, the length of time spent in each phase can vary. For example, some individuals will immediately recognise the value of the intranet and be persuaded; the denial und resistance phases are bypassed. The exploration and confidence phases are reached immediately. Others will deny the need for change right up to and even beyond the launch of any new IT project. Until the benefits of the new system are clearly demonstrated to them, they will not recognise the need for a new way of doing things. After the launch of the project, some individuals will still resist it. The reasons are complex: an intranet may be seen as usurping the individual's traditional role as an information provider; it may represent an open approach to information sharing which is contrary to the personal philosophy of certain individuals; it may be seen as too complicated, too technical because it works differently from most other applications on the PC. Through training and trial and error, individuals explore the system and their self-confidence grows. Gradually as people explore the new system further they will gain confidence with it, eventually taking responsibility and ownership for parts of the system and pride in the benefits that it offers.

The Need for a 'Killer App'

There will a variety of applications such as firm-wide calendars, litigation diaries and lists of frequently asked questions (FAQs) that will all be of assistance to users, if relocated to the firm's intranet. Ideally, law firms should perform a communication audit to determine which applications can be easily transferred and which would maximise the benefit to users. What is most important, however, is that users can see at least one clear and distinct benefit of using the intranet. If users do not like what they see, they can simply choose not to use it. No amount of clever technology will make up for the fact that if users cannot find what they want quickly and easily, they will simply stick to their tried and trusted methods of obtaining information. Thus the intranet should contain at least one application that meets users' needs better than all the alternatives, that persuades users that they should not only adopt this technology but that they cannot live without it - a so-called killer application or 'killer app'.

The history of information technology is littered with numerous examples of killer apps. For accountants, the spreadsheet was the killer app, the tool that persuaded many to invest in the PC. Desktop publishing was a killer app for the graphics design industry (and in the process made the Apple Macintosh the standard within the industry). Email was the Internet's first killer app. So what is the killer app for the intranet? In larger law firms it is likely to be something as humble as the telephone directory. The reason is that for most large organisations, producing a phonebook is a major administrative task. Every individual in every department has to be issued with a large book, or a folder containing all relevant contact details. Phonebooks become out of date as soon as they are published, as people leave, join, are promoted, change job titles and so forth. Indeed, in some larger global organisations, producing an up-to-date phonebook is such an enormous task they simply do not attempt it; each office is responsible for its own phone list. From the employee's point of view, not having a proper phonebook is an irritation that can also become embarrassing when a customer or client cannot be routed to the appropriate person within the organisation. Alternatively, it becomes an irritation as updates have to be constantly inserted and removed. Employees who are pushed for time will not always update the directory, with the result that out-of-date information is circulating within the organisation and employees will not be able to rely on the directory.

By contrast, a centralised phonebook on the intranet can be quickly updated and 'republished' on a daily or even hourly basis. Of course, being available on a web site, it is always available. Changes can be effected immediately and are available to all. There are additional benefits: the list of names and numbers can link to more detailed information such as job title, biographical details, c.v.s, lists of responsibilities, external memberships, publications, and so forth. Something as simple as a phonebook can justify the intranet investment through the savings on printing hard copies. British Telecom are known to have saved £20 million by putting their own internal phonebook on their intranet (Bailey, 1998). If implemented in a structured manner, this type of application can also give the firm access to new information. For example, the web developer can create search facilities not just allowing users to find colleagues via their first name or last name, but also giving users the facility to find out how many people work in particular departments, the make-up of those departments in terms of ratios of Partners to assistants, and so forth. In pre-intranet times this type of detailed information was available to very few individuals, usually the top management of the firm. Using the intranet, such information is democratised; it is available to all.

Intranet Management: Centralised V. Decentralised

A lot of the early adopters of intranets were the larger software and telecoms providers where small groups of technically adept employees had immediate access to a web server (see the Glossary for a definition). These groups of resourceful employees would quickly set up a small internal web site for their own use and for the purposes of internal marketing. As the internal IT departments discovered these developments, they attempted to rein in such activities on the (entirely correct) grounds that this *ad hoc* approach was a recipe for chaos.

There are clear justifications for having a centralised approach. If all intranet content is administered by one or more individuals, they can quickly and easily pick out those areas on their site or sites where there is content that is either dead or is not being utilised (by examining their own web site statistics). In terms of consistency of slyle, there are clear benefits. If there are as many internal web sites as there are departments (or in the case of law firms, practice area groups), the end result will be inconsistent layout and navigation styles (meaning that users have to learn how to use a different web site for each department or group) and duplication of information. The final justification involves the use of new technologies. There are thousands of new companies bringing out web-based products virtually each day, whether database integration products, discussion forums or workflow products. By having a centralised approach to intranet development, an organisation can deploy these new technologies to all users instantly by simply adding a new piece of software to a single web server or group of servers, instead of having to reinstall software across multiple servers at multiple locations.

There are, however, some arguments for having a decentralised approach. Having one or two people manage an intranet creates a bottleneck in the flow of information from information 'producers' to information 'consumers'. This problem should not be underestimated. The Information Technology department will quickly become immersed in adding and removing information to and from the intranet site or sites. This is a fairly low-level task; it does not make best use of the IT skills available. It also detracts the IT department from other tasks such as developing new services for the intranet and extending its reach. If a bottleneck remains, the information producers may decide not to send any further information forward for inclusion on the intranet. This action will negate all the rhetoric about intranets facilitating more open information and knowledge sharing.

Establishing the Intranet Franchise

The solution is to *decentralise the ownership of content*, i.e. the actual information that goes on the intranet, and at the same time *centralise the technological infrastructure*. In other words, give other employees the ability to add, edit and remove information to and from the intranet while at the same time retaining control over the way in which the pages are presented. This can be achieved in one of two ways. The first is to separate entirely the content from the layout by storing all information that goes on the intranet in a database. There are specific products that have been developed for this very purpose. Software can be bought off the shelf, or with the necessary technical expertise such tools can be developed in-house. The content can then be added, updated and deleted very easily by individuals with no technical expertise whatsoever. Meanwhile the layout (the way in which the information is presented) and underlying technology can be controlled and managed centrally by design and technical professionals. The second method is to invest in some of the newer collaborative web development software that is now appearing. Whatever method is chosen, the benefits will quickly become apparent. Instead of simply adding, editing and removing content those responsible for maintaining the intranet will be freed to concentrate on developing more and better web-based tools. Similarly, each department will 'own' and control their own information. The IT department is simply the initiator and manager of the technical infrastructure. However, safeguards should be developed in terms of guides to writing on the Web. Guidelines will need to be produced. These will evolve over time.[3] The effect of content devolution is that the intranet stops becoming a project owned by the IT department and instead becomes a project owned by every department or practice area that has the ability to contribute, in other words everyone!

EVALUATING THE BENEFITS

For many law firms, it is still too early to evaluate the benefits of their intranet. However, like every IT application it should be evaluated. There are two types of evaluation:

formative evaluation - that which influences the design and development, and summative evaluation - that which provides evidence of effects and achievements. There are many different evaluation tools available. At one end of the spectrum there are the *ad hoc* collection of users' responses using tools such as on-line discussion forums and on-line questionnaires through to assessing user feedback via techniques such as recording/logging user behaviour, structured interviews, focus groups, observation and participant observation surveys. The techniques chosen will depend on the purpose and also on the resources available.

Problems Associated with Intranets

From the user's point of view, information overload is likely to be the biggest problem associated with Intranets. According to a 1998 KPMG research report into information management, over 44 per cent of respondents were concerned about information overload. The last thing that lawyers need is yet another information source that will bombard them with information that they don't need. The benefits brought by email are already being diluted by the diminishing 'signal to noise' ratio (i.e. the amount of actually useful and relevant email compared with the irrelevant and the useless). It is intended that intranets should provide users with only the essential information, that the signal to noise ratio should be higher.

From the firm's point of view, increased access to information and know-how via the firm's intranet carries a risk that individual lawyers will use know-how documents inappropriately. The ability to access large quantities of seemingly relevant information may lead the lawyer into a false sense of security. Thus, instead of speaking with colleagues, the lawyer may instead simply take copies of documents off the firm's intranet and use them uncritically.

Intranets, like public web sites, can suffer if there is a lack of evangelisation. While some parts of an intranet may become well used, others may be neglected. Again this comes back to the need for a killer app. Indeed, there may be the need for several killer apps littered throughout the intranet to ensure that the less well-known by-ways are also explored. Unfortunately, lawyers are under increasing pressure to spend time billing rather than exploring services that may or may not be of use. Once a new service is established it must be extensively advertised internally to ensure that it is used.

From the content contributor's point of view time may be a problem. If the firm is large and has many content contributors, then (given the current state of the technology) these individuals will need to find the time necessary to create materials that can be added to the intranet. However, in time it will be possible for users to simply click a button that says 'publish this on the intranet and create links for any other document that should reference it' and it will happen.

WHERE ARE INTRANETS GOING?

In terms of actually changing the way a law firm does its business, intranets will become truly revolutionary when law firms open them up to their clients, to counsel and to court officials, in other words, when they become extranets. Just as Federal Express have opened up their parcel-tracking system to their customers via the Web, in due course, law firms will either choose to (or be forced to) open up their systems to provide their own clients and contacts with information relating to the particular legal matters in hand. These systems may include all relevant client documentation, but may also include summaries of actions to date, action points from previous meetings, meeting schedules and the like. We will see different types of information made available according to the nature of the visitor. For example, the firm may wish to provide (or the client may demand) a summary of billing to date, time not billed and access to all previous bill narratives. The truly intelligent intranet application will also work with all of the parties' existing software so that changes made on the client/matter intranet site will be reflected elsewhere. This type of application becomes particularly useful where there are more than two parties to the litigation matter. If there are several co-defendants, then sharing documents will be quicker and more efficient and therefore cheaper for the client. From an IT support perspective, instead of having to deal with hardware or software incompatibility problems between client and solicitor or solicitor and counsel, all parties to the action will have a single interface access to up-to-date, accurate and genuinely useful information. Perhaps the logical extension of this concept is for the courts themselves to establish specific web sites. Thus, to answer the original question, 'where are intranets going for law firms?', they will be extended outside the firm as extranets.

ACTION POINTS

1. Determine your firm's culture and work with it - don't try to change it! It will change itself over time.
2. Build a prototype intranet site as a proof of concept.
3. Find and implement a 'killer app' on the intranet.
4. Centralise the technology, but decentralise the content. Give employees the ability to manage information about themselves and their department, practice area or group.
5. Evangelise the intranet - establish awareness sessions and training for new joiners.

6. Beware of information overload, technology sceptics and the time constraints of content contributors.
7. Evaluate constantly.

FURTHER READING

Bernard, R. (1998). *The Corporate Intranet.* 2nd edition. John Wiley and Sons, New York.

Gonzalez, J.S. (1998). *The 21st Century Intranet.* Prentice-Hall Computer Books, Rhinebeck, New York.

Greer, T. (1998). *Understanding Intranets.* Microsoft Press.

NOTES

1. A document management system is a piece of technology that allows users to store information about the documents that they create which can then be searched on later. Document management systems can also offer audit facilities, which show the life of the document and security features which can limit the users who can read, print and amend the document, and so forth.
2. Such as PRINCE (Projects in Controlled Environments) or SSADM (Structured Systems Analysis and Design Method).
3. There is, however, an excellent *Guide to Web Style,* available on the Internet at http://www.sun.com/styleguide/ which offers useful advice on how to write for the Web, whether private or public.

BIBLIOGRAPHY

Bailey, Liz (1998). 'Why your clients need an intranet now', *Webspace Magazine,* April, p.26.

Handy, Charles (1995). *Gods of Management.* Arrow Books Limited, London, pp.9-20.

Pal, A. (1996). *Intranets and IT Nirvana.* Ovum Reports. A White Paper (available at http://www.ovum.com/innovate/gr2/gr2wp.html).

Yeates, D. and Cadle, J. (eds) (1996). *Project Management for Information Systems.* Pitman Publishing, London, p. 4.

4 KNOWLEDGE MANAGEMENT AND INTRANETS

WHAT IS KNOWLEDGE MANAGEMENT?

There is a significant business literature emerging on knowledge management, which suggests that the successful exploitation of 'knowledge assets' or so-called 'intellectual capital' is a key to competitive advantage in the future. The goal is simple: to discover what the organisation knows, where that knowledge lives, how it can be found in future, made useful and relevant and how it can be delivered to the right person at the right time.

The term itself is probably an oxymoron. Knowledge cannot be 'managed' *per se* because it is too amorphous. Only the systems that filter, categorise, condense and deliver knowledge can be managed. But some of the above goals are being tackled under this all-embracing banner. So does this theory offer anything new or is it simply 'old wine in new skins'? There are those who believe that knowledge management is no more than a repackaging of information management, which in turn is no more than a repackaging of document management. Such analysis is harsh and somewhat simplistic. It is true that some software suppliers and management consultancies have jumped on this particular bandwagon, repackaging their products and services. (Cynics would say that they have done so in order to counter the post-year 2000 and post-Euro drop in corporate IT spending.) However, there is more to knowledge than simply documents and there is more to knowledge management than just intranets.

CASE STUDY: XEROX AND A LESSON FOR INTRANET DEVELOPERS

Xerox are probably best known as the manufacturer of photocopiers. There is a (possibly apocryphal) story of how Xerox spent many years and many thousands of dollars back in the 1980s attempting to build a so-called expert system* that would encapsulate all of the knowledge held by their various employees about how to fix notoriously complex photocopiers.The project team lumbered from crisis to crisis and after many years, were still no nearer to producing a working system. In the end the Xerox management sacked their chief technologist and instead hired an anthropologist to observe the work of the photocopier engineers. The conclusion of the anthropologist was that the expert system project should be abandoned altogether and instead all engineers should be issued with two-way radios. That way, this particular group of experts could be brought together over the airwaves at any time to discuss a problem that one of their number might have. Xerox duly purchased the two-way radios and the expert system project was abandoned, never to be completed. Technology that attempted to capture knowledge was not the solution. Instead, the solution was a 'technology' (i.e. two-way radios) that facilitated the sharing of experience.What was required was unhindered information flow and the ability to group-tackle problems.

---

* An expert system is a computer program that attempts to mimic the way in which human beings reason through the use of IF.. .THEN rules. By responding with yes, no and maybe to various questions, it is intended that the program can deduce what the problem and the solution might be. An example of a rule embedded in an expert system designed to fix a photocopier might be 'IF paper is jamming at point X, THEN check the placement of the toner cartridge'. The expert system would then ask the user if he/she has checked the placement of the toner cartridge, and based on the response, the system would ask further questions until, eventually, the problem is solved.

The Legal Information Environment

Managing knowledge in a law firm is a key problem, arguably *the* great unsolved problem from an IT perspective. Most law firms now recognise that the documents they create are a huge yet untapped asset. At the same time, lawyers want to work in a perfect information environment: an environment where exactly the right type and the right amount of information is delivered to them wherever they may be when they need it.

By contrast, lawyers, like most other knowledge workers are drowning in a sea of irrelevant information and trivia: newspapers, emails, faxes and paper documents are all part of the problem. Generally information technology only makes a bad situation worse. What is more, new (IT-inspired) information channels appear with each passing year: web sites for example, whether internal or external, add to the problem. They do not solve it. Technology has also given legal publishers the ability to deliver 'potentially relevant information' to the desktop of lawyers on a daily basis, whether via on-line databases such as Lexis-Nexis or Lawtel, CD-ROMs, or via traditional paper-based publishing. Lawyers are in an impossible position. They feel the need to know about every potentially relevant legal development; they cannot afford not to know about a case or issue of public policy that may affect their client's interests.

But lawyers are also their own worst enemies. They are not only information gatherers, they are also information hoarders. Given a large office containing filing cabinets and in-built shelving, they feel almost duty-bound to fill them. Furthermore, in the absence of an organised information or knowledge management initiative, many lawyers will consider information hoarding as necessary for their professional survival. Over time, the lawyer will come will come to believe that it is in their own best interests. The logic is compelling: by hoarding information. It is always available there is no need to compete with other lawyers, or chase around the firm for a copy of a particular piece of information. They can also act as gatekeeper on their own information, ensuring that only certain individuals gain access to their own personal know-how collection. This obsession with information hoarding reaches its logical conclusion when the lawyer in question comes to believe that a monopoly on particular information will lead to personal indispens-ability within the firm - an insurance policy against redundancy. This is an understandable but a wholly irrational belief.

The only truly organised information resource for the entire firm is the library or information centre. Here, books, periodicals and practitioner encyclopaedias are categorised, ordered, shared and most importantly, managed. Many of the medium-to-large law firms have attempted to utilise the existing information management capabilities of information professionals to create a so-called 'info-bank' or 'brief-bank' solution.

The Info-Bank/Brief-Bank Solution

Law firms have also recognised that legal documents produced both in-house and elsewhere are a huge dormant asset, which if managed properly can prevent the reinvention of the wheel. Since the early 1990s many law firms have invested in document management 'solutions', products which allow the user to create a profile of a document being created and then search for those documents at a later date. In addition, they may have developed their own internal know-how projects. Many of the larger firms have spent significant time and effort establishing so-called info-banks, corporate depositories for legal information that one could not find in either traditional legal textbooks or practitioners texts. A typical info-bank might include firm precedents, information on foreign lawyers, information about counsel including c.v.s, papers from conferences (either given or attended), useful counsel opinions, court transcripts, and so forth. The size of an info-bank can range from a few hundred documents to tens of thousands. On this topic Susskind writes:

> a variety of approaches to in-house know-how systems have been attempted and adopted with varying degrees of success. This remains perhaps the most challenging aspect of IT Development for lawyers offering the promise of a means of harnessing the most valuable resource of practitioners - their expertise - which is all the more powerful when combined with that of others.
>
> *Susskind, 1996*

In many of the larger law firms, intranet projects are seen as a useful new way of addressing the issue of know-how.

However, once again, such an initiative is based on an assumption that is flawed. The mere existence of a particular type of technology does not turn a knowledge-hoarding organisation into a knowledge-sharing one just as the existence of a telephone system does not necessarily lead to incisive intelligent conversations between two individuals. The replacement of an existing 'info-bank' technology with a more up-to-date and (perhaps) user-friendly web-based system is certainly a forward step. (A web-based system has the potential to allow users to access the system from wherever they can find access to the Internet - from their home, from a hotel or from a web-based kiosk.)

But in terms of knowledge management it is only part of the solution and not an end in itself. Studies have shown that managers get two-thirds of their information and knowledge from face-to-face meetings or phone conversations. Only one third comes from documents (Davenport, 1994). Thus, a knowledge management strategy that focuses entirely on intranets as a mechanism purely for document delivery is a one-dimensional strategy and unlikely to create the more radical change that is required. The overall goal of the intranet should be to improve knowledge sharing between lawyers and thereby alter the culture of the firm in a positive way. Knowledge management is people management and much more about cultural change than the implementation of intranets. Information technology is only the enabler - a means to the end not the end in itself.

There has been relatively little in the way of substantive research into know-how in UK law firms. One of the few surveys of the subject [1] found that the take-up of such projects was broadly comparable across all regions of the UK. However, as the size of the firm increased, one could observe a greater interest in know-how projects. This is not altogether surprising. Larger firms have a broader and deeper body of knowledge to capture. They also have greater financial resources at their disposal. The survey also found that the majority of firms had conducted a review of the existing services provided by the Library and Information Services Department and further that some 96 per cent of those 'firms with a know-how system said that it had added to the range and scope of the services which they were able to provide'. Furthermore the development of a know-how project had increased the need for the skills of library and information services professionals. How successful these projects have been is difficult to assess. The survey offered scant indications, as few firms were willing to share their experiences in this regard. Neither were actual technologies used discussed, because again they were viewed as a source of competitive advantage. In reality, the technology adopted is highly unlikely to be a source of competitive advantage 'because essentially the same technology is available to everyone, it cannot provide a long-term edge to anyone' (Davenport and Prusak, 1998). Content is more likely to prove decisive - the knowledge itself is the competitive advantage.

A One-Sided Debate

The contrast between the two sides of the IT debate - information and technology, is startling. The literature on information and knowledge management in the UK law firm is sparse. We have for example, one small research report and a few pages in a leading text. By comparison the marketing literature and free seminars on technology 'solutions' available to corporate organisations is vast.

The result is that we have become obsessed with technology: the latest hardware upgrades, the latest operating systems, the latest applications and the latest buzzwords. We have been seduced by impressive marketing tools and techniques and often willingly upgrade for the sake of upgrading. Yet at the same time we acknowledge that such upgrades will make not the slightest difference to overall productivity. Why is this? Part of the reason is that information and knowledge are intangibles - it is far simpler (and, from the vendor's point of view, easier to turn a profit) by pointing one's finger at a lawyer's computer system and saying 'you need a better one' than to examine poorly defined information systems and methodologies which may reflect uncomfortably on the internal culture of the firm. Another fundamental reason is that we lack a common vocabulary with which to commence such a debate.

ESTABLISHING THE VOCABULARY

There are three fundamental information management concepts that require definition: data, information and knowledge. The first is simple - data is raw facts and figures. Information can be defined as 'data processed into meaningful patterns' (Lindsey Scott, 1998). Data becomes information by adding value. In other words, knowledge workers and information professionals do things to data to make it more useful. Davenport and Prusak identify five methods by which knowledge workers add value to information: contextualisation - users gain an understanding of the purpose for which the data was gathered; categorisation - users understand how a single piece of information fits into the overall body of knowledge and can gain easier access to it; calculation - the data may have to be analysed mathematically or statistically; correction - knowledge workers or information professionals may have to remove errors; condensation - the data may have to be summarised

A non-dictionary definition of knowledge might be 'that which enables the generation of new information from existing information'. If we take a step back from the semantics, most people would agree that there is some form of interplay between information and knowledge. The concept of knowledge implies a body of information that is of a higher value or calibre, that offers meaning or insight. The distinction between knowledge and information should be made clear, 'knowledge is a personal subjective process emerging from previous experiences and current events, while information is objective data about the environment' (Roos *et al.*, 1997). Knowledge has other characteristics: 'knowledge is aware of what it doesn't know ... unlike data and information, knowledge contains judgement. Not only can it judge new situations and information in light of what is already known, it judges and refines itself in response to new situations and information' (Davenport and Prusak, 1998). 'Knowledge, unlike information, is about beliefs and commitments' (Nonaka and Takeuchi, 1995). Knowledge is information made actionable. Knowledge also evolves: the knowledgeable person who does not continue to learn soon becomes dogmatic and opinionated. There is a further twist in the professional services context. Unlike a university researcher, a law firm is not interested in the pursuit of abstract knowledge *per se,* but in applied knowledge or know-how, or alternatively 'the use of knowledge combined with experience'.[2]

Why Consider Knowledge Separately?

There are plenty of useful quotations from management literature on the importance of information and knowledge in today's marketplace. Tom Peters writes 'Success in the marketplace today is directly proportional to the knowledge that an organisation can bring to bear, how fast it can bring that knowledge to bear and the rate at which it accumulates knowledge' (Peters, 1994). Superior knowledge is not merely a source of competitive advantage but a prerequisite. Peter Drucker argues that in the new knowledge-based economy, knowledge is not simply another resource alongside traditional factors of production, namely labour, capital and land but the only meaningful resource (Drucker, 1993). In short, knowledge replaces all other production factors. A realisation of this magnitude ought to lead to a cultural revolution in the workplace. If we agree that knowledge is the only meaningful asset in the workplace, it should alter our entire approach to the management of knowledge. Fundamental questions should be asked: where is this knowledge? Who is using it and how? How can it be measured? And most importantly - how can its potential be leveraged? But lawyers would look upon this debate and argue that they have always been knowledge workers - they synthesise, condense, simplify and apply information to create new information; in other words they have been adding value to information for centuries. So what is new here?

Being such a new area of study, there is no definitive model of knowledge management - it is currently no more than a collection of ideas and themes. Even if there were a single theory of knowledge management, it would probably not apply to law firms in its entirety. Knowledge management tools and techniques are industry-specific: the way in which a law firm uses its knowledge is manifestly different from, say, a car manufacturer. For example, a law firm does not go through iterative cycles in attempting to refine a physical product which can be mass produced. By and large, law firms apply a body of specialised knowledge to a unique client problem in order to provide a customised solution. The solution may be highly customised - a unique 'one-off' or it may be a solution that is a variation on a well-known theme. Furthermore, it may be that the firm can replicate aspects of the solution elsewhere but often, particularly on complex matters, it cannot.

Knowledge assets will exist in many places - on paper, in electronic records, in the business logic that defines corporate systems (whether IT or otherwise) or in people's heads. The essence of a knowledge management strategy in a law firm context is getting as much knowledge out of information cul-de-sacs such as people's heads and embedded into corporate systems and into the heads of others. What every law firm seeks (or should seek) is a methodology that allows the systematic capture, development and use of legal and quasi-legal knowledge. The means by which this is achieved will vary. It is likely to involve some form of technology, perhaps an internet-based solution, but combined with this is the need for significant cultural change. Such change will only be achieved when there are incentives and rewards for knowledge creators to share their knowledge and when a corporate culture exists which promotes and demonstrates the benefits of corporate knowledge sharing.

THREE MODELS OF KNOWLEDGE MANAGEMENT

Model I: The Learning Loop

A simple model of knowledge management envisages a so-called 'learning loop' within the organisation (see Figure 4.1). On one part of the loop, there exists a knowledge base which is utilised in the course of the work of the firm. By combining this knowledge with an employee's own knowledge and utilising the knowledge of others, the employee can perform certain actions or deliver particular outcomes. This in turn may provide further insights which can be fed back into the knowledge base and be reused by others. However, this is a very shallow model as it does not distinguish between the different types of knowledge that may exist within the organisation.

Model 2: Intellectual Capital

An alternative is to look at information and knowledge as one body of intellectual capital (for further discussion see Roos *et al.*, 1997) alongside the more traditional notions of resources such as plant, machinery and other assets. Intellectual capital theory attempts to explain the difference between the value assigned to a corporation by a stock market and the value assigned by the balance sheet. The leading pioneer of this approach is Leif Edvinsson, Corporate Director of Intellectual Capital for Skandia, the Swedish financial services corporation. According to Edvinsson, intellectual capital can be divided into a number of component parts:

Human Capital

Human capital (a firm's employees) is loaned rather than owned and is withdrawn when an employee leaves the firm. It has also been called 'migratory knowledge' (Badaracco, 1991). Roos *et al.* sub-divide this category still further, into competence, attitude and intellectual agility.

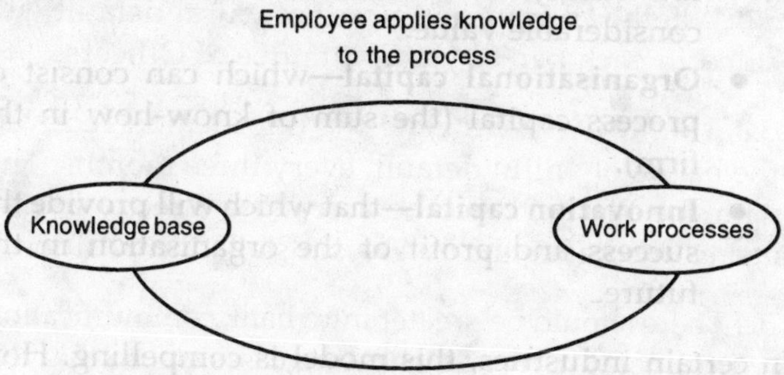

Figure 4.1. The learning loop.

Structural Capital

This is the know-how contained in the firm's processes and systems (not necessarily IT systems). Skandia define structural capital as all the intellectual capital that remains in the company when employees go home at night. It will consist of infrastructure, processes and culture. Good examples of structural capital in the retail sector might be product supply chains - the mechanisms by which large supermarket chains ensure that they have the right produce, of sufficient quality in the right place at the right time, in other words, a process. Structural capital can also exist in brand names and trademarks which are more easily valued by traditional accountancy methods. Structural capital can then be further divided into:

- **Customer capital**—this is defined as a firm's relationship with its clients or customers or all of those things that bind a particular customer to a particular organisation. Where a company competes for one-off purchases and competes mainly on price, there is likely to be little customer capital. However, where there are likely to be long-standing relationships and price is likely to be only one of many factors (as is the case for law firms), then customer capital will have considerable value.

- **Organisational capital**—which can consist of process capital (the sum of know-how in the firm).
- **Innovation capital**—that which will provide the success and profit of the organisation in the future.

In certain industries, this model is compelling. How else, for instance, can one explain the fact that in early 1999, Microsoft had net fixed assets of less than $1 billion but a market valuation of nearer $400 billion? The market has valued Microsoft so highly because it recognises that the company has significant human and structural capital, items which cannot appear on the traditional balance sheet. In the law firm context, however, this intellectual capital model is helpful only up to a point. Law firms, being partnerships, are not listed on any stock exchange nor do they tend to publish annual reports. It is difficult to assign a monetary value to the intellectual capital of lawyers, except by asking for a view from a lawyer's peer group. In addition, many law firms are heavily reliant on their individual 'stars' - in other words, their human capital has far more value than their structural capital. However, it does at least help us to categorise different forms of knowledge.

Model 3: Tacit and Explicit Knowledge

Perhaps the most persuasive model and one that is

most relevant to the law firm context is that espoused by two Japanese academics. Their theory is as follows. Knowledge can be divided into explicit knowledge - that which is formal and systematic, can be more easily processed, transmitted electronically and stored in databases; and tacit knowledge - that which is 'highly personal and hard to formalise, making it difficult to communicate or share with others' (Nonaka and Takeuchi, 1995). They, believe that there are four modes of knowledge conversion that are created when tacit and explicit knowledge interact. They define these four modes as socialisation, externalisation, combination and internalisation.

Socialisation

> a process of sharing experiences and thereby creating tacit knowledge such as shared mental models and technical skills... apprentices working with their masters and learning craftsmanship not through language but through observation, imitation and practice.
>
> *Nonaka and Takeuchi, 1995*

The Xerox story illustrates the importance of socialisation: shared experiences via two-way radios. The real-world problems could not be solved by trying to capture all of the engineers' knowledge in a computer program or even in a document. Instead, technology (in this case two-way radios) could be used to improve communication. A solicitor's traineeship is another good example of knowledge transfer through socialisation. The belief is that through a traineeship, trainee solicitors learn to think like practising lawyers rather than law students.

Externalisation

This is 'the process of articulating tacit knowledge into explicit concepts ... taking the shape of metaphors, analogies, concepts, hypotheses or models' (Nonaka and Takeuchi; 1995).

Combination

Explicit to explicit - 'a process of systemising concepts into a knowledge system. Individuals exchange and combine knowledge through such media as documents, meetings, telephone conversations or computerised networks' (Nonaka and Takeuchi, 1995). Good examples of the combination approach to knowledge creation are the many law firm know-how projects established to capture legal knowledge in the form of legal documents. Clearly there cannot be direct explicit to explicit knowledge transfer - knowledge cannot be created by computers directly - humans must play an intervening role.

Internalisation

From explicit to tacit - 'when experiences are internalised ... into individuals' tacit knowledge bases in the form of shared mental models or technical know-how' (Nonaka and Takeuchi, 1995). Reading a book is a good example of taking explicit information and from it, creating an internal mental model.

Rather than looking at knowledge sharing as a mechanism that threatens the role of the individual, this model encourages companies to provide the individual employee with an opportunity to demonstrate his or her expertise and ensures that individual abilities are widely recognised and appreciated. It also encourages traditional techniques such as storytelling as a method of sharing knowledge. But the application of these techniques is dependent on the culture of the organisation. Here we can return to the analysis devised by Handy, as explained in the previous chapter. Japanese corporate culture is based on a very complex yet fluid form of the Apollo-based culture. The significance of group thinking above individual thinking is paramount. Japanese companies are known (and one suspects, quietly ridiculed in some quarters in the UK) for their emphasis on the continual development of the brand of the company both to customers and employees, with their emphasis on doing things their way, and the continual reinforcement of their values through the company song and slogan. Either the individual conforms to their ways of working or the individual leaves. Hence socialisation techniques such as storytelling within the Apollo-based culture will work quite successfully.

By contrast, the prevailing attitude in most UK law firms will be a combination of Zeus, Apollo and Dionysus. The notion of group story-telling seems bizarre. It is hard to envisage too many City lawyers feeling comfortable sharing their 'war stories' with their more junior colleagues over a cup of sake or a gin and tonic! However, ideas such as storytelling should not be entirely dismissed. Storytelling is a non-intrusive way of exchanging knowledge. Whether gossip on the stairs or exchanges outside the boardroom, they are the lifeblood of any organisation. After all, what did this chapter begin with but a story? Knowledge management techniques must be chosen and applied in ways that are appropriate to the prevailing culture of the firm.

From Theory to Practice

All of the above is interesting, at least in an academic sense. But what relevance docs knowledge management have to the very practical subject of intranet development? In the previous chapter, we addressed the need for a killer app an application that would persuade potential users to use an intranet. What knowledge management does is to bring an extra dimension to this type of development. Instead of simply being a useful tool for names and numbers the phonebook application can be extended still further to include information that might be deemed important to a knowledge management initiative. By inviting the lawyers themselves to include information about their specialist legal skills within a phonebook-type application, an intranet can make a significant contribution to capturing knowledge about who knows what. This is different from a biographical summary. Instead, it includes information about what the individual lawyers believe that they are really good at and would like to be known for throughout the firm. Susskind calls this 'know-who' as opposed to 'know-how' (Susskind, 1996) and they are both equally important.

The recently merged company, BP-Amoco, have taken precisely this step. A small group of knowledge management pioneers have developed a mechanism so that users can update their own details via the intranet. They have also included space for individuals to identify, from a lengthy list of specialisations, their own particular strengths. So far, nearly 11,000 of the 100,000 employees have updated their own details. This has given the new company a much better appreciation of the skills available within the company. It has also given employees the opportunity to make connections with their counterparts elsewhere, and most importantly, has created a sense of community within the newly merged company, often across vast distances. Employees quickly realise that they are not struggling on particular problems in isolation. The concept can be extended still further so that individuals are permitted to create their own 'home pages' about their projects or research interests on the company intranet. Similarly, 3M encourage scientists from across disciplines to collaborate and share their ideas and have introduced what is known as the '15 per cent' rule. This allows employees up to 15 per cent of their time on their own projects which has developed an intranet environment for 'creating an endless stream of new products, sometimes based on existing knowledge, more often by re-combining existing knowledge in different and creative ways' (*Management Today*, 1997). This is a far cry from simply posting documents on an intranet. But 3M are a company with a culture that celebrates individual autonomy and entrepreneurial spirit. Experience in other industries is beginning to show that communities of shared interests are as important for the transfer of knowledge as simple document search and retrieval.

ISSUES FACING THE LEGAL KNOWLEDGE MANAGEMENT 'CHAMPION'

With hindsight, we can see that many first-generation know-how projects implicitly adopted a one-dimensional model of knowledge management based around document management and document centralisation in a know-how information bank. Using the terms defined by Nonaka and Takeuchi, this is combination - explicit to explicit knowledge transfer. As we have seen above, there is a far richer model of knowledge management available not only based around capturing documents but also creating the opportunities for the sharing of expertise and know-how. Document management is part of the solution but it is not the whole solution.

Cultural Hurdles to Knowledge Management

The hurdles are numerous. They are also firm-specific. Each firm will encounter these hurdles in slightly different ways.

Individuality

Lawyers are not noted for their team-based approaches to legal work or for their willingness to share their expertise. The problems begin at law school. Legal education, whether black-letter or otherwise is based on the testing of the individual for legal knowledge and the application of that knowledge. Business education by contrast encourages the group-tackling of projects. Similarly, from the first day in the average firm, lawyers are encouraged by the firm to be client-focused, often at the expense of an inward-facing knowledge-sharing focus. Indeed, in some of the larger law firms it is not unknown for a lawyer to undeıstand their client organisation better than their own. Lawyers do not tend to group-tackle projects and therefore accumulate specialised individual expertise more quickly than their professional counterparts in accountancy or management consultancy. Even in large litigation or corporate matters, each lawyer tends to take responsibility for a particular area of work, such as the drafting of a particular document or section of a document, or working on a particular legal issue. Although few will admit it, specialist lawyers tend to know a great deal about relatively little. As the acknowledged expert in an area, a lawyer may harbour concerns regarding the quality of the work that a non-specialist lawyer might produce. These latter concerns can usually (but not always) be overcome through 'health warnings' and referral information on documentation. Taken to extremes, some lawyers can come to resent others doing work which they perceive to be their own domain. The pressure towards individuality is also increasingly exerted by clients. One of the fundamental problems that a law firm now faces is its reliance of individual stars within the firm. Clients increasingly want to hire individual lawyers and will often pay a premium to ensure that a star works on their particular matter. By contrast, the firm will want a new client to hire *the firm* not individual lawyers. But unless knowledge is shared und managed across the whole firm, this problem will only get worse. A knowledge management initiative is a key measure by which this tendency can be countered.

Time

If know-how is perceived as a task purely for support staff and not as a legitimate expenditure of fee-earners' time, lawyers will be more concerned about short-term billing targets than building corporate knowledge. Any time spent sharing knowledge is time not spent billing and in a law firm, time really is money. While the knowledge management gurus might view such arguments as patently short-termist in a world where the only real resource is knowledge, they are very serious concerns of law firm finance directors. Most law firms have a time-based culture where the emphasis is clearly on billable hours and recording time. Thus lawyers increasingly feel the pull of their laptops and dictaphones. Such cultures are simply not conducive to knowledge sharing unless driven by a management initiative.

Resources

A recent KPMG report concluded that many organisations are too lean to exploit knowledge management to the full. It states '49 per cent of respondents said that people wanted to share knowledge but do not have the time. This was considered a greater drawback than the cultural issues popularly accepted to be barriers'. It goes on 'it could be that organisations ... are so lean that they cannot give their employees the time necessary to develop and share knowledge'.[3] Like other organisations, large law firms have been trimmed of their support staff, but unlike traditional corporate organisations, law firms have not endured the decade of downsizing. Nevertheless, many law firms are fairly lean organisations and only, the very largest can afford to employ specific information or knowledge managers.

Success

It is often said that success is the enemy of innovation.

Many of the larger law firms have done very well from providing legal advice to clients, growing year on year, expanding overseas and paying their Partners handsomely without any recourse to knowledge management or even particularly innovative use of IT. For someone attempting to introduce new thinking into the firm, this can be a major impediment.

A Lack of Incentives

The existence of the internal marketplace for knowledge may be either informal and *ad hoc* or it may be non-existent. In such environments, left without further instructions, lawyers will rarely see the benefits of sharing knowledge. The solution is to create marketplaces both physical and virtual for knowledge exchange and the discussion of ongoing matters. Technology alone is not a solution. The firm must back up its commitment by demonstrating the value it places on knowledge exchange. As Roos *et al.* (1997) point out, 'the difficult part is creating an environment where people can communicate. Technical systems can help but a technical system in itself does not ensure communication'. Thus technology and cultural change must go hand in hand. Technology can be used as an opportunity to change behaviour but it has to be introduced carefully, cautiously and in a structured manner.

Overuse of Technology

It is also possible to overuse technology and there are occasions when it can inhibit and undermine intended information sharing. For example, a recent report entitled *Nil by Mouth* by Investors in People (1998) highlighted the dangers of employees overusing email at the expense of human contact. Once the benefits of email become clear, employees are less likely to meet and talk with their colleagues (hence the title of the report). The introduction of email is usually welcomed as an important step forward in enhancing the abilities of employees to communicate with one another, particularly where the organisation is spread across several different offices or countries. What is can also do is isolate individual employees, increase the danger of boredom at work and increase the likelihood of the employer failing to take advantage of employees' talents. Email can also be used to bureaucratise an organisation. Individuals can fall into the habit of simply firing off emails rather than taking responsibility for a particular issue. Email is a quick way of passing the buck. The conclusion of this report is clear: technology should be used but its implications and impact need to be carefully studied and monitored. Similarly, if an intranet is used in place of regular face-to-face meetings between a manager and employees, it is likely to increase any existing sense of isolation and dislocation, not reduce it.

CASE STUDY: MCKINSEY & COMPANY -AN EXAMPLE OF BEST PRACTICE

McKinsey & Company* are possibly the best example of an organisation successfully using knowledge management in a professional services context. They have a two-pronged approach of combining technology with cultural change. While embracing the importance of Intranets and collaborative groupware-type products, McKinsey recognise the need for practical measures such as post-study debriefs during which the group asks itself what did we learn from this matter and what could we do better next time?' Every McKinsey employee is set a learning agenda in which he or she li given targets for the coming year in terms of personal development. All consultants are assessed annually on the amount of information they submit to the knowledge base and on the amount of use they make of the knowledge

---

* Management Consulting: the natural environment for managing knowledge? Tim Roberts. McKinsey and Company, talk given at Leveraging High Fee-earners: Knowledge Management in Professional Services Firms, 15 July 1997.

> base. Partners are explicitly evaluated' on their contributions to the firm's knowledge base. One of the criteria for election to partnership includes 'thought leadership'. By this is meant the new ideas and knowledge that the candidate has added to the firm's knowledge base. Even the most junior fee-earning staff are assessed on their ability to make use of the firm's resources. McKinsey have established a clear link between an employee's ability to contribute to the growth of knowledge and individual salary enhancements. Perhaps one of the most interesting and unusual characteristics of McKinsey is the peer recognition and respect that is gained from performing a research project on a new area of potential work and presenting it to the firm. Far from being perceived as a second-class task, a project which adds to the firm's corporate knowledge base is considered to be a task of significant importance (and quite an honour) to any McKinsey consultant at any stage of their career. Such projects may be based on an idea for client work, enabling the firm to capture new work ahead of a competitor, or may allow the firm to be prepared for events before they occur. So far as this author is aware, no law firm embraces such a far-sighted approach. Clearly, lawyers have much to learn from such organisations.

ACTION POINTS

1. Establish and agree what you mean by knowledge and knowledge management within your organisation.
2. Recognise that there is more to knowledge management than simply documents e.g. tacit v. explicit knowledge.
3. Develop your know-*who* as well as your know-how via the intranet.
4. Acknowledge the impediments: time constraints, lack of resources, and recognise that successful law firms have no reason to change their (bad) habits.
5. Give everyone incentives to share knowledge - whether financial or recognition.

6. Look for best practice in other industries and apply it.
7. Recognise that technology is a only a factor in knowledge management - it does not drive it.

FURTHER READING

Davenport, T.H. and Prusak. L. (1998). *Working Knowledge - How Organisations Manage What They Know.* Harvard University Press.

Nonaka, I. and Takeuchi, H. (1995). *The Knowledge Creating Company.* Oxford University Press, Oxford.

Roos, J., Roos, G., Dragonetti, N.C. and Edvinsson, L. (1997). *Intellectual Capital- Navigating the New Business Landscape.* Macmillan Business Press, Basingstoke.

NOTES

1. 'Know-how' and Information Provision in Legal Firms, Webb, Sylvia P., *Report of an exploratory study of current developments in Britain* - February to May, 1996, British Library Research and Innovation Report 1.
2. Ibid.
3. Knowledge Management - Research Report 1998, p.3, available on the World Wide Web at http://www.kpmg.co.uk

BIBLIOGRAPHY

Badaracco, J.L. (1991). *The Knowledge Link: How Firms Compete through Strategic Alliances.* Harvard Business School Press.

Davenport, T.H. (1994). 'Saving IT's soul: human-centred information management', *Harvard Business Review*, Harvard Business School Press, March-April, p.121.

Davenport, T.H. and Prusak, L. (1998). *Working Knowledge - How Organisations Manage What They Know.* Harvard University Press, pp. 10-16.

Drucker, P.F. (1993). *Post Capitalist Society.* HarperBusiness, New York.

Investors in People (1998). *Nil By Mouth.* Investors in People and Andersen Consulting, London.

Lindsey Scott, A. (1998). 'Xerox Professional Services, Knowledge Management—how to implement it using document management'. Paper presented at Document '98, a conference organised by Miller Freeman and staged at the NEC Birmingham, 12-15 October 1998.

Management Today (1997). 'The knowledge within', August, p.28. Haymarket Press on behalf of Management Publications.

Nonaka, I. and Takeuchi, H. (1995). *The Knowledge Creating Company*. Oxford University Press, pp.8-69.

Peters, Tom (1994). *Liberation management: Necessary Disorganisation for the Nanosecond Nineties*. Macmillan, London.

Roos, J., Roos, G., Dragonetti, N.C. and Edvinsson, L. (1997). *Intellectual Capital: Navigating the New Business Landscape*. Macmillan Business Press, Basingstoke, pp. 17-25.

Susskind, Richard (1996). *The Future of Law*. Clarendon Press, Oxford.

5 ELECTRONIC COMMERCE

WILL E-COMMERCE SHAPE THE LAW MARKET?

Over the course of the next decade, we are going to see radical changes in the way in which the world does its business. Such changes are only just beginning. In this chapter we look at a number of different industry-specific e-commerce case studies. These studies demonstrate how the industries are already being affected by e-commerce. However, there is an inherent danger in extrapolating conclusions from one-off successes. The truth is that no one really knows which industries will be affected and which will not, nor do we know whether a business model in one sector is applicable to another. E-commerce is like a tornado rolling across the countryside: some industries will be pulverised while others will be left virtually untouched. At present, knowing where the tornado is heading is very difficult to judge. Obviously the key question for lawyers is - is it heading our way? This is not yet clear. A few of the very largest law firms have taken the initiative, as have a slightly larger number of smaller firms. Perhaps most well known are Linklaters with the 'Blue Flag' product and Clifford Chance with 'NextLaw'.

What is already apparent is that if there is going to be one winner from global electronic commerce generally, it will be the consumer. There is going to be a fundamental shift in the balance of power away from the producer or service provider and towards the consumer. We are just at the beginning of a radical economic shake-out. There are both exciting and frightening times ahead.

Characteristics of the Electronic Marketplace

This new networked economy will have some characteristics quite unlike those of the old industrial economy. There will be a tendency towards temporary monopolies. Just as IBM dominated the mainframe marketplace, and Microsoft currently dominates the PC software marketplace, we will see small companies become massive dominant forces in their chosen marketplace within a matter of years or even months. The example of Amazon.com as the world's largest electronic bookseller is a demonstration of what is to come in the future; in price-sensitive markets speed is critical. There is also a tendency for the winners in a particular competitive market to dominate, occupying most or all of that particular marketplace. Before the Internet or even the PC, we saw this phenomenon with another late-twentieth-century technology -video cassette recorders. Two standards emerged: VHS and Betamax. In retrospect we now accept that Betamax was the superior standard but for a variety of different reasons it failed to gain the necessary support and VHS now dominates. We will see the same phenomenon with new technologies in the new networked economy: those who are first to the market and can gain the best support will dominate the market, regardless of whether theirs is the best technology. This dominance will be so complete that the competition may as well abandon their own competing product, accept that the battle is lost and look to win the battle in the next technology race. Thus, the speed to market is critical.

How Big is Electronic Commerce?

The predictions are still decidedly bullish: 'Worldwide business over the web is expected to total between $200 and $300 billion by 2001 ... a hundred-fold increase in a few short years' (*The Economist*, 1998). Fifty per cent of all new-car buyers will use the Internet to influence their purchase by the year 2000 (Power & Associates, 1998). E-commerce will be a trillion dollar marketplace by the year 2000 and about 70 per cent of the transactions will be business-to-business commerce, said Internet guru, Nicholas Negroponte in 1997. While this estimate was wildly optimistic at the time, Forrester Research now predicts that by 2003, business-to-business commerce on-line will jump to $1.5 trillion, from $48 billion in 1998'.[1]

E-commerce is not simply some passing management fad such as total quality management or business process re-engineering. What electronic commerce brings is the ability to reach a massive new global audience at a greatly reduced cost: a truly different way of doing business. But the rules of engagement are also quite different: it is a market system where the customer's demands are absolute and one where customer loyalty is difficult to engender yet imperative for survival.

Some Basic Definitions

E-commerce can take two forms: either business-to-business, or business-to-consumer. The World Wide Web and software that interacts with the Web will form the core system of e-commerce. Given the current relatively low penetration of the Internet into the consumer domain, the majority of Internet business over the next five years is likely to be business-to-business. However, as we see the Internet made available via other consumer devices such as the television, the telephone (and perhaps even the microwave door), we will see an increase in the amount of business-to-cousumer e-commerce Confusingly, different companies use different terminology. Some organisations use the all-embracing term, electronic business (or e-business) to describe a new way of doing business using the Internet. This covers everything from sending business-to-business email through to web-based transactions. E-business is very cheap to get started: all that is required is an Internet account which allows for email communications and web browsing. It is also very cost effective: 'the total cost of processing a paper-based invoice with a couple of revisions can amount to £60. Done on e-mail it is 60p'.[2] However, our interest here is primarily with business-to-business e-commerce.

The Typical E-Commerce Business Process

Every industry has business processes. In the law firm context, the key business process follows the cycle of client instructions, file opening, credit checks and initial advice through to the completion of the deal or settlement of the dispute followed by the submission of a final bill, file closure and the archiving of the file. In the retail or manufacturing sectors the business processes are more complex and varied. In e-commerce, the typical business process is largely the same. It is as follows. A buyer logs on to a web site to examine a catalogue of products. From the catalogue, various items are selected by being placed in a virtual shopping basket. Having made a choice or choices the consumer must then submit an order. The consumer will be authenticated before the order is taken, i.e. the consumer will prove that they actually are who they say they are. Once the order is taken it will be fed into an internal IT system (often referred to as an Enterprise Resource Planning system which will manage the stock in the warehouse). From there, the information is fed directly to the warehouse shipping department and the product is then shipped to the buyer (the so-called 'fulfilment' of the order).

FOUR CASE STUDIES IN E-COMMERCE

Below, we look at a number of different marketplaces where the Internet is creating considerable pressure on the existing competitors, while offering the consumer ever greater choice and value. However, for every successful e-commerce venture, there are probably 10 that fail. A clear perspective and a few words of caution are essential. A few very successful ventures do not make a revolution. An understanding of what is happening in disparate industries is essential. Only by recognising and understanding changes in commerce generally will lawyers be able to ready themselves for the likely changes in their own legal practice over the next few years. In addition, before we are carried away on this media-inspired 'tsunami', we should recognise that a future opportunity does not equate to present reality. While the research groups and new-media pundits forecast massive growth, the figures on current e-commerce are not all that impressive.

For example, a report by the Organisation for Economic Cooperation and Development (OECD) concluded that despite astonishing projections of the future of electronic commerce, those numbers, when viewed in the context of overall commerce, were minuscule. The estimated revenue from e-commerce totaled $26 billion in 1997, but that represented only 0.5 per cent of total retail sales for the OECD's seven largest economies (*The Wall Street Journal*, 1998a). Also, if we were to believe the media hyperbole, we would believe that e-commerce is a wholly new phenomenon. It is not. The financial community have been using electronic networks and electronic data interchange (EDI) to transfer funds around the world for many years. Similarly, every day millions of consumers have their credit card details checked electronically. These are both examples of commerce occurring electronically. However, the term e-commerce is now synonymous with the use of Internet-based technology.

There are some significant hurdles to be overcome before the full potential will be realised: the need for customer privacy and security and the development of consumer trust being the largest. However, these aspects are primarily cultural rather than technical hurdles. There is even now some modicum of evidence to suggest that even these barriers are being overcome. The fact that the uptake of electronic commerce has been somewhat slower than expected should not lead to complacency. What it does demonstrate is two points: first, that it is not too late for organisations that have not embraced e-commerce to establish and implement their own e-commerce strategy. Second, it demonstrates the importance for lawyers to be ready to advise their clients on the legal aspects of electronic commerce.

STUDY I: COMPUTER HARDWARE AND SOFTWARE

Not surprisingly, computer hardware ranks as the number one product sold over the Internet. This is closely followed by computer software. For example, Cisco, the makers of computer routers, hubs and switches (hardware devices that allow networks to talk to one another) have the world's largest and most successful electronic commerce site (see Figure 5.1). Cisco doubled the size of their business in one year between 1995 and 1996. How? Due to the need for businesses to get access to the Internet, more and more organisations needed Cisco products. The problem that Cisco faced was how to scale up the business without increasing costs. Their pre-Internet method of doing business was to accept many hundreds of thousands of faxed orders and manually to key them into their ordering system. They were facing the prospect of being unable to deal with new orders: in other words, a crisis caused by the growth of the business. Cisco looked to the Internet to solve the problem created by the Internet, by setting up a 'networked commerce' web site.

Cisco are now selling an average of $10 million worth of products a day (and over $20 million on a good day!) which equates to roughly $4 billion a year, processing over 1,000 orders a day and generating nearly 60 per cent of all their business via a single web site address. Cisco dominate the business-to-business marketplace, taking more on-line orders than the entire European electronic commerce market in 1997. Why are Cisco so dominant? First, they benefit from a technology-literate customer base: all of their customers (predominantly network managers or IT professionals) will have access to the Web from their workplace and probably from their home too; they are comfortable using the Internet and understand both its strengths and limitations. Second, this approach cuts out the middleman. IT managers no longer need IT product resellers. Instead they can browse a web site containing some 12,000 Cisco products, examine product configuration information and even be advised about their proposed configuration of products, check the order status, track the product order and view invoices and credit notes, all in the comfort of their own office. Cisco's is a giant among e-commerce sites and they are taking full advantage of the benefits that it offers.

Computer software is another industry that is benefiting from e-commerce. Increasingly, software manufacturers are inviting users to download copies of their newest software from their public web sites. The software may be time-limited as a 30-day evaluation copy or it may have limited functionality. If the users decide that they would like to obtain a full version, instead of dispatching a box containing manuals and a CD-ROM or floppy disks, in return for credit cards details the user will obtain a licence key that unlocks the door to full software functionality. This is convenient for the user and cheaper for the manufacturer. One slight fly in the ointment for the software industry is that currently only about 15 per cent of all software products can be downloaded from the Web (according to recent surveys by both Forrester Research and Softletter.com, an industry-based newsletter). We can expect these limitations to be overcome in due course. As one IT analyst with the Aberdeen Group puts it,'At some point, you'd have to be an idiot to go down the street to buy software' *(Investor's Business Daily*, 1998), Purchasing the necessary licences for large organisations requires a lot of paperwork, which is why doing it electronically is so attractive.[3] According to International Data Corporation, site licensing (i.e. licensing of multiple copies of software) is one area of software sales that will be conducted 100 per cent over the Net by 2008.

CASE STUDY 2: BOOKSELLERS

The Internet poses a significant threat to existing names in the bookselling marketplace. The winner from all of this competition is once again the customer who will benefit from a wider portfolio of books to choose from and cheaper prices.

The success of Amazon.com (see Figure 5.2), the first electronic bookseller, is now well known. Amazon.com achieved web site sales of $148 million in 1997, up an astonishing 838 per cent from the previous year *(FinancialTimes*, 1998). It is now the world's largest bookseller, with a market valuation of $ I I billion but has yet to make a profit in its four-year existence. Why has it been so successful? Part of the reason is that Amazon.com was first. (If it is not already apparent from previous chapters, on the Internet being first is everything.) Second, books: are an ideal product to sell on the Internet. The Internet-browsing public are, on the whole, relatively well-off. Given that they are on the Internet in the first place, it is a pretty good bet that they enjoy reading and learning. In addition, the book buyer doesn't really need to see the product: as long as there is a table of contents and a few book reviews written by independent third parties that is sufficient. Amazon.com can offer the customer an inventory of 4.7 million titles, far in excess of any physical bookshop, and pride themselves on their speed of 'fulfillment' (the time taken between the order being placed and the product being delivered. Amazon can deliver a US title from the USA to the UK in as little as three days). They also heavily discount their titles, aiming to pass on the savings to customers. The fact that the company does not have a network of hundreds of physical outlets means that Amazon.com can advertise their books at discounts of up to 40 per cent.

Amazon.com are not satisfied to sit on their laurels, however. They have since paid $55m for three small Internet booksellers in the UK in order to obtain a foothold in this European marketplace and the Amazon.co.uk web site is now online, selling 1.2 million UK titles and 200,000 US titles, again at up to 40 per cent off the usual High Street price! They are also diversifying into other product areas such as videos. Amazon.com are capitalising on being first. This is as logical as it is lucrative for the company. Internet users who have successfully completed a book purchase are likely to be more willing to return to the Amazon site to purchase other products, whether books or otherwise, because Amazon.com is an Internet brand name that they will trust The company has also invested heavily in marketing the Amazon.com brand and in their own internal IT. In terms of marketing, Amazon.com have signed up nearly 100,000 web sites to channel buyers to the site. In terms of their own IT investment, the company makes extensive use of so-called collaborative filtering software so that they can perform all manner of analysis on people's spending habits. The site now offers the user-related products that might prompt impulse purchases. Having selected a title on the Amazon.com web site, users are directed to a section entitled 'Related titles' which tells the user that 'other customers who bought the book you are interested in, also bought copies of the following...'. It will then list three or four closely related titles, inviting the visitor to look at these as well. The site also offers reviews written by other customers and occasionally by the author. The idea here is that Amazon can present itself not so much as a bookseller but as a community where book-lovers meet. Events of 1998 demonstrated just how serious the threat of Amazon.com is considered to be by the traditional booksellers. Bertelsmann, the world's largest English-language publisher, bought half of the giant Barnesandnoble.com web presence at a price of $200 million, hoping to develop and capitalise the brand name on this, the largest US traditional bookseller. Similarly, W. H. Smith, the well-known UK High Street bookseller paid £9.4m for one of Amazon's rivals, The Internet Bookshop - incidentally paying 265p per share, a massive premium on the 85p per market share price (The *Independent*, 1998). Although W. H. Smith managed to generate £ 1.7 million worth of sales in the first half of 1999, they may be too late to generate a global brand name that can compete with the American start-up. Amazon.com, as one of the first success stories of e-commerce, has established the predominant brand in the marketplace. Amazon will be hard, if not impossible, to emulate.

Figure 5.2. Amazon.com - the best-known e-commerce site. http://www.amazon.com is reproduced here with the kind permission of Amazon.com. Inc.

The Changing Book

Although Amazon.com have been quick to exploit an immature market, it will interesting to see if they can also exploit changes in the nature of the book itself. For example, the first electronic book or 'e-book' has now appeared. 'The Rocket E-book weighs only 22 ounces, can hold at least 4,000 pages... is claimed to have a battery life of up to 33 hours and costs US$499. Electronic books are downloaded from the Internet via a PC where they can be stored. The size of the LCD screen however is only 4 by; 3 inches' (*Internet Business*, 1999). The paper book will not disappear: it has many excellent features which have been refined over centuries - a table of contents, an index, page numbering, footnotes, etc. But a user cannot search the traditional book for keywords or phrases. Publishers of reference works will increasingly produce an e-book version of their popular titles. Lawyers in particular with their need for access to lengthy practitioners' 'bibles' will benefit from having searchable reference works to hand at all times. It may be that within a few years, Amazon.com will be acting as an intermediary between the author and the book purchaser and instead of dispatching a paper copy of a book, they will instead be authorising the downloading of a digital stream of information.

CASE STUDY 3: CONSUMER BANKING

Internet-based banking poses a major threat to the traditional banking industry in the business-to-consumer domain. It will also mean that telephone banking is probably no more than a passing trend. Again, the cost savings are an overwhelming justification. This was illustrated by a study by Booz, Allen and Hamilton, a firm of management consultants, which showed that the costs of a transaction in the traditional High

Street branch of a bank is $ 1.08 whereas over the Web it is $0.13 (*Internet Business*, 1998). Thus banks, both established and newcomers, are setting up Internet-based banking services (see Figure 5.3) and are able to pass some of the savings to their; customers, luring them away from traditional banking methods with offers such as higher interest rates on current accounts and the convenience of banking at home. This form of banking benefits the customer because it offers access to financial advice at any time, from anywhere, no early closing and no queuing. In addition, such banks offer very favourable rates of return partly because of the savings in office overheads. The traditional High Street banks with their large workforces and expensive leases simply will not be able to compete. Also, if customers can manage their own accounts by transferring money electronically, it is harder for the banks to justify their charges. Web-based banking services are also more secure than regular Internet services. Most consumer banking services have developed dedicated extranet services: instead of using the Internet via an ISP to access the bank's system, the consumer dials the bank directly over a traditional telephone line. The banks just happen to use web-based technologies to make these services available. According to the *Online Banking* Report, currently 5 per cent of the US population do some form of on-line banking, but by the end of 2001, that number will increase to 21 per cent of the population (The *Wall Street Journal*, 1998b). Even more popular in the USA is the idea of on-line share trading: nearly 40 per cent of all share trades take place over the Internet. Towards the end of 1998,a number of different UK financial services groups, including household names such as Barclays Bank, began to offer share trading over the Web (*The Times*, 1999) offering prices in real time (i.e. as they change). It seems likely that the US experience will be repeated elsewhere in the world.

CASE STUDY 4: THE MUSIC INDUSTRY

In 1990, the music industry was dominated by the big labels such as Sony, Polygram, Warner, Universal and EMI. In 1998 we witnessed the increasing fragmentation of the industry as small independent labels proliferated. We are also witnessing a boom in the number of pirate CD-ROMs available. Why is this happening? One reason is the Internet. According to the

International Federation of Phonographic Industries (IFPI) 'around 3 million tracks are downloaded from the Internet every day. Some are legitimate samples ("try before you buy") but the vast majority are pirated' (The Economist, 1998). The Internet gives both legal and illegal distributors equal access to the means of distribution.

So far, playback of the illegally downloaded tracks from the Internet has been pretty inconvenient. For example, few people are prepared to jog around their local park with their laptop computer strapped to their back simply in order to listen to music that they downloaded from the Web! It is still a lot more convenient to use more traditional (i.e. 1 0-year-old) methods such as buying a CD and portable CD-player. But all this is likely to change. Indeed it is already changing. Human ingenuity being what it is, where there is a gap in the marketplace, someone somewhere will fill it In October 1998, the Recording Industry! Association of America lost an application in the US courts to have a product called the 'Rio' banned. The Rio is a portable consumer product similar in many Ways to the now ubiquitous Sony Walkman. The Rio can store digitised tracks which are downloaded off the Internet, in other words 'roll your own' digital music. The technology used is a standard called MP3.[4] This technology will deflate any track down to one-sixteenth of its size; meaning that it can be transmitted across the Internet in minutes rather than hours. For $300, or £ 175 in the UK (a price that will surely plummet), the Rio[5] allows the user to store and replay tracks downloaded from the Internet at CD-like quality. There is also a web site called MP3.com (see Figure 5.4) which offers a massive range of music tracks available electronically, covering everything from jazz through to 'techno' and hip-hop. MP3.com have signed up an estimated 10,000 bands. The idea here is that undiscovered bands dan submit their music for inclusion on the site and visitors are free to download any tracks without charge.

The music industry is facing a double whammy, however. Not only is it faced with ever more sophisticated piracy, it is also seeing the proliferation of small recording companies. Unlike the 1980s, it is not so much the small Independent labels such as Island and Chrysalis that are the cause of concern. Instead, artists are discovering, much to the chagrin of the major recording studios, that because of the Internet, they do not actually need a recording contract at all. For about £5,000 aspiring artists can purchase a state-of-the-art package of hardware and software and set up their own recording studio using equipment virtually identical to that which one might find in a professional studio. Having recorded enough tracks, they can then establish their own web site on which to give away their music in order to create a following. Once they have done this, they can then set up a site where visitors can order CDs or can download further tracks in return for a credit card number. The best-known example of a DIY record label is 'Righteous Babe'. This label was established by its one and only artiste -Ani DiFranco. So far she has sold approximately 2 million albums on CD. Because there is no middleman, she keeps all of the profits herself. What is there to stop others from following in her footsteps and establishing their own record label? Only a lack of initiative.

In the 1970s and 1980s, the recording industry heavily promoted a campaign against unauthorised and illegal home taping using cassettes, arguing that home taping was 'killing music'. Nevertheless, consumers still taped music for their friends, and the recording industry survived. This time, however, amateur reproduction will be more sophisticated. If the quality of the reproduction is as good as the original recording and dissemination is far easier because the reproduction can be sent to millions via email or downloaded from web sites, what role is played by the music distribution companies? This is a potential doomsday scenario for the major record labels. Their role as gatekeeper separating artist from fan has been severely eroded.

The music industry has recognised that it has to fight technology with technology and it is investing heavily in an equivalent standard and group of products that will allow the industry to retain some measure of control. In other words, the industry is betting on technology for its survival. The standard is the Secure Digital Music Initiative (SDMI).[6] The major record labels are working with hundreds of different manufacturers from Panasonic to Casio to implement their own standard which limits the ability of the consumer to download tracks without payment.

NOT ALL E-COMMERCE IS SUCCESSFUL

In the early phases of e-commerce, it became clear that web-based shopping had failed to capture the imagination of most shoppers. For example, the financial results for 'Barclay Square', the UK's first virtual shopping mall, were less than impressive. Other examples abound. 'E-Christmas' was a UK web site set up for service during the run-up to Christmas 1997 and was backed by Microsoft and UPS, the world-wide courier company. It was designed to assist those web-users who were challenged for original gift ideas, with a wide selection of possible presents and access to over 140 different merchants. It was thought that such a site would offer the added benefit of allowing users to browse from the comfort of their own homes and avoid the overcrowded shops. However, the merchants involved in E-Christmas were clearly not the recipients of others Yuletide excess: 'although 180,000 people are estimated to have visited the site, a total of only 350 products were sold between 10th November 1997 and 8th January 1998' (The Economist Group, 1998b). Why did this site fail? Part of the blame for the E-Christmas fiasco can be placed on poor site design, weak search facilities and delays with technology. However, more generally, it may be that the blame may also lie with the poor marketing by the merchants themselves - a mismatch of products and customers. Not surprisingly, those involved took a more upbeat view: 'we had more sales than the Wright brothers paying passengers on their first flight' said one key participant.[7] This stoic response showed a faith in the technology that may ultimately have been justified. For example, in December 1998, a year later, *Newsweek* proclaimed that 'Christmas.com' had arrived, and delivered a surprisingly upbeat commentary on how consumer-oriented e-commerce is finally beginning to take off. The report estimated that 17 million Americans spent in the region of $2.3 billion on Christmas presents via the

Web in 1998 (*The Wall Street Journal*, 1998c). What is so surprising is that the technology has not changed. There has been no significant advance in terms of security standards or privacy controls. Instead it appears that a year of experience and familiarity with using the Internet is breeding confidence in the user community. This breakthrough has yet to be matched in Europe. This demonstrates a key cultural difference between the US and Europe. In the USA, there is a consensus that IT generally can provide a competitive advantage. In Europe, IT is used to reduce costs or simply to keep up with the competition.

Is Electronic Commerce A Level Playing Field?

What makes e-commerce different is that instead of being the domain of large financial institutions (as was the case with EDI), the technology that makes electronic commerce possible is now available to all. Thus e-commerce would appear to have much to offer the smaller corporate organisations: it gives them an opportunity to compete in marketplaces that they could not previously have dreamt of entering. For example, before e-commerce, if a small company wanted to go into retailing children's toys, it would set up a small shop somewhere, probably well away from the main High Street due to the high costs associated with renting high-profile premises. Over time, the business might grow sufficiently so that the company could open stores in other locations. However, it could probably never compete with the main High Street brand names because of its lack of purchasing power, its lack of brand awareness, the relative scarcity of its stores and their locations. In other words, the costs of competing with the major players was so great that either the smaller company had to content itself with its current market or grow through the purchase of a larger competitor, Similarly, the problems of entering a related marketplace were large.

To start from scratch would mean time spent creating new relationships, of studying the dynamics of the new market, building brand awareness in the new market, and so forth.

By contrast, with electronic commerce the cost of entering a new market is the cost of establishing a transactional web site, which compared with the cost of establishing a chain of High Street locations is minimal. Impressive but costly premises on the main High Streets are no longer assets to be sought after. Indeed, quite the reverse. These premises are an unnecessary expense, a drain on resources. Instead all that is required is a web site, some good internal IT systems, a large warehouse and a good relationship with one of the major worldwide couriers. What happens when the more well-known brand names in toy retailing enter the e-commerce marketplace? If they are slow, then the new electronic brand will be sufficiently established and trusted that the established brand will struggle. The problems faced by Bertelsmann in establishing Barnesandnoble.com as the number one electronic bookseller are evidence enough. Barnes and Noble may be the biggest name in the offline world, but Amazon.com, the four-year-old upstart, is number one and virtually synonymous with on-line bookselling.

On one level it would appear that any organisation can compete with any other organisation: all that is required is a transactional web site. However, Internet surfers will always prefer to do all their shopping from one site, fill one virtual shopping basket and see one transaction on their credit card statement. Thus, one company such as Amazon.com can begin by selling books on-line but can rapidly extend the brand into other marketplaces. So who will succeed in e-commerce and who will fail? Those corporate organisations that will thrive will benefit from having a recognisable and trustworthy brand name, access to significant IT resources, in particular database technology, and an innovative culture that supports and encourages the extended use of IT. Good examples of companies that possess all of the above are the major UK supermarkets: they are well placed for electronic-commerce. Their names are well known and trusted by consumers; they have a reputation for spending heavily on IT - witness for example their introduction of the reward cards, which are used increasingly to analyse consumer behaviour. They are also innovative, having recently moved into consumer banking. Thus if Tesco, Sainsbury's or any of the other major supermarket brands want to begin their e-commerce ventures by selling their existing product lines over the Internet but then extend their product range by selling, for example, used cars, foreign holidays, furniture or even china ornaments on the Internet, they can and (more worryingly for any traditional seller of such products) they may.

So does this mean that electronic commerce for all consumer products will eventually be dominated by a few very large companies? Not necessarily. The Web is a niche medium not a mass medium. Thus a company that specialises in particular products, can develop its own e-commerce site and thrive on it, as long as it is done quickly. This is exactly what Elizabeth Botham & Sons, a small family bakers in Whitby, North Yorkshire is doing (see Figure 5.5). Having eschewed the traditional information-based site, the firm has been selling cakes, breads, hampers, specialty teas and coffees by mail order since 1995 to customers all over the world. This company is a specialty baker and has no pretensions of competing head to head with any supermarket chain. But for niche goods, where customers' needs will not be addressed by the bigger supermarkets, such companies can and do thrive. Evidence of this company's success should provide some comfort to those law firms with fewer resources available: they need not be left behind in the race toward legal electronic commerce.

FURTHER READING

Kosier, D. (1997). *Understanding Electronic Commerce*. Microsoft Press.

NOTES

1. Forrester Research figures from the *New York Times*, 14 April 1999.
2. BT, Preparing for E-business booklet.
3. Tech Web - a free email newsletter, 15 September 1998.
4. Short for Motion Picture Expert Group, Audio Layer 3.
5. The Rio PMP300 from Diamond Multimedia Systems uses microchips to store up to 60 minutes of music and runs on two AA batteries.
6. The music industry is trying to rush out this new standard in a matter of months, It may be that despite its haste, it is already loo late.
7. James Roper, managing director of IMRG, quoted in 'An Unhappy E-Christmas'. Information Strategy, April 1998, published by the Economist Group, p.8.

BIBLIOGRAPHY

The Economist (1998). 'A note of fear', 31 October, p.87.

The Economist Group (1998a). 'Prepare for impact - executive briefing', Information Strategy special supplement, April, p.5.

The Economist Group (1998b). 'An unhappy E-Christmas', Information Strategy, April, p.8.

Financial Times (1998). 18/19 April.

The Independent (1998). 'Smith's turns to on-line retailing', 9 June, p. 19.

Internet Business (1998). 'The virtual warehouse', BPA International, May, p.40. *Internet Business* (1999).

The shape of books to come', BPA International, February, p. 15.

Investor's Business Daily (1998). 28 April.

J.D. Power & Associates (1998). Survey by market researchers, *Business Week*, 9 March.

The Times (1999). 'Tell Sid: the Net sells shares', Interface Section, 13 January, p.5. *The Wall Street Journal* (1998a). 28 September.

The Wall Street Journal (1998b). 15 May.

The Wall Street Journal (1998c). 'Forrester Research suggest that 8.5 million U.S. households purchased gifts online leading up to Christmas 1998, up from 2 million leading up to Christmas 1997', 30 December.

6 LEGAL ELECTRONIC COMMERCE

E-commerce does not affect all marketplaces equally. So how will the legal marketplace be affected? This chapter addresses this vital issue. What is becoming clear is that electronic commerce is coming to the legal profession whether the profession likes it or not. Two of the largest law firms have already embraced high value e-commerce, while a number of smaller firms have been offering low value e-commerce (i.e. access to basic legal services over the Internet) for some time. But what about the vast majority of law firms that do not have the resources of the 'magic circle' of firms yet are not interested in the marketplace for low-value services such as on-line wills? There are numerous business opportunities to be exploited, at least for the time being. What are they, and where are they? This chapter attempts to address these questions.

It has been said that the best form of defence is attack; in other words, in order to ensure their survival, all law firms need to apply the lessons being learnt by the first wave of legal e-commerce suppliers. Those that act now will prosper. Those that wait for the competition to storm their own citadel will find that their defences are weak. Their traditional sources of work could be severely eroded.

Developing a Legal E-commerce Strategy

Harvard Business School professor, Michael Porter,

writes 'the essence of strategy formulation is dealing with the competition' (Yeates and Cadle, 1996). Information systems can change the basis of the competition by increasing the cost of switching suppliers, generating new services to forestall external threats of substitution, creating barriers to entry, or helping the customer to dominate the supplier. While no barriers to entry can be erected here, law firms can, through the use of extranet-type services, increase the cost of changing suppliers, and forestall external threats of substitution.

Traditionally, there are four reasons why any organisation should invest in IT:

- business survival;
- competitive advantage; improved efficiency;
- external business forces (such as mergers, EU directives, etc.).

The main two business drivers in this context are likely to be business survival and competitive advantage. Improved efficiency may be a by-product of e-commerce. External business forces (such as mergers and EU directives) are not relevant here. Thus the third and fourth bullet points are not discussed below.

Business Survival

In a world where everyone obtains their information and knowledge on-line, clients will come to expect this convenience of service from their lawyers as much as from their supermarket, their bookshop or their local doctor.

Many medium-sized law firms have developed strategies based around particular niche practices. In order to defend these niches against the predatory instincts of the competition, they need to provide such services electronically, not merely extending the law firm 'brand' with an information-based web site, but with sites that provide legal services to their existing clients for a fixed fee. Of course these firms can attempt to plunder the markets of the bigger competition but they will have to establish their presence before their competitors do.

Just as Amazon.com can extend their brand from books into videos or software or any other consumer product, there is absolutely nothing to prevent a firm with a successful track record in legal e-commerce from developing services into new areas where traditionally they do not have a strong reputation. The Web presents an opportunity to penetrate hitherto undeveloped markets. The current markets for legal electronic commerce are virtually non-existent and being first is critical. Users of successful e-commerce sites develop a sense of trust in these sites. Existing customers are therefore more likely to recommend and use any new legal service provided by an existing e-commerce provider than to switch to any equivalent service provided by its competitors.

Competitive Advantage and Business Efficiency

The competitive advantage is not in the technology *per se* but in being the first law firm to implement it in a given marketplace. Where the technology is available to all, there can be little long-term competitive advantage in the technology itself. The development of web-based legal services in particular niches will provide the firm with significant competitive advantage: attracting favourable views and support from clients, and media interest, lowering costs and in all likelihood, increasing market share. Extranets also offer efficiency gains. If properly implemented, lawyers will be able to add and delete information to and from the extranet from any location and without knowing anything about the underlying technology; it is possible to envisage lawyers performing this type of legal work from their homes or whatever locations suit them. Consequently, the need for lavish office premises will be reduced. There may be an increased use of home working and flexible working arrangements. This type of legal work may offer many lawyers the flexibility they crave, an alternative to 12-hour days in the office. Delivery of legal advice via extranets also saves on office expenses - the expensive letterheaded paper, envelopes and delivery expenses will all be reduced.

Choosing an Area for E-commerce Development

Having established reasons for entering the e-commerce marketplace, law firms need to examine the services that they currently provide. One of the simpler ways of performing this analysis is to use a method defined by Maister. The theory is as follows. A firm will have a portfolio of legal work consisting of three different types: expertise, experience and efficiency, alternatively defined as 'brains', 'grey hair' and procedure.

Expertise/Brains Projects

'Brains projects usually involve highly skilled and highly paid professionals. Few procedures are routinizable. Each project is a one-off' (Maister, 1993). Legal projects such as privatisations of infrastructure and utility companies are good examples. Of course, the clients attempt to find legal advisors with related experience but such projects also require a high degree of original thinking. Each would have their own unique legal challenges. Not surprisingly there is a higher tariff associated with this type of work. Original innovative thinking can easily justify higher fees.

Experience/Grey-Hair Projects

'Clients with grey hair problems seek out firms with experience in their particular type of problem. In turn the firm sells its knowledge, its experience and its judgement. In effect, they are saying "Hire us because we have been through this before; we have practice at solving this type of problem'" (Maister, 1993). There are numerous examples of grey-hair-type projects. Indeed, the vast majority of medium to large law firms survive and prosper through their marketing of such projects, selling their experience and expertise in particular niche areas. Areas of legal practice that begin as brains projects can become grey-hair-type projects. For example, a few City firms have managed to monopolise the legal work surrounding privatisations because they can legitimately claim that they have done that type of work before.

Efficiency/Procedure Projects

These are 'well recognised and familiar types of problems' where 'the steps necessary to accomplish this arc somewhat programmatical' (Maister, 1993). Good examples of procedural projects might be debt collection or residential conveyancing where, although experience is useful, the problems are sufficiently familiar that they can often be delegated to well organised but less widely experienced workers. The basis for competition here is generally price. This type of work can often only be profitable if it is undertaken in high volume.

Every law firm will have a differing combination and balance between these three different types of work. The very largest firms will probably have a combination of brains and grey-hair work and may not bother at all with procedure-based legal work. (However, there are some hybrid law firms that will do almost any type of legal work.) The medium-sized firm may undertake some brains-type projects but such projects may be infrequent or performed by a few key individuals. Instead, such firms rely on the marketing of their experience and expertise in particular areas of law. At the opposite end of the profession, the High Street firms may gain much of their income from procedure-type projects such as high-volume residential conveyancing, debt collection or personal injuries disputes. Having considered the nature of the legal services that the firm provides, the firm needs to consider which of these services can be most easily extended to the on-line world. Of course, there is absolutely nothing to prevent a law firm from establishing an e-commerce site in areas of law in which they have little or no existing reputation. Realistically, however, few firms would be willing to stake their reputation on both new technology *and* legal advice about which they know very little. Instead, most will prefer to choose an area of development where they already have expertise and strength in depth. Even those law firms that claim to offer a full service will have particular specialisations where they are stronger.

Using a Business Matrix

In determining business decisions, analysts often rely on methods such as SWOT (Success, Weaknesses, Opportunities, Threats) analysis or BCG Matrix analysis (see Figure 6.1). This latter matrix models the relationship between an organisation's current services and how the firm's management wishes to manage them. Market growth is presented along one axis and market share along the other. It is intended that this analysis will show which services are good bets for the future and which are not.

'Wild cats' are those products that have good growth potential in the marketplace. 'Stars' are those products that are profitable now and are also expected to do well in future. ('Stars' are the embodiment of the well-known 80/20 rule, namely that 80 per cent of the profits of an organisation are likely to come from 20 per cent of its products or services.) 'Cash cows' are high- income earners. 'Dogs' are those products that make little or no contribution to the organisation. Most lawyers will recognise the potential of on-line legal services for turning 'wild cat' practice areas (those with low market share but a potential for high market growth) into 'stars' (high market share and high growth).

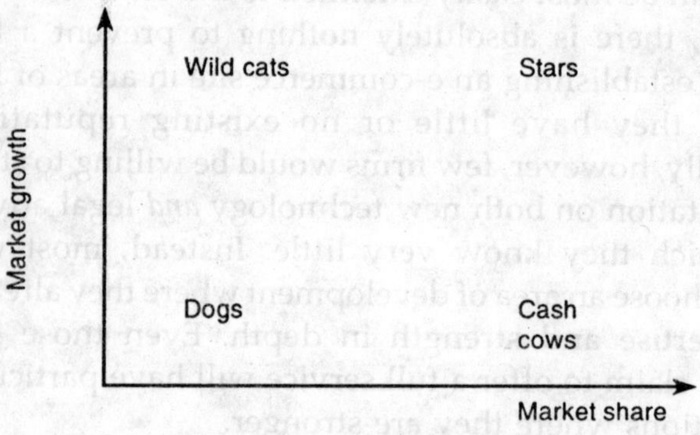

Figure 6.1 The business matrix.

Experience or Procedure or Both?

Having considered the strengths of the firm's legal work, the next task is to develop a short-list of practice areas which can be more easily transferred on line. There are two options: experience-based legal advice and/or procedure-based legal services. Experience-based legal work attracts a higher premium than procedure-based work. The problem, however, is that not all experience-based legal services can be easily transferred. The key here is finding areas of work involving a high degree of legal compliance. Examples include banking and financial regulation, planning and environmental law, health and safety, data protection and aspects of employment law. A firm with existing expertise in such areas could extend its market reach onto the Internet. For example, a firm claiming to offer expertise on employment law could offer a site containing the full text of particular EU directives, together with expert legal advice on what this means in particular scenarios; areas where the law has changed recently; Acts of Parliament that have implemented particular directives; and so forth. However, the area of law must be fast moving. A client in need of advice about how to comply with the relevant regulations in an area of law that does not change would be more easily pleased with an annotated textbook than with a subscription-based web site. Ideally, the area of law should be multi-jurisdictional. Thus, the law firm could begin by offering legal information on the law in the UK and gradually extend its product to cover other countries as its popularity grows. For the experienced lawyer the actual content is not particularly difficult to develop in itself. However, initial development of materials will be extremely time-consuming unless the research has already been performed, for example for lectures, articles or as part of a pre-existing marketing initiative. Since the extranet system should be based around questions and answers, considerable time will also be expended converting the materials to this format. Materials produced elsewhere will probably not exist in this format.

There will also be a significant human resource implication. The product will require the commitment of key legal experts within the firm to maintain and improve the site's content. It will require sales and marketing individuals - after all, if no one actually purchases a subscription, the product will make no return on investment. Finally, it will require technical resources. The system must be kept running 24 hours a day, seven days a week. All of the above must be factored into any project plan.

Extranets and Case Management

In theory, procedure-based work such as debt collection, residential conveyancing and personal injuries claims can be transferred more easily onto the Internet. Given that such services are based around a series of procedure and routines, they may already involve a high degree of IT usage. For example, there are numerous software packages available for the management of high-volume debt collection, residential conveyancing and personal injury disputes. It ought to be a relatively small step to make the information contained within this software available over the Internet. However, this will depend on the software provider and underlying software tools used. In terms of the efficiency and cost savings, the resultant media coverage and the new business that will result, it is likely to be a giant leap for the firm, in terms of growth and fee income. But as with all Internet services, getting there first is critical. The firm that can claim to manage twice the number of matters with the same number of staff while simultaneously undercutting the competition on price per matter will become a significant force in their chosen legal marketplace.

It is not only high-volume legal work such as residential conveyancing that would benefit from such innovation. High value non-contentious work could also be managed via an extranet, whereby the client could log into the system using a password, view the latest drafts of documents and examine the changes. The client could also view memoranda written on the file.

There are also significant potential productivity gains to be achieved. In any legal practice, lawyers may spend up to 20 per cent of every day dictating and drafting letters to clients informing them of the latest action on a file or simply confirming the contents of a telephone conversation. This is inefficient for the lawyer and it is costly to the client - the time will be recorded and probably passed on in the next bill. Yet this is not legal advice as such—this is simply good housekeeping. H would be far more efficient if a lawyer could either dictate or type a note directly into a case management database that is accessible over the Web. The client, meanwhile, using a case matter number and a password could access the system and view the latest information. This is not idle speculation about what might be nice in an ideal world. All of this is achievable now with technology available today.

Likely Benefits of Case Management Extranets

This type of extranet application would allow clients to see what is going on with their legal matter, in the same way that they could look up a train timetable on the Internet. Where the firm involved is handling a large number of similar types of contentious matters on behalf of a single client (for example, acting on behalf of an insurance company or trade union), such an application would be even more useful. Such a service would allow one person within the client organisation to manage a massive number of potential claims. In the best case scenario (no pun intended), this type of access to information is likely to dramatically improve client satisfaction. A case management extranet would provide the client with access to information when they want it, not when the lawyer chooses to provide it. An extranet would give more power to the client to drive the litigation process instead of handing it over entirely to their legal advisors. Clients will become more equal partners in the litigation process. Some lawyers may view this prospect with trepidation. But such views will not survive in the technology-driven legal practice of the future.

There are benefits, however. Cost reduction is one, potential for increased market share is another. First, cost reduction. The introduction of a case management extranet will allow lawyers to concentrate on more substantive legal issues instead of sending out routine letters to their clients simply informing them of minor events in the course of the legal matter. In turn, this should lead to fewer disputes over fees. After all, clients are much happier to pay for legal advice than for glorified administrators and paper-chasers. Second, such systems offer the potential for increased market share. If lawyers can spend less time on each matter, they can potentially take on more clients and more matters. If charging a fixed fee for the work then these efficiency gains will have a direct positive implication on profitability.

However, a case management extranet will not completely replace the need for regular written communication with the client. Until clients are familiar with communicating with their legal advisors in this way, lawyers will need to send out reports outlining major events in the course of the transaction or dispute. If the only form of communication is via a web page then the onus will be placed on the client to visit the web site. A lawyer cannot force clients to log onto the firm's extranet. By contrast, a letter sent directly to the client is more likely to be read. However, if the correct type of software is used, even the dispatch of the weekly or monthly report can be automated.

THE RESPONSE FROM LAW FIRMS

What have UK law firms done so far? The answer is very little. In terms of experience-based extranet services, with the exception of two of the very largest of international firms there is little to show for this revolution in legal services. In many ways, this is quite disappointing and suggests a lack of entrepreneurial thinking on the part of most law firms. Unlike companies selling consumer products, law firms have fewer hurdles to overcome. They offer a product which is pure 'value-added' information; they do not have to resolve the problems of fulfilment (i.e. the ability to deliver a product to the purchaser as quickly as possible). Furthermore, the only major legal e-commerce sites that have been established use subscription mechanisms. This avoids the need for on-line credit card validation and authorisation. Instead subscribers send a cheque to the law firms in question and in return obtain a password.

The major stumbling block would appear to be that most lawyers have serious concerns over their professional liability and insurance implications. In part, it also reflects the inherent conservatism of many lawyers. If lawyers are unwilling to embrace technology as a mechanism for improving internal efficiency, they are even less likely to commit the firm to the potential liability of a web site offering legal advice. But, as the previous chapter showed, the need to lead new markets on the Internet is absolutely paramount. As is often the case, the drivers of change in the legal profession will be the clients. When clients can obtain information from their other professional advisors electronically, they will come to expect the same services from their lawyers.

The Linklaters and Clifford Chance Experiences

There are exceptions, however. Linklaters (now Linklaters and Alliance), the London-based international law firm, opted to forego the more traditional marketing-based web site and in 1996 launched their 'Blue Flag' service. Blue Flag is a legal risk management service designed to provide commoditised legal advice on European financial and banking regulatory issues (hence the name Blue Flag). This service is designed to appeal to those concerned with legal compliance working in fund management, securities houses, investment and commercial banks and provides step-by-step legal advice on tap to subscribers for a fixed annual fee. Not surprisingly, having established the service, Linklaters have now extended it to cover other (non-European) jurisdictions where they have expertise.

The benefits to clients of this Blue Flag type of system are clear. Consider the following fictional scenario:

An in-house lawyer works in a large corporate organisation. The company is considering a purchase of a major overseas rival. The lawyer in question has been asked to present a paper to the board on the legal implications of this move. In-house lawyers, being generalists rather than specialists, might be tempted to instruct a firm of respected lawyers to be certain that they have all of the pertinent issues covered. However, they are also likely to be concerned about the resultant bill. Thus, they turn to Blue Flag. Here they can search for relevant information in the knowledge that it has been produced by a highly reputable firm of solicitors, they can print it out and present it to the Board and file it as though it were any other piece of legal advice. The task is completed more quickly and at no additional cost to the company. It is hardly surprising that the service is proving so successful. How have Linklaters achieved this in such a small space of time? They were very fortunate to have already produced much of the content that makes up the site and have it readily available in electronic form. All that was required was a degree of innovative thinking about how the information could be delivered to clients, i.e. via the Web rather than CD-ROM or paper.

Clifford Chance launched their own extranet service known as NextLaw in the second quarter of 1998. This product covers data protection regulation world-wide. 'A client can find out how to comply with data transfer rules in 30 jurisdictions and print off a customised legal advice report' (Joy, 1998). Clifford Chance were in the similar happy position of having sufficient resources and much of their legal materials readily available; two of their key data protection lawyers already produce a paper-based guide to data protection world-wide.

How much do these systems earn for these firms? Not surprisingly, both firms are fairly reticent about making exact figures known. Blue Flag is said to have made £1.5 million in fees in its first year. However, it is also said that the Blue Flag site cost roughly £500,000 to establish. According to Christopher Millard, a Partner at Clifford Chance, the firm spent over £1 million in research and development. In terms of charging, the Blue Flag system costs '£7,800 a year in subscriptions plus up to £9,600 in update fees. There's an initial subscription of up to £4,750 for each of the 16 other European jurisdictions plus an annual £2,000 update charge... Clifford's NextLaw has an annual subscription of £2,000 for each jurisdiction and clients must take at least ten' (Joy, 1998). But direct fees are not the only benefit. It is also said that the amount of referral work that Linklaters is receiving as a result of this venture has greatly increased.

Whose Technology? Who Cares!

Many law firms will argue that they do not have the resources of a Linklaters or a Clifford Chance to invest in high technology. This is true - Linklaters and Clifford Chance are two of the largest firms in the UK and worldwide. But there are alternative options. Susskind has suggested that law firms should club together to share their spending power (Joy, 1998). However, there is little precedent for law firm cooperation and there is likely to be even less incentive to cooperate where any resulting product is perceived as giving another firm a competitive advantage.

There is an alternative. What appears to have occurred to no one is that a law firm need not invest in its own technology at all. If law firms are jumping on the intranet technology bandwagon, then they can be sure that their clients are too. Thus it makes perfect sense to approach the firm's 20 largest and most important clients and offer to provide legal advice electronically on the client's intranet. Legal advice on compliance issues, on how to avoid specific liabilities, or on specific points of law that should always be considered, could all be offered via the client's intranet. With the right technological infrastructure, such information could be updated from the lawyer's desktop. Clients that would consider paying a subscription for a dedicated law firm extranet site would quite happily pay to have a lawyer updating the legal section of their own intranet for a fixed fee. The investment here is minimal - the only resource required is lawyers' time which is paid for through subscriptions. The benefits will undoubtedly include improved client satisfaction and access to apparently free legal advice for all employees. Such services will also increase the cost to the client of changing legal advisors. Ultimately, it is possible to envisage different levels of legal advice available electronically, with clients expecting a lawyer to offer some measure of legal information on their own intranet for a minimal charge, with links to a subscription-based extranet hosted by the law firm themselves that costs more. Lawyers need to be far more inventive in their charging mechanisms for such services.

Legal E-commerce and the Smaller Firm

Legal e-commerce is not only for international multi-office law firms such as Linklaters and Clifford Chance. At the opposite end of the legal services spectrum, there are numerous firms that are embracing the Web as a medium which can generate new business. In many ways these smaller firms are better placed to take advantage of the opportunities presented by the Web. On the Internet, speed is essential. While smaller firms clearly do not have the financial resources of the likes of Clifford Chance and Linklaters, they do not have a management structure involving numerous committees, leading to excessive delay. A streamlined management structure allows for quicker decision making and for IT projects to move ahead more swiftly.

The Kaye Tessler & Co. web site is perhaps the best-known example of a small firm using its site in innovative ways. The site goes far beyond the traditional brochureware marketing approach. Instead, users can fill in a web-based form which covers all of the information their lawyers might need in order to produce a valid will. Users can then choose to pay for the service (£40 plus VAT) by credit card either submitted electronically, or over the phone or by cheque. Wills can be sent by email, fax or post. By cutting down on the time taken during initial instructions, Kaye Tessler have successfully turned what was a loss-leading service into a profitable one. Not content with an on-line will service, Kaye Tessler have expanded their services into other areas. They now offer on-line questionnaires which are the equivalent of an initial interview with a solicitor on all of the following areas: conveyancing, tenancy agreements, matrimonial disputes, unfair dismissal, small claims and debt collection. Again the benefit here is speed. If the firm can spend less time per transaction, they can take on more transactions. Given that smaller firms tend to charge a fixed rate for such matters, this equates to increased profitability.

There are other examples. Michael Anvoner & Co.[1] offer a web-based wills service for expatriates working abroad. Merriman White's web site[2] allows users to fill in details of a potential personal injuries claim and submit it by email. The claim is then assessed free of charge. Similarly, Mellor and Jackson,[3] a small firm based in Oldham, Lancashire, offer free conveyancing quotations via their web site, as do Fidler and Pepper[4] along with on-line wills and on-line case management (see below). These are examples of using the Web to cut out one stage in the legal process. However, in each case the actual service is delivered in a variety of different ways - via email, post or fax rather than the Web.

A firm in the north west of England has claimed the prize as the first law firm to offer a full web-based conveyancing system. Gorvin Smith Fort, a firm of solicitors based in Stockport, recently implemented a new web-based service,

> '[that] will allow clients and estate agents to request a quotation via the Internet... [the] Case Management System can then produce a quotation ... thereafter, the client or agent can enquire on the status of the case via Gorvin Smith Fort's homepage using their unique password at anytime until the case is completed.'[5]

Arguably, every law firm that has a high-volume caseload will have to follow this lead. Firms that do not will probably find their caseload diminishing by the year, as clients move their legal business to law firms that do offer these services. It has happened in the consumer banking sector. There is no reason to think the same market forces do not apply to this area of legal practice.

Threat from 'Non-Lawyers'

While lawyers currently have a supposed monopoly on the delivery of legal services, this has not prevented the appearance of 'desktop lawyer'-type packages for the PC. The idea of providing consumers with legal documents such as wills, court forms, basic contracts, and so forth has been around for some time and has made relatively little impact on the work of most law firms. However, this idea is now being extended to the Internet. For example, Dixons' Freeserve,[6] now the largest ISP in the UK, have a service called the Freeserve Desktop Lawyer which offers users access to legal documentation via their web site. This service, launched in April 1999, offers the user access to document templates drafted by 11 Stone Buildings, a set of barristers. With these templates, users can assemble their own documents for use in a variety of different circumstances. The service is supported by a free helpline to a call centre run by solicitors who can help with assembling documents and, if required, referral to a local solicitor for further assistance as well as providing a legal magazine. Although the documents have been created by lawyers, Dixons are not a law firm in the traditional sense. Yet this has not prevented them from marketing a service that could undermine traditional law firm marketing techniques.

What are the consequences of such developments? There are two opposing views - one negative and one positive. First, the negative view. For many small firms of solicitors relying on high volumes of low-value legal work, this type of legal service could be the thin end of wedge. For some of the more elementary legal services, this may negate the need for a solicitor entirely. If any Internet user can log onto any web site (whether law firm or otherwise), download legally valid documents and obtain advice on when such documents should and should not be used, then the likelihood of such individuals walking through the front door of a law office are severely diminished. The positive view is that this type of service will have no effect on traditional legal services. It will simply mean that more people use legal documents to conduct their own affairs. Indeed, this is likely to increase the realisation on the part of Internet users that perhaps they need to consult a lawyer more and not less. The merits of each argument will be examined in more detail in the Conclusion.

IMPEDIMENTS TO LEGAL E-COMMERCE

Corporate Inertia

Realistically, the first issue to be overcome internally will be corporate inertia. Developing on-line services is entrepreneurial. Lawyers are generally not good entrepreneurs. Given that many of them spend every day advising their clients on risk management and guiding them *away* from potential risks, they have an inherent dislike of risk-taking.

The Rewards Structure

Besides the professional indemnity implications, compliance-based extranets have significant implications for the way in which law firms reward and remunerate their fee-earners. Having built an extranet, it must be fed with high-quality and up-to-date legal information. This requires the input of specialist lawyers. Clifford Chance's Next Law product is said to require 'updating by a team of eight to ten lawyers and IT specialists'. Traditionally, lawyers progress up the career ladder towards partnership by demonstrating a variety of different skills such as outstanding technical (i.e. drafting) abilities, excellent client-handling techniques, demonstrations of negotiating prowess, the ability to bring in new work, and so forth. By contrast, the skills involved in developing information for a compliance-based extranet application are more akin to textbook writers. If these abilities are not highly valued within the firm's rewards structure, the lawyers involved are unlikely to be interested in contributing to the extranet project.

Law firms with less foresight than Linklaters and Clifford Chance may also look at the opportunity cost of having a lawyer involved in an extranet project and question the value of his or her contribution.

Human Resources Issues

Not having the right combination of people is also a potential impediment. While a legal e-commerce project is similar to a general web-site project in many respects in that it will involve web programmers and graphics designers, it is likely also to involve security experts and marketing people. Not every law firm will have such skills in-house.

Services v. Products

Lawyers reward themselves based on whether they meet their target of billable hours. Extranets work on entirely different principles. The level of profitability will depend on the number of subscribers. The more subscribers there are, the higher the profits. Extranets are products in their own right and must be treated as such. Yet traditional economic terms associated with products such as 'return on investment' are relatively meaningless in the law firm, except in the most abstract sense. Law firms will need to learn a vocabulary more usually associated with product-based sectors of the economy such as manufacturing and consumer goods retailing. They will need to learn new techniques in marketing products, pre-sales and after-sales services. This is a considerable learning curve in its own right.

If law firms are to embrace the product-based approach to legal services, then a considerable cultural change will be required. It is already evident in relation to intranets and knowledge management, that cultural change, not IT implementation, is the greatest challenge in the law firm.

Taking risks only really appeals to those who have nothing to lose; successful law firms have done very well over the past 40 years using the current business model. There seems to be little reason to change. E-commerce is very new and has the appearance of being very risky. It would not be surprising if law firms believed that they have a great deal to lose. Thus it remains to be seen whether they are ready to embrace the changes necessary to succeed in e-commerce.

THE BOTTOM LINE: WHAT DOES IT ALL COST?

Estimates in this area are no more than the proverbial wet forefinger in the air. As we saw earlier, large-scale legal e-commerce projects such us Blue Flag and NextLaw are not cheap - Clifford Chance are quoted as having spent nearly £1 million in order to launch Next Law. However, this figure is likely to include the opportunity cost of lawyers not performing their required billable hours. The figure may also have been inflated simply to make competitor law firms believe that they could not afford to compete. The reality is that they cannot afford *not* to compete. But while the top few firms can afford to invest hundreds of thousands of pounds in new technology, most law firms cannot. So what should the typical law firm expect to spend on their e-commerce project?

Procedure-based products are easier to cost because there are products that can be purchased and implemented immediately with little or no additional work required. All that is needed is the hardware to run the package and a connection to the Internet. A typical installation of a web-enabled case management system, allowing clients to access details about their own cases or transactions, will cost in the region of £10,000 including computer hardware.

For grey-hair/experience-based products law firms should be budgeting for a project costing a £10,000 to £15,000 minimum investment. While this may seem to be a considerable outlay, compared with the cost of opening new offices in city centres across the country it is minimal. There are many variables to be factored in, however. First there is the cost of the hardware. A basic powerful PC or server will cost a minimum of £3,000. (A state-of-the-art PC server will cost between £10,000 and £20,000.)[7] Then there is the software that will run on the server. Here there is a variety of different packages to choose from and the decision will depend on what services are being offered. In the case of most law firms, they will be offering users simple access to on-line documentation. Depending on how such documentation is to be created and delivered, costs can vary from only a few hundred pounds to several thousand. Of course, the computer must be connected to the Internet. Leased lines cost in the region of £1,500 to install and approximately £500 per month to run. This is, however, an absolute minimum. Most e-commerce products will require so-called 'fault tolerant' connections which cost considerably more. Finally, the firm is likely to require the assistance of specialist e-commerce consultants. Not surprisingly these services are not cheap: £500 per day would be the absolute minimum fee. Contract web designers charge from £300 per day. Readers should bear in mind, however, that EasyJet, the low-cost no-frills airline, launched their web-based ticket-booking system using in-house developers for less than £20,000. It can be done for much less than the millions envisaged by Clifford Chance.

ACTION POINTS

1. Determine whether your product should be procedure based or experience based. If procedure-based work is already performed and case management tools are already used, extend onto the Internet to provide a quick and impressive return on investment (why not do both?).
2. Bear in mind that grey-hair/experience-based legal products are more profitable. With

experienced-based products, the firm is competing less on cost, speed and volume and more on experience and client confidence in a 'safe pair of hands'.

3. Play to your strengths - utilise your existing reputation in the marketplace and extend it into related areas. If your firm has a niche, make that niche electronic before the competition does. The experience from early e-commerce ventures demonstrates that being first is essential.
4. Consider giving a small amount of legal content away to clients for their own intranets. From there, draw them into your dedicated extranet site. Make your site an essential part of your client's work. It will increase the cost of clients changing their legal advisors as well as beating off the competition.
5. Budget for the project but also budget considerably more for the resulting business support that will be required.
6. In terms of technology, don't reinvent the wheel if possible. Work with existing providers of e-commerce and document management solutions.
7. Recognise the cultural hurdles to be faced and overcome.
8. Recognise that the competition may not be other law firms - Freeserve could be just the start. The banks, building societies and the supermarkets may all be viewing your legal business as a worthy candidate for their own e-commerce ventures.
9. Recognise, too, the rewards that are out there - fortune favours the brave.

FURTHER READING

As yet no one has produced a dedicated book on legal e-commerce. However, it is early days. Some helpful reading includes:

Christian, Charles (1998). *Legal Practice in the Digital Era.* Bowderdean, London. Susskind, Richard (1996). *The Future of Law.* Clarendon Press, Oxford.

NOTES

1. http://194.223.185.18/mac/wills.htm
2. http://www.merrimanwhite.co.uk/
3. http://www.mnj.co.uk/
4. http://www.fidler.co.uk
5. Extract from article in Solnotes the on-line newsletter of Solicitee at http://www.solicitec.com/solnotes.htm
6. http://www.freeserve.co.uk/
7. If this seems like a lot of money for a single machine, bear in mind that the High Street banks invest up to £1 million in a single mainframe machine that will handle 50,000-100,000 transactions each day.

BIBLIOGRAPHY

Joy, Peter (1998). 'Online legal services - the law on tap', *Commercial Lawyer,* August, pp. 54-5.

Maister, D.H. (1993). *Managing the Professional Service Firm.* Free Press Publishing, Simon and Schuster, New York.

Yeates, D. and Cadle, J. (eds) (1996). *Project Management for Information Systems.* Pitman Publishing, London.

7 ON-LINE PRACTICALITIES

Whether as a firm or individual, the process of actually getting onto the Internet means that there are many choices to be made. In this chapter we demonstrate how the beginner can get started and what the new user will expect to find.

THE INTERNET CONNECTION

There are a number of ways to access the Internet. Individuals who own a PC with a modem can simply open an account with an Internet Service Provider (ISP). For the law firm, the choice will depend on what (if anything) may already be in place in the way of technical infrastructure. It will also depend on the budget available. But no matter what the budget or method of connection, access to the Internet will also be via an ISP.

Understanding the Role of the ISP

An ISP is simply a commercial organisation that has fast direct links to the Internet and which, for a fee, acts as a gateway to the Internet. There are currently over 200 ISPs to choose from in the UK, ranging from the local one-man-and-a-dog organisations to global telecommunications companies such as British Telecom and Worldcom. Over the past two years, companies as diverse as Tesco, the well-known UK supermarket chain; Dixons, the UK High Street electrical retailer; Nationwide, the UK's largest building society (or mutual society); and even Arsenal Football Club have all decided to enter the ISP market.

Understanding 'Bandwidth'

Bandwidth is the term used to describe the amount of data that can be passed through a wire at any one time. Most consumers have no choice but to connect to the Internet from their home by modem, using their existing telephone line. Currently, this has low bandwidth capabilities. A modem is a device that is either attached to or sits inside the PC, allowing the user to connect to their ISP via a traditional telephone line and thus connect to the Internet. The modem (which stands for modulator/demodulator) translates the 1s and 0s used by computers into an analogue (i.e. sound-wave) signal. This signal is passed along the copper wire that makes up most of the residential telephone network. A modem at the receiving end translates this signal back into 1s and 0s. The problem with this approach is that modems have a limit on the speed that they can support, which is currently 56,000 bits per second, or 56 Kbps. The majority of modems work at either 28,800 Kbps or 33,600 Kbps. While this may sound quite fast, it is not. A 5,000 word, or 10-page document will be in the region of 50 kilobytes. At the opposite end of the spectrum, a short video clip may be as much as 10,000,000 bits (approximately 1,200 kilobytes). Without going into the mathematics, transferring large documents over even the fastest modem link will be a slow and painful process and the transfer of video unthinkable. Graphics files are much larger than plain text, audio bigger still and video the largest file type of all. As users want more and more multimedia content, modems become less and less viable.

A further problem is that a modem connection makes continuous use of a phone line while the user is on-line. As most individual offices only have one phone line connection, the individual effectively cannot be contacted by phone while they are on-line. However, some telecommunications companies are now addressing this problem with solutions that allow users to have both a normal phone service and access to the Internet via the telephone line. In addition, most cable companies are now offering Internet access alongside their television and telephone services using their own telecommunications.

Connecting the Firm to the Internet

The connection from a law firm to an ISP will be via modem links, ISDN or via a so-called 'leased line'. Most ISI's offer both modem links or leased lines some offer ISDN services too. A leased line is exactly what it says - a fibre-optic cable leased from the ISP, who in turn may have leased it from BT or other large telecommunications company. Many of the larger law firms lease fast-line connections from ISPs thus providing themselves with 24-hour/seven-day-a-week access to the Internet for a fixed price. A middle ground that is faster than a modem but not as fast as a leased line is to have one or more ISDN lines installed. ISDN stands for Integrated Services Digital Network. As the name suggests, this service is entirely digital from end to end, i.e. there is no analogue modem-based conversion. In the UK this is now a cost-effective solution and can offer speeds far in excess of those provided by the average modem. Again, without getting too technical, there are two flavours of ISDN, the faster of which can give up to 124 Kbps (or four times the speed of the average 33.6 Kbps modem). However ISDN requires specific computer hardware (ISDN adaptors) in order to work.

Which Solution to Choose?

In purely technical terms, the choice of connection will be dictated by how much bandwidth is needed. In layperson's terms, bandwidth is the size of the pipe through which Internet data is pushed. Most Internet users will want fast access to Internet web sites with their graphics, sound or even video files. Here, Internet connections via modems will be feasible in theory but incredibly frustrating. Larger law firms would also find that supporting hundreds of modems puts an intolerable strain on support resources - a major logistical headache. By contrast, leasing a line for which the firm is not responsible is very straightforward and introduces no additional support overhead. In addition, a leased line is a fixed cost; users are not paying local call charges because the line is already paid for. Thus a leased line is probably the best solution for larger firms. However, there is no reason why a firm cannot start with modems or ISDN and move to a leased line when the need is evident.

Having decided to get on-line, there are a large number of questions that need to be considered. A list of questions to ask in relation to each service is included in Appendix C. It is also wise to consider whether the chosen shortlist of ISPs are members of the UK Internet Service Providers Association and/or its European equivalent.[1] A list of ISPA members can be found on the ISPA web site.[2] Members of these organisations have signed up to a code of conduct that is designed to be a sign of quality in the services that they provide.

If using a dial-up ISP the first question is whether the provider has a local point of presence (or PoP). Internet pundits will often claim that one of the greatest things about the Internet is that it can be accessed for the price of a local phone call. However, this is only the case if the ISP has a local point of presence. This issue does not apply to leased-line users, as the firm will be paying a flat fee rather than for each minute spent on-line. After that, the question of charging arises. Speed of access should also be considered. If the ISP is small, it may have invested little in its own connection to the Internet. Having a state-of-the-art leased-line connection to an ISP is no guarantee that state-of-the-art connectivity will be achieved. An Internet connection is only as fast as the slowest link. Thus if the ISP itself has slow links out onto the Internet, then the fee paid for the connection between office; and ISP is wasted. This means that email will take longer to be delivered and web access will be slower. The size and financial capital of the ISP should also be taken into account. The ISP marketplace has become very cut-throat and the smaller ISPs are unlikely to be economically viable in the long term. We are likely to see a shake-out of the ISP market as the marketplace matures and the bigger High Street names begin to dominate. Finally, in terms of support, the questions that need to be asked are: what is the reputation of the ISP for dealing with customers' problems and what are the hours of operation? Lists of all Internet Service Providers can be found at the back of any of the Internet-oriented magazines currently available.

The Changing Dial-up ISP Marketplace

Part of the reason why the Internet has been slower to take off in the UK than in North America is the cost of a local phone call. In the USA and Canada where local calls are free for the residential consumer, Internet access is also effectively free. In the UK, users have to pay the cost of local calls. In September 1998, BT raised the stakes in the ISP consumer marketplace with their 'Click+' initiative by offering pay-as-you-go Internet access of a penny-. a-minute above and beyond the normal cost of a local call. BT do not bill users - they simply add the charge to the user's telephone bill. The established ISPs saw this as unfair competition - a large telecommunications company using its financial muscle to enter the ISP marketplace, by offering a service without charge. BT (being the size that it is) can afford to subsidise free access. In addition, BT are likely to be the beneficiary of increased consumer use of the Internet with the number of line rentals, the number of second-line installations and the amount of telephone usage all likely to increase substantially. However, BT were not the first to propose the effective abolition of a monthly standing charge. Cable and Wireless announced a similar service in August 1998 called 'Internet Lite'. Similarly, Dixons, in conjunction with telecommunications giant Energis, responded with their 'Freeserve' service which offers free access apart from the cost of a local call (but with support calls charged at £1 per minute). The potential of the Internet marketplace was successfully demonstrated by the fact that by October 1998, Freeserve were the second largest ISP after AOL (America On-Line). By January 1999, they had overtaken AOL to become the largest with nearly 1 million subscribers. However, the dominance of Freeserve and their ilk may prove to be short-lived; Freeserve are only making money from the expensive support calls. They also rely on the pricing structure which is partly set by the telecommunications regulator. In response, by February 1999 many of the other major ISI's such as Virgin and Tesco were also dropping their monthly charges. As at April 1999, Freeserve are still the largest ISP with over 1.3 million subscribers and almost all ISPs are now looking to drop their monthly charges.

Why Have Companies Become ISPs?

Why has there been this rush by non-technology companies to become ISPs? It may seem an unlikely marketplace for Tesco, Dixons and the Nationwide Building Society to compete. It can be explained thus: these companies all place an increasing reliance on information. They are information companies as much as they are grocers, electrical retailers or mutual building societies. Being a provider of

Internet access gives them information about their customers. It is also about extending the brand name and having the ability to offer new electronic services: customers tend to prefer dealing with a brand name that they recognise. It provides free advertising for new products and special offers. A further benefit to these companies is control. In Cyberspace, where the competition is only a mouse-click away, having the first point of contact with the customer has become very important. To an extent the ISP can also control the way in which the customer accesses the Internet, by steering them away from the web sites belonging to the competition.

BROWSING THE WEB

Having obtained the necessary Internet connection via a dial-up ISP or a leased-line connection from the workplace, and having also installed the necessary software, there are a few basic issues that need to be addressed.

When users open up the web browser application on their computer, the browser will present a web page by default. This will probably be the home page of the ISP. This page (and every other page on the Web) will have a unique address known as a URL (Uniform Resource Locator. URL is usually pronounced u-r-1 rather than 'earl'.) Thus the easiest way to navigate around the Web is simply to type in the address or URL, if it is known. The relevant web page will be delivered automatically to the user's screen.

But what if a particular web site address is unknown or the user has no idea whether a web site might even exist? Unfortunately, there is no authoritative fully indexed guide to all available Internet web sites. Instead, there are three main methods for finding sites: search engines, directories and, finally, guesswork.

Search Engines

A number of companies have attempted to index all known web sites. In other words, they have attempted to create the equivalent of a phone book for the whole of the Internet.These companies run so-called 'Search engine web sites'. Search engine sites create their listings automatically through the use of 'spidering' software (spiders crawl the Web). Spiders are software applications that are specifically written to search for and index the web sites that they find. Search engine web sites send out spiders to make copies of the pages they find on the Web. These are stored in an index, effectively a huge digital catalogue of web pages. When a word is typed into a search engine site, the software running behind the site flips through this catalogue to find web pages that appear to match what the user is looking for.

There are in the region of 400 search engines currently available, some claiming to cover the whole of the Internet, others on specific topics such as law, or geographical areas such as Europe or the UK. Most web users limit themselves to the well-known search engines such as AltaVista, Infoseek, Lycos, Excite, Webcrawler and Hotbot. Each search engine works in a slightly different way, and getting to know how an engine does complex searching (e.g. searching for phrases, using AND, OR or NOT parameters, etc.) can take some time. Thus, for convenience, most users limit themselves to one or two search engines with which they feel comfortable. The cost of switching to a different engine is high because of the learning curve involved. Thus search engine sites tend to retain their visitors.

The key search engine sites have also added extra services such as searches for email addresses and so-called 'personalised' searching. A consequence of this is that the major search engines have become the first point of entry onto the Internet for most users. The media have been quick to label these sites as 'portal sites', the new megabrands of the digital economy. To an extent the label is justified. Many of the companies that own these search engine sites have become the darlings of American stock exchanges. If the New York Stock Exchange was to be believed, in early 1999 AOL was worth more than Disney or Time Warner, and Yahoo! was worth twice the entire News Corporation media empire. Will these few portal sites become dominant Internet brands? Probably not. The Web is democratic; there is nothing to prevent a user from going directly to the sites that interest him or her. That said, search engine sites are extremely important for giving both new and experienced users a tool with which to navigate around the Internet.

How Good are Search Engines?

Unfortunately, none of the search engines index everything on the Web. In fact, one research report concluded that 'as of November 1997 the number of pages indexed by HotBot, AltaVista, Excite, and Infoseek were respectively roughly 77M, 100M, 32M, and 17M and the joint total coverage was 160 million pages'. This compares with an estimated total of 320 million web pages (at the time). The same report continued 'the most startling finding is that the overlap is very small: less than 1.4 per cent of the total coverage, or about 2.2 million pages were indexed by all four engines'.[4] Other research[5] confirmed that coverage by the major search engines was indeed patchy, with HotBot apparently indexing approximately 34 per cent of the total web content, AltaVista 28 per cent and Excite 14 per cent. Clearly these are not very satisfactory figures.

Search engines, like most text retrieval engines, are also pretty stupid. Context is not addressed. For instance, a search for the word 'chips' on any of the major Internet search engines will offer the user information about computer chips, potato chips, casino chips and more than likely, a web site or two in appreciation of the 1970s TV show 'CHiPs' ('Ponch and Jon still ride the Information Superhighway here ...'). Like most other search engines before them, these engines find and count the number of keywords in order to establish the importance of the site - which is not necessarily reflective of the true importance of a particular document or site.

Better search engines are appearing, however. For example, the bizarrely named Google search engine developed by Stanford University (http://www.google.com) uses a different approach. It uses a mechanism that rates a site based on who links to it. The ranking depends not simply on the number of sites that link to the site, but on the linking sites' own importance rating. Google is still under development but has so far indexed 60 million web pages. The developers of Google are so confident about the results that can be obtained by using their search engine that they offer users an 'I feel lucky' button so that after typing in their search term, they can avoid having to trawl through the 20 most relevant hits and instead go directly to what Google believes to be the most relevant hit. What is so surprising is that it actually appears to work.

Directories

Yahoo! is the best-known example of a directory-based search engine. It is also one of the biggest commercial success stories of the Internet. Originally, Yahoo! attempted to categorise web sites as it found them, employing college students to find and categorise new sites and then write a short description about the sites they had found. However, as the Web grew, they had to abandon this approach. Instead, in order to be listed with Yahoo!, the web site owner must submit details about their site electronically. Indeed, such is the success of Yahoo! that the owners are even contemplating a charge for all submissions. Yahoo! has since been floated on the US stock market, making its founders multi-millionaires. It has also become much more than a simple search facility. It has become one of the key so-called portal sites for the Web. Other traditional search engine sites such as those listed above have also begun to offer directory-based services.

Guesswork!

Once the naming conventions of the Internet are understood, it is possible to make an educated guess as to the Internet address of many organisations. For example, every user of the Internet will have heard of Microsoft and know that it is a corporation based in the USA. All US (and many non-US corporations) register their web sites with the com suffix. Therefore, it would be a reasonable guess to assume that Microsoft's web site is http://www.microsoft.com, and that is indeed the case. Other less well-known companies often register the names of their products as web site addresses. Therefore, educated guesswork can work quite effectively. However, guesswork only works some of the time. A name such as Microsoft is straightforward. But what about a name like Norton Rose, the well-known London law firm? Would that be http://www.nortonrose.com or would it be http://www.norton-rose.com (with a hyphen) or perhaps http://www.norton rose.com (with an underscore)? All are potentially valid web site names. Or perhaps it might be any of the above but with a .co.uk suffix? Or perhaps they do not even have a web site.[6] Such complexities can quickly lead to frustration on the part of the user. In addition, a failure to register a domain name can create problems. For example, the American Bar Association is often referred to as the ABA. However, looking up http://www.aba.com takes the user into the web site of the American Bankers' Association. (The American Bar Association's web site is at http://www.abanet.org.) This example demonstrates two things -first, the importance of registering a domain name as quickly as possible before another organisation with a similar-sounding name does so. It also demonstrates that educated guesswork can only work some of the time.

Browser Features: the Basics

Having found useful web pages, it is quite likely that the user will want to revisit them. All web browsers have a facility called Bookmarks or Favorites. By adding a bookmark the browser will store the web address so that the user can revisit the site by selecting its name from the list of bookmarks. This is a much easier way of remembering relevant web sites than having to write down any useful addresses. Other essential navigation features include the Back and Forward buttons, the Go button and the Home button. Having been on-line for a few minutes, the average user will probably have visited a number of different web pages or web sites. In order to navigate back to a page previously visited, the developers of web browsers introduced the Back and Forward buttons which do exactly what one would expect them to do. The web browser can remember the pages that the user has visited and their sequence. The Go button or menu will list every page visited during the current session on the Internet. Thus, instead of pressing the Back button 30 times, the user can simply click on Go, find the relevant page from the menu and access it directly. The Home button will bring the user back to where he or she started. (It is interesting to see how the simplicity of the web browser is being reflected in other non-Internet software. The metaphors of Backwards, Forwards and the Home page and the convention for single mouse-clicks are now being increasingly used in non-web software.)

GETTING STARTED WITH EMAIL

Email is likely to be the service that offers the initial appeal to new Internet users. It is a quick and effective means of electronic communication. Getting started with email is also very simple. Many law firms will already have their own internal email. Most email packages can also send and receive Internet email. There are a large number of email packages available, either as standalone software or integrated into other software. For example, both of the major web browser tools tome with excellent email facilities built in. Alternatively, an ISP can usually provide the user with a package that will address all of the essential functions. It is not possible, nor is it appropriate here, to look at all of the different email packages commercially available. Each package varies in its capabilities, its handling of attachments, the ability to create email lists, personalised groups, and so forth. A law firm should make its own decision according to its present and future needs and its current computing environment.

Email 'Netiquette'

'Netiquette' is short for network etiquette. It is important for new users to appreciate the subtleties of using email. Communicating by email is quite unlike communicating face-to-face or over the telephone. The recipient cannot observe any of the visual or aural nuances; they cannot see any facial expressions nor can they hear a tone of voice. Therefore it is important that new users take care with the drafting of their emails when starting to use this new medium. There is at least one entire book (Angell and Heslop, 1994) and a number of documents freely available on the Internet which set out in much more depth the preferred elements of email communication. Although not strictly netiquette as such, new users should also bear in mind that it is extremely easy for users to forward email to other email users. The decision to forward an email is entirely within the discretion of the recipient not the original sender. Therefore users should review the content of every potentially sensitive email very carefully before sending it, as it may be seen by people other than the intended recipients. Law firms should also develop their own 'acceptable Internet email usage policy' and should ensure that the entire firm complies with it.

It is not necessary, although it is good practice, to include a signature at the base of every email. A signature is a standard block of text included at the base of every message that might include a name, an email address and an organisation name. Other optional elements might be a phone number, web site address, and perhaps a postal address. In the case of law firms, it is a wise practice to include a disclaimer at the base of every email sent out as from from the firm. Most email systems allow users to include a signature automatically so that it does not have to be typed out at the end of every message.

Spam

One of the scourges of modern life is junk mail. The Internet is not immune. If anything, the problem is worse on the Internet. Junk email is known as 'spam'.[7] There is no effective method of avoiding spam. It is simply one of the hazards of being on the Internet, but hardly a justification for not having email. It would be bizarre indeed if a company refused to have a postal address on grounds that they might receive junk mail in the post now and again. There is some evidence emerging that spam is becoming a problem for UK businesses. For example, according to a 1998 report, commissioned by Novell and produced by Benchmark Research, spam was costing UK businesses up to £5.1 billion a year in lost time and wasted resources. The difference between junk mail that uses the postal service and spam is that with the former, the cost is born entirely by the sender. It costs the recipient nothing to receive junk mail through the post. However, with spam, the cost is born equally between sender and recipient, because both will be paying for access to an ISP for their email. Furthermore, there is no additional cost associated with sending spam to a million email users as opposed to one Internet user; it is this abuse of email's ease of use that is so objectionable. The same report showed that 75 per cent of corporate employees receive up to five junk emails a day and that this was beginning to cancel out some of the savings gained by the introduction of email. This is probably an overstatement. Junk email can be quickly deleted just as junk mail in the traditional post can be discarded. Some regulatory attempts are being made to limit the amount of spam on the Internet, with pressure being brought on Internet Service Providers not to offer email services to the main offenders. However, the problem remains.

Viruses by Email

In the minds of most users computer viruses are closely associated with email. Email is the easiest way to spread a virus. A virus is a piece of software that replicates itself by incorporating itself into other programs used by that particular computer. Viruses cannot be caught by simply opening and reading an email, but one of the easiest ways to obtain a virus is via email attachments. Therefore, every Internet user should also have virus-checking software installed that checks email attachments for viruses. This software should also be kept up to date as new viruses can appear very quickly indeed. In addition, every PC user should adhere to a simple rule, namely if you receive a program in the mail, and you don't know the sender, or you weren't expecting a program, delete it. There is also an extremely useful web site run by IBM on information about hoax virus scares at: http://www.av.ibm. com/ breakingnews/hypealert/.

OTHER INTERNET SERVICES

The Web and email are the two essential Internet services. Those listed below are of less importance to the average user who may, however, occasionally come across them or need to obtain access to them. Thus they are included for the sake of completeness.

Gopher

Invented at the University of Minnesota (it also happens to be their mascot) the Gopher service was a predecessor to the Web. A Gopher service allows the user to access documentary information resources on the Internet using a simple text-oriented menu-driven hierarchy. What this means in English is that users could drill down through various directories to find information that interested them. Gopher services are now more rare on the Internet as usage of the graphically-enhanced Web increasingly dominates. Almost all web browsers can access both Gopher and web services. Internet users will still occasionally encounter Gopher sites.

Usenet

Usenet is another variation on an electronic discussion list. The majority of Usenet groups are not managed by a single individual. In other words, they are unmoderated and therefore are tantamount to an electronic, discussion-based free-for-all. To quote directly from the Usenet Frequently Asked Questions (FAQ at http://www.mug.com/help/what_is_usenet.html), 'Usenet is a world-wide distributed discussion system. It consists of a set of "newsgroups" with names that are classified hierarchically by subject. "Articles" or "messages" are "posted" to these newsgroups by people on computers with the appropriate software - these articles are then broadcast to other interconnected computer systems via a wide variety of networks'. This is an asynchronous one-to-many form of communication similar to listserv-type email discussion lists. In order to access Usenet newsgroups, a user needs to have a special 'newsreader' program. There are many thousands of Usenet groups and new groups are established virtually every day.

Individual Usenet groups are usually controlled by a single person, the 'owner'. That person, often in conjunction with members of the group will decide the parameters of the discussion. Some newsgroups are moderated, that is, they will have strict guidelines governing acceptable content and tone of the discussion taking place. Not surprisingly, it is unmoderated Usenet groups that give rise to the largest number of 'flame wars' (the exchange of highly personalised abusive messages).

Usenet also contains large numbers of discussion groups that some organisations and individuals would wish to see restricted or even banned. Some may well be illegal in certain jurisdictions. In addition, given the high percentage of unmoderated groups, the so-called 'signal-to-noise ratio' (that is, the amount of discussion is actually useful as opposed to that which is merely opinionated) can be quite low.

FTP and Telnet

File Transfer Protocol (or FTP) is the method by which a user can send a copy of a file from one computer to another across the Internet. There are two forms of FTP. In the first, you sign on to the remote host computer using a login or ID code which is supplied to you by the administrator of the host. The second form of FTP, known as 'anonymous FTP', allows any user to sign on as a guest provided they offer some basic details about themselves such as an email address. Anonymous FTP is a very useful Internet function in that it allows Internet users to obtain digital information, either documents or computer software, without charge. Computer software houses often make software updates and so-called 'bug-fixes' available to the world using anonymous FTP as it is far cheaper than using the traditional mail service.

Telnet is a simple Internet service that allows a remote user to access the facilities of their home network as if they were directly connected to it. For example, a user could retrieve their email from their own mailbox using Telnet. Similarly a number of reference libraries world-wide have made their library catalogues available over the Internet using Telnet.

Talk and Internet Relay Chat

A one-to-many communication, Internet Relay Chat (IRC) is the citizen's band radio of the Internet. Unlike other Internet services, IRC allows the user to engage in synchronous conversation by typing into a keyboard and watching his or her own comments and the responses of others appear directly on screen, key by key. There are many thousands of IRC channels offering discussion on a wide variety of topics. However, given that conversations can occur between users from widely differing cultures and backgrounds, the results can often be quite anarchic. IRC has its own culture and netiquette.[8] Talk is a more controlled and comprehensible one-to-one version of IRC. All that is required for this service is a terminal emulation program (usually available in the UNIX operating system), an email address and of course, someone at the other end willing to respond.

These are the major services that a user can obtain from the Internet. There are others such as MUDs which can stand for any of: Multi User Dimension, Multi User Dungeon or Multi User Dialog. This service allows multiple users to interact and is primarily used for games purposes. Another area that has not been addressed in this chapter is the emergence of three-dimensional worlds on the Internet built using a language called VRML (Virtual Reality Markup Language). In due course, users will see many current two-dimensional web sites replaced by three-dimensional sites built using VRML. However, such developments are still some way off.

THE LEGAL WEB: WHAT IS OUT THERE FOR THE UK LAWYER?

Having obtained access to the Internet, the next question is what is useful to the practising lawyer? This section does not provide a guide to all relevant web sites and newsgroups. There are far more comprehensive guides already available (Holmes and Venables, 1997).

The UK is not blessed with the types of resources one can find in the USA (courtesy of the Legal Information Institute at Cornell University) or their counterparts in Australia (the Australian Legal Information Institute). Part of the problem has been the issue of Crown copyright. Although Her Majesty's Stationery Office (HMSO) do have their own web site, UK lawyers do not have the right to access legal information that their US and Australian counterparts enjoy. The reason why is that first, the UK does not yet have a Freedom of Information Act and second, the HMSO is now a Government agency, which means that it has its own cost recovery targets. Since its only product is legal and quasi-legal information, not surprisingly, it is unwilling to provide a free web site containing statutes, statutory instruments, and so forth. There are cracks emerging, however. There are now electronic copies of judgments available from most divisions of the High Courts,[9] all judgments from the House of Lords since November 1996, [10] Practice Directions from various courts, an increasing number of forms and leaflets offering guidance on court procedures, Hansard from both Houses of Parliament and large quantities of Select Committee publications all available on the Web without charge. This hardly constitutes an electronic law library on the scale of either the US or the Australian ventures but it is at least a start. Scotland has its own equivalent resources.

It is important to recognise the limitations of the World Wide Web. Many lawyers using the Internet for the first time mistakenly believe that it is some kind of information nirvana. It is not. While it can be incredibly useful for certain forms of legal research, such as finding obscure articles on new and developing areas of law, or for finding out about the legal or commercial opposition, many lawyers are surprised to discover they cannot use it to look up a specific point of law. In addition, they would be foolish to expect to find a level of organisation and categorisation of legal materials that they might expect to find in a standard legal reference text or the average law library. Judgments on the Web have no case notes nor are they indexed in any meaningful way. The situation is far from perfect. Thus lawyers cannot yet forego their subscriptions to more traditional forms of access to legal information, but the Web is not without its uses.

On the more positive side, we are seeing the development of legal academic e-journals on the Web. These are either the electronic publication of existing legal academic journals (so-called 'parallel publishing') or they are original publications designed specifically for the Web.

In the UK there are at least two new peer-reviewed legal e-journals: the *Web Journal of Current Legal Issues* (published by the University of Newcastle) and the *Journal of Information, Law and Technology(JILT)* published jointly by the University of Warwick and Strathclyde. But two new e-journals does not amount to a revolution in legal electronic publishing. Given that the Web offers academics and traditional legal publishers the same means of publication and distribution, in other words a level playing field, why have we not seen a cottage industry of academics establishing their own e-journals? Part of the reason is that academics are increasingly required to publish in particular journal titles which are invariably well established and owned by the major legal publishers. With so many journals available, it is not sufficient to be published in any journal. For academics to progress their careers, they need to be published in the very 'best' journals in the field. New electronic journals will take some time to establish sufficient reputations in each field of academic inquiry in order to attract the highest quality of academic writing. In addition, the economics of running an electronic journal are complicated. The administration necessary to support a subscription-based system of invoicing and cheque-clearance is significant. The established legal publishers enjoy economies of scale with a few staff responsible for a portfolio of academic journals. University law schools running a single' electronic journal cannot afford to put such systems in place. Hence the few UK legal electronic journals that exist are currently available free of charge.

ACTION POINTS

1. Determine your needs for Internet access - modem, ISDN or leased line?
2. Familiarise yourself with the essential basics of the web browser forward, back, stop and home buttons.

3. Learn and apply the three basic ways of accessing web sites - search engines, directories and guesswork.
4. Pick a single search engine and learn how to use it in depth.
5. Recognise the limitations of search engines - none of them index everything on the Internet.
6. Learn the basic netiquette of using email (see Appendix D) and be ready to deal with spam (junk email) and potential viruses.
7. Familiarise yourself with some of the legal resources that are available to the UK lawyer.

FURTHER READING

Holmes, Nick and Venables, Delia (1997). *Researching the Legal Web.* Butterworths, London.

An excellent guide to what is available to UK lawyers on the Web.

NOTES

1. http://www.euroispa.org
2. http://www.ispa.org.uk
3. http://www.altavista.digital.com; http://www.infoscck.com; http://www.lycos.com; http://www.excite.com; http://www.Webcrawler.com; http://www.hotbot.com
4. A technique for measuring the relative size and overlap of public web search engines, Krishna Bharat and Andrei Broder, paper given al the 7th International World Wide Web conference, Brisbane, April 1998, available on the Web at: http://decWeb.ethz.ch/WWW7/1937/coml937.htm
5. NEC Research Institute report - April 1998.
6. They do - http://www.nortonrose.com
7. The origins of the word 'spam' as a term to describe junk email are obscure: one of Monty Python's less well-known sketches.
8. More information about IRC can be found on the World Wide Web at http://www.undernet.org including an FAQ and at http://www.mirc.co.uk/ ircintro.html. The mIRC site also allows users to download software that will get them started on IRC.

9. See http://www.courtservice.gov.uk/highhome.htm
10. See http://www.open.gov.uk

BIBLIOGRAPHY

Angell, D. and Heslop. B. (1994). *The Elements of Email Style.* Addison-Wesley, New York.

Holmes, Nick and Venables, Delia (1997). *Researching the Legal Web.* Butterworths, London.

8 WEB TECHNOLOGY

WHERE IS THE WEB NOW?

The pace of technological innovation on the Internet is truly awesome. Moreover, it is developing exponentially, creating further innovations ever more quickly. It is an unstoppable force, the engine of a new emergent networked economy, as important as the invention of the steam engine to industrialisation. The Web is truly revolutionary: a disruptive technology. It has not only created a paradigm shift in thinking within the IT industry, it has unleashed economic changes few could have predicted. It would be no exaggeration to say that the Web is the future of computing. For example, Microsoft, the world's largest software company, performed a multi-billion dollar U-turn and reworked its entire strategy so that all of its existing and future software products could interact with the Internet World Wide Web. Similarly, as a result of the Internet phenomenon, a two-man start-up company called Netscape Communications Corporation was floated on the New York Stock Exchange and at the end of its first day of trading had a market value of $3 billion. The World Wide Web browser has now become ubiquitous and is set to become the electronic window on information of all descriptions whether originating on the Internet, a corporate database or CD-ROM. We are already seeing the Web migrate into other applications such as Personal Digital

Assistants, mobile phones and, in due course, we will see the Web appear on digital TV. The technology will continue to develop literally by the day.

Internet Genealogy

The history of the Internet (see Figure 8.1) can be traced to a US defence-related research initiative in the mid-1960s leading to the development of the ARPAnet (or Advanced Research Projects Agency network). Following the successful launch of the first Soviet Sputnik in 1957,

[1950s] [1960s] [1970s] [1980s] [1990s] [FAQ] [Sources]

Hobbes' Internet Timeline v 4.1

by

Robert H'obbes' Zakon
Internet Evangelist
The MTTRE Corporation

The author wishes to acknowledge the *Internet Society* for hosting this document, and the many Net folks who have contributed suggestions and helped with the author's genealogy search. Now he's on a new *quest* that you may be able to help with.

19505

1957

USSR launches Sputnik, first artificial earth satellite. In response. US forms the Advanced Research Projects Agency *(ARPA)* within the Department of Defense (DoD) to establish US lead in science and technology applicable to the military (:amk)

Figure 8.1. Hobbes' Internet Timeline - an essential history lesson on the Internet. http://www.info.isoc.org/guest/zakon/internet/history/hit.html is reproduced here with the kind permission of the author, Robert Zakon, and the Internet Society.

the US defence establishment decided that a new computer system was required in order to keep pace with the Russians in the space race. However, this new computer system could not be located in one place because such a system could be destroyed by a Soviet missile attack. Thus in designing this new system, one of the primary criteria was to build a distributed network, one that would survive any nuclear attack. ARPAnet began its existence as a network of a mere four computers. It was then split into a military network (MilNet) and a public network. Since that time, a large number of other additional networks have been attached to the original ARPAnet: BitNet, JANET, and so on. As it developed, the Internet slowly moved away from its defence-oriented childhood and became the plaything of academic researchers. However, it only took its first real steps towards adulthood in the early 1990s when its commercial potential was recognised following the development of the World Wide Web.

THE THREE PHASES OF COMPUTING

The first computers starting in the late 1940s were so-called mainframes: enormous constructs accessed via dumb terminals. These terminals were 'dumb' in that they had no computing power of their own - they were simply a means of getting at the computing power contained in the central computer. When PCs came along in the 1980s, the computing industry was turned on its head. Instead of communicating with the computer remotely, the operator now had immediate, access to the computing power. Computers were no longer used for complex mathematics. They were also used as better typewriters, to create documents and also to generate graphics.

Having installed a number of PCs within an organisation, it was a natural step to attempt to make these computers communicate with one another. Thus modern networking was born. Out of this chaos and upheaval came a new model for corporate computing called the Client/Server model. Corporate organisations have been attempting to develop client/server models of computing for over 10 years now. The term sounds complicated but the concept is actually quite simple: a 'client' is just a software application on a computer. In order for the client to perform, it must communicate with the server. A server is a more powerful computer that delivers or 'serves' information to a client computer. The benefit of this computing paradigm is that the actual computing tasks are shared between two machines. The problem from a development point of view is that computer programmers would spend huge amounts of time writing the same piece of client software over and over again for different operating systems. The arrival of the Web has allowed the technology community world-wide to take stock of what has been created to date and question some previously accepted ideas. For example, Larry Ellison, chief executive of Oracle, declared in September 1998 that 'client/server computing is now officially dead' and that implementing a traditional client/server model is a 'colossal error' (*Computing*, 1998). This would less surprising were it not for the fact that for the past 10 years, Oracle have spent millions of dollars trying to persuade organisations that client/server computing using Oracle products was a perfectly sensible and cost-effective thing to do! All the same, it is gratifying to see that even someone as rich and powerful as Larry Ellison can admit that his company's entire strategy was wrong.

The Web Browser as The 'Universal Client'

The Web has changed the rules. The Web is a form of client/server computing but with key differences. Some might say that the Web presents an entirely different model of computing. It ignores incompatibilities between different operating systems. As long as the machine in question is running a particular Internet protocol, that is all that is required. Thus a web server (the machine that actually holds or hosts the web pages) may be running on a UNIX operating system. The web browser, the client software, can run on Windows, UNIX, Macintosh or any other flavour of operating system. The point is that it doesn't matter. A Macintosh web server can serve web pages to a Windows web browser and vice versa. What is more, the web server needs to store only one version of the information to be 'served' because the client program will interpret that information and create the display as appropriate. The great thing about the Web is that in future every computer, indeed every electronic device, will have a form of Web interface; it might not look like a current web browser, but the underlying technology will be based around the Web. The hope is that developers will only have to produce software that runs on a web server. If it will run on a web server then it will be viewable through any web-enabled device. In effect, the web browser will become the universal client. One may well ask then if the humble web browser running just one protocol can access all manner of information and we can fit pieces of software into mobile phones, personal digital assistants and any other consumer device we care to mention, why do we all need expensive complex PCs? This is a very interesting question.

THE TECHNOLOGY 'GLUE'

The Internet is based around two key technologies: packet-switching (a means by which data to be transmitted across the network is encapsulated in addressed 'packets' or envelopes); and a set of software protocols known as Transmission Control Protocol/Internet Protocol (TCP/IP). Protocols are sets of specifications that allow computers to exchange information regardless of their make, type or operating system. One of the major problems of modern computing is incompatibility. An IBM-based PC will speak one language, whereas an Apple Macintosh speaks another and UNIX machines speak a different language altogether. Protocols provide all computers with a common language and there are different protocols for email, for file transfer and for accessing web sites. Any computer that can recognise the TCP/IP set of protocols is what is known as 'Internet-enabled'.

Packet-Switching

Packet switching was one of the key inventions that meant the network could withstand a Soviet nuclear attack. The concept behind packet-switching was that any data to be transmitted across the network would be encapsulated in addressed 'packets' or envelopes. These packets would be examined by special purpose computer hardware known as 'routers' for the packets' addresses. The routers would consider the current best route to the final destination based on available information. Routers constantly scan accessible networks looking for breakages and data traffic jams. Thus packets with the same destination need not necessarily take the same route. Moreover, information packets tend not to take the most direct route between two points. Once the data reaches its destination, the addressee computer 'unpacks' the packets, removes the envelope and offers the data to the user. The packets also check themselves to see if any of the information they are carrying has been corrupted and if it is has, to resend it.

TCP/IP

TCT/IP' is a suite of protocols consisting of various layers that ensure communication across the Internet occurs smoothly. It is far more important for the non-technical reader simply to be aware of its existence rather than how it works and what each protocol does that is a book in itself.[1] Internet Protocol (IP) was created to carry data - the same collection of 1s and 0s that underlies every program, document and image created using a computer. IP is a very flexible protocol for sending information across a network that has many different possible starting points and many different possible destinations. Because IP packets can travel from their starting point to their destination without staying linked together during the journey, they don't have to look for pathways across networks large enough to carry large chunks of information, but can instead scatter and exploit the smallest pathway across the network.

HTTP://WWW: WHAT'S IN A NAME?

Every computer that provides a service on the Internet will have both a domain name and an IP address.

IP Addressing

IP addresses currently consist of four sets of numbers each between 1 and 255. An example of an IP address might be 162.134.7.36.

IP addresses can be thought of as telephone numbers for computers on the Internet and they are allocated in the same way. Thus, to a degree, IP addresses can be analysed in the same way as one can analyse a telephone number by looking up the area code. However, it is slightly more complicated than this. Not everyone who is on the Internet will have a fixed IP address. Instead, Internet Service Providers and corporations often prefer to allocate IP addresses to the users dynamically (i.e. when an individual decides to go on-line he or she is allocated an IP address from a pool of addresses for the duration of that on-line session).

The analogy between IP addresses and telephone numbers can be extended. Just as phone numbers in the

UK have been changed frequently to cope with the expansion of the traditional telephone service, some time in the near future the Internet is also going to have all of its numbers changed. The current version used on most of the Internet is version 4 (IPv4). As IP becomes the globally accepted protocol for communications, the Internet will run out of numbers, just as UK phone companies are running out of phone numbers. The reason is partly due to the way in which the Internet authorities allocate IP address blocks. This has been quite inefficient. IP addresses are split into what are known as classes - A, B and C. A class-A address gives an organisation access to over 16 million IP addresses. Class-A addresses are rarely allocated directly to organisations other than network service providers. Class-B addresses give the organisation access to 65,500 IP addresses, while even very large organisations may only require 20,000. By applying for a class-B address block, the organisation will receive 65,500 addresses and never use 45,500 of them! The next generation of IP numbering (IPv6), instead of being a 32-bit number, will be a 128-bit number. This will allow for millions of new IP addresses but will also be far more efficient in its allocation of those numbers. A new version of the IP protocol will also offer additional functionality such as authentication, assurance of data integrity and confidentiality. The good news is that IPv6 is a superset of IPv4. In other words, the new version of IP will understand the old version. Thus, organisations can move to IPv6 when they are ready -evolution not revolution.

Internet-Naming Conventions: the Domain Name System (DNS)

IP addresses are hard to remember and easy to type incorrectly. Thus the Domain Name System (DNS) was established because users prefer computer names to numbers. It is far easier to remember someone's name than their telephone number. The system that converts domain names into IP addresses is known as the domain name system. It is a database (i.e. an electronic list of domain names together with corresponding IP addresses) held on dedicated computers world-wide. It is constantly updated. Thus, if a user establishes a commercial web site selling motorcycles parts, called www.motorcycles.com, and decides to physically relocate the web site from one machine to another, all they have to do is ask their Internet Service Provider to update the relevant record on the DNS database on their behalf so that all traffic looking for www.motorcycles.com is redirected to the new location. There is no need to actually change the name of the site. This system offers commercial web site developers a great deal of flexibility: the files that make up any web site can be located anywhere in the world and can be moved according to need.

Origins of the DNS

Unfortunately, when the idea of a DNS was mooted in the United States, little regard was given to the potential of an international naming convention. For instance, the six original top-level domains made no reference to any country, presumably because it was assumed that all domains would be located in the United States! For the first few years after the establishment of ARPAnet, this was not a problem - the first international connection to ARPAnet did not occur for four years. Thus there remain six top-level domain (TLD) names (.com for company, .org for organisation, .gov for government, .net for network organisations, .edu for academic establishments and .mil for military networks). Recent discussion by the International Ad-hoc Committee has led to proposals for a further seven TLDs in order to reduce the pressure for top-level domain names. These are .firm, .store, .Web, .arts, .rec (for recreation/ entertainment), .into and .nom for individual or personal nomenclature.

The DNS is also a hierarchy. Beneath each of these top-level domains are sub-domains. For example, the official residence of the President of the USA, the White House, is a domain of its own within the .gov top-level domain. In addition there are now also geographical domains for over 250 countries world-wide.[2] These country-specific TLDs are run by companies, universities or any other nominated suitable organisation. UK domain names are managed by Nominet.[3] However, the web site owner will normally have no direct contact with the organisation responsible for top-level domain registrations. If they want to register their web site, they normally contact their ISP which, for a small fee, will deal with this administrative task.

To make matters even more complicated, each country has its own variations on accepted naming conventions. For example, the UK and Japan use '.ac' (for academic) not '.edu' (for education) and '.co' instead of '.com' for their commercial domains. There are many other anomalies. The legacy of the original naming convention remains: most web sites in the United States still do not use the .us ending to indicate a US location. Instead, US commercial organisations simply use '.com'. The status of having a domain name that is not geographically specific has caught on - many non-US organisations (including many UK law firms) have chosen to register their organisation with the '.com' registration.

All top-level domain names are currently administered by Network Solutions, a company registered in the US, which, up until September 1998, had exclusive rights to register Internet domain names under a contract with the National Science Foundation, a publicly-funded body in the USA. However, early in 1998 the Clinton administration announced plans which called for the effective privatisation of the domain name registration framework, so that this currently extremely lucrative business would be shared between a number of competitors. A new body called ICANN (The Internet Corporation for Assigned Names and Numbers) was established in September 1998 to 'take over responsibility for the IP address space allocation, protocol parameter assignment, domain name system management, and root server system management functions'.[4] In April 1999, ICANN announced the names of five new registrar companies including AOL, Register.com, France Telecom, and a consortium of address registration businesses. Following a test period, other companies were also permitted to register top-level domain names.

Analysing the Domain Name

Experienced Internet users can analyse a domain name and learn something about the host computer or its owners. Domain names are most easily analysed from right to left. For example, the computer called 'law.aberdeen.ac.uk' tells us that this computer is based in the United Kingdom, is in the academic domain (all UK academic organisations will have a domain name ending in .ac.uk), is based at Aberdeen University and is probably law related. Alternatively, a (fictional) computer with the name of 'spock.law.indiana.edu' tells us that this computer is based in the educational domain at Indiana University (all US academic organisations will have a domain name ending in .edu), again is probably law related and that the computer administrator is probably a Star Trek fan! However, a name such as nike.com tells the user nothing about where the host computer is located. It tells us only that Nike is a commercial organisation that could be based anywhere world-wide. To make matters more complicated and confusing, a .uk address does not mean that the web site is necessarily based in the UK. It simply means that the web site in question probably has some affiliation with a

UK company or organisation and that the domain name was registered through Nominet. But as we saw above, the files that actually make up that web site could be anywhere in the world!

Deciphering the URL

A URL consists of up to three parts: the protocol, the name and, possibly, the file location. Thus, for example, the following URL, http://www. w3c.org/WWW/style.htm tells the user that this is a site on the World Wide Web and therefore that a browser such as Internet Explorer or Netscape Navigator should be used to access it. How do we know this? http (which stands for Hypertext Transfer Protocol) is the protocol used to transfer information from web sites to end-users. The www in the above address is also an obvious clue! Most web sites include the www but it is not mandatory (for example, http://cnn.com is a valid web site address). We can see that the site belongs to the 'organisation' domain (.org) and finally we can see that the file we are interested in (style.htm) is located in a sub-directory called WWW. Most static web sites (i.e. ones that do not use databases) consist of pages of HTML. Hence the filenames will end .htm or .html. However, Internet users will increasingly come across pages with endings such as .asp, .nbp, .cfm and .dll. (Incidentally, when using a web browser, it is usually not necessary to type in the http:// part of the web site address - most web browsers assume that the user wants to access a web site by default.)

So what is HTTP and how does it work? The Hypertext Transfer Protocol allows any web browser to connect to any web server. The web browser will either request information (using the 'get' command) or send information to a web site (using the 'post' command). Servers will either send information back to the browser (if the command was a 'get') or will use the information provided (if the command was a 'post'). The server then closes the connection. As far as the user is concerned, he or she either browsed a web page or posted some information via a web-based form. One of the most powerful aspects of HTTP is that the connection is opened and then closed again. This means that it can cope with millions of people connecting with the server every day. If the server software did not close the connection after the request, the server would quickly tie itself in knots and crash the machine on which it is hosted. Hence HTTP is a very powerful protocol in that it can cope with millions of requests each day. By the same token, one of the *least* powerful aspects of HTTP is that the connection is opened and then closed again. From a programmer's point of view, HTTP is stateless: it knows nothing about what has happened previously or what is going to happen next. It simply provides information electronically in response to a request and then closes the connection. This problem manifests itself when developing a complex web site. For example, if users have answered a series of questions about themselves in order to make a purchase on a web site, the last thing they want to do is to have to answer the questions all over again, simply because the web site has 'forgotten' them. Programmers can address this Statelessness in a number of ways (so-called 'cookies', state management, usernames and logins are all used) but this Statelessness remains a key difficulty when developing complex applications for the Web.

THE LANGUAGE OF THE WEB

This section is intended to give the reader a basic understanding of how web pages are created. There are a myriad of books and on-line resources available about HTML and how to build web sites. However, it is hoped that it will be clear from this section that the basic elements of HTML can be learnt in minutes.

Understanding HTML

The World Wide Web was invented by a technical writer not a programmer. Programmers, being an elitist group, would say that it shows. HTML or Hypertext Mark up Language is not really a computer language in the traditional sense. It is a scripting language, i.e. a developer intertwines a piece of HTML code with ordinary text and graphics. HTML is an offshoot of SGML (Structured Generalised Markup Language), the mother of all document-scripting languages. SGML is extremely complicated and its complexity has prevented its widespread adoption. HTML is far simpler to use and implement.

The easiest way to show how HTML works is to demonstrate it via a simple web page looking at the page from both the developer's and the end-user's point of view. Below is an example of a simple home page consisting only of text and HTML tags. In order to create this page, a web developer would type the following into any text editor:

```
<HTML>
<HEAD>
<TITLE>This is a test homepage</TITLE>
</HEAD>
<BODY>
<Hl>This is a very simple Web page - </H1>
<P>This is a piece of text and this piece of text is
<B>bold</B> und this is <I>italicised</I>
</BODY>
</HTML>
```

When opened in a web browser the same file would look like Figure 8.2.

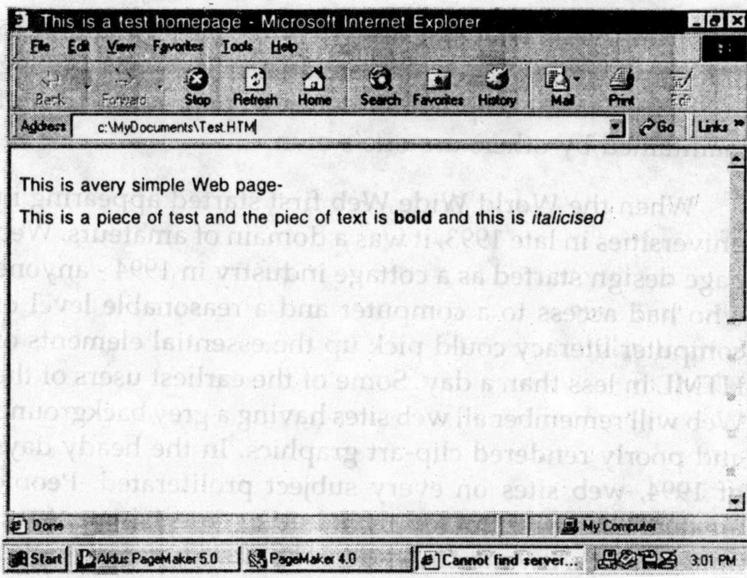

Figure 8.2. A simple web page.

Looking through the mark-up, we can see that the text between the two title tags appears at the top of the browser; the <H1> tag creates a large heading; the <P> tag creates a new paragraph; the <B> and </B> tags embolden the text between them; and the and </I> tags italicise the text. This tagging process is very simple indeed. There is a range of other tags that allows for different-sized headings, underlining, the creation of tables, the inclusion of graphics, and so on. Most importantly, there is a tag that allows the developer to create hypertext links between different sections of the same document and between different web documents, whether created by the developer or by anyone else on the Internet. The web page developer is also free to link to any other page on the Internet, and despite the protestations of some (more ignorant) lawyers, they can do this with or without the permission of other web page developers. The system is completely open. It is, however, good manners to inform other web site designers of one's intention to link sites together. There are circumstances where linking might lead to the impression that web pages created and maintained by others are one's own.

When the World Wide Web first started appearing in universities in late 1993, it was a domain of amateurs. Web page design started as a cottage industry in 1994 - anyone who had access to a computer and a reasonable level of computer literacy could pick up the essential elements of HTML in less than a day. Some of the earliest users of the Web will remember all web sites having a grey background and poorly rendered clip-art graphics. In the heady days of 1994, web sites on every subject proliferated. People created web pages not for profit but for entertainment and amusement. Anyone could do HTML and everyone did. Developing a series of 'plain vanilla' web pages was a simple exercise. However, 'simple to do' soon became synonymous with 'simple to do badly'! Indeed, all too often web developers confused the ability to publish web sites with an obligation to publish. It soon became clear that designing a visually compelling and interactive web site (i.e. a site where users can submit their personal details, ideas or information, or participate in an on-line discussion) was a more complex undertaking. Within a year, the professional web site became clearly distinguishable from the 'one man and his word processor' counterpart.

In addition, web site developers encountered a technical barrier, namely the limitations of HTML. HTML was not really designed for page layout but for document description. A myriad of start-up technology companies such as Netscape (now part of AOL), along with the more established technology corporations such as Sun and Microsoft, saw these limitations for themselves and introduced new technologies to the Internet finding new applications of old technologies to create so-called 'workarounds' that could overcome HTML's limitations. Examples of these new technologies and workarounds included Java, CGI scripts, Javascript/Jscript, VBScript, tables and frames. Thus from starting out as a simple extension of word processing, web site design and development has become a specialised high-tech cross between computer programming, graphics design and information management. That said, it is still possible for one person to create a fairly simple yet professional-looking site, but it is no longer the straightforward exercise it once was.

Meta Tags

An important tag that is often overlooked by beginners is the meta tag. The word 'meta' is short for metadata. Metadata is just a technical term for information about information. A library catalogue is a good example of traditional metadata - it describes the contents of the library collection. Meta tags on web pages are a means by which the web developer can describe the contents of the page. Meta tags are very important for increasing the chances of a web site being found and properly indexed by a search engine. When visiting a site, search engines' spiders will look first for meta tags. If they exist, the details contained there will be passed to the main index of the search engine. If they do not, the search engine will attempt to index the web page itself. Thus meta tags are the most effective way for controlling how search engines index a web site. As the Internet continues to increase in size, meta-data will become increasingly critical in order to allow users to find resources.

There are also emerging standards such as Dublin Core[5] that set out what should and should not be included within the metadata. One of the main reasons why search engines return so much useless information to users in the way of results is that not all web sites use meta tags.

Search engine sites cannot perform searches for the names of authors of documents or for documents produced between two distinct dates or other forms of complex searching. Instead, they rely on the use of keywords. Metadata attempt to overcome this limitation.

While the simplicity and transparency of HTML may seem quite appealing at first, it soon becomes apparent to the web developer that the language is actually quite limited. It consists of fewer than 100 tags, which may seem like a lot but is not. While it is simple enough to put a few pages together for basic information dissemination, once the user wants to add more complex functions such as electronic links to databases for catalogue-based web sites, or to use forms for collecting information about visitors to a web site, develop on-line forums for electronic discussion, or attempt to personalise the web site according to the visitor's tastes and interests, HTML is completely insufficient. In the words of the *Economist*, 'writers of HTML are starting to feel as if they are trying to do calculus with an abacus' (*The Economist*, 1998a). Neither is HTML designed for complex document layout.

Once the limitations of using HTML became clear, the computer industry quickly set about extending its functionality by integrating other (existing and new) computing languages. Thus working behind the scenes of the average web site is the electronic equivalent of a Frankenstein's monster, consisting of pages of HTML-tagged text and graphics together with programs written in any of the following: CGI (Common Gateway Interface) scripts written in Perl, Javascript, Visual Basic Script, perhaps some Java and other proprietary computer and scripting languages. From the user's point of view a web site may look simple. From the developer's point of view it is rarely so. In fact, HTML is not being used for its original purpose at all. It was designed as a document description language - to describe the various elements that make up a document. Instead it is being used as a document-formatting language.

It is also virtually impossible to do anything useful with a document once it has been formatted in HTML, other than publish it on a web site. Because the content and the formatting are contained within the same file, in order to reuse the content, all of the formatting must be removed. The simplicity of HTML is part of the reason why the Web has been so phenomenally successful. But in order for it to be developed still further, radical changes are required.

The Future of HTML: XML

Conscious of the limitations of HTML the computing community (and in particular the World Wide Web Consortium) has been busy developing and agreeing a standard for a hotter alternative. This new language is called Extensible Markup Language (or XML for short). Despite the name, XML is not an extension of HTML. It is like HTML in that it is a tag-based language but instead of having a limited lexicon of fewer than 100 tags, XML has an infinite number. Using XML, organisations can actually create their own tags to develop a mark-up language all of their own. Why would they want to do this? In XML, tags can be invented that best describe the contents. This will make searching a great deal easier and more effective. Thus, on a legal document, a web site developer can use existing tags such as <author>, <title>, <document type>, but can also make up new tags that might be specific to the legal context, such as <client>, <case name>, <case/docket number>, <counsel>, <opposition's counsel>, <argument>, <fact>, <opinion>, <obiter dicta>, and so on. However, web browsers have to be able to read and make sense of these tags. In order to do so, every XML document will be linked to an appendix known as a Document Type Definition or DTD. This will contain detailed information about how the web browser should interpret the tags. Developing these DTDs will be a slow and arduous process but ultimately this hard work will be rewarded, allowing web users to perform all manner of complex searching.

In addition, XML makes documents usable by other computer programs. Instead of being simply a format for publishing electronically, web documents could be reused to create new information. XML-enabled software will be able to extract all of the contents from a web page and transmit that information into a database or into a word-processing package for further editing. Using XML, the way in which documents are exchanged between organisations will be transformed. To take another example from the legal context, in order to file documents with a court, an overworked junior staff member or court clerk has to physically take documents down to the court, hand them to a member of the court staff who then manually re-keys the relevant data into their own internal database. In an XML-based world, the documents will be transmitted electronically, the relevant information will be automatically stripped out of the document and new documents (either web-based or paper-based) can be created automatically. XML anticipates a world in which one company's computer system will be able to read and make sense of any other organisation's documents automatically with no human intervention. This is truly revolutionary and in the legal context described above would speed up the administration of justice and reduce costs both for the client and for the public purse. HTML has given Internet users the ability to publish information freely and quickly. XML will give them the ability to make that information interact, to create further new and useful information. The implementation of XML will be as revolutionary as the Web itself.

SOFTWARE IS FREE ON THE INTERNET

The remarkable developments of the Internet have had interesting side-effects. For example, there is an increasing amount of software that is available free of charge. Much of this software is limited in some way: either it becomes useless once a trial period of 30 days has expired, or it offers a limited functionality. However, some software developers have apparently thrown caution to the wind and released the source code to their products. (Source code is the original programming code which reveals how the software actually works.) For example, Netscape Communications made two important announcements in early January 1998. First, they announced that the Netscape Communicator product would be available free of charge. (Microsoft had always made its browser freely available and so this was simply the inevitable response to the competitive challenge from a much larger competitor.) Second, however, Netscape announced that the source code for their best-selling flagship product would also be freely available. Some viewed this move as commercial suicide as Netscape's business plan was based around the sale of this web browser product. It was, in the words of one industry commentator, 'the computer-industry equivalent of revealing the recipe for Coca-Cola' *(The Economist,* 1998b) and what is more, the equivalent of allowing anyone to improve the recipe. At the time, Netscape and Microsoft were locked in a commercial battle over which browser would prove more popular with the web-surfing public. So why did Netscape take this seemingly suicidal step? The aim was 'to turn the entire Internet into a vast research division for Netscape's browser software' *(The Economist,* 1998b). A new organisation called mozilla.org was established, complete with web site to 'provide a central point of contact and community for those interested in using or improving the source code' of Netscape

Communicator. The Mozilla Organisation was the largest single step taken by an IT company towards making genuinely valuable source code available free of charge. Netscape 5 is the result of this collaborative exercise.

The idea was not new, however. The most popular web server software currently used on the Internet, despite the best attempts of both Microsoft and Netscape, is Apache. This software is available free of charge. There are other examples of so-called open-source programming. GNU/ Linux is a variant of the popular UNIX operating system. Linux will run on computer hardware that most people would now think of as useless (that is, state-of-the-art PCs circa 1993). The core of Linux was created in 1991 by Linus Torsvald, a Finnish programmer. Having created it, he turned it over to the wider international community of computer programmers to add new features, fix bugs and produce documentation. In 1998, GNU/Linux began to capture the hearts and minds of corporate organisations as a credible alternative to operating systems such as Microsoft Windows NT. According to the International Data Corporation, Linux tripled its market share of the operating-system market in 1998 to 17.2 per cent, outpacing the growth of Windows NT.

These methods of software distribution are examples of what is commonly described as 'copyleft' (a mirror of copyright). The idea behind copyleft is that any programmer can make alterations and improvements to a piece of software and submit them for inclusion in the next release. You can even sell your own version. However, the source code, the recipe, must remain open. Open-source programming has been likened to academic research rather than business - you discover something new and instead of selling the encapsulation of the idea, you hand it over to the wider community. However, it relies on the motivation of computer programmers many of whom are more interested in reputation than money. This is the complete reverse of the usual business model within most of the software industry.

For example, Microsoft hire huge numbers of programmers who are motivated by ever-more valuable stock options. As a result, Microsoft have become the largest and most successful software company in the world. Even they now accept (amongst themselves if not to the outside world) that the open-source programming model can be quicker and more effective. See, for instance, the so-called Halloween memo - an internal Microsoft memo leaked to the press which details reactions of key Microsoft executives to Linux and includes an admission that even they cannot keep up with the ability of the open-source community to produce fixes to problems.

Could this be the start of a new trend towards making software freely available? The computer giant, Sun, appears to be using a form of open-source programming with some of their newer technologies such as Jini. Could software companies survive not by selling software but by selling associated consultancy services? Whether intentionally or not, the Internet is encouraging users to expect something for nothing: free browsers, free evaluation software via the Web, even free operating systems. If this trend continues, we are going to see another paradigm shift in the IT industry and the Internet will be the showcase for all of this new free software.

FUTURE DEVELOPMENTS

This section is not meant to be a 'crystal ball' from which readers can determine the 'next big thing'. Instead, it is meant to highlight some of the key developments and give a sense of the overall thrust of changes. The Internet is developing in all manner of directions, in terms of infrastructure, software development and pervasiveness. The fact is that no one can predict where the Internet is going. Given recent history, it is quite likely that there will be at least one major technical development that apparently comes from nowhere and is anticipated by no one.

Within the past three years we have seen the emergence of Java as a new computing language designed to work on the Web. We have seen Microsoft, the world's largest software company, reanalyse their whole strategy and redesign all of their existing corporate software products to interact with the World Wide Web. We have also seen the emergence of new commercial forces in the computing industry: Netscape, Yahoo! and AOL. These are turbulent technological times and the turbulence is set to continue.

From a Passive Medium to an Active One

From its beginnings as an essentially passive medium, whereby the user obtained an electronic copy of a static document, it is now quite common for Web users to fill in forms in order to take part in surveys, register preferences or even purchase everyday items electronically. This interactivity has allowed Web-based commerce to develop at a frightening pace. In addition, computer programmers have introduced animation, sound and even video onto web pages. Furthermore, the introduction of new technologies such as Java[6] has made it possible for software to be distributed over the Internet at the time of need. This, in turn, has called into question the current model of computing based around expensive and complex Personal Computers. If software can be paid for and downloaded at time of need, why pay for and store infrequently used software on one's own PC? Easier maintenance and lower cost of ownership have also become key issues in the IT industry, in part as a result of the Internet.

Internet 2

The importance of the research origins of the Internet has not been lost on the US Government. Having paid for nearly 90 per cent of the research that makes the Internet what it is, they are determined not to lose their advantage. Internet 2 is only one part of the jigsaw. Other projects include the White Houses Next Generation Internet (NGI) and the National Science Foundation Very High Bandwidth Network Service (VBNS).

The Internet 2 initiative will link up 120 research universities in the USA to a super-fast fibre-optic network, offering speeds of between 100 and 1,000 times faster than the current service. Most large commercial and academic organisations currently lease a 'T I' line, almost 50 times faster than the average modem. It is claimed that Internet 2 will offer speeds up to 400 times faster than a Tl line, making TV-broadcast quality video conferencing entirely feasible. Internet 2 will also provide a playground for innovative research into all manner of new forms of communication and collaboration such as virtual reality and 3-dimensional environments. However, in order to take advantage of such speeds, a fibre-optic network will be required. In the USA, this communications backbone is fairly well advanced. This is not the case in Europe. This may mean that a two-tier Internet may emerge in the early years of the next century unless swift action is taken.

The US Government have also invested in a Next Generation Internet initiative which is researching security, robustness and reliability. They are also testing out networks with speeds of between 100 and 1,000 times the current speed of the Internet backbone.

In future, we will also probably see ISPs offering different levels of service. While it is possible to purchase an increasingly large pipe to connect to the Internet, if you sign up to an ISP, you get one level of service. There is no facility available for the user to communicate electronically with their ISP to the effect that they want a higher-quality service immediately because they are about to video-conference. Instead, the same level of service persists whether for email or for video transmission. In future, this will change: organisations will purchase different levels of Internet access according to their immediate needs.

ADSL

There is an ongoing debate in computing circles about whether DSL (Digital Subscriber Line) will or will not supersede ISDN, a current technology favoured by the large telecommunications companies in Europe. Like most other Internet technology, DSL was invented for something completely different: its original purpose was to allow the delivery of video-on-demand down plain old copper telephone wire (often referred to as 'POTS'). DSL has various flavours, the most popular being ADSL (the 'A' standing for Asymmetric). It is claimed that DSL offers speed of up to 50 times faster than the typical 28.8 Kpbs modem, instant connections (unlike traditional modems with their tedious dial-up routines) and simultaneous voice and data connections over the same line. (In other words there will be no need for a second phone line.) It is also more secure because it offers a dedicated connection to the Internet. However, it only works over short distances (less than 3 miles). It is currently being tested in the UK (BT were piloting ASDL services in April 1999). The exact way in which it works is beyond the scope of this text.

Cable Modems

An alternative to ADSL and one that seems to be developing more quickly as a viable alternative to ISDN lines, is the cable modem. Cable modem operators (such as NTL) claim that this technology will offer speeds of 256 Kbps as opposed to 128 Kbps for standard ISDN. However, the one problem with cable modem is that the performance degrades as more users use the service.

Internet Via Satellite

Satellite offers two key advantages over ISDN, ADSL or any form of cable-based service. The first is that satellite-based services can reach people in remote locations where it might not be feasible or economic to lay additional cables. The second is that satellite services allow for organisations that need to deliver the same set of bulk data to multiple clients. There are a number of initiatives underway to create global networks to deliver Internet-based information. For example, Teledesie is a $15 billion network comprising 288 low earth orbit satellites. Its competitor, Skybridge, is a $4.2 billion network of 80 satellites. Both intend to offer some form of data transfer services (i.e. email) as well as voice-based services. It will still be a few years before these companies offer commercial services, but if they work, they may beat off the threat of ADSL. By the same token, just because the system works it does not necessarily mean they are profitable. For example, Iridium[7] is a global telecommunications system which means that anyone with an Iridium telephone handset can phone anywhere in the world, bouncing a signal from satellite to satellite. It is nothing short of a technological marvel. However, since its launch, Iridium has not sold a single handset in the UK and is in Chapter 11 bankruptcy protection in the US.

Internet Telephony

One of the other potential benefits of the Internet is the ability to make phone calls. The theory is very appealing. A home user with a connection to the Internet through an ISP, could for the cost of a local call, phone any other

Internet user world-wide, thus by-passing expensive international call costs. While this is all feasible, making such calls over the Internet is not going to be practical in the near future. The problem is getting adequate bandwidth across the whole of the Internet so that there is no delay at either end. However, for a corporation with offices in a variety of locations which may already pay a fixed fee to connect various offices together to transfer data, it makes sense to use the same services for the routing of voice-based communications. We will probably see a convergence of voice and data using the common Internet protocols. The telecommunications, organisation that can deliver both services to its clients will prosper. (Those that cannot will soon be insolvent.)

The fact is that no one knows exactly where the Internet is going. Literally thousands of start-up companies are constantly delivering new Internet products to the world. The vast majority of these fail to reach the notice of mainstream web developers even though they may be extremely good ideas. A few break through into the Internet marketplace and usually make their creators millionaires. The remainder will try again. There are also plenty of examples of second-best technologies becoming the established standard (VHS and Betamax, for example. Macintosh fans would draw a parallel with the PC and the Apple Macintosh). The existence of a particularly good technology does not mean it will be adopted. Whatever happens it will be fascinating to watch.

ACTION POINTS

1. Recognise that the technology of the Internet is constantly changing. Be prepared to update your knowledge regularly.
2. Take note of the key trends - ADSL, cable modems

and Internet by satellite - and be looking to implement them when they are available.

3. Read the technology press but avoid over-hyped technologies - history suggests that they will not deliver many of their supposed benefits.

NOTES

1. For a non-technical introduction to TCP/IP, see Yale University's Introduction to TCP/IP web site (http://pclt.cis.yale.edu/pclt/comm/tcpip.htm)
2. Interested readers will find a complete listing of countries and their domain name codes at ftp://ftp.nw.com/zone/iso-country-codes
3. http://www.nominet.net
4. Quotation taken from ICANN homepage on web site - http://www.icann. org/abouticann.html.
5. See http://www.oclc.org
6. Developed by James Gosling of Sun Microsystems. For more information on Java, see Sun's excellent web site http://java.sun.com
7. http://www.iridium.com

Computing (1998). 'Oracle finds a new base', 17 September, p.l.

The Economist (1998a). 'Untangling the Web', 25 April, p.l16.

The Economist (1998b). 'Netscape breaks free', 28 March, p.86.

9 SECURITY AND THE INTERNET

UNDERSTANDING THE RISKS

No discussion of the Internet and electronic commerce is complete without an overview of the security implications. As the law firm extends its reach electronically via the Internet, proper security measures become paramount. However, the security concerns in a law firm context are different from those involved in traditional e-commerce. Few law firms have developed or are developing systems where credit card details are passed across the Internet. Thus this chapter does not dwell on the inner workings of encryption security standards such as Secure Socket Layer (SSL), Secure Electronic Transactions (SET) or the operating features of digital certificates. Instead, it looks at Internet security and IT security in the wider context of overall corporate security and discusses some of the specific Internet-related technologies available that may be implemented.

We live with risk every day. Every time we hand over a credit card at a shop or a restaurant or provide credit card details in the course of a telephone conversation, we run the risk that once our back is turned or the conversation terminated, those credit card details will be used by others without our consent. But in such situations, the risks are known - we understand the risk but do it anyway. With the Internet, there is an additional fear of the unknown.

Once details are submitted via a web site, the user has no idea where they will reside in future. It is this fear of the unknown that has allowed speculation to develop that the Internet is a 'dangerous place'. It is very easy to get wrapped up in the hypothetical risks associated with using it. Instead, Internet users need to put the risks in their proper perspective and manage their own behaviour accordingly.

The Cost of IT Security

IT security is complex, detailed and riddled with three-letter acronyms. Most people try to avoid learning anything about the subject if at all possible. Unfortunately, security is also perceived to be a negative item on the corporate balance sheet. It costs a great deal yet apparently offers no tangible benefits. Hence it tends to come low down the list of budget priorities. But this attitude ignores the fact that the cost of establishing a security system is far less than the cost of intrusion. For example, the US Department of Defense estimates that a single virus outbreak will cost an organisation an average of $8,000 in lost time, reduced productivity, and possible reinstallation of software. What the Department of Defense cannot calculate, however, is the cost of lost confidence. For example, who would want to do business (particularly legal business) with an organisation whose security is known to have been breached?

What Does Computer Security Actually Mean?

Unless one knows what the goal is, how can one know whether it has been achieved? The IT industry uses the following baseline measure. An information transfer is considered secure if it complies with the following four parameters: privacy, authenticity, accountability and integrity.

- Privacy is achieved if the contents of a message remain private when passing across the Internet.

- Integrity means that the message is not altered when passing across the Internet.
- Authentication is knowing who you are talking to and knowing they are who they say they are.
- Accountability is having both parties agree that a particular exchange took place.

The first lesson that needs to be learnt is that risk cannot be entirely eliminated - it can only be managed. No computer network, whether a corporate Local Area Network or Wide Area Network is entirely secure. Security issues on the Internet are made doubly difficult because the Internet was built for resilience not for security. It is, after all, no more than a very high-speed postal service, delivering information from one computer to another via a series of nodes. Until 1993, the main purpose of the Internet was the free transfer and sharing of academic information and research (i.e. information that was intended for widespread dissemination) and this overall purpose is reflected in its current infrastructure. Thus all Internet security measures have to be 'bolted on top' of the existing Internet infrastructure. The consequence is that holes in any security infrastructure are inevitable.

How Big is the Problem?

A 1997 FBI survey of the top *Fortune* 1000 companies concluded that the overall cost of computer crime in that year was a staggering $55 billion! Given that being hacked into is embarrassing for both individual and corporation, most companies are understandably reticent to admit that they have been kicked into or suffered computer crime through fraud and blackmail. Thus this enormous figure is likely to be a conservative estimate. The problem is very big.

KNOW THE ENEMY

H is important to distinguish between the various types of individuals involved in hacking. Films such as *Wargames* built upon a pre-existing stereotype of the hacker as an adolescent or college student male hacking late into the night. The reality is slightly different. There are three different types of individuals:

Hackers

This group hack into networks not to cause damage or disrupt services but because they see network security as a challenge, a safe to be unlocked. Thus they consider themselves to be slightly more ethical than those who hack for profit. However, the term 'hacker' is often used pejoratively.

Crackers

These people hack into networks in order to vandalise systems, to cause damage, or disruption to services. However, a cracker does not necessarily work outside of the organisation.

'Phone Phreaks'

The exploits of phone phreaks have now passed into the annals of Internet mythology. A small band of crackers in the USA used various flaws in the software controlling public telephone networks so that they could obtain free long-distance phone calls at the expense of AT&T. The flaws were plugged and phone phreaks no longer exist. They are now either hackers or are burglars turned policemen and become computer security consultants.

What can They Do?

Ask this question to any vendor of computer security products and they will respond with a lengthy inventory of potential evils. Below are just some of the potential evils that can be exacted on hapless individuals or corporations.

Most corporate organisations possess powerful computers on which they store all of their documents and databases. Once a cracker has gained access to an organisation there is nothing to stop him (and it usually is him) from leaving a small piece of code that uses that processing power whenever it is needed. The cracker can come back and pick up the results later once the software has completed its tasks.

Other clever but illegal methods include the unauthorised use of computer storage. Why upgrade your own PC if you can break into someone else's network and use all of the resources available there? Additional threats include mail spoofing - the ability to send email so that it looks as though it originated from your organisation. So-called 'denial of service' is another. This is the ability to reduce the available email, web access or fax services by bombarding an organisation with email messages, web requests or bogus fax deliveries. One clever manoeuvre is for individuals to break into the computer systems of large companies, install software that slows the system down to a snail's pace, then call the organisation pretending to be experts in speeding up computer systems. They are then invited in, fix the problem which they created in the first place and get paid handsomely for the privilege!

Newer arrivals on the cracker scene include web site vandalism (by changing vital information such as prices on e-commerce web sites or the introduction of viruses) and web spoofing - creating a replica of a web site and directing web traffic to a spoof version not to the authentic version. Vendors will also point out that some hacking and cracking software products can be obtained for free from web sites on the Internet that allow someone with virtually no understanding of computers to hack networks and make web servers unusable. All of the above makes for frightening or exciting reading depending on one's point of view.

However, some of the myths about IT security need to be dispelled - a sense of realism is required. First, in terms of numbers, the group that constitutes malicious hackers or crackers world-wide is quite small. The Internet is not rife with hackers. out to destroy any and all corporate organisations.

Second, it is far easier to sabotage a computer system than it is to defraud or blackmail an organisation via its computer systems. Fraud or blackmail would require contacts within the organisation and increases the likelihood of betrayal and discovery which may lead to criminal prosecution and a possible jail sentence. Every would-be hacker will consider whether the benefits outweigh the risks. In most cases they do not. A March 1998 survey by the Computer Security Institute and the FBI confirmed that sabotage was far more popular than fraud. A massive 74 per cent of all computer break-ins were virus related (i.e. an attempt by an unknown computer programmer to introduce a hostile computer program into any other computer system. It is a form of non-specific sabotage). Unauthorised access accounted for 39 per cent of all of break-ins. Telecom fraud and financial frauds accounted for 14 per cent and 13 per cent respectively.

Third, it is incorrect to think that all of the 'bad guys are out there' and all of the 'good guys are in here'. Hacking is also done internally. The reality is that the disgruntled employee is as much of a security threat as the stereotypical adolescent male hacker. Poor security standards and poor enforcement encourage the dishonest or disgruntled employee to take advantage of such opportunities. The threat does not diminish once the employee has left the organisation. Technically-literate former employees may know how to break into an organisation electronically. Indeed, they may themselves have programmed in any number of backdoor entry points into a particular system. Very often, due to negligence or ignorance on the part of the remaining staff, passwords remain valid on various systems for years after the departure of the employee. The risks posed by employees include disclosure of confidential data to competitors or to the general public. The importance of this should not be underestimated. While the cost of computer hardware continues to plummet, the value of information continues to increase.

THERE IS NO SOLUTION: ONLY RISK MANAGEMENT

Unfortunately, there is no silver bullet in IT security. Computer security management is a state of mind rather than the purchase and good management of software and hardware and it must be a state of mind that is shared by all employees rather than a single individual. Many vendors of computer security products will lead the ignorant customer to believe that their products are the answer. But they are simply taking advantage of customer naivety. Computer security is probably 51 per cent people related and 49 per cent technology related. Thus 51 per cent of the solution is the development and continual review of an IT security policy.

An IT security policy should not be developed in isolation. It is only one aspect of an overall security policy and this starts at the front door of the organisation. Most small- to medium-sized organisations only think about an IT-based security policy after a breach has occurred. This is reactive fire-fighting not management. What is required is proactive general security management. For example, a comprehensive security policy should look at who comes into the firm, and should include the following questions. How are visitors and contractors monitored? Do they have badges? Are they accompanied? How easy is it for them to tailgate employees through any security doors? Are door codes changed regularly? Who has keys? What are the policies of the organisation in relation to confidential information - are documents shredded or simply thrown away? Are there security audits - how often do they take place? A firm can spend all the money in the world on clever IT security solutions, but if someone can bluff their way into the office and actually sit down at a computer hosting mission-critical data or services, it is all a colossal waste of time and money.

Large technology companies are so sensitive about information management that they instigate clear desk policies and enforce strict waste disposal of all documentation include such seemingly mundane information as phone lists. They also impose strict control of what is permitted in conversation outside of work. Some technology companies even operate a 'three strikes and out' policy: in other words threes failures to comply with any aspects of their security policy means that the employee can be sacked. While this may seem somewhat draconian, it also demonstrates the value that such companies place on their security procedures.

As part of the general security management initiative, firms should look at the control of users' passwords. Passwords are considered by most users to be an annoying necessity. Consequently, they try to make their password as easy as possible to remember. They pick the name of their partner or their pet, or use their birthday, and to make matters worse, they usually write it down. With a few pieces of personal information it is likely that passwords can be guessed correctly. Users should be made to change their password every few months and should not be permitted to use a password that they have used previously. Also, the hacker's job can be made far more difficult by the use of a few random numbers or characters - thus instead of using the name 'sarah' as a password, the character string of 's@r@h' will defeat many intruders. Passwords are also used extensively on the Internet - most Internet users will have come across web sites where they have to enter a user name and a password in order to access the site. How many employees use the same password over and over again? Again, this is a risk. The risk can be managed but only through education. Eventually, the problems associated with passwords will disappear as the problems created by technology are solved by technology: fingerprint and even iris recognition will replace plain-text passwords.

British Standard BS7799

Ultimately, law firms should be aiming to comply with or even be certified under British Standard BS7799 - an increasingly important standard that details how an organisation should securely store, handle and process information. It provides a framework for in-house security efforts. The British Standards Institute (BSI) provide supplementary information about BS7799 on their web site. This is, however, the ideal scenario. The reality is somewhat different.

A KPMG survey published in March 1997 summarised the responses of 1,500 finance directors of UK organisations with a turnover in excess of £10 million. The following conclusions emerged:

- Of those interviewed only 45 per cent of respondents had any kind of security policy;
- 73 per cent of companies surveyed had no designated security officer;
- 77 per cent had no formal procedure for reporting security incidents;
- 98 per cent had not implemented BS7799 or anything similar;
- 65 per cent of organisations with access to the Internet did not know what connections were made;
- Only 30 per cent of the 45 per cent with a security policy addressed the Internet;
- 25 per cent were not registered under the Data Protection Act, thus potentially breaking the law.

Clearly we have a long way to go.

THE TECHNICAL SOLUTIONS

The remaining 49 per cent of the security solution is technology based. Where a large organisation has leased a line to connect to the Internet, the obvious step is the purchase of a firewall. A firewall is a combination of hardware and software used to prevent Internet traffic from entering an organisation and to monitor Internet traffic leaving the organisation. The firewall sits between the organisation and their ISP and should be the only point of access between the firm and the Internet.

While the purchase of a firewall is essential, it leads most organisations into a false sense of security. A firewall is not an end in itself - it is simply a means to an end - part of the solution to be used in conjunction with other security measures, and as part of a properly implemented IT security policy. The reality is that in most organisations a firewall is only one of many potential entry points. If users have modems on their PCs linked to the ISP then installing a firewall is tantamount to bolting the front door but leaving the side windows open. In addition, if the firewall is not set up correctly (as is often the case) it may as well not be there.

Firewalls can be used for monitoring outgoing Internet traffic. According to International Data Corporation, most companies that purchase firewalls set them up only to monitor or prevent in-bound traffic. Security-conscious organisations should also be logging outbound Internet traffic, and seeing who is doing what on the Internet, by automatically examining web pages and software that have been downloaded, as well as monitoring people logging into the corporate network through the firewall. However, there are Data Protection implications here. The firm must be able and willing to provide employees with any and all information held in relation to their web-surfing habits.

Security and the Web Site

While Intranets are the current hot topic in computing, little has been written about the security threats to a web site. The web site for most law firms is the shop-window for their legal services and usually no more than that. The site will not usually contain information about clients, matters, bills outstanding, charge-out rates, etc., although this will probably change as more law firms move from simple marketing web sites to e-commerce, embracing the changes anticipated. One might assume that there would be little of interest in a marketing web site to the cracker. However, increasingly the web site may be the first contact a potential client has with a law firm. Just as one would be very careful to protect the corporate identity of the firm, one should have in place measures to ensure that the corporate identity is equally protected in Cyberspace. This would be particularly important where the firm is known to be involved in high-profile and controversial legal work. A website is also an advertisement — it presents a challenge to the would-be cracker. It says 'come and get me'. Unfortunately, most web sites are established with relatively little thought given to their ongoing protection and the implications for protecting the 'brand'.

Some well-known web sites have been cracked with photographs and text being replaced by 'less complimentary' materials. Interested readers can view a selection of 'before' and 'after' web sites at http://www.2600.com, a favourite haunt of hackers and crackers. Among those web sites that have been cracked are the UK Labour Party, the UK Conservative Party, the Los Angeles Police Department and, surprisingly, UNICEF. Unless a law firm is known to be acting for high-profile individuals or organisations, many lawyers may think that their site is likely to be fairly low down the list of potential hacking targets. However, law firms should rely on their own security measures not on the ignorance or benevolence of individual hackers. While it is fathomable (though wholly unacceptable) that someone might hack web sites belonging to political parties or controversial organisations, one might ask why UNICEF, a non-partisan and humanitarian organisation, was targeted by hackers? The answer would appear to be because it was easy!

Security risks exist at a number of levels on a web site: the coding that makes up the site; the server software (i.e. the software that turns a computer into a machine capable of making information available over the Internet); the operating system; and in the protocols used. The ways in which such security can be compromised are fairly technical in nature, usually specific to particular products and beyond the scope of this book. Hackers can, for example, exploit security holes in web server software using so-called SYN attacks (short for synchronisation transaction) where they flood the web server with requests for information. Web server software developers have released patches to deal with such attacks but these are reactive responses after the damage has been done and many Webmasters do not bother to download the patch to prevent its reoccurrence. Hackers can also take advantage of the coding that makes up many web pages. For example, many web sites often provide users with access to databases. Using an aspect of the code that is often necessary to make databases interact with the web pages, hackers can access sites and obtain access to the databases. There are many sources of information which can help the non-technical reader understand the risks posed.[1]

Where a web site is hosted by a third party, in other words, outsourced, how certain can the law firm be that security is being taken seriously? Web site development and hosting is often cost-effective but it can also be an abrogation of responsibility for security. Therefore, a firm should ask itself what security measures are in place to identify and manage the risks? This will depend on how the web site is assembled. If the coding has been produced internally, one can presume there is less of a risk. However, if the coding is done by a third party, i.e. a web site design consultancy, then their work should be examined by a knowledgeable programmer, either someone who works for the firm or by another programmer hired specifically for this task. If the web site is hosted externally, the firm needs to consider what, if any, mechanisms are in place to prevent unauthorised intrusions. Does the host organisation have security policies supplemented by mechanisms such as firewalls to prevent unauthorised access? It is important for a law firm to ask these questions before the web site is outsourced. Changing web site hosts is a time-consuming exercise.

Security and the Intranet

Intranets pose a different security risk for law firms. If the cracker can obtain access to the intranet by penetrating the firm's firewall or gaining physical access to the firm's offices, then intranets may offer the illicit intruder easy access to different types of information. Unlike a normal file storage system that may use codes to describe the contents of different files and directories, an intranet is designed to be user-friendly and allow for quicker access to information. Depending on what is available on the intranet this may include commercially sensitive and confidential information: lists of clients, client documentation, billing information, performance targets, and so forth. Intranets are also increasingly offering users the ability to search and access the entire internal network. Again, part of the solution is to establish internal firewalls between different parts of the network and to exclude certain users based on their user, profiles. It is also a question of educating users about computer security generally. Many large commercial organisations hire computer security experts (that is benevolent hackers, also known as 'tiger teams') to attempt to break through the firewalls and see what can be recovered from the corporate network.

Security and the Extranet

By their very nature, extranets present the greatest threat to security. In the business-to-consumer domain, they present an exciting challenge to external hackers with the promise of credit card goodies to be found inside. A 1998 survey on security awareness found that 'web sales sites recorded 13 per cent more breaches than non-sales sites' (*Information Week*, 1998). It is likely that in future much of the hacker interest will focus on poorly defended extranet sites.

As yet, there have been no high-profile stories about e-commerce sites being hacked and credit cards details being used fraudulently. Could this be because no hacks have occurred? This is unlikely. Much more likely is that the victims have tried to keep the events as quiet as possible. Security and e-commerce may yet prove to be the Achilles' heel of the Internet. It would only take one well-publicised theft of credit card information from a well-known e-commerce such as the Amazon.com site to bring the e-commerce hyperbole crashing down to earth. The last thing that is needed is a high-profile story about hackers getting hold of thousands of credit card details from a single web site which would effectively undermine the trust of the web-surfing and electronically purchasing public.

Most law firm extranet sites will be business-to-business rather than business-to-consumer and are therefore unlikely to offer the hacker access to credit card details. However, depending on the type of extranet site, there are potential security risks. If the extranet service is procedure based, it may offer hackers access to lawyer-client communications and this exposure could be potentially fatal to client confidence in the firm. If the firm offers access to its expertise via an extranet and the site is insecure, then the enterprising hacker could take copies of various pages and publish them on various public web sites. The reason why clients are prepared to pay so much for services such as Blue Flag and NextLaw is because this knowledge is so rare - these products represent the combined experiences of many lawyers over a number of years. If such services can be hacked and the information placed in the public domain, the value of such information would rapidly diminish. As we saw in April 1999 with the publication of a list of MI6 officers on the Internet, once information is placed on one web site, it is virtually impossible to prevent its replication onto other web sites. The need to purchase expensive subscriptions to dedicated extranet sites is immediately diminished.

THE TECHNICAL SECURITY SOLUTIONS

Computer security technology and standards is a massive topic. It would be impossible to address all of the different tools and protocols currently available. In any event, many of the tools and protocols are not relevant to the average law firm. Thus, this section provides an overview of the most significant to this readership. However, the technology is developing rapidly. Readers are strongly advised to investigate each tool or protocol further before implementing them.

The purchase of several different security products brings with it a sense of security. However, the use of disparate products can leave gaps which can be exploited by the skilled hacker. Ultimately we will see comprehensive security products emerge that plug such gaps. For the time being, however, all corporate organisations have to mix and match their security products and hope to fill all of the gaps. It is not satisfactory but it is all there is at present.

Background

The Internet is a postal service. Messages are passed from node to node on the Internet as plain text, unless some form of encryption is used. Encryption scrambles a message so that it cannot be read without a key which is known to the intended recipients. Thus encryption makes data indecipherable. Once the message is received, decryption unscrambles the scrambled message.

The development of Internet-related computer security

products has taken place in a political context surrounding the use of strong encryption products. In the USA, this has pilled freedom-of-spcech advocates and the entire computing industry against the law enforcement community and specifically the FBI. In addition, different countries have adopted different approaches to the control of security products. For example, the US Government regulate the export of strong encryption products in the (tenuous) belief that their export will compromise national security. The argument runs as follows. If strong encryption can be used by terrorists, criminals or hostile countries, this will limit the ability of the relevant US authorities to act to protect the 'national interest'. Similarly, Singapore limits the export of strong encryption products. European countries have fewer restrictions although there are exceptions. For example, in France the use of encryption is illegal because it is viewed as a form of munitions! In fact, the only thing that has been limited by such regulations is the ability of US technology companies to compete in the world market for encryption products because they cannot be exported. Anyone can download strong encryption products from countries such as Germany and use them to outwit the FBI, the CIA or any other law enforcement agency. As the technology industry has repeatedly pointed out, the encryption genie is out of the bottle.

Authentication IS the Issue

Those who have focused on encryption to the exclusion of all other issues are also missing the point. Fundamentally, the most important issue is authentication. In layperson's terms, authentication means 'I am who I say I am'. If I am not who I say I am and I conduct business across the Internet then whether it is done using encryption or not, it is still fraud!

People use authentication every day. At its most basic,

we authenticate one another when we recognise one another. If you look at the face of a work colleague you identify that person as having a particular name and authenticate that person in your own mind. We also use authentication whenever a cheque is signed and examined against a bank guarantee card. In IT, there are different ways in which a user can be authenticated. Passwords are the most popular yet basic form of authentication. They are also very weak. (It is likely that passwords will eventually be replaced by biometric authentication methods such as fingerprints, iris recognition or face recognition.)

Password protection can be enhanced through the use of a 'physical token'. These are small credit-card-like devices that a user must have in order to get access to the network or particular sections of the network. There are different variations. For example, SecurID tokens have a small LED screen that creates a random number every minute. In order to access a system, the user must have a username, a password and be in possession of a token so that they can type in the random number when they log in. If the number doesn't match the expected number, access is denied. Other types of tokens require users to enter a PIN number on the credit-card token. This, in turn, creates a random number. This number is then entered on the computer and the user can then gain access to the required resource. The drawback of physical tokens is that each token costs a fixed fee and they have to be changed regularly. Where there are only users, however, it is a very secure option.

Digital Certificates

On the Internet, where there are potentially millions of users needing to be authenticated, the possession of physical tokens is simply not feasible. The consequence is that technology companies are developing alternative standards based on so-called digital certificates. Digital certificates are akin to a driving licence - proof that you are who you say you are. They are pieces of software that are appended to the web browser. Digital signatures rely on what is known as a 'public key infrastructure'. A public key infrastructure is a complex subject that will not be fully explored here. Digital certificates provide authentication which allow users to identify themselves to web servers so that they can communicate securely or gain special access to web site information. Users enroll themselves and receive digital certificates from a certificate authority such as 'Verisign.[2] The idea is that the presentation of a digital certificate will provide a more straightforward means of identification and access control compared with user ID and password methods or physical tokens. The problem is that generally, most Internet users cannot be bothered to enroll with a certificate authority because they see no benefit. To most people it is like upgrading to the latest version of Internet Explorer or Netscape Navigator - it is a lot of work for no apparent benefit and unless there is a compelling reason, most people just do not bother. Consequently, digital certificates have yet to reach a critical mass of users.

E-Commerce Encryption Standards: SSL and SET

Any examination of current Internet security must include a description of the major emerging standards for electronic commerce, namely SSL and SET. While no law firms are currently using a model for legal services transactions using credit cards, this may become commonplace in future.

SSL (Secure Socket Layer)

SSL (or Secure Socket Layer) is currently the only choice for organisations wishing to establish secure electronic commerce sites. The competing standard, SET (Secure

Electronic Commerce), has yet to capture the imagination of the Internet-surfing public for reasons outlined below. SSL protects both buyer and merchant, or information producer and information consumer by securing both ends of the 'pipe' using so-called 'public key cryptography'.[3] (The way in which key cryptography works is very complicated. It involves the creation of a unique string of numbers using a mathematical algorithm. An in-depth exploration would be detailed and long-winded and would probably only interest a tiny minority of this book's readership.) Technically, SSL sits between TCP/IP and HTTP. SSL initiates what is known as a 'security handshake'. This handshake involves the two parties agreeing on the level of security that they will use and fulfils any authentication requirements for the connection. Thereafter, SSL's only role is to encrypt and decrypt the stream of information that is sent in either direction. It is currently used extensively across the Internet.

SET (Secure Electronic Transactions)

SET is an 'open, global standard detailing the secure use of payment cards over open networks such as the Internet' (*Secure Computing*, 1997). Technically, SET is a serious contender as the predominant security standard for electronic commerce. But there are problems with implementing it. Started in 1996, it has the backing of two of the largest credit card providers, Mastercard and Visa. On the technology side, it has the backing of IBM and a number of other major Internet software development companies. SET is the first full attempt to create a secure environment across the whole transaction. Unlike SSL, it gives a high degree of protection to all of; the parties involved in the transaction: buyer, merchant, bank and credit card processors. Thus it is particularly appealing to the financial services industry. From the user's point of view, the idea is that those sites that have a 'SET mark' (an indicator similar to a British Standards 'kitemark') carry an implicit guarantee that card holders can use their cards on these sites, certain in the knowledge that their details will not be intercepted.

It is now nearly three years since the publication of the standard and SET has still to catch on. The sceptics argue that SET is costly, overly complicated and ultimately unnecessary. Meanwhile the web-surfing public are happily entering their credit-card details into SSL-based web sites and e-commerce is growing exponentially. This is in spite of the absence of a fully integrated security system. The problem is that each party to the transaction needs a digital certificate[4] to sign, encrypt and decrypt the messages being sent. As discussed above, digital certificates are complicated and not fully understood by most Internet users. It is therefore difficult to persuade users to adopt them. Advocates of SET would argue that web users and businesses with e-commerce sites that do not take advantage of SET are risking huge potential liabilities. However, the longer SET remains sidelined, the harder it will be for the credit card issuers to persuade users to change their habits and adopt SET as the preferred security standard.

THE CHANGING ROLE OF THE LAWYER IN THE INFORMATION SOCIETY

> It is not simply about the networking of technology but about the networking of humans through technology. It is not an age of smart machines but of humans, who through networks can combine their intelligence, knowledge and creativity in the creation of wealth and social development. It is an age of vast new promise and unimaginable opportunity, but it is also an age of peril.
>
> *Tapscott, 1995*

Commercial web browsers were released only 7 years ago and already some key themes are becoming apparent to the legal profession. 'Commoditisation' - the user-friendly repackaging of legal information via the Internet, 'disintermediation' - the death of the middleman, and the emergence of a new type of capitalism - a truly networked economy.

The last theme is going to have fundamental implications for wider society and lawyers will be affected as much as any other group.

THE COMMODITISATION OF LEGAL SERVICES

There can be no doubt that information technology, instead of simply automating existing processes, is just beginning to transform the legal services industry in certain specific areas. As far as the client is concerned the transformation is likely to be wholly positive - there will be more legal information more widely available, and that information will be available more quickly and efficiently than before. It is still debatable/as to whether it will be any cheaper. The jury is still out on whether this transformation will be wholly positive for the legal profession. The key question that remains unresolved is whether legal e-commerce in the form of extranets offering the sum of many lawyers' expertise and experience will *replace* traditional legal services or whether they will be considered as additional services to complement the existing methods of legal practice. Will lawyers discover a huge untapped need for legal services or will every law firm simply cannibalise their own client base?

There are two opposing views. Susskind's conclusions about these changes are upbeat. He anticipates that as legal information is repackaged in a more user-friendly format using information technology (via kiosks and information systems provided by Government, law firms, and legal publishers), a huge untapped market for legal services will be unleashed. Individuals and businesses will begin to understand much more clearly their rights and obligations and will be more willing to pursue them. This is what Susskind terms 'the latent legal market' (Susskind, 1996). The theory is that both client and lawyers Will be better off - the client will have access to better legal information and the lawyer will find clients needing more legal services.

Other commentators such as Charles Christian are less convinced. He criticises Susskind's book as follows:

> At its heart is the beguiling argument that a great many people do not use conventional legal services (in other words consult lawyers) because the whole process is so user-hostile, complicated, expensive and otherwise unattractive that these people are alienated from the law. But, says the good professor, if the law were packaged in a different way, so that it was accessible to everyone, in other words the latent legal market, more people would use it than do today.
>
> *Christian, 1998*

Christian is not convinced, dismissing the latent legal market as no more than an urban myth. He goes on: 'the fact is that the law is like dentistry. Although we all know that we should look after our teeth and that the prevention of tooth decay is better than a filling or dentures, few people voluntarily set foot in the dentist's surgery'.

So who is right and who is wrong? I believe that they both are. Certainly Christian's views are correct up to a point - for every user of the Freeserve Desktop Lawyer service, that is probably one less client walking through the front door of the average law office on the High Street. Yet, by contrast, anecdotal evidence from the Blue Flag experiment suggests that the number of referrals has increased greatly as a result of this service. Presumably subscribers are realising that the legal issues surrounding their affairs are more complicated than they may seem and consequently they instruct a law firm in the traditional way. The fact is that all on-line legal services are not alike. To use a medical analogy, comparing Freeserve's Desktop Lawyer with Blue Flag is like comparing a visit to the doctor because of a twisted ankle with a visit to a Harley Street specialist because of a rare skin complaint - the problem, the treatment and the cost are on a completely different scale.

If both Susskind and Christian are correct up to a point, then those medium-to-large firms that do invest in the Blue Flag type of extranet application will become even larger and richer than they are now. Meanwhile on the High Street, the smaller firms that do not have the resources to invest in extranet-type applications, or any form of information technology for that matter, will be severely affected by non-traditional providers of legal services such as Tesco, the Nationwide Building Society and Virgin. It can only be a matter of time before these companies or similar ones develop their competitor products to Freeserve's Desktop Lawyer and consequently, unless remedial action is taken. High Street firms will slowly wither and perish. This is a grim scenario for the average small firm. So how might they survive? One solution might be for smaller firms that have traditionally survived on legal work based around residential conveyancing, debt collection, wills and probate and family law, to move into more specialised areas of legal practice such as employment law, taxation, commercial litigation, and so forth. Speculating a little further, life in the legal profession might become really interesting if the medium-sized firms, i.e. those that have survived doing all types of legal work, recognise that there are no longer sufficient profit margins in high-volume, low-value legal services and attempt to move up the legal practice 'food chain' into areas such as banking, corporate finance, telecommunications, information technology, and so forth to compete on cost with the larger firms - extranet against extranet.

So is this scenario the real future of legal practice? Will the Internet create a cut-throat marketplace for legal services, controlled entirely by the consumer in which they download legal information or legal products in the form of software and where the notion of the lawyer-client relationship becomes an interesting but quaint artefact that died out in the early years of the twenty-first century? Two factors militate against such a scenario.

First, the market for legal services is what economists describe as 'sticky' - there is an element of quality built into such services. When buying a consumer item such as a pair of Levi's jeans, which are identical anywhere in the world, the consumer will gravitate towards that web site which offers the best price for the identical item. But the purchasing of legal services such as the drafting of an employment contract or an IT outsourcing contract has little in common with the purchase of a pair of jeans. While clients do 'comparison-shop' for legal services, cost is only one factor. Quality of service is fundamental and it is very difficult for clients to determine the quality of legal services until after those services have been provided.

Second, there are limits on what can be achieved in terms of commoditisation. Most traditional legal services are about a particular set of business problems and providing a customised legal solution to solve those problems. Lawyers will continue to develop business relationships where the complexity and the uniqueness of the legal or commercial situation means that it cannot be commoditised. In addition, there will always be a role for the face-to-face business relationship between lawyers and clients where a high degree of trust and understanding is required. Moreover, a simple precedent together with document assembly software delivered via the Internet (or on a floppy disk for that matter) cannot capture the knowledge gained by years of experience of drafting similar documents or all of the subtleties of industry practices. A high percentage of legal expertise is tacit knowledge and it is extremely difficult to convert tacit knowledge into explicit knowledge. Experienced lawyers possess a wealth of tacit knowledge that cannot easily be transferred. If knowledge cannot be written down in a document, that document cannot be published on a web site. Thus there will always be a role for legal advice delivered in the traditional way. Complex legal matters will remain the domain of the legal expert and will be charged for in the traditional way.

Even Clifford Chance, one of the early innovators with extranet services believe that on-line services could account for 20 per cent of the firm's business within five years. (This may be over-ambitious but it provides an indication of the aspirations of one of the very largest firms.) This still leaves 80 per cent of legal services delivered in a traditional way. The Internet is not a doomsday scenario for all law firms. It is not 'the end of the world as we know it'. However (and it is a very big however), as Charles Christian states in the Foreword to this book, the Internet is both a new business opportunity and a threat to the traditional forms of legal services. It must be embraced and made to work for the law firm.

DISINTERMEDIATION

In a world where an individual can comparison-shop from the comfort of their own home for anything and everything, who needs the traditional middlemen such as estate agents or travel agents? Simply surf around, find the best, fill in the form with credit card details and receive the goods of your choice by post. Disintermediation is the cumbersome term used to describe this simple idea of removing the intermediary in any transaction. It has been predicted that the role of the intermediary will disappear. It has been suggested by others that it will simply change.

In a law firm context, disintermediation will manifest itself in a number of different areas and in different ways. Perhaps the most interesting area is in relation to the future role of the law librarian.

The Internet is already affecting the ways in which lawyers access legal information. There was a time when in order to borrow a book from an academic or public library, the user would present him or herself at the enquiry desk, fill out a form and return at least three hours later once the book had been found. Now, most library users are permitted to walk freely amongst the books and browse to their heart's content. Thus, the librarian's role changed from gatekeeper to search facilitator. The Internet will eventually change the role of the librarian once again. With the World Wide Web, anyone has free access to a massive, yet totally chaotic electronic library available via a very simple piece of software that sits on his or her PC. In the traditional library context, the librarian can offer special, often unique, insights into the way in which to find information. On the Internet, unless the librarian is physically present at the lawyer's PC every time a search is performed this is impossible.

Searching for information on the Internet is currently an imprecise art, where a single keyword can produce millions of hits or no hits at all. That said, searching on the Internet will only become easier, quicker and more precise. The role of the librarian as research assistant will be reduced, perhaps disappear altogether. The current vast array of electronic legal information resources currently available on CD-ROM will also available in Internet-ready format. This is already happening. Legal publishers that used to provide electronic materials on tapes, then on CD-ROMs are now willing to provide these same materials via the Internet or, alternatively, will make available the newest versions of their products onto a firm's intranet every night. Furthermore, the courts themselves are publishing materials on their own court service web sites (for example see http://www.courtservice.gov.uk).

What role will the law firm librarians fulfil in this new world of instantaneous and ubiquitous information? This is a question that all law librarians should be asking themselves: the library profession urgently needs to reassess its own role before others reassess it for them and decide that they have no future in the digital era. One possible role for the future law librarian is ensuring that only quality electronic information reaches the desk of the fee-earner, in a sense, a return to the role of gatekeeper. The difference this time, however, is that the role of the librarian is to keep the information from the user rather than the user from the information. With so much information available and so much of it irrelevant, busy lawyers may happily employ librarians to help them manage it. This filtering role would be achieved by the creation and management of tailored indexes, and thesauruses so that the lawyer obtains only that information which is clearly useful, authenticated and relevant.

The more entrepreneurial-minded of librarians, or information professionals as they may prefer to describe themselves, will recognise that their skills of categorisation, search and retrieval and understanding of information needs, offer great potential to any large organisation. In a world awash with information, the professional who can steer a course through to the information that is actually required, may be considered more valuable than ever before. Far from signalling the death of librarianship as a profession, the Internet may signal a resurgence of recognition in the value that librarians can bring to an organisation. What librarians may have to accept at the same time is that their primary role as custodians of the physical record is dead.

Another more specialist role for future librarians will be as digital corporate archivists. There are already some worrying reports emerging about the lifetime of digital data *(Computing,* 1998). Despite assurances from the IT industry about the longevity of digital data, the infinite lifetime of CD-ROMs, for example, is not assured. Some organisations are already discovering that data created no more than 20 years ago is already unreadable due to breakages in the magnetic storage data and that the process of data conversion can do as much harm as good. Migration of data carries a threat of data loss and/or corruption. This is particularly important in the law firm context where non-contentious matters may turn litigious many years after their conclusion. Traditionally, the librarian carries the responsibility for the ongoing access to information whereas IT technicians are more interested in developing new systems. Are librarians competent or willing to take the role of digital archivists? Probably not at present. What is clear, however, is that the preservation of the corporate electronic memory will become a full-time occupation and someone, whether library or IT professionals, must take responsibility.

INTERESTING TIMES ...

What role then for the lawyer in these 'interesting times'? Clearly some of the larger law firms are likely to prosper as a result of large impressive e-commerce offerings. But what is the future of the smaller firm? Indeed, does the smaller law firm have a future, in a world where the legal marketplace is open to new non-traditional competitors that can enter the market by simply developing a web site?

Small firms have one card left to play. In many ways, new technology favours the smaller specialist law firm. If a group of experienced lawyers can offer the same service as a City law firm via the Internet, but from less than ostentatious offices in a small provincial town where the overheads are a fraction of those in the City, then those cost savings can be passed on to the client. Where the client is able to discern that they are obtaining an equivalent quality of service from a small firm using technology effectively, they may decide to change their legal advisors. It may be that within a few years, we will see a trend away from the 'mega-firms' to smaller specialist niche firms that are able to offer the same service for less cost. Could it be that the impressive city centre offices with their glass-fronted corner sites, far from being a demonstration of power and prestige, instead become an expensive burden? The Internet has shown itself capable of incredible power in terms of democratising access to information and increasing competitiveness in different marketplaces, driving a metaphorical coach and horses through traditional market structures. There is no reason to think that the legal services marketplace is immune.

There are exciting and scary times ahead for the legal profession. The Internet must not be dismissed as some passing fad. It is a new marketplace - a new opportunity. This is 1492 - a New World. Law firms can be part of this

New World, and embrace the new digital economy, or they can be part of the old world and watch their tradition of practices being slowly eroded.

The choice is entirely within your own making.

ACTION POINTS

1. Recognise that Internet security is only one small part of overall IT security, which in turn is part of overall corporate security. The best Internet encryption and authentication is no use if the organisation is exposed elsewhere.
2. Recognise that there is no such thing as total security only risk management.
3. Put the risk in its proper perspective and manage your user behaviour accordingly.
4. Think about your organisation from the hacker's perspective. Examine the potential risk areas and put in place all reasonable safeguards.
5. Do not fall into the trap of believing that a firewall is the first and last line of defence in Internet security - it is not.
6. Educate your users - make sure their passwords are not obvious, easily available or semi-permanent.

FURTHER READING

Ford, W. and Baum, M.S. (1997). *Secure Electronic Commerce: Building the Infrastructure for Digital Signatures ana Encryption.* Prentice-Hall, Inc., New Jersey.

Grant, G.L. (1998). *Understanding Digital Signatures: Establishing Trust over the Internet and other Networks.* McGraw-Hill, New York.

Stirling, Bruce (1994). *The Hacker Crackdown, Law and Disorder on the Electronic Frontier.* Penguin, London.

Interestea readers can read more about phone phreaks, hackers and crackers in this excellent and highly readable book.

The most up-to-date and some of the best information to be found on Internet security is to be found actually on the Internet, e.g. Usenet groups such as alt.security and comp.security.misc should be examined.

There are other important security-related web sites such as the Computer Emergency Response Team (CERT, at http://www.cert.com) and the World Wide Web security FAQ (http://www.w3.org).

NOTES

1. See, for example, the *Guide to Content Security*, produced by Content Technologies Limited, which sets out all potential security problems relating to emails and web content.
2. http://www.verisign.com
3. http://www.rsi.com
4. To be more precise, each party needs a SET-compliant X.509 digital certificate.

BIBLIOGRAPHY

Christian, Charles (1998). *Legal Practice in the Digital Age - the Quest for the Killer Legal App.* Bowderdean, London, pp.27-8.

Computing (1998). The vanishing world of data', 30 April, p.48 (originally published in *Business Week).*

Price Waterhouse Coopers (1997). 'Global Information Security Survey', p. 6.

Secure Computing (1998). 'Trading securely on the Internet', October, p. 20.

Susskind, Richard (1996). *The Future of Law.* Clarendon Press, Oxford.

Tapscott, Don (1995). *The Digital Economy, Promise and Peril in the Age of Networked Intelligence.* McGraw-Hill, New York.

APPENDIX A

USEFUL GENERAL INTERNET SITES AND SOFTWARE RESOURCES

Below are a selection of different options for search engines, sites for promoting and maintaining web sites, web development tools, web server software, databases, middleware tools, and significant Internet technologies. The list is by no means complete. Instead, it is designed to give the user, whether web-surfer, new web developer or Internet project-manager an idea of the possible options available.

SEARCH ENGINES

AltaVista

http://www.altavista.com—One of the most comprehensive directories on the Web, formerly owned and developed by Digital, now owned by Compaq, computer hardware manufacturers, who announced in early 1999 that they were proposing to create a separate company called AltaVista and eventually float it on the New York Stock Exchange.

AOL Netfind

http://www.aol.com/netfind/ - One would expect AOL, the world's largest on-line service provider, to have a comprehensive guide to on-line resources. (Underneath this is actually the Excite search engine in the USA and Canada and the Lycos search engine in Europe.)

Askjeeves

http://www.askjeeves.com - The concept behind this site is the use of natural language. It also directs the user to other search engine sites if the question cannot be answered from the AskJeeves index itself.

Excite

http://www.excite.com - Another major player in the marketplace. It also offers a news-tracking facility.

Hotbot

http://www.hotbot.com - From the publishers of *Wired* magazine, this search engine also allows you to search newsgroups as well as web pages.

InfoSeek

http://www.infoseek.com - Again one of the earliest entrants. It is very popular and also provides good quality results. It also incorporates a directory structure developed by people not machines.

Lycos

http://www.lycos.com - Currently one of the best-known search engine 'brands'. It is one of the oldest and proof that being first is everything. Currently it does not have a comprehensive index nor is it particularly swift at indexing new sites. It was purchased by the US Home Shopping Network for $6 billion in February 1999.

Yahoo!

http://www.yahoo.com - The leading directory service on the Internet - this site attempts to categorise web sites to create some form of order from the chaos. Yahoo! also has country-specific web sites such as www.yahoo.co.uk.

The competition between the major search engines is fierce and cannibalistic; brands are constantly buying up smaller competitors and merging to form bigger and better brands. In addition, old-media companies (such as Disney, Time Warner, etc.) are buying interests in these new-media companies. The best method of keeping up to date with changes in this marketplace is to use the Search Engine Watch site -http://www.searchenginewatch.com.

PROMOTING, MONITORING AND MAINTAINING WEB SITES

Exploit

http://www.exploit.com - Similar to Submit-It.

Link Exchange

http://www.linkexchange.com - A scheme that allows web site owners to exchange banners or adverts with other sites. This tends to bring in a completely different web-browsing audience.

NetIntellect

http://www.netintellect.com - A competitor product to Webtrends.

Submit-It

http://www.submit-it.com - A web site that allows the web developer to submit details about their site for a small fee. A web site can be submitted to a small number of sites free of charge. It has a wide variety of services and pricing arrangements.

Web Site Garage

http://www.websitegarage.com - An extremely useful site that remotely checks your site for various features such as optimised graphics size, speed of downloading, quality of the HTML, browser compatibility, spelling, and so forth. It also provides a web site bit counter. Users pay a monthly subscription. It is very easy to use and it all functions from the web site, i.e. there is no software to download and install.

Webtrends

http://www.Webtrends.com - The best-selling tool for monitoring web sites in terms of visitors, pages visited, times/dales, browsers used, navigation paths, etc.

FINDING NEWSGROUPS

DejaNews
http://www.dejanews.com - A directory of all newsgroups that make up Usenet.

Liszt
http://www.liszt.tom - Similar to DejaNews.

TOOLS FOR CREATING WEB PAGES

There is a wide variety of different tools available, many free of charge. They range from WYSIWYG (What You See Is What You Get) tools to ones that allow the user to develop directly using HTML. The choice of tool depends on the existing skills of the user and on the intended complexity of the site.

Dream Weaver
http://www.macromedia.com - One of the very best WYSIWYG tools on the market from a designer's point of view. This tool comes from long-standing developers of multimedia software. Macromedia also make the Director and Shockwave Flash products which allow developers to create quality animated web sites.

Frontpage
http://www.microsoft.com - One of the most popular simply because it is from Microsoft.

Homesite
http://www.allaire.com - One of the very best HTML editors. It incorporates very useful features such as HTML validation.

HotMetal Pro
http://www.sq.com - A mature product for those who prefer to hard-code their HTML.

Netobjects Fusion

http://www.netobject.com - Netobjects was a start-up company that now has a variety of stand-alone and collaborative web-development tools. Now partly owned by IBM and Novell.

Pagemill

http://www.adobe.com - The web development offering from Adobe, one of the best-known on-line publishing software companies.

INTERNET SERVER SOFTWARE

Apache

http://www.apache.com - Despite the best efforts of Microsoft, Apache is still by far the most popular web server software on the Internet. It is a UNIX-based tool that is available free of charge.

Lotus: Domino

http://www.lotus.com - Web server software designed to work in conjunction with Lotus Notes databases.

Microsoft

http://www.microsoft.com - Internet Information Server (IIS) comes bundled with the NT Server software. A cut-down version of the IIS Web Server comes bundled with NT Workstation software and with Windows 98. IIS is used extensively in corporate environments partly because so many add-on products will work with it and also because the corporate environment is wholeheartedly embracing NT as a robust network operating system.

Netscape

http://www.netscape.com - Developers of the Enterprise Server Suite, as well as one of the two most popular browsers and of SSL, the most popular form of web-based security.

Novell

http://www.novell.com - Not surprisingly, their products are designed to work in conjunction with Novell Netware.

Oracle

http://www.oracle.com - Again, a web server designed to work in conjunction with existing Oracle databases.

DATABASE TOOLS

Borland

http://www.borland.com - Developers of a range of database tools such as Delphi and dBASE.

Microsoft

http://www.microsoft.com - SQL Server is Microsoft's industrial strength database offering.

Oracle

http://www.oracle.com — The world's biggest database company has been quick to recognise the major business opportunity that the Web presents and has responded accordingly. Oracle have a reputation for robust scalable database products and are rapidly turning themselves into a Internet-oriented company.

Sybase

http://www.sybase.com - One of the four leading database vendors. Sybase is used widely in the financial services industry but has made little inroads in legal services. They are currently losing market share as large corporations move towards either Oracle, Informix of Microsoft SQL Server.

MIDDLEWARE

Middleware is the term used to describe the glue that allows a database to talk to the Web and vice versa. Some of the middleware tools available are proprietary, i.e. they only work with certain databases. Others are designed to work with a variety of different databases and on different operating systems.

Active Server Pages

http://www.microsoft.com - A fairly complex method for linking databases to the Web. A worthwhile solution if there is technical expertise available, in particular programmers with experience of writing Microsoft applications.

Cold Fusion

http://www.allaire.com - Much simpler than Active Server Pages and just as effective. Uses a tag-based Cold Fusion Markup Language (CFML) which will appeal to those coming from an HTML background. This is an easy to understand, mature package with a huge following world-wide. It also runs on different user platforms.

Tango Enterprise

http://www.pervasive.com - A robust system that does not require high-level programming abilities.

There are many other web application platforms available, each with their own strengths and weaknesses (e.g. WebEnterprise from Forte Software (www.forte.com), HahtSite from Haht Software (www.haht.com), Apptivity from Progress Software (www. progress.com)).

OTHER SIGNIFICANT INTERNET TECHNOLOGIES

ActiveX

http://www.microsoft.com - This is Microsoft's attempt

to counter the threat posed by Java. ActiveX, COM and DCOM are all methods to extend the capabilities of the Internet web browser.

Java

Originally developed for consumer electronics, Java is a new programming language created by Sun Microsystems (http://www.sun.com) that became well known (and much over-hyped) from 1995 onwards. Java is a combination of two different computer-programming languages, namely C++ and Smalltalk. It uses a syntax similar to C++ but includes some improvements and has an internal structure similar to Smalltalk. (C++ is a so-called object-oriented version of an equally popular and powerful computer language known as C.)

Before Java, all computer programs had to have separate versions of the software written for different computing platforms. Java uses a clever trick of running on a so-called 'Virtual Machine' or ('VM') to get around these problems. The Virtual Machine is simply a small piece of software that runs on a user's computer. All Java applications can then run on that user's computer, regardless of operating system, via the Virtual Machine. All popular web browsers include a Virtual Machine. This offers the potential for software developers of 'Write Once, Run Anywhere', i.e. it avoids the need to develop eight or 10 different versions of the same piece of software.

At first glance it would appear that Java is tailor-made for use on the Internet - Java developers could build components in Java that were lightweight and easily downloaded over a network. A drawback is that Java is an interpreted rather than a compiled language and is therefore slower than programs written in C++. Java has no relationship with HTML. It is not a programming language for the beginner.

Javascript

Javascript is a scripting language developed by Netscape that extends the somewhat limited functionality of HTML. It bears little relationship to Java except in the name. It bears some characteristics of the C programming language and like C, is a complete programming language. It can work in conjunction with HTML to perform extended functions such as form validation, image enhancement and to perform calculations. It can perform these functions without submitting the entire form to a web server (unlike CGI scripting). It is a very powerful language - a great deal can be achieved with a few lines of Javascript.

Shockwave

http: / /www.macromedia.com - Shockwave and Flash are mechanisms that give the user the ability to create dynamic and animated web sites.

APPENDIX B

USEFUL LEGAL RESOURCES ON THE WEB

There are many useful directory sites for UK lawyers. The UK legal directory sites will be of more use to most readers as they are maintained by dedicated professionals (and gifted amateurs) so that the links are up to date. The subsequent lists contain addresses which may change. If the address cannot be found, check the UK legal directory sites for the most up-to-date address.

UK AND INTERNATIONAL LEGAL DIRECTORY SITES

- The National Centre for Legal Education - http://www.law.warwick.ac.uk/ncle/
- Delia Venables Portal to Legal Resources in the UK and Ireland -http://www.venables.co.uk/legal/welcome.htm
- Infolaw - Information for Lawyers Limited's Gateway to the UK Legal Internet - http://www.infolaw.co.uk/
- Lawlinks - legal information on the Internet compiled by Sarah Carter -http://libservb.ukc.ac.uk/library/netinfo/intnsubg/lawlinks.htm
- The World Wide Web Virtual Law Library - a massive, but US-oriented site -http://www.law.indiana.edu/law/v-lib/lawindex.html
- The Law Society - http://www.lawsoc.org.uk/db/legallinks/display_links.asp

PRIMARY UK SOURCES

- Acts of Parliament - http://www.hmso.gov.uk/acts.htm

- Statutory Instruments — http://www.hmso.gov.uk/stat.htm
- House of Commons - http://www.parliament.uk/commons/HSECOM.HTM
- Commons Hansard - http://www.parliament.the-stationery-office.co.uk/pa/cm/cmhansrd.htm
- House of Lords Judgments - http://www.parliament.the-stationery-office.co.uk/pa/Id 199697/ldjudgmt/ldjudgmt.htm
- House of Lords Hansard - http://www.parliament.the-stationery-office.co.uk/pa/Id 199697/ldhansrd/pdvn/home.htm
- HMSO - http://www.hmso.gov.uk/

ESSENTIAL SITES

The following sub-sections each consist of three essential sites:

UK Sites for Lawyers

- The new Civil Procedure Rules - http://www.open.gov.uk/lcd/civil/procrules_fin/cproc.htm
- CCTA Government Information Service — http://www.opcn.gov.uk
- Local Government - http//:www.local.gov.uk

European Legal Web Sites

- Europa - the main European Union site - http://europa.eu.int
- European Parliament - http://www.europarl.eu.int
- EUR-Lex - http://europa.eu.int/eur-lex/en/index.html

BUSINESS LAW SITES

- Business Information Sources on the Internet - http://www.dis.strath.ac.uk/business/index.html
- UK Business Net - http://www.ukbusinessnet.com/intro.htm
- Lawmoney - http://www.lawmoney.com/

UK Legal Practioner Sites

- The Law Society - http://www.lawsoc.org.uk
- Hieros Gamos - http://www.hg.org/hg2.html
- International Centre for Commercial Law - http://www.icclaw.com/

Practitioner Magazine Sites

- *The Lawyer* - http://www.the-lawyer.co.uk
- *Law Society Gazette* - http://www.lawgazette.co.uk/
- *In Brief*- http://www.inbrief.co.uk/

On-Line Journal Sites

- Electronic Law Journals - http://elj.warwick.ac.uk/juk/
- UCLA list (US-based) http://www.law.ucla.edu/Research/journals.html
- Findlaw (US-based) - http://lawschools.findlaw.com/journals/index.html

Legal Technology Sites

- Society for Computers and Law - http://www.scl.org
- Infolaw - in particular their directory of legal technology suppliers - http://www.infolaw.co.uk/
- Delia Venables site - in particular her directory of legal software and IT suppliers - http://www.venables.co.uk/legal/softwarl .htm

APPENDIX C

GETTING ON-LINE: KEY QUESTIONS TO ASK

USING A DIAL-UP CONNECTION

Questions to Ask

1. Does the Internet or On-line Service Provider (ISP/OSP) have a local point-of-presence, i.e. can the Internet be accessed for the price of a local telephone call?
2. What is the monthly fee (if any) per individual account?
3. Is free web space included in the deal in case your firm wishes to develop a web site at a later stage?
4. Are email accounts included in the offer?
5. How fast is their access? Currently the fastest modems (56 K) have two standards. Are both supported? Most ISPs support one standard but not the other - make sure that the standard support is the one that you currently use or might use.
6. Is there a freephone or local call-rate technical support line and is it available 24 hours a day/ seven days a week?
7. How knowledgable is the ISP's technical support? (This is not always easy to establish for the new user. It may also depend on the individual contacted.)
8. Does the ISP provide other 'on-line services' - such as technical support web pages?
9. Is there full access to newsgroups?
10. How long does it take to get connected?

11. What connection speed is most frequently obtained?
12. How often is the service unavailable or engaged tones encountered?
13. How often are users cut off?
14. How fast is web-browsing/file download speeds?

USING A DEDICATED CONNECTION

Questions to Ask

1. What is the speed of the connection?
2. What is the installation charge?
3. What is the monthly/annual rental charge?
4. What other costs are there, if any?
5. Who does the ISP connect to?
6. What assistance/technical support is available?
7. Is there a service guarantee?
8. What are the long-term financial prospects of the company offering the service?

10 E-COMMERCE: PROPOSED LEGAL FRAMEWORK

A proposal for a Directive to establish a coherent legal framework for the development of electronic commerce within the Single Market has been put forward by the European Commission. The proposed Directive would ensure that information society services benefit from the Single Market principles of free movement of services and freedom of establishment and could provide their services throughout the European Union (EU) if they comply with the law in their country of origin. Such services are defined as those provided normally against remuneration, at a distance, ay electronic means und in response to the individual request of a customer. The proposed Directive would establish specific harmonised rules only in those areas strictly necessary to ensure that businesses and citizens could supply and receive information society services throughout the EU, irrespective of frontiers. These areas include definition of where operators are established, electronic contracts, liability of intermediaries, dispute settlement and role of national authorities. In other areas the Directive would build on existing EU instruments which provide for harmonisation or on mutual recognition of national laws. The Directive would apply only to service providers established within the EU and not those established outside.

"The Single Market's legal framework, combined with the single currency, provide the European Union with a unique opportunity to facilitate the development of electronic commerce", commented Single Market Commissioner Mario

Monti. "Electronic commerce adds a new dimension to the Single Market for consumers in terms of easier access to goods and services of better quality and at lower prices. Electronic commerce will promote trade, stimulate innovation and competitiveness and create sustainable jobs. This proposal should ensure that the Union reaps the full benefits of electronic commerce by boosting consumer confidence and giving operators legal certainty, without excessive red tape."

The global electronic commerce market is growing extremely fast and could be worth ECU billion by the year 2000. Worldwide, 86 million people were connected to the Internet by the end of 1996 and by 2000, this is expected to reach 250 million individuals. Within the EU, estimated that more than 400,000 jobs related to the information society were created between 1995 and 1997 and that one in four news jobs is derived from these activities.

Scope

The proposal for a Directive, which was foreseen in the Commission's April 1997 electronic commerce Communication (see IP/97/313), covers all information society services, both business to business and business to consumer services, including services provided free of charge to the recipient - e.g. funded by advertising or sponsorship revenue and services allowing for on-line electronic transactions such as regulated professions (such as lawyers or accountants), the proposal lays down the general principle that the on-line provision of services is permitted and that national rules on advertising shall not prevent professions from operating Web-sites. However, these would have to respect certain rules of professional ethics which should be reflected in codes of conduct to be drawn up by professional associations.

Implementation

Rather than inventing new rules, the proposal would seek to ensure that existing EU and national legislation were effectively enforced. The development of a genuine Single Market - based on mutual confidence between Member States - is stimulated by strengthening enforcement mechanisms. The proposal would seek to do so by encouraging the development of codes of conduct at EU level, by stimulating administrative co-operation between Member States and by facilitating the setting up of effective, alternative cross-border dispute settlement systems. The proposal would also require Member States to provide for fast, efficient legal redress appropriate to the on-line environment and to ensure that sanctions for violations of the rules established under the Directive were effective, proportionate and dissuasive.

Mutual Recognition/Derogations

The proposed Directive would clarify that the Single Market principle of mutual recognition of national laws and the principle of control in the country of origin must be applied to information society services so that such services provided from another Member State are not restricted for reasons falling within the scope of the proposal which would not cover taxation, personal data (the free movement of which is covered by Directive 95/46 - see IP/98/925), the activities of notaries, representation and defence of clients before a court, gambling activities. Furthermore, the proposed Directive would not interfere with the application of the Brussels Convention on jurisdiction, recognition and enforcement of judgements in civil and commercial matters and the Rome Convention on the law applicable to contractual obligations.

The proposed Directive would also allow Member States on a case by case basis to impose restrictions on information society services supplied from another Member State if necessary to protect the public interest on grounds of protection of minors, the fight against hatred on grounds, of race, sex, religion or nationality, public health or security and consumer protection. However, such restrictions would have to be proportionate to their stated objective. Moreover, such could only be imposed (except in cases of urgency) after :

- the Member State where the service provider was established had been asked to take adequate measures and failed to do so and
- the intention to impose restrictions had been notified in advance to the Commission and to the Member State where the service provider was established.

In cases of urgency, the reasons for the restrictions (and the urgency) would have to be notified in the shortest possible time to the Commission and to the Member State of the service provider. Where the Commission considered proposed or actual restrictions were not justified. Member States would be required to refrain from imposing them or urgently put an end to them.

PROPOSAL FOR A EUROPEAN PARLIAMENT AND COUNCIL DIRECTIVE ON CERTAIN LEGAL ASPECTS OF ELECTRONIC COMMERCE IN THE INTERNAL MARKET

Executive Summary

Electronic commerce offers the Community a unique opportunity for economic growth, to improve European industry's competitiveness and to stimulate investment in innovation and the creation of new jobs. But such benefits will not be optimised unless the many legal obstacles which remain to the on-line provision of services (particularly important for cross border trade and for SMEs) are eliminated. The present proposal intends to remove such obstacles thereby allowing our citizens and our industry to benefit in full from the development of electronic commerce in Europe.

The Commission's 1997 Communication on electronic commerce[1] set a clear objective of creating a European coherent legal framework by the year 2000. This proposal meets that objective. It builds upon and completes a number of other initiatives[2] that, together, will eliminate the remaining legal obstacles, while ensuring that general interest objectives are met, particularly the achievement of a high level of consumer protection. This proposal will reinforce the position of the Community in the international discussions on the legal aspects of electronic commerce which are currently underway in a number of international fora (WTO, WIPO, UNCITRAL, OECD). The Community will thus secure a major role in international negotiations and significantly contribute to the establishment of a global policy for electronic commerce.

The proposal is based on the orientations set out by the Commission in the 1997 Communication. It provides a light, enabling and flexible approach. Particular attention has been paid both to the special nature of the Internet and to the role of interested parties and of self-regulation. The proposal meets the principles of subsidiarity and proportionality by covering only those issues where a Community initiative is indispensable. These issues, which were identified in the Commission's 1997 Communication, have been subsequently endorsed by the European Parliament[3]. They are the subject of work at Member State and international level and are being discussed by industry and other interested parties.

At present, there is uncertainty in a number of areas about how existing legislation can be applied to the on-line provision of services. There is divergent national legislation already in place or currently being discussed. Furthermore, diverging jurisprudence is emerging. The proposal therefore seeks to remove the obstacles that result from such conditions, for service providers established in Europe, by tackling five key issues that together form a coherent framework to bring about the free circulation of on-line services. These issues are all interrelated because obstacles to electronic commerce services can arise at each step of the economic activity (from the promotion and the sale of a good or service to the settlement of disputes) and because none of these obstacles can be removed in isolation (for example, clarifying a service provider's liability is not possible without defining its place of establishment). Accordingly, the European Parliament, in its recent resolution, has asked the Commission to speed up the process of presenting a proposal for a directive which would address these issues in a coherent way.

These five issues are the following :

(1) Establishment of Information Society Service Providers

The proposal removes the current legal uncertainty surrounding this issue by providing a definition of the place of establishment in line with the principles established by the Treaty and the jurisprudence of the Court of Justice. This is a key element for the proper functioning of the Single Market. In addition, the proposal prohibits special authorisation schemes for information society services and sets out some information requirements that the provider must fulfil in order to ensure transparency of its activities.

(2) Commercial Communications (Advertising, Direct Marketing, Etc.)

Commercial communications are an essential part of most electronic commerce services. It if therefore important to clarify and facilitate their use. The proposal thus defines what constitutes a commercial communication and makes it subject to certain transparency requirements to ensure consumer confidence and fair trading. In order to allow consumers to react more readily to harmful intrusion, the proposal requires that commercial communications by e-mail are clearly identifiable. In addition, for regulated professions (such as lawyers or accountants), the proposal lays down the general principle that commercial communications are permitted provided they respect certain rules of professional ethics which should be reflected in codes of conduit to be drawn up by professional associations.

(3) On-line Conclusion of Contracts

Electronic commerce will not fully develop if concluding on-line contracts is hampered by certain form and other requirements which are not adapted to the on-line environment. To this end, Member States States shall be obliged to adjust their national legislation. In addition, the proposal legal insecurity by clarifying in certain cases the moment of conclusion of the contract, whilst fully respecting contractual freedom.

(4) Liability of Intermediaries

To facilitate the flow of electronic commerce activities, there is a recognised need to clarify the responsibility of on-line service providers for transmitting and storing third party information (*i.e.* when service providers act as "intermediaries"). To eliminate the existing legal uncertainty and to bring coherence to the different approaches that are emerging at Member State level, the proposal establishes a "mere conduit" exemption and limits service provider's liability for other "intermediary" activities. A careful balance is sought between the different interests involved in order to stimulate co-operation between different parties thereby reducing the risk of illegal activity on-line.

(5) Implementation

Rather than inventing new rules, the Commission has sought to ensure that existing EC and national legislation is effectively enforced. By strengthening enforcement mechanisms, the development of a genuine Internal Market - based on mutual confidence between Member States - is stimulated. Such strengthening is achieved by encouraging the development of codes of conduct at Community level, by stimulating administrative co-operation between Member States and by facilitating the setting up of effective cross-border alternative dispute resolution systems. For similar reasons the proposal also requires Member States to provide for fast, efficient legal redress appropriate to the on-line environment.

EXPLANATORY MEMORANDUM

I. OBJECTIVE

Electronic commerce provides the Community with a unique opportunity to create economic growth, a competitive European industry and new jobs. The legal framework of the internal market and the euro are key tools for exploiting this opportunity.

Electronic commerce is global and requires increased international co-ordination. The European Union has launched a dialogue on the implications of the global electronic market place within the framework of the Global Business Dialogue. The latter seeks to ensure a coherent approach between public and private sectors at the global level.

However, pending the establishment of a set of rules covering the different areas at global level, the Union must act in order to establish within Europe a genuine single market for electronic commerce. This single market must ensure that European businesses and citizens are able to receive and supply information society services throughout the Community, irrespective of frontiers. Indeed, the legal framework of the internal market forms a major asset for electronic commerce, and electronic commerce forms a major asset for the internal market:

— for the *construction of Europe,* electronic commerce in the area without frontiers will bring together the peoples of Europe, promote trade between them and increase knowledge of their cultural diversity;

— for *European citizens and consumers,* electronic commerce will provide increased access' to goods and services of better quality at lower prices and heighten attention for the protection of citizens at Community level, not only at national level;

— for *European enterprises,* especially SMEs, electronic commerce will provide considerable opportunities for growth and will encourage investment in innovation;

— For *employment growth within the Community.* Even if it is not possible to estimate the total number of people currently employed in electronic commerce activities, these activities offer a true employment potential. For example, according to recent estimations more than 400,000 information society related jobs were created within the Community between 1995 and 1997. It is estimated that one in four new jobs is derived

> from these activities; that there are 500,000 unfilled vacancies requiring information society skills and that 60% of these are in SMEs seeking to develop their electronic commerce activities.

The Commission has already set out the approach it is pursuing to ensure that this potential can be realised. In its communication. *"A European initiative in electronic commerce"*[4] it announced the creation of a legal framework for the internal market based on the principle of country of origin control. The features of this approach include, in particular, avoiding over-regulation, basing regulation on internal-market freedoms, taking account of business realities and meeting general interest objectives effectively and efficiently. The Commission emphasises the urgency of implementing this policy as the measures set out in the communication must be taken by the year 2000.

The Commission's work, based on these principles and studies as well as consultations with interested parties, has identified a number of legal problems which must be resolved quickly at Community level. In its work the Commission has taken particular account of the opinion of the *European Parliament*, as expressed in its resolution of 15 April 1998[5] on the communication from the Commission, which urged the Commission to present a proposal for a Directive on information society services in order to clarify the regulatory framework and to safeguard the rights of users of electronic commerce.[6] The Commission has also taken account of the opinions of the Committee of the Regions and of the Economic and Social Committee,[7] of the consultations held with interested parties on the basis of the Communication and of other initiatives on the information society.

II. NECESSITY OF A LEGAL FRAMEWORK FOR THE INTERNAL MARKET

Electronic commerce consists of information society service[8] activities. These consist of a large variety of on-line services, for example, the sale of goods or services or the free provision of information remunerated by commercial communication. These services do not develop in a legal vacuum; they are already subject to a series of national, Community or international rules. However, having regard to the aims of the internal market (Article 7a of the EC Treaty), the principles of freedom of establishment (Article 52 of the EC Treaty) and of the freedom to provide services (Articles 59 and 60 of the EC Treaty), certain aspects of the existing legal framework must be clarified in order to increase legal security : Indeed, certain legal barriers hamper the exercise of these freedoms by an information society service provider, or a citizen (using these services or make their exercise less attractive.

1. Lack of Clarity in the Existing Legal Framework

Differences in certain legal provisions applicable to information society services in different member States can result in a situation where, as an exception to the principle of free movement and subject to conformity with the case law of the Court of Justice, one Member State may make the provision of a service from another Member State conditional on supervisory measures or the application of its own legislation. In practice this means that a service provider wishing to offer a service throughout the internal market must, in addition to the compliance with the rules of the country in which he is established, ensure that the service is compatible with the law of the other 14 Member States.

A significant lack of legal certainty characterises the current legal framework. This legal uncertainty arises over the lawfulness of measures taken by one Member State concerning services provided by providers established in another Member State (are they justified in relation to the principle of freedom to provide services or of secondary Community law applying that principle?) Legal uncertainty also arises in determining the requirements to be met by Information society services (to what extent does a particular rule apply to such services?) Cases which have already been decided diverge, indicating that there is a serious lack of legal certainty whose adverse effects are strongly amplified in a cross border situation.

Moves in certain Member States to enact new legislation are apparent and there are already differences in approach which entail a real risk in the short term of fragmenting the internal market. Some Member States have already enacted legislation specifically addressing information society services (D) while others have begun a large scale amendment of their rules B, F, FIN; I, NL); lastly, in some Member States specific issues are the subject of surveys, draft proposals or new legislation, (for example, regulated professions (A, F, D, I); liability (F, NL, S. UK); and contracts (A, B, D, NL, DK, S)).

2. Significant Economic Costs

The current legal framework gives rise to significant costs for operators wishing to develop their activities across borders. The results of a survey undertaken within the *"Commercial Communications"* newsletter[9] demonstrate the significance and specific nature of these costs.

The significance of legal costs : 64% of respondents undertook a legal analysis of the regulatory situation and notably regarding the cross-border situation. Of the 36% who did not, 43% had not yet done so because they were still in pilot phases and 30% because they could not afford to undertake such an evaluation.

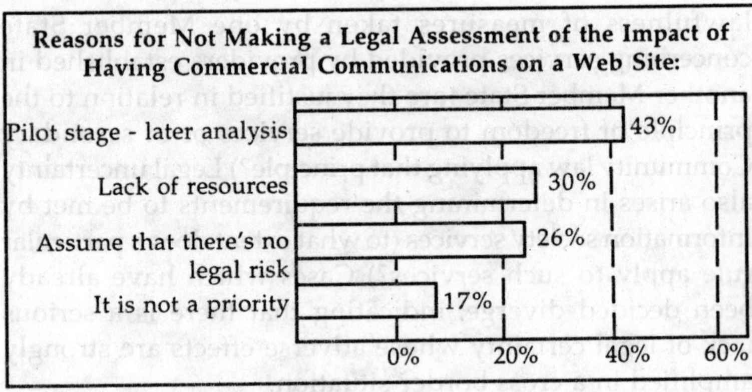

Reasons for Not Making a Legal Assessment of the Impact of Having Commercial Communications on a Web Site:

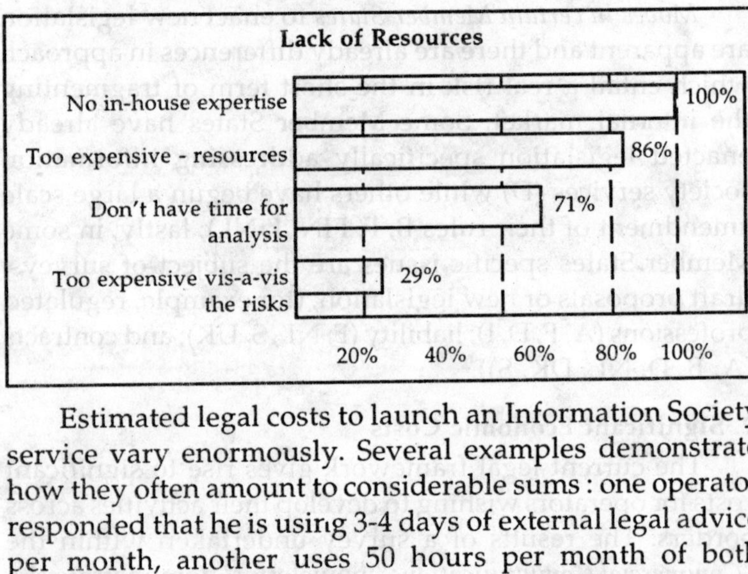

Lack of Resources

Estimated legal costs to launch an Information Society service vary enormously. Several examples demonstrate how they often amount to considerable sums : one operator responded that he is using 3-4 days of external legal advice per month, another uses 50 hours per month of both internal and external legal advice (amounting to approximately 70,000 DM per year), another used fifty days of both in-house and external legal advice to launch a new service and an SME indicated that it had to employ a lawyer on a full-time basis. One of the key operators in the electronic commerce market noted that he has to rely on 8 in-house lawyers dedicating 45 hours per week and 18 outside legal advisers who on average supply 175 hours of advice per week. For the UK market alone, this operator estimated that a review of the regulatory framework for his information society service cost him 60,000 ECU.

The specificity of the legal costs associated with electronic commerce : of those who have undertaken a legal analysis, no less than 40% believe that the legal uncertainty that characterised electronic commerce was greater than for other lines of business. The cross-border dimension of the activity also distinguishes it since 64% evaluated legal aspects other than those in their own country and 57% believed it was essential to evaluate how the activity would be treated in other Member States. Moreover, of those who did not make a legal assessment, only 26% denied that there was a risk and 30% would have done so if they had had the resources to.

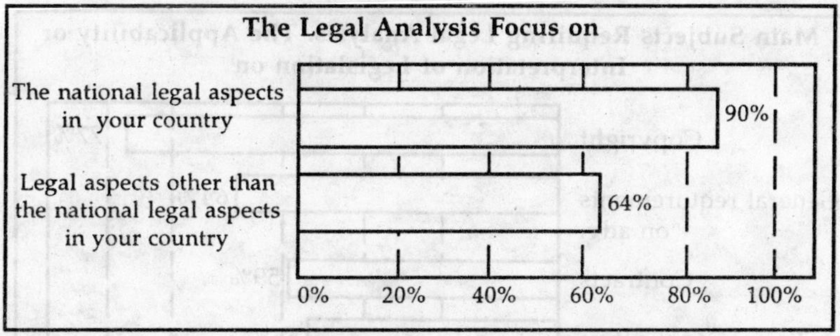

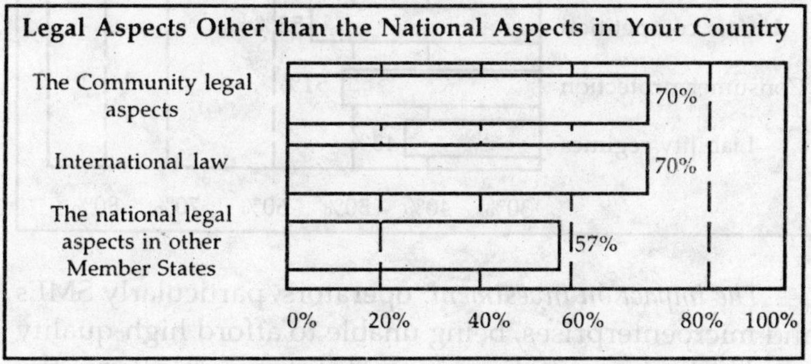

The key areas giving rise to legal costs : The survey allowed for the identification of the legal issues giving rise to the most significant problems :

3. The Impact on Investment by and Competitiveness of European Companies

At present, an operator wishing to engage in electronic commerce across the internal market almost invariably has no certainty that his service will not be subject to the control of, or the imposition of direct or indirect restrictions by, other Member States in addition to the Member State in which he is established. In view of this risk, the business must seek legal advice (from lawyers, consultants, etc.) in each Member State and negotiate with the authorities of those States in order to be sure that their activities are lawful there.

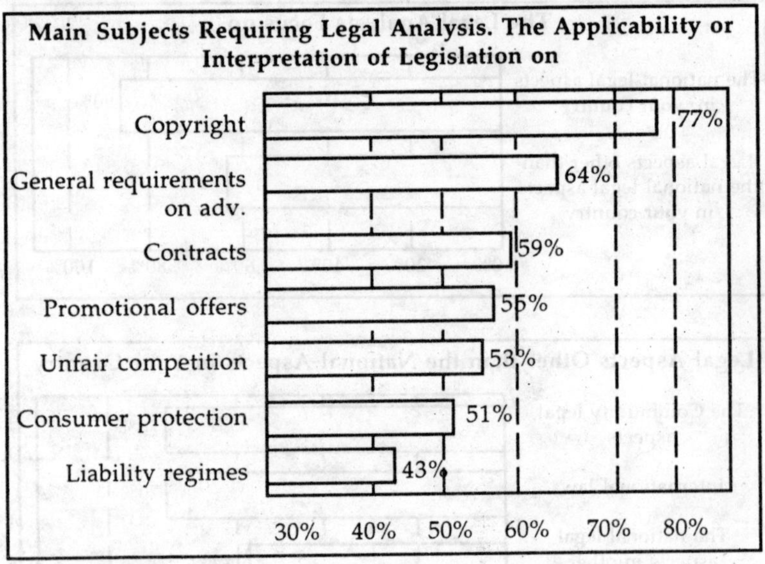

The impact on investment: operators, particularly SMEs and microenterprises, being unable to afford high-quality legal advice, are discouraged from exploiting the opportunities afforded by the internal market and investing in the European development of their businesses;

The impact on the competitiveness of European enterprises : operators must plan their service so that it is compatible with the requirements of all Member States. This is a disincentive for investment in innovation and may lead to the services being designed to meet the requirements of the most severe restrictions. This means that some SMEs and microenterprises are less competitive than businesses with the funds to invest in an evaluation of the risks of securing access to the new market in electronic commerce while remaining within the law.

4. The Lack of Confidence on the Part of Consumers

Consumers, and more generally, recipients of services may feel that they are in an unclear and vague situation with few guarantees as to the level of protection afforded and they may therefore be unwilling to conclude on-line contracts and exploit new opportunities.

III. ISSUES TO BE ADDRESSED

1. The Establishment of Operators

What requirements must be met by an operator wishing to provide information society services? This can only be determined by ascertaining the Member State in which the operator is established so that the relevant rules concerning establishment can be identified. There are wide divergences of approach and many factors giving rise to legal uncertainty in this area:

— *determining the place of establishment* of an on-line service is particularly difficult; is it determined by the server which hosts a site, the ability to have access to a site in a Member State, or is it a simple letter box? The position in the Member

States is very vague in this area and national authorities, operators and consumers are not clear as to which rules apply;

— some confusion also exists over the issue of *authorisation arrangements or declaration arrangements.* In most Member States, services that can be classified as information society services do not generally require a specific authorisation. Some Member States have rules requiring declarations while in others there are no prescribed formalities. Uncertainties become apparent when new kinds of services are established and it may be difficult to classify them under existing categories (press, telecommunications, audiovisual, etc.);

— Given the principle of freedom of establishment (Article 52 of the Treaty) which must be enjoyed by all persons wishing to provide services over the Internet, such a situation is unsatisfactory and calls for clarification to facilitate the exercise of this freedom.

2. Commercial Communications

Commercial communication, (advertising, direct marketing, etc.), by its nature, forms part of most electronic commerce services and is an area where obstacles to the internal market are particularly marked :

— *existing definitions* in this area (for example "advertising", "sponsorship") give rise to uncertainty when they are applied to on-line services. For example, in most Member States it is unclear whether simply having an Internet site, establishing a hypertext link, or using a domain name constitutes commercial communication. This is particularly harmful because, depending on the interpretation of existing definitions, rules which may or may not be suitable, will be triggered;

— the disparity in the rules on the *advertising of regulated professions* forms a clear obstacle to the development of professional services over the Internet. The use of a site by a professional service is often considered to be commercial communication and Member States laws on regulated professions differ markedly on this point; many Member States strictly prohibit advertising, for example, in the case of lawyers and doctors, in other Member States the rules are decidedly more flexible, in particular for the legal professions;

— national rules on *unfair competition* may have a very restrictive effect as their interpretation may result in prohibitions or restrictions on certain commercial practices, such as promotional offers or rebates and discounts. The effect is particularly serious in the case of new and innovative marketing practices and in view of the need to employ them on the Internet to make the business stand out among the other services available;

— *transparency* requirements, (for example, an indication that it is an advertising message or is sponsored, etc.), are vague and very, divergent. In most Member States there is no clear and general obligation to indicate on an Internet site that commercial communication is involved or to indicate on whose behalf it appears. On the other hand, in some Member States requirements of this type may arise under general rules on consumer protection or fair trading or conversely under specific rules;

— new, *intrusive* commercial communication practices, such as "spamming", or advertising in discussion forums etc., raise issues which have already resulted in court cases or have led Member States to adopt legislation.

3. Electronic Contracts

Apart from financing by commercial communication, on-line transactions (contractual undertakings, on-line payments, subscriptions) are another source of revenue on the Internet. Specific obstacles restricting the possibility of concluding on-line contracts across frontiers have been identified :

— *some formal requirements* prevent contracts from being concluded electronically, or result in a considerable lack of legal certainty as to their lawfulness or validity. This may take the form of requirements which obviously rule out electronic contracts, (for example, a requirement that a contract be drawn up on paper), or more frequently, difficulty arising from the interpretation to be given to requirements such as "in writing" (*i.e.* on paper), "in a durable medium", "an original". Such legal uncertainty clearly works against on-line transactions; some Member States are therefore considering amending their rules and the courts have already given rulings on this matter. At Community level, the recent proposal for a Directive on electronic signatures does not deal with formal requirements other than signature;

— *the particular acts* performed by the parties with a view to concluding electronic contracts may result in considerable legal uncertainty as to the conclusion of the contract. In particular, the same act of clicking on the "OK" icon may have different legal implications' in different Member States (does it constitute acceptance of an offer to provide a service or a customer's offer to contract?) and can give rise to uncertainty as to the time when the contract was concluded (the time of receipt or of sending the acceptance?). This major divergence between the national legal systems, linked to the specific nature of the technological context, results in uncertainty in cross-border contractual relations, particularly for consumers, and is inimical to the development of the trust which is necessary for electronic commerce (one party may consider, on the basis of his own legal system, that the contract has been concluded while the other party, on the basis of his national rules, believes that he is not yet bound).

4. Liability of Intermediaries

There is considerable legal uncertainty within Member States regarding the application of their existing liability regimes to providers of Information Society Services when they act as "intermediaries", *i.e.* when they transmit or host third party information (information provided by the users of the service). These activities have been the subject of the different Member States' initiatives adopted or currently being examined on the issue of liability.

In view of the limited degree of knowledge providers have about the information that they transmit or store via interactive communication networks, the main problem that arises is the allocation of liabilities between on-line service providers transmitting and storing illegal information and the persons who originally put such information on line.

Questions also arise as regards the ability of providers to control the information they transmit or store.

In this context, divergent principles have been adopted in those Member States which have introduced new legislation specifically addressing this issue. Equally divergent approaches are being discussed in those Member States which are assessing the need to legislate. Moreover, despite the limited case law available in Europe, divergences in rulings and reasoning by the courts can already be noted.

For the internal market these divergences could be the source of obstacles for the cross border provision of information society services (for instance if a Member State decides to block access to information stored in the server of a service provider established in another Member State whore the applicable liability regime is deemed to be unsatisfactory). In some Member States, the situation may also inhibit activities such as the provision of hosting facilities. Indeed the current situation creates an incentive for providers to establish such activities in Member States with favourable regimes (forum shopping). The situation also leaves different parties (service providers, content providers, persons whose rights have been violated and consumers in general) under considerable legal uncertainty.

5. Settlement of Disputes

Court actions or out of court redress for unlawful behaviour or disputes concerning the Internet in cross-border cases are not always sufficiently effective or appropriate to induce businesses to provide services and customers, in particular consumers, to use them. Yet the Court of Justice has clearly[10] established that access to justice is a corollary of the freedoms of the area without internal frontiers. Moreover, the European Parliament has emphasised the need for arbitration.[11] This failure of the law to take account of the specific nature of the Internet and of cross-border situations emerges at various levels :

— the *slowness of the remedy* : unlawful acts on the Internet will produce loss and harm, characterised by their speed and wide geographical scope. In the context of the remedies for these problems, the effectiveness of emergency measures are sometimes dissuasive a should be improved;
— *the costs in relation to the nature of the activities* : apart from disputes between professionals, disputes concerning the Internet may be on a small scale, involving small amounts (micropayments) or disputes between private individuals using an information society service (e.g. classified advertisements) which do not justify a full court action an are better served by out of court remedies. However, the conditions for implementing out of court measures are often not suited to an on-line context (lodging the original of an arbitral award with a tribunal, presence of the parties, notification, etc.);
— the procedures available to the *national authorities*, the co-operation between them and access to those authorities are not always transparent and effective. This aspect must be considered more systematically, covering information society services as a whole.

6. The Role of National Authorities and the Principle of Country of Origin

In electronic commerce there is a great deal of uncertainty in determining which Member State has jurisdiction over a particular activity. In some cases the same activity may be subject to the supervision, and within the jurisdiction, of a number of Member States. As different links in the economic chain of a particular activity (the content provided, hosting, access to the Internet commercial communication, etc.) may be connected to the territory of a number of Member States, there may be multiple points of supervision and thus of legal frontiers. Yet, in other cases, some activities are not subject to supervision by the Member State on whose territory the service provider operates.

This uncertainty as to "who supervises what" is prejudicial to the free movement of information society services and the control of such services. It is therefore necessary to improve *the level of mutual confidence* between national authorities by clarifying the application of the principle of free movement of services. This principle (articles 59 and 60 of the EC Treaty) tends towards control in the country where the provider is established (since, except under derogation, Member States may not restrict services coming from a service provider established in another Member State).

In practice the lack of a clear interpretation of "information society services", "service provider" and "establishment" means that the allocation of roles among Member States in the control of service providers remains unclear. In particular, the uncertainty over the meaning of "establishment" prevents national authorities' responsibilities from being clearly determined.

Moreover, the *lack of information* on the origin of the service provider and on his activity. National legislation shows that in most Member States, there is no systematic obligation to provide information on the site as such (*i.e.* apart from any offer made in a commercial contract).

Finally, the fact that operators cannot be certain that

their service will not be subject to the application of restrictive measures in another Member State also requires clarification.

IV. THE APPROACH ADOPTED

1. Address Only What is Strictly Necessary for the Internal Market

The approach is to interfere as little as possible with national legal rules and to do so only where it is strictly necessary for the proper functioning of the area without frontiers. In fact, the principal of mutual recognition and the body of existing Community law help reduce the need for new rules. Moreover, the parties involved can themselves deal effectively with many of the issues. This therefore reduces the remaining issues which call for regulatory intervention. Accordingly, the Directive does not need to cover complete areas of law, it can target specific aspects.

2. Encompass All Information Society Services

The Directive applies to "information society services", *i.e.* all services normally provided against remuneration, at a distance by electronic means and on the individual request of a service receiver. This definition, has already been adopted in Directive 98/34/EC of the European Parliament and of the Council, laying down a procedure for the provision of information in the field of technical standards and regulations[12] and in the draft proposal for a Directive on the legal protection of services based on, or consisting of, conditional access).[13] This definition encompasses a large number of very different economic activities which may be carried out on line. These include the following :

- a business to business or a business to consumer service;
- a service consisting of the sale of goods or services,

as well as services which are free to the recipient (the funding often being secured by commercial[14] communications);

- services allowing for on-line electronic transactions of goods such interactive teleshopping, on-line shopping malls, etc. (the fact that the good is not delivered on-line does not imply that interactive teleshopping is not an information society service);
- a very wide *range of sectors and activities*, for example electronic newspapers, educational services, on-line encyclopaedias, sales services for certain products such as motor vehicles, tourism services, professional services (lawyers, doctors, chartered accountants, etc.). estate agents, virtual supermarkets, classified-advertisement services, BBS, job-search services, search engines, entertainment services, video-game services, services providing access to the World Wide Web, discussion forums, etc).

It is essential to cover all of these activities since all these services should be able to benefit from the internal market and, in legal terms, be guaranteed that they can develop without regard for frontiers; moreover, the development of the Internet economy shows that the same service provider can supply a large number of services across frontiers.

3. Address the Issues in the Same Instrument

Remaining obstacles must be addressed in the same instrument in order to cover the different stages of the economic activity of the relevant services. To be able to engage in such an activity it is necessary first of all to set up the business, carry out commercial communication activities, conclude contracts with customers, deal with any disputes involving liability and find procedures for resolving any disputes, etc. As the Commission indicated in its communication of 16 April 1997, it has identified the central elements in this economic chain requiring regulation at Community level to remove the cross-border obstacles to those activities.

It is essential that the various stages of the activities should be dealt with jointly in the same instrument enabling operators in practice to invoke the guarantee provided by the Directive so that there really are no frontiers affecting their activities. A Member State would otherwise remain able to adopt measures affecting one of those elements of a business's activities and thus frustrate the Community objective of achieving the proper functioning of the area without internal frontiers.

Moreover, addressing the obstacles in the same instrument ensures coherence by grouping issues that are interdependent. The provisions of the Directive form a response to issues which must be considered as a whole because the proposed solutions are in most cases common to a large number of information society services and are interlinked.

4. Refrain from Dealing with External Aspect

Until an international regulatory framework is established, the Directive only covers service providers who arc established in a Member State. It does not cover, at this stage, information society services provided by a person established in a third country.[15] In practice this has the following consequences :

— service providers who are not established in the *Community cannot exploit the opportunities afforded by the area without internal frontiers* guaranteed by the Directive. To do so, they must establish themselves in a Member State;

— This directive does not prejudice;

— the Community's international rights and obligations;

— the results of the various discussions within international organisations on the legal aspects of electronic commerce.

This approach was adopted because the Directive has as its primary objective to ensure that the internal market functions properly and further because the Community is already participating actively in the various efforts to establish a global framework for the information society.

It is clear that the Internal Market approach followed in this Directive, and in particular the application of the country of origin rule, cannot be taken, at this stage, as a model for possible future international negotiations, in view of the fact that this approach can only be followed when a sufficient degree of legal integration exists.

5. Taking Account of Fundamental Rights and Liberties

Activities involved in information society services constitute both services within the meaning of Articles 59 and 60 of the Treaty and information within the scope of the principle of freedom of expression laid down in Article 10 of the European Convention on Human Rights. These activities may therefore qualify for protection under the principle of freedom to provide services, freedom of establishment and freedom of expression. This essential feature justifies the application of the principles of the internal market, in particular Article 3, according to which Member States are *prevented from restricting services* provided by a service provider established in another Member State who is already subject to control and to the legal system there.

6. Establish a Light, Evolutionary and Flexible Framework

The Directive takes account of the fact that electronic commerce is at an early stage of its development, the need to avoid restricting that commerce by hasty and ill-adapted rules and the ability of parties to determine many of the issues themselves. Moreover, the directive relies upon the 'acquis' of a number of directives already adopted to achieve an Internal Market. Accordingly, the priority is not to develop a set of new rules, but rather on the one hand, to coordinate the amendment and modernisation of national law where it is not suited to electronic commerce and, on the other, to guarantee the effective and efficient application of existing rules. This explains, for example :

— the fact that the Directive focuses solely on the basic requirements which must be transposed by Member States irrespective of the categories or rules to which they will be anchored;

— the provisions which leave it to interested parties or the national authorities to adopt the *means of implementing* certain provisions of the directive. The directive *encourages the development of codes of conduct* at European level because numerous electronic commerce issues can be regulated by the interested parties themselves without there being any need for legal intervention;

— the fact that the directive, to account for the specific nature of certain areas or activities foresees *exceptions to the internal market principles* in so far as they are justified by the jurisprudence of the European Court of Justice.

7. Ensure a High Level of Consumer Protection

In view of the importance of electronic commerce for the European service industry, and of the fact that its development is as yet in its initial stages, it is important that such commerce is not restricted and that its growth is promoted while effectively meeting general interest objectives such as consumer protection. Thus, the directive provides for a number of provisions which will reinforce the protection of consumers and increase their trust in new services in Europe, in particular :

— it will *lessen the risk of illegal activities* via the Internet in Europe by establishing effective control by national authorities at the origin of the activity (in the Member States where the company in questions is established); it has the effect of making national authorities more responsible for their obligation to ensure the protection of the general interest not only within their borders but also throughout the Community and in the interests of citizens of other Member States.

— it imposes on operators *information and transparency obligations* upon operators which are indispensable for the consumer to take well-informed decisions;

— it establishes certain new guarantees as regards *contractual relations,* in particular the obligation to make available to users the means of correcting handling errors, the clarification of the moment of conclusion of electronic contracts, and the requirement that providers send a receipt;

— it guarantees *better redress systems* by promoting codes of conduct by allowing the use of electronic in out of court dispute settlement mechanisms (conciliation, arbitration), by facilitating efficient and fast legal redress, and by establishing contact points, at Member State level, to assist consumers.

Moreover, the directive leaves for Member States the possibilities of adopting, for consumer protection reasons and under certain conditions, measures restricting the free circulation of Information Society services, notably in the area of contracts concluded with consumers.

It should be noted that the Rome convention's criteria determining the law applicable to contractual obligations, which allow for derogations in favour of the consumer would be met, for example, in the case where the conclusion of the contract was preceded by a specific invitation by e-mail sent to the consumer's country and where the consumer undertook the steps necessary to conclude the contract in his country.

Finally, given the *speed* and geographic *scope* of damages caused by illegal internet activities, it is desirable that Member States allow for the act initiating a national Court action to be sent by appropriate electronic means and in a language other than that of the Member State of jurisdiction.

ANNEX : COMMENTARY ON INDIVIDUAL ARTICLES

CHAPTER I. *GENERAL PROVISIONS*

Article 1

This article clarifies the primary objective which is to ensure that, following the coming into force of this directive, information society services will be able to fully benefit from, except under derogation, the free movement of services between the Member States. It is also clarifies the scope of application particularly by indicating that the Community "acquis" is maintained.

Article 2: Definitions

Subparagraph (a) "Information Society Service"

This definition was taken from Article 1(2) of Directive 98/34/EC[16]. In this Directive, in accordance with the definition of services laid down in Articles 59 and 60 of the Treaty, information society services are defined as "any service, that is to say, any service normally provided for remuneration, at a distance, by electronic means and at the individual request of a recipient of services" In addition, the Article defines the following terms: "at a distance,", "by electronic means, "at the individual request of a recipient of services.

It must be noted that the definition of information society services does not cover internet televised broadcasting when it solely represents an additional means of transmitting an integral or unaltered set of television programmes as defined in Article 1(a) of directive 89/552/EC, which have been broadcast over the air, by cable or by satellite.

Subparagraph (b) "Service Provider"

This definition is based on Articles 59 and 60 of the Treaty and their interpretation by the case law of the Court of Justice. Any person providing an information society service constitutes a service provider. Service providers include the following:

- natural and legal persons;
- in the case of legal persons, all forms of company are included.

Subparagraph (c) "Established Service Provider"

This definition makes it possible to determine the Member State in whose jurisdiction the information society service provider is situated. The definition adopted is based on the judgement of the Court of Justice which provided that *"the concept of establishment within the meaning of Article 52 et seq. of the Treaty involves the actual pursuit of an economic activity through a fixed establishment in another Member State for an indefinite period"*[17]. This definition is based on qualitative criteria concerning the actual nature and stability of the economic activity rather than formal criteria (a mere letter-box) or technology (establishment of technical means, etc.) which readily enable operators to evade supervision.

By focusing on the real nature of the activity, the definition, on the one hand, is sufficiently flexible to be applied by national authorities on a case-by-case basis, and, on the other, enables the Member State in which the service provider is established to exercise effective authority over it and, if necessary, to take measures or impose sanctions which will produce real effects.

Furthermore, it should be noted that the Court has recognised that the same operator can be established in several Member States. In such cases, the Court has had reason to clarify, in the field of television, that when there exist several establishments belonging to the same TV broadcasting organisation, the Member State with supervisory, powers shall be the one where this organisation has the "centre of its activities."[18]

Thus, the following, for example, do not amount to an establishment on the territory of a Member State:

— *the location of the technology used*, e.g. the hosting of web pages or of a site;
— *the ability to access an internet site* in a Member State (any other approach would mean that an operator would be considered to be established in several or indeed fifteen Member States);

— the fact that a service provider established in another Member State offers *service targeted* at the territory of another Member State (in fact, the internal market enables businesses particularly SMEs, to tailor their offers to specific niche markets in other Member States).

Subparagraph (d) "Recipient of the Service"

This definition is based on the definition of services within the meaning of Articles 59 and 60. The recipient is the person using a service, for example, a person using a service which consists of organising a discussion forum and leaving a message there.

Subparagraph (e) "Commercial Communications"

— The proposed definition covers the various forms which commercial communications can take and is consistent with the Commission's new policy in this area set out in its communication entitled *"The follow-up to the Green Paper on commercial communications in the internal market"*.[19]

The reference to direct and indirect promotion aims to prevent circumvention of the ban on commercial communications for certain products and services.

In view of this wide definition and of the need for legal certainty, it has been specified that the promotion of a product, service or image of an enterprise created by a third party independently of that enterprise, for example, consumer-testing services, comparisons, or competitions for the best product or service, etc does not constitute commercial communication.

Given this definition, the following would not constitute commercial communications :

— mere *ownership* of a site;
— provision of information not constituting promotion;
— a hypertext link to a web site for commercial communications when it is created without any financial nexus to or any other consideration from the person owning the site *(i.e.* independent promotion);
— mention of the domain name or an e-mail address, logo or brand name when it is made without a financial nexus to or other consideration from the owner of the domain name, address, logo or brand name *(i.e.* independent promotion).

Subparagraph (f) "Coordinated Field"

This definition makes it possible to determine the national provisions in respect of which the Member States are to ensure compliance under Article 3. It therefore covers all requirements which may apply to a person acting as a provider of information society services or to information society services.

Article 3: The Internal Market

This article has as its *objective* the implementation of the principle of freedom to provide services under Article 59 of the Treaty. This implementation is based, on the one hand, on determining the Member State responsible for ensuring the legality of the activities in an information society service and, on the other, orr the prohibition on other Member States from restricting the freedom to provide these services.

Thus, paragraph 1 requires the Member State in which the service provider is established (as defined in Article 2) to ensure that his activities comply with the national law of the country (including, of course, applicable Community regulation).

This provision does not seek to substitute either the 1980 Rome Convention on applicable law for contractual obligations or the 1968 Brussels Convention on judicial competence which continue to apply. Nor does the directive prejudice ongoing work on judicial competence in the context of the revision of the Brussels Convention.

Paragraph 2 prohibits in principle all forms of restriction to the freedom to provide information society services, *i.e.* any actions on the part of a Member State liable to hamper or otherwise make the free provision of services less attractive. However, possible exemptions from the principle are provided for in Article 22(2) and (3).

CHAPTER II. PRINCIPLES

SECTION 1: ESTABLISHMENT AND INFORMATION REQUIREMENTS

Article 4: Principle of Non-authorisation

The *purpose* of this article is to give effect to the principle of freedom to provide services by facilitating access to the supply of services on the Internet. Thus, it establishes a sort of "right to a site" which can be exercised by any operator, company or self-employed person deciding to use the Internet to provide a service.

Paragraph 1

— The solution adopted has been to clarify the existing situation by asking Member States not to introduce any requirement of prior authorisation, though subject to paragraph 2. This is a qualitative obligation covering not only formal authorisation requirements but also any procedures which might have the same effect, such as, for example, the need to wait to receive a confirmation of receipt following a declaration.

Paragraph 2

Sub-paragraph (a) of this paragraph is to ensure that requirements for access to activities which are not specific to information society services continue to be applicable. Thus, for example, if legislation requires professional qualifications or authorisation by a professional body or authorisation to carry on the activities of a travel agency, it will continue to apply in full to any operator wishing to carry, on such activities on the Internet.

Sub-paragraph (b) covers general authorisation requirements and individual licenses established by directive 97/13/EC of 15 December 1997.[20]

Article 5: General Information to be Provided

Paragraph 1

This paragraph refers more specifically to the information concerning the service provider. The obligation to supply information supplements those which exist in certain national laws and in Directive 97/7/EC on the protection of consumers in respect of distance contracts,[21] which is specifically concerned with *contractual relationships*. Thus, even if there is no contract, the service provider will have to make available the information specified in this paragraph.

The information in question must be *easily accessible* while the service is being icon or logo with a hypertext link to a page containing the information which is visible on all the site's pages would, for example, be sufficient to meet this requirement.

***Paragraph* 2**

The information referred to in this paragraph is vital for protecting the consumer and other recipients of the service and for ensuring fair trading. A price indicated in Euros will meet this requirement.

SECTION 2 : COMMERCIAL COMMUNICATIONS

Article 6 Information to be Provided

Subparagraph (a) establishes the principle that the commercial communication must be clearly identifiable as such. This would be the case, for example, for a header the content of which left no doubt as to its nature. By contrast, identification would not be clear, for example, if the commercial communication is hidden, or in the case of an article which praised the qualities of a product and was commissioned and financed by a commercial operator without that fact being mentioned, or again in the case of a site entirely sponsored by a private interest for the purposes of advertising, but not mentioning that fact.

Subparagraph (b) establishes that the person on whose behalf the commercial communication is carried out must be clearly identifiable. This would be the case, for example, if the banner carried the name of that person. In the case of commercial financing, an icon or logo with a hypertext, link to a page containing the information which is visible on all the site's pages would, for example, be enough to meet this requirement. As regards banners, it must be clarified that a person for whom the commercial communication is undertaken need not be directly identified on the banner. For example, it would suffice if hypertext links to the banner allowed for such identification.

Subparagraph (c) establishes that promotional offers must be transparent. Such offers are not prohibited, but they must contain sufficient information so as not to leave any ambiguity as to their nature, and their conditions must be specifically indicated. In view of the possibilities which exist on the Internet for supplying information, such a requirement will make it easier to protect the consumer and safeguard fair trading without imposing a significant financial burden on operators.

Subparagraph (d) requires transparency with regard to promotional competitions and games and stipulates that the conditions for taking part in them must be indicated, for example by means of an icon or logo with a hypertext link. The promotional competitions and games in question are those which serve the purpose of commercial communication and not gambling, which is excluded from the Directive's scope (Article 22(1)).

Article 7: Unsolicited Commercial Communication

This Article deals with "spamming" practices, *i.e.* the sending of unsolicited e-mail to consumers or discussion groups. The need to protect the consumer demands solutions over and above those which already exist in Article 10(2) of Directive 97/7/EC[22] and Article 12(2) of European Parliament and Council Directive 97/66/EC concerning the processing of personal data and the protection of privacy in the-telecommunications sector.

This article requires unsolicited communications to have a specific message on the envelope so that the recipient can instantly identify it as a commercial communication without having to open it.

Article 8: Regulated Professions

Paragraph 1

This paragraph sets out the general principle that commercial communication is permitted for regulated professions to the extent necessary for these professions to be able to provide an information society service and provided it meets the professional rules of conduct applicable to them. Such rules exist in all Member States and in all professions and meet legitimate general interest objectives.

In practice, the issue for a service provider wishing to use the Internet to offer services falling under the rules applicable to regulated professions or to carry out commercial communication in respect of those services is to determine what types of information may be communicated under the professional rules of practice relating to advertising.

***Paragraph* 2**

Given the considerable differences of approaches prevailing and the fact that this sector has a tradition of self-regulation, it is intended *to encourage the bodies representing regulated professions at European level to identify the necessary adjustments and common solutions, in compliance with Community law,* in the interest of the professions themselves but also in the interest of consumers and the competent national authorities.

Two types of information merit particular attention from the bodies in question : the provision of information on *specialities and fees*. This information is vital to economic activity and to consumer protection. Other indications might also be important and merit examination, in particular, illustrations, photographs, logos; cases resolved with the agreement of customers: indication of names of customers; customer testimonials of services provided.

Finally, if necessary, the Commission might take action to define what types of information are compatible with the ethical rules of conduct in association with the Member

States in the context the Committee set up under Article 23.

SECTION 3 : ELECTRONIC CONTRACTS

Article 9: Treatment of Electronic Contracts

Paragraph 1

— This provision requires the Member States to make it possible in reality for electronic contracts to be used. It complements the proposal for a directive for a common framework for electronic signatures[23] which solely addresses the issue of the legal validity of electronic signatures without touching other aspects of the legal validity of electronic contracts. This means that the Member States have an *obligation to succeed*, carry out *a systematic review* of those rules which might prevent, limit or deter the use of electronic contracts and to carry out *this review in a qualitative way, i.e.* not seek simply to amend the key words in the rules (e.g. "paper") but to identify everything which might in practice prevent the "effective" use of electronic contracts.

The scope of the analysis to be carried out by the Member States covers all the stages of the contractual process, and not solely that of the actual conclusion of the contract, and the question of the medium used for the contract. The various stages of the contractual process are : the invitation to treat or the contract offer itself, negotiations, the offer (where there has been an invitation to enter into a contract), the conclusion of the contract, registration, cancellation or amendment of the contract, invoicing, archiving the contract.

In concrete terms, for the purposes of incorporating

this Article into their legislation and enforcing the obligation, the Member States will have to :

— repeal provisions which manifestly prohibit or restrict the use of electronic media;

— not prevent the use of certain electronic systems as intelligent electronic agents;

— not give electronic contracts a weak legal effect, the result of which would be to favour in practice the use of paper contracts;

— adapt the formal requirements which cannot be met by electronic means or, as will more often be the case, which give rise to legal uncertainty because it is not certain how they are to be interpreted or applied to electronic contracts. This does not affect the requirement of a signature, which is already covered by the proposal for a Directive on a common framework for electronic signatures.[24] Legal uncertainty as to the interpretation of formal requirements is the most frequent obstacle to the effective use of electronic contracts. Examples of formal requirements which the Member States will have to examine and. where appropriate, amend are :

Requirements as to the medium used for the contractual process : that the contract be on "paper", that the contract be "written", that a "letter" (letter of confirmation, letter of intent) be sent, that a "document" be presented, that a specific "form" be used, that there be an "original copy" of the contract, that there be a certain number of "original copies" (e.g. one per person), that the contract be "printed" or "published".

Requirements as to human presence : that the contract

be negotiated or concluded by natural persons or in the presence of both parties, that the contract be negotiated or concluded in a specific place.

Requirements as to the involvement of third parties : that the contract be prepared or authenticated by a notary, that the contract be concluded in the presence of witnesses, that the contract be registered or lodged with a person or authority.

As regards fiscal aspects of invoicing, it should be noted that specific measures at Community level will be necessary to remove the barriers that exist as a consequence of the divergence in requirements imposed at national level.

Paragraphs 2, 3 and 4

The purpose of these derogations is to introduce a degree of flexibility and to take account of situations when restrictions to the use of electronic contracts might be justified. They can also be adapted by implementing measures. Moreover, to ensure transparency. Member States are asked to indicate the types of contract which will be covered by this derogation.

Article 10: Information to be Provided

In order to ensure a high standard of fair trading and consumer protection, this Article pursues an objective of transparency regarding the various stages of the contractual process, in particular the need to describe in advance what different steps are necessary before the formal conclusion of a contract. This aspect specific to the formation of electronic contracts is not dealt with by Directive 97/7/EC.

Paragraph 2 emphasises the importance of the quality of the act of consent.

Paragraph 3 aims to allow the recipient of the service to have access to relevant codes of conduct concerning contractual aspects that the service provider is subject to.

Article 11: Time at Which the Contract is Concluded

The Article addresses a specific situation :

— a contractual process in which the recipient of the service only has the choice of clicking "yes" or "no" (or the use of another technology) to accept or refuse an offer;

— a concrete offer made by a service provider (the situation in which the service provider only issues an invitation to offer is not covered).

In view of the significant degree of legal uncertainty surrounding this type of situation, the Article seeks to determine clearly the time at which a contract is concluded (paragraph 1). Paragraph 2 requires the service provider to put in place appropriate means for the recipient to be able to identify and correct handling errors, such as confirmation windows allowing him to be able to ensure that the recipient has indeed accepted his offer.

SECTION 4 : LIABILITY OF INTERMEDIARIES

This section establishes limitations on the liability of Information Society service providers, when they act as "intermediaries", as regards illegal acts initiated by others.

Only the activities involved in serving as on-line intermediaries are covered. These activities are characterised by : (i) the fact that the information is provided by recipients of the service and (ii) the fact that the information is transmitted or stored at the request of recipients of the service. The term "recipient" of the service should be understood to cover a person who places information on-line as well as a person who accesses and/or retrieves such information. The term "information" as used in this section should be understood in a broad sense.

Other types of activities which also constitute Information Society services are not addressed since no new problems specific to the Internet have been identified as arising. Thus for example, the sale of plane tickets by an on-line travel agency (even if the agency sells the tickets on behalf of the airline company) cannot be considered as mere conduit or storage of information of third parties and therefore does not fall within the limitations established by this directive.

Limitations to liability are established in a horizontal manner, *i.e.* they affect liability for all types of illegal activities initiated by third parties on line (e.g. copyright piracy, unfair competition practices, misleading advertising, etc.). It should be clear, however, that the provisions of this section do not affect the underlying material law governing the different infringements that may be concerned. This section is restricted to the establishment of the limitations on the liability. If a service provider fails to qualify for such limitations, the nature and scope of his liability will be established on the basis of Member States legislation.

The distinction as regards liability is not based on different categories of operators but on the specific types of activities undertaken by operators. The fact that a provider qualifies for an exemption from liability as regards a particular act does not provide him with an exemption for all of his other activities.

Article 12: Mere Conduit

Article 12 establishes an exemption from liability as regards acts of transmission of information in communication networks where the service provider plays a passive role as a conduit of information for third parties (the recipients of the service).

This liability exemption covers both cases in which a service provider could be held directly liable for an infringement and cases in which a service provider could be considered secondarily liable for someone else's infringement (for instance as an accomplice). As regards the types of activities covered by this article claims for damages cannot be directed against the provider for any form of liability. Equally, the provider cannot be subject to prosecution in a criminal case. The article does not exclude, however, the possibility of an action for injunctive relief.

Paragraph 1

The application of the exemption requires that the information transmitted is "provided by the recipient of the service". When the service provider is transmitting his own information he cannot be considered any longer as performing an intermediary - *i.e.* a "conduit" - activity. The same holds if the provider modifies the information itself during the course of the transmission.

To be granted an exemption from liability, three conditions must be fulfilled cumulatively.

The requirement that the provider does not initiate the transmission means that the provider is not the person who makes the decision to carry out the transmission. The fact that a provider automatically initiates a transmission at the request of a recipient of his service does not mean that the service provider initiated the transmission in this sense.

The requirement that the provider does not select the receivers of the transmission does not imply that the provider is disqualified from the exemption in the case of the selection of receivers as an automatic response to the request of the person initiating the transmission (e.g. a user's request to have an e-mail forwarded to a mailing list broker).

The third requirement is that the provider neither selects nor modifies the information contained in the transmission.

***Paragraph* 2**

Intermediate and transient storage taking place during the transmission of the information in order to carry it out, is covered by the "mere conduit" exemption.

Only those acts of storage that take place during the course of transmitting the information and which do not serve any purpose other than the carrying out of the communication will benefit from the exemption. These acts of storage do not include copies made by the provider for the purpose of making the information available to subsequent users. Such acts will be addressed in article 13.

The term "automatic" refers to the fact that the act of storage occurs through the ordinary operation of the technology. The term "intermediate" refers to the fact that the storage of information is made in the course of the transmission. The term "transient" refers to the fact that the storage is for a limited period of time. However, it should be clear that the information cannot be stored beyond the time that is reasonably necessary for the transmission.

Article 13: "Caching"

This article addresses temporary forms of storage most often referred to as "system caching". This form of storage is undertaken by the service provider with a view to enhance the performance and the speed of digital networks. It does not constitute as such a separate exploitation of the information transmitted. Thus, copies of the information, made available on line and transmitted by third parties, are temporarily kept in the operator's system or network for the purpose of facilitating the access of subsequent users to such information. Such copies are the result of a technical and automatic process and they are "intermediate" between the place in the network where the information was originally made available and the final user.

To benefit from an exemption for potential liability arising from this type of storage, the provider must respect certain conditions.

Article 14: Hosting
Paragraph 1

Article 14 establishes a limit on liability as regards the activity of storage of information provided by recipients of the service and at their request (e.g. the provision of server space for a company's or an individual's web site, for a BBS, a newsgroup, etc.).

The exemption from liability (both as regards civil and criminal liability) cannot be granted if a service provider knows that a user of his service is undertaking illegal activity (actual knowledge).

The exemption from liability, as regards claims for damages, cannot be granted if the service provider is aware of facts and circumstances from which the illegal activity is apparent.

Service providers will not lose the exemption from liability if after obtaining actual knowledge or becoming aware of facts and circumstances indicating illegal activity, they act expeditiously to remove or to disable access to the information.

This principle, established in the second indent of the paragraph, provides a basis on which different interested parties may lay down procedures for notifying the service provider about information that is the subject of illegal activity and for obtaining the removal or disablement of such information (sometimes referred to as "notice and take down procedures"). It should nevertheless be stressed that these procedures do not and cannot replace existing judicial remedies.

The Commission is actively encouraging industry self-regulatory systems, including the establishment of codes of conduct and hot line mechanisms[25].

***Paragraph* 2**

This paragraph establishes that if a recipient of the service acts under the authority or the control of the provider, article 14 does not apply. It should be stressed that the relevant control is the control of the recipient's acts and not the control over the information as such.

Article 15: No Obligation to Monitor

This article establishes that no general obligation should be imposed on providers to screen or to actively monitor third party content. This general rule does not affect the possibility of a court or law enforcement agency requesting a service provider to monitor, for instance, a specific site during a given period of time, in order to prevent or fighting specific illegal activity.

CHAPTER III. IMPLEMENTATION

The purpose of this Chapter is to ensure that the Directive is properly implemented in the interests of the public and service providers and it is justified by the need to ensure the proper functioning of the internal market, in particular the application of the principle of country of origin laid down by Article 3.

Article 16: Codes of Conduct

This Article therefore encourages the creation of codes of conduct at European level. It is wholly consistent with the policy adopted at Community level both by Council Recommendation 98/ 560 of 24 September 1998[26] and with the Council Decision adopting a Multiannual Action Plan promoting safe use of the Internet of....

In order to ensure that these codes of conduct are consistent with Community law, subparagraph (b) encourages interested parties to inform the Commission of any draft codes. By contrast, under Directive 98/34/ EC,'[27] voluntary, agreements to which a public authority is party must be notified in accordance with the terms of the Directive.

This provisions will be particularly important for the implementation of certain other provisions, such as Article 8.

Article 17: Out of Court Dispute Settlement
Paragraph 1

This Article establishes an obligation to allow effective recourse to these remedies, in particular by electronic means, where they comply with the principles set out in paragraph 2. This type of mechanism would appear particularly useful for some disputes on the Internet because of their low transactionai value and the size of the parties, who might otherwise be deterred from using legal procedures because of their cost. The legal framework of these dispute-settlement mechanisms in the Member States should not be such that it limits the use of these mechanisms or makes them unduly complicated. For example, in the case of specific mechanisms for disputes on the Internet, these could take place electronically.

Paragraph 2

These principles apply solely to disputes concerning consumption and are already set out in Commission Recommendation 98/257/EC,[28] adopted on 30 March 1998, on the principles applicable to the bodies responsible for out-of-court settlement of consumer disputes and are explained in the Commission Communication of 30 March 1998 on the out-of-court settlement of consumer disputes.[29]

Article 18: Court Actions

This Article is concerned solely with issues which must be addressed to ensure the proper functioning of the internal market, and it is directly linked to the Community objective of guaranteeing the freedom to provide services as defined in Article 3 of the Directive, in particular by not calling into question the mutual confidence between Member States.

Paragraph 1 relates to *legal remedies in urgent cases* (e.g. applications for the adoption of interim measures). The Member States must take measures to make such remedies effectively available and will therefore have to examine whether their procedures are adapted to tackling illicit conduct or disputes on the Internet.

Article 19: Co-operation Between Authorities

The purpose of this Article is to give national authorities the means of meeting their task of monitoring information society services and to ensure effective co-operation between Member States and between the Member States and the Commission.

Paragraph 4 requires Member States to set up within their administration contact points that can direct and assist the recipients of services, in particular consumers.

Article 20: Electronic Means

The purpose of this Article is to allow implementing measures to be adopted concerning the electronic means which might be considered appropriate for the purposes of meeting the obligations which refer to such means of communication (Articles 17(1) and 19(4)). Such measures must be taken with a view to facilitating cross-border communications under adequately secure conditions.

Article 21: Sanctions

This is a standard provision for internal market Directives.

CHAPTER IV. DEROGATION

Article 22: Derogations

In view of its wide scope and the need to ensure a degree of flexibility and leeway in its application, the Directive provides for three types of derogation :

Paragraph 1 : The general derogations to the scope of application cover *taxation* and the areas covered by directive 95/46/EC.[30] There could be certain interference between the latter and this directive on electronic commerce. Given that directive 95/46/EC already ensures the free circulation of personal data between the Member States, the area it covers has been excluded from the scope of application of this directive. The fiscal aspects of electronic commerce are also excluded and are under review in the work that has been launched by the Commission Communication "Electronic commerce and indirect taxation."[31]

Moreover, certain activities listed in Annex I are also excluded because it is not possible to guarantee the freedom to provide services between Member States given the lack of mutual recognition or sufficient harmonisation to guarantee an equivalent level of protection of general interest objectives.

Paragraph 2: derogation from the internal market clause:

The country of origin principle, as envisaged in this Directive, requires certain derogations in the specific cases cited in Annex II. Indeed, certain specific areas cannot benefit from the country of origin principle because in these fields:

- it is *impossible to apply the principle of mutual recognition* as set out in the case law of the Court of Justice concerning the principles of freedom of movement enshrined in the Treaty, or
- it is an area where mutual recognition cannot be achieved and there is *insufficient harmonisation* to guarantee an equivalent level of protection between Member States;
- there are *provisions laid down by existing Directives which are clearly incompatible* with Article 3 because they explicitly require supervision in the country of destination.

Paragraph 3 : derogations from the freedom to provide services in specific cases :

Paragraph 3 allows measures to be taken in very, specific cases to restrict the freedom to provide information society services which would normally be considered incompatible with Article 3(2).

These derogations are subject to a series of conditions relating to the measures' characteristics (subparagraph (a)) and the conduct of the Member State taking them (subparagraph (b)).

Moreover, an emergency procedure has been devised

to take account of the speed at which loss and damage can occur.

Moreover, the derogations are subject to a supervision procedure by the Commission. It goes without saying that the Commission's approach in this context will be flexible, and, in particular, will seek to avoid cases of disguised or disproportionate restrictions to the free movement of the relevant services. Having said this, the Commission will fully account for the Member States' need to enforce, laws seeking to protect fundamental societal interests. It would, for example, be out of the question for the Commission to prevent a Member State from applying a law which would forbid the arrival of racist messages.

CHAPTER V

Article 23 sets up the Consultative Committee charged with assisting the Commission in implementing its powers of enforcement. The subsequent articles are standard for directives.

PROPOSAL FOR A EUROPEAN PARLIAMENT AND COUNCIL DIRECTIVE ON CERTAIN LEGAL ASPECTS OF ELECTRONIC COMMERCE IN THE INTERNAL MARKET

The European Parliament and the Council of the European Union,

Having regard to the Treaty establishing the European Community, and in particular Articles 57(2), 66 and 100a thereof,

Having regard to the proposal from the Commission,[32]

Having regard to the opinion of the Economic and Social Committee,[33]

Acting in accordance with the procedure referred to in Article 189b of the Treaty,[34]

(1) Whereas the European Union is seeking to forge ever closer links between the States and peoples of Europe, to ensure economic and social progress; whereas, in accordance with Article 7a of the Treaty, the internal market comprises an area without internal frontiers in which the free movement of goods, services and the freedom of establishment are ensured; whereas the development of information society services within the area without internal frontiers is vital to eliminating the barriers which divide the European peoples;

(2) Whereas the development of electronic commerce within the information society offers significant employment opportunities in Europe, particularly in small and medium sized enterprises, and will stimulate economic growth and investment in innovation by European companies;

(3) Whereas information society services span a wide range of economic activities which can, notably, consist of selling goods on line; whereas they are not solely restricted to services giving rise to on-line contracting but also, in so far as they represent an economic activity, to services which are not remunerated by those who receive them, such as those offering on-line information; whereas information society services also include on-line activities via telephony and facsimile;

(4) Whereas the development of information society services within the Community is restricted by a number of legal obstacles to the proper functioning of the internal market which hamper

or make less attractive the exercise of the freedom of establishment and the freedom to provide services; whereas these obstacles arise from divergences in legislation and from the legal uncertainty as to which national rules apply to such services; whereas, in the absence of co-ordination and adjustment of legislation in the relevant areas, obstacles might be justified in the light of the case law of the Court of Justice; whereas legal uncertainty exists with regard to the extent to which Member States may control services originating from another Member State;

(5) Whereas, in the light of Community objectives, of Articles 52 and 59 of the Treaty and secondary Community law, these obstacles should be eliminated by co-ordinating certain national laws and by clarifying certain legal concepts at Community level to the extent necessary for the proper functioning of the internal market; whereas, by dealing only with certain specific matters which give rise to problems for the internal market, this Directive is fully consistent with the need to respect the principle of subsidiarity;

(6) Whereas, in accordance with the principle of proportionality, the measures provided for in the Directive are strictly limited to what is needed to achieve the objective of the proper functioning of the internal market; whereas, where action at Community level is necessary, and in order to guarantee an area which is truly without internal frontiers as far as electronic commerce is concerned, the Directive must ensure a high level of protection of general interest objectives, in particular consumer protection and the

protection of public health; whereas according to Article 129 of the EC Treaty, the protection of public health is an essential component of other Community policies; whereas this directive does not impact on the legal requirements applicable to the delivery of goods as such, nor those applicable to services which are not information society services;

(7) Whereas this directive does not aim to establish specific rules on international private law relating to conflicts of law or jurisdiction and is therefore without prejudice to the relevant international conventions;

(8) Whereas information society services should be supervised at the source of the activity in order to ensure an effective protection of public interest objectives; whereas, to that end, it is necessary to ensure that the competent authority provides such protection not only only for the citizens of its own country but for all Community citizens; whereas, moreover, in order to effectively guarantee freedom to provide services and legal certainty for suppliers and recipients of services, such information society service should only be subject to the law of the Member State in which the service provider is established; whereas, in order to improve mutual trust between Member States, it is essential that this responsibility of the Member State of origin be clearly expressed;

(9) Whereas the place at which a service provider is established should be determined in accordance with the case law of the Court of Justice; whereas the place of establishment of a company providing services via an internet website is not the place at which the technology supporting its website

is located or the place at which its website is accessible; whereas, in conformity with the case law of the Court[35] in the case where the same supplier has a number of establishments, the competent Member State will be the one where the supplier has the centre of his activities; whereas in the case where it is particularly difficult to assess in which Member States the supplier is established, cooperative procedures are established between the Member States and the consultative committee can be convened in urgent cases to examine such difficulties;

(10) Whereas commercial communications are essential for the financing of information society services and for developing a wide variety of new, free of charge services; whereas in the interests of consumer protection and fair trading, commercial communications, including discounts, promotional offers and promotional competitions, must meet a number of transparency requirements and that these requirements are without prejudice to Directive 97/7/EC of the European Parliament and of the Council on the protection of consumers in respect of distance contracts[36]; whereas this directive does not affect existing directives on commercial communications in particular directive 98/43/EC[37] of the European Parliament and of the Council relating to the advertising and sponsorship of tobacco products;

(11) Whereas Article 10(2) of European Parliament and Council Directive 97/7/EC on the protection of consumers in respect of distance contracts[38] and Article 12(2) of European Parliament and Council Directive 97/66/EC concerning the

processing of personal data and the protection of privacy in the telecommunications sector[39] address the issue of consent by receivers for certain forms of unsolicited commercial communication and are fully applicable to information society services;

(12) Whereas in order to remove barriers to the development of cross-border services within the Community which professional practitioners might offer on the Internet, it is necessary that compliance be guaranteed at Community level with professional rules aiming, in particular, to protect consumers or public health; whereas codes of conduct as Community level would be the best means of determining the rules on professional ethics applicable to commercial communication; whereas the drawing up or, where appropriate, adaptation of such rules should in the first place be encouraged by, rather than laid down in, this Directive; whereas the regulated activities covered by this Directive should be understood in accordance with the definition established in article l(d) of Council Directive 89/48/EEC on a general system for the recognition of higher-education diplomas awarded on completion of professional education and training of at least three years' duration;[40]

(13) Whereas each Member State must amend its legislation containing requirements, in particular form requirements, which are likely to curb the use of contracts by electronic means, subject to any Community measure in the field of taxation that could betaken on electronic invoicing; whereas the examination of the legislation requiring such adjustment should be systematic

and cover all the necessary stages and acts of the contractual process, including the archiving of the contract; whereas the result of this amendment must be to make contracts concluded electronically genuinely and effectively possible in law and in practice; whereas the legal effect of electronic signatures is dealt with by European Parliament and Council Directive *98/.../EC* on a common framework for electronic signatures;[41] whereas it is necessary to clarify at what point in time a contract entered into electronically is considered to be effectively concluded; whereas the service recipient's agreement to enter into a contract may take the form of an on-line payment; whereas the acknowledgement of receipt by a service provider may take the form of the on-line provision of the service paid for;

(14) Whereas, amongst others, Council Directive 93/13/EEC[42] on unfair terms in consumer contracts and European Parliament and Council Directive 97/7/EC of the European Parliament and of the Council on the protection of consumers in respect of distance contracts[43] are the essential means established at Community level to protect consumers in contractual matters and these directives also apply in their entirety to information society services; whereas this Directive only complements them; whereas are also included in these means established at Community level Directive 98/6/EC[44] concerning consumer protection relating to the indication of prices of products offered to consumers, Directive 84/450[45] EEC concerning misleading advertising, Directive 90/ 314/EEC[46] on package travel, package holidays and package tours,

Directive 87/102/ EEC[47] concerning consumer credit; whereas this directive is without prejudice to Directive 98/43/EC[48] which was adopted in the framework of the internal market and other directives relating to the protection of public health;

(15) Whereas the confidentiality of electronic messages is guaranteed by Article 5 of Directive 97/66/ EC concerning the processing of personal data and the protection of privacy in the telecommunications sector; whereas in accordance with that Directive Member States must prohibit any kind of interception or surveillance of such electronic messages by others than the senders and receivers;

(16) Whereas existing and emerging disparities in Member States' legislation and case law concerning civil and criminal liability of service providers acting as intermediaries prevent the smooth functioning of the Internal Market, in particular by impairing the development of cross-border services and producing distortions of competition; whereas service providers have a duty to act, under certain circumstances, with a view to prevent and stop illegal activity; whereas the provisions of this Directive constitute the appropriate basis for the development of rapid and reliable procedures for removing and disabling access to illegal information; whereas such mechanisms could be developed on the basis of voluntary, agreements between all parties concerned; whereas it is in the interest of all parties involved in the provision of information society services to adopt and implement such procedures; whereas the provisions of this

Directive relating to liability are without prejudice to the development and effective enforcement, by the different interested parties, of technical systems of protection and identification;

(17) Whereas each Member State must, where necessary, amend any legislation which is liable to hamper the use of out of court dispute resolution systems based on electronic means; whereas the result of this amendment must be to make the functioning of such mechanisms genuinely and effectively possible in law and in practice, including across borders; whereas the bodies responsible for such out of court settlement of consumer disputes must comply with certain essential principles, as set out in Commission Recommendation 98/257/EC on the principles applicable to the bodies responsible for such settlement of consumer disputes; [49]

(18) Whereas it is necessary to exclude certain activities, as indicated in the annex, from the scope of this Directive given that the freedom to provide services in these fields cannot be, at the current time, guaranteed under the Treaty or existing secondary legislation: whereas excluding these activities does not preclude the future adoption of instruments which might be necessary for the proper functioning of the internal market; whereas taxation, particularly value-added tax imposed on a large number of the services covered by this Directive, must be excluded from the scope of this Directive and that in respect to this, the Commission also intends to extend the application of the principle of taxation at source to the provision of services within the Internal

Market thus allowing for overall coherence in its approach;

(19) Whereas as regards the derogation in Annex IT, contractual obligations concerning contracts concluded by consumers must be interpreted as including information on the essential elements of the content of the contract, including consumer rights, which have a determining influence on the decision to contract;

(20) Whereas this Directive does not apply to services supplied by service providers established in a country outside the Community; whereas, in view of the global dimension of electronic commerce, it is appropriate to ensure that the Community rules are consistent with international rules; whereas this Directive is without prejudice to the results of discussions within international organisations (WTO, OECD, UNCITRAL) on legal issues; whereas the Directive is also without prejudice to the discussions within the Global Business Dialogue which were launched on the basis of the Commission Communication on "Globalisation and the Information society - The need for strengthened international coordination";[50]

(21) Whereas, in accordance with the Council Resolution of 29 June 1995 on the effective uniform application of Community law and on the sanctions applicable for breaches of Community law in the internal market[51] and the Commission communication of 3 May 1995 on the role of sanctions in implementing Community internal market legislation[52] the Member States need to ensure, that, when Community acts are

transposed national legislation, Community law is duly applied with the same effectiveness thoroughness as national law;

(22) Whereas the adoption of this directive would neither prevent the Member States from taking into account the various social, societal and cultural implications which are inherent to the advent of the Information society nor hinder cultural, notably audiovisual, policy measures, which the Member States might adopt, in conformity with Community law, taking into account their linguistic diversity, national end regional specificities and their cultural heritage; whereas, in any case, the development of the Information society must assure that Community citizens can have access to cultural European heritage provided in the digital environment;

(23) Whereas the Council of Ministers, in its resolution of 3 November on the consumer aspects of the information society, stressed that the protection of consumers deserved special attention in this field; whereas the Commission will examine the degree to which existing consumer protection rules provide insufficient protection in the context of the information society and will identify, where necessary, the deficiencies of this legislation and those issues which could require additional measures; whereas, if need be, the Commission should make specific additional proposals to resolve such deficiencies that will have thus been identified;

(24) Whereas Council Regulations 2299/89, 3089/93 and.../98 establish a code of conduct governing the operation of Computer Reservation Services; whereas this Directive is without prejudice to the above Regulations.

(25) Whereas Council Regulation 2027/97 and the Warsaw System place various obligations upon air carriers regarding the provision of information to their passengers, inter alia, about the liability of the carrier; whereas this Directive is without prejudice to the requirements of the above Regulation or the Warsaw System.

HAVE ADOPTED THIS DIRECTIVE :

CHAPTER I GENERAL PROVISIONS

Article 1 Objective and Scope of Application

1. This directive seeks to ensure the proper functioning of the internal market particularly the free movement of information society services between the Member States.
2. This directive approximates, to the extent necessary for the achievement of the objective set out in paragraph 1, national regulations applicable to information society services;

Article 3: Internal Market

(1) Each Member State shall ensure that the information society services provided by a service provider established on its territory comply with the national provisions applicable in the Member State in question which fall within this Directive's co-ordinated field.

(2) Member States may not, for reasons falling within this Directive's co-ordinated field, restrict the freedom to provide information society services from another Member State.

(3) The obligation in paragraph 1 covers the provisions set out in Section 3 of this directive only to the extent that the law in that Member

State is applicable according to its rules of international private law.

CHAPTER II PRINCIPLES

SECTION 1 : ESTABLISHMENT AND INFORMATION REQUIREMENTS

Article 4 Principle of Non-authorisation

1. Member States shall lay down in their legislation that access to the activity of information society service provider may not be made subject to prior authorisation any other requirement the effect of which is to make such access dependent on a decision, measure or particular act by an authority.
2. Paragraph 1 shall be without prejudice to authorisation schemes
   (a) which are not specifically and exclusively targeted at information society services, or
   (b) which are covered by directive 97/13/EC[53].

Article 5: General Information to be Provided

1. Member States shall lay down in their legislation that information society services must render easily accessible in a direct and permanent manner to their recipients and competent authorities the following information :
   (a) the name of the service provider;
   (b) the address at which the service provider is established;
   (c) the co-ordinates of the service provider including his electronic-mail address which allow for him to be contacted rapidly and communicated with in a direct and effective manner;

(d) where the service provider is registered in a trade register, the trade register in which the service provider is entered and any registration number in that register;

(e) where the activity is subject to an authorisation scheme, the activities covered by the authorisation granted to the service provider and the co-ordinates of the authority providing this authorisation;

(f) as concerns the regulated professions: any professional body or similar institution with which the service provider is registered; the professional title granted in the Member State of establishment, the applicable professional rules in the Member State of establishment and the Member States in which the information society services are regularly provided;

(g) in the case where the service provider undertakes an activity that is subject to VAT, the VAT number he is registered under with his fiscal administration.

2. Member States shall lay down in their legislation that prices of information society services must be indicated accurately and unequivocally.

SECTION 2: COMMERCIAL COMMUNICATIONS

Article 6: Information to be Provided

Member States shall lay down in their legislation that commercial communication must comply with the following conditions :

(a) the commercial communication must be clearly identifiable as such;

(b) the natural or legal person on whose behalf the commercial communication is made must be clearly identifiable;

(c) promotional offers, such as discounts, premiums and gifts, where authorised, must be clearly identifiable as such, and the conditions which must be met to receive them must be easily accessible and be presented accurately and unequivocally;

(d) promotional competitions or games, where authorised, must be clearly identifiable as such, and the conditions for participation must be easily accessible and be presented accurately and unequivocally.

Article 7: Unsolicited Commercial Communication

Member States shall lay down in their legislation that unsolicited commercial communication by electronic mail must be clearly and unequivocally identifiable as such as soon as it is received by the recipient.

Article 8: Regulated Professions

1. Member States shall lay down in their legislation relating to commercial communication by regulated professions that the provision of information society services is authorised provided that the professional rules regarding the independence, dignity and honour of the profession, professional secrecy and fairness towards clients and other members of the profession are met.
2. Member States and the Commission shall encourage professional associations and bodies to establish codes of conduct at Community level in order to determine the types of information

that can be given for the purposes of providing the information society service in conformity with the rules referred to in paragraph 1.

3. Where necessary in order to ensure the proper functioning of the internal market, and in the light of the codes of conduct applicable at Community level, the Commission may stipulate, in accordance with the procedures laid down in Article 23, the information referred to in paragraph 2.

SECTION 3 : ELECTRONIC CONTRACTS

Article 9: Treatment of Electronic Contracts

1. Member States shall ensure that their legislation allows contracts to be concluded electronically. Member States shall in particular ensure that the legal requirements applicable to the contractual process neither prevent the effective use of electronic contracts nor result in such contracts being deprived of legal validity because of the fact that they have been concluded electronically.
2. Member States may lay down that paragraph 1 does not apply to the following contracts :
   — contracts requiring the intervention of a notary;
   — contracts which, in order to be valid, are required to be registered with a public authority;
   — contracts falling within the scope of family law;
   — contracts falling within the scope of the law of succession.

3. The list of derogations provided for in paragraph 2 may be amended by the Commission in accordance with the procedure laid down in Article 23.
4. Member States shall submit to the Commission a complete list of the categories of contracts covered by the derogations provided for in paragraph 2.

Article 10: Information to be Provided

1. Member States shall lay down in their legislation that, except when otherwise agreed by professional parties, the manner of the formation of a contract by electronic means must be explained by the service provider clearly and unequivocally and prior to the conclusion of the contract. Such information shall include, in particular:
   — the different stages to follow to conclude the contract;
   — whether or not the concluded contract will be archived and will be accessible;
   — any means which exist of correcting handling errors.
2. Member States shall lay down in their legislation that the different steps to be followed to conclude a contract by electronic means be set out such as to ensure that parties can reach a full and informed consent.
3. Member States shall lay down in their legislation that, except when otherwise agreed by professional parties, the service providers must indicate any codes of conduct to which they subscribe and information on how these codes can be consulted by electronic means.

Article 11: Moment at Which the Contract is Concluded

1. Member States shall lay down in their legislation that, save as otherwise agreed by professional parties and in the case where a recipient is required to express his consent to accept a service provider's offer by using technological means, such as clicking on an icon, the following principles apply :

— the contract is concluded when the recipient of the service :

- receives from the service provider, by electronic means, an acknowledgement of receipt of the recipient's acceptance, and
- confirms receipt of the acknowledgement of receipt;

— the acknowledgement of receipt is deemed to be received and the confirmation is deemed to have been given when the parties for whom they are destined are able to access them;

— the acknowledgement of receipt by the service provider and the confirmation of the service recipient must be sent as quickly as possible.

2. Member States shall lay down in their legislation that, save as otherwise agreed by professional parties, the service provider must make available to the recipient of the service appropriate means allowing him to identify and correct handling errors.

SECTION 4: LIABILITY OF INTERMEDIARIES

Article 12: Mere Conduit

1. Where an information society service is provided that consists of:

   - the transmission in a communication network of information provided by the recipient of the service; or
   - the provision of access to a communication network.

   Member States shall provide in their legislation that the provider of such a service shall not be liable, other than for injunctive relief, for the information transmitted on condition that the provider :

   — does not initiate the transmission,

   — does not select the receiver of the transmission, and

   — does not select and does not modify the information contained in the transmission.

2. The acts of transmission and of provision of access referred to in paragraph 1 include the automatic, intermediate and transient storage of the information transmitted to the extent that this takes place for the sole purpose of carrying out the transmission in the communication network and that the information is not stored for a period longer than is reasonably necessary for the transmission.

Article 13: Caching

Where an information society service is provided that consists of the transmission in a communication network of information provided by a recipient of the service. Member States shall provide in their legislation that the provider shall not be liable, other than for injunctive relief, for the automatic, intermediate and temporary storage of that information done for the sole purpose of making more efficient the information's further transmission to other recipients of the service upon their request, on condition that:

(a) the provider does not modify the information;

(b) the provider complies with conditions on access to the information;

(c) the provider complies with rules regarding the updating of the information, specified in a manner consistent with industry standards;

(d) the provider does not interfere with technology, consistent with industry standards, used to obtain data on the use of the information; and

(e) the provider acts expeditiously to remove or to disable access to the information upon obtaining actual knowledge that:

— the information at the initial source of the transmission has been removed from the network, or

— that access to it has been disabled, or

— that a competent authority has ordered such removal or disablement to take place.

Article 14: Hosting

1. Where an information society service is provided that consists of the storage of information provided by a recipient of the service, Member States shall provide in their legislation that the provider shall not be liable, other than for injunctive relief, for the information stored at the request of a recipient of the service on condition that:

— the provider does not have actual knowledge that the activity is illegal and, as regards claims for damages, is not aware of facts or circumstances from which illegal activity is apparent; or

— the provider, upon obtaining such knowledge or awareness, acts expeditiously to remove or to disable access to the information.

2. The provisions of this article shall not apply when the recipient of the service is acting under the authority or the control of the provider.

Article 15: No Obligation to Monitor

1. Member States shall not impose a general obligation on providers, when providing the services covered by articles 12 and 14, to monitor the information which they transmit or store on a general obligation to actively seek facts or circumstances indicating illegal activity.
2. Paragraph 1 shall not affect any targeted, temporary surveillance activities required by national judicial authorities in accordance with national legislation to safeguard national security, defence, public, security and for the prevention, investigation, detection and prosecution of criminal offences.

CHAPTER III IMPLEMENTATION

Article 16: Codes of Conduct

1. Member States and the Commission shall encourage :

(a) the drawing up of codes of conduct at Community level by trade and professional associations or organisations designed to contribute to the proper implementation of this Directive, and in particular Articles 5 to 15;

(b) the transmission of draft codes of conduct at national or Community level to the Commission so that the latter may examine their compatibility with Community law;

(c) the accessibility of these codes of conduct in the Community languages by electronic means;

(d) professional associations or organisations to inform Member States and the Commission of their assessment of the application of their codes of conduct and their impact upon practices, habits or customs relating to electronic commerce.

2. In so far as they may be concerned, consumer associations shall be involved in the drafting and implementation of codes of conduct drawn up according to paragraph 1 (a).

Article 17: Out of Court Dispute Settlement

1. Member States shall ensure that, in the event of disputes between an information society service provider and its recipient, their legislation allows the effective use of out of court dispute settlement mechanisms including by appropriate electronic means.
2. Member States shall ensure that bodies responsible for out of court settlement of consumer disputes apply the principles of independence and transparency, the adversarial principle, and the principles of effectiveness of procedure, legality of the decision, liberty of parties and representation.

3. Member States shall encourage bodies responsible for out of court dispute settlement to inform the Commission of the decisions they take regarding information society services and to transmit any other information on the practices, usages or customs relating to electronic commerce.

Article 18: Court Actions

1. Member States shall ensure that effective actions can be brought against information society services' activities by allowing measures to be taken as rapidly as possible by way of interim injunctions in order to remedy an alleged infringement and to protect the interested parties from being subject to further damages.
2. Acts in breach of the national provisions incorporating Articles 5 to 15 of this Directive which affect consumer interests shall constitute infringements within the meaning of Article 1(2) of Directive 98/27/EC of the European Parliament and Council on injunctions for the protection of consumers' interests[34].

Article 19: Co-operation between Authorities

1. Member States shall ensure that their competent authorities have the appropriate powers of supervision and investigation necessary to implement this Directive effectively. Member States shall ensure that service providers supply the national authorities with the information necessary to implement this Directive.
2. Member States shall ensure, with a view to allowing the effective implementation of this Directive, that their national authorities co-operate with the authorities of other Member States and

shall, to that end, appoint a contact person, whose coordinates they shall communicate to the other Member States and to the Commission.

3. Member States shall, as quickly as possible, provide the assistance and information requested by authorities of other Member States or by the Commission, including by appropriate electronic means.

4. Member States shall establish in their administration contact points, which shall be accessible by electronic means and from which recipients and service providers may :
   — obtain information on their contractual rights and obligations,
   — obtain the coordinates of authorities, associations or organisations from which recipients of services may obtain information about their rights or with whom they may file complaints and
   — receive assistance in cases of disputes.

5. Member States shall ensure that competent authorities inform the Commission of any decisions taken in their country regarding proceedings or disputes relating to information society services and practices, usages and customs relating to electronic commerce.

6. The rules governing cooperation between national authorities as referred to in paragraphs 2 to 5 shall be laid down by the Commission in accordance with the procedure set out in Article 23.

7. Member States may ask the Commission to convene urgently the committee referred to in Article 23 in order to examine difficulties

concerning the application of Article 3(1) of this Directive.

Article 20: Electronic Means

The Commission may take measures, in accordance with the procedure provided for in Article 23, to ensure the proper functioning of electronic means between Member States, as referred to in Articles 17(1), 19(3) and 19(4).

Article 21: Sanctions

Member States shall determine the sanctions applicable to infringements of national provisions adopted pursuant to this Directive and shall take all measures necessary to ensure that they are enforced. The sanctions they provide for shall be effective, proportionate and dissuasive. Member States shall notify these measures to the Commission no later than the date specified in Article 24(1) and shall inform it of all future amendments to them without delay.

CHAPTER IV DEROGATIONS

Article 22: Derogations

1. This Directive shall not apply to :
   — the field of taxation;
   — the areas covered by directive 95/46/EC[55]
   — the activities of information society services referred to in Annex I. This list of activities may be amended by the Commission in accordance with the procedure laid down by Article 23.
2. Article 3 of this Directive shall not apply to the fields referred to in Annex II.
3. By way of derogation to Article 3(2), and without prejudice to court actions, the competent authorities of Member States may take measures

to restrict the freedom to provide information society service subject to such measures being consistent with Community law and with the following provisions :

(a) the measures shall be :

(i) necessary for one of the following reasons:

— public policy, in particular the protection of minors, or the fight against any incitement to hatred on grounds of race, sex, religion or nationality;

— the protection of public health;

— public security;

— consumer protection.

(ii) taken in respect of an information society service which prejudices the objectives referred to in the preceding indent or which presents a serious and grave risk of prejudice to those objectives;

(iii) proportionate to those objectives;

(b) prior to taking the measures in question, the Member State has :

— asked the Member State referred to in Article 3(1) to take measures and the latter did not take measures or measures taken were inadequate;

— notified the Commission and the Member State in which the service provider is established of its intention to take such measures;

(c) Member States may lay down in their legislation that, in the case of urgency, the conditions stipulated in point (b) do not apply. Where this is the case, the measures shall be notified in the shortest possible time to the Commission and to the Member State in which the service provider is established, indicating the reasons for which it considers that there is urgency.

(d) the Commission may decide on the compatibility of the measures with Community law. Where it adopts a negative decision, the Member States shall refrain from taking any proposed measures or shall be required to urgently put an end to the measures in question.

CHAPTER V ADVISORY COMMITTEE AND FINAL PROVISIONS

Article 23: Committee

The Commission shall be assisted by an advisory committee made up of representatives of the Member States and chaired by a representative of the Commission. The committee shall draw up its own rules of procedure.

The Commission representative shall submit a draft of the measures to be taken to the advisory committee. The committee shall deliver its opinion on the draft within a time limit which the chairman may lay down according to the urgency of the matter, where appropriate by vote.

The opinion shall be recorded in the minutes. In addition, each Member State shall have the right to request that its position be recorded in those minutes.

The Commission shall take the utmost account of the opinion delivered by the committee. It shall inform the committee of the manner in which it has taken account of the opinion.

Article 24: Implementation

1. Member States shall bring into force the laws, regulations and administrative provisions necessary to comply with this Directive within one year of its notification and shall inform the Commission thereof.

   When Member States adopt these provisions, these shall contain a reference to this Directive or shall be accompanied by such reference at the time of their official publication. The methods of making such reference shall be laid down by Member States.

2. Not later than three years after the adoption of this Directive, and thereafter every two years, the Commission shall submit to the European Parliament, the Council and the Economic and Social Committee a report on the application of this Directive accompanied, where necessary, by proposals to adapt it to developments in the field of information society services.

Article 25: Entry into Force

This Directive shall enter into force on the twentieth day following its publication in the Official Journal of the European Communities.

Article 26: Addresses

This Directive is addressed to the Member States.

DIGITAL MILLENNIUM COPYRIGHT ACT

The new Digital Millennium Copyright Act creates safe

harbors from copyright infringement liability for service providers. Under the Act, a "service provider" includes anyone who operates a server linked to the Internet or a proprietary online service. Because only service providers who register with the Copyright Office can take advantage of most of these safe harbors (and because copyright holders should comply with the Act in giving notices of infringement) we strongly recommend that all clients and friends of the firm take notice of this new legislation. Anyone who provides hosting services on the Internet should register an agent with the Copyright Office as soon as possible in order to ensure access to this liability-limiting legislation. You should also consider making adjustments to your subscriber agreements to take these new provisions into account. (Under the Act, "subscribers" can be anyone using your services, whether or not they pay you.)

Why Was This Act Needed?

Copyright infringement is a strict liability offense—even if you don't know you've copied material belonging to someone else, you can be subject to an injunction or damages order from a federal court. This poses a problem for online service providers, who may unwittingly "copy" material posted by their subscribers. It also poses a problem for anyone with infringing material residing on his or her server.

The online service provider industry has argued strenuously over the last three years that it should not be held liable for infringing material posted by others because it has no way to police what is transmitted on its networks. Copyright holders, on the other hand, have argued that online service providers should bear responsibility because they are in a better position to prevent violations. The new Act represents a compromise between these camps.

What Does the Act Do?

The new Act includes provisions designed to insulate service providers (those providing Internet access and those operating proprietary networks) from copyright infringement liability. Providers will remain responsible for their own content, but will not be held responsible for content posted by others provided they meet the Act's requirements. Once a provider has notice of an infringement, it may qualify for a safe harbor from liability by taking down the allegedly infringing material: there are also procedures for restoring such content if the allegations are not pursued. Providers need to register with the Copyright Office in order to provide copyright holders and subscribers with an address at which the notices and counter-notices established by the Act can be received—and to be eligible for related safe harbor protections.

What Are the Safe Harbors?

In general, to the extent a service provider is merely sending on, saving, caching, or pointing to material automatically (without originating or modifying the material), it may be able to qualify for a limitation of its infringement liability. Service providers must also post a policy for terminating subscribers (users, even if non-paying, of the service provider's system), and must accommodate and not interfere with reasonable, industry-standard technical measures used to identify or protect copyrighted materials.

The Act protects service providers based on the function the service provider is performing. Here are some of the specific requirements the Act sets forth for its safe harbors:

1. Transit Functions

The safe harbor applies only if somebody other than the service provider:

(a) Initiates or directs the transmissions : and
(b) Selects the material to be transmitted and the recipients of the material.

This safe harbor does not apply if the service provider:

(a) Maintains a copy of the material for longer than reasonably necessary for transmission; or
(b) Modifies the material's content during transmission.

2. *System Caching*

The safe harbor applies only to material that is :

(a) Made available online by somebody else such as an original website;
(b) Transmitted by the original site to somebody requesting the material;
(c) Stored only temporarily and automatically for the purpose of making the material available for requests by other subscribers; and
(d) Unmodified in its content.

To qualify for this safe harbor, a service provider must:

(a) Comply with rules specified by the original site governing refreshing, reloading, or otherwise updating material if these rules are consistent with generally accepted industry standards;
(b) Not interfere with technology that records and relays information about the use of the material (such as measuring the number of "hits" on particular websites);
(c) Limit access to cached material to subscribers meeting substantially the same conditions (such as registering, subscribing, paying a fee, etc.)

that are required to access the material directly on the original site; and

(d) Promptly remove or disable access to cached material upon receiving a notification of claimed infringement from a copyright owner where the notification also states that the material has been removed or disabled from the original site, or that a court has ordered the material to be removed or disabled from the original site.

3. Storing Material at the Direction of Subscribers

This safe harbor applies on the following conditions :

(a) A service provider must remove or disable access to material if it: (i) has actual knowledge of infringement, (ii) is aware of facts and circumstances that would make infringement apparent, or (iii) receives a notification of claimed infringement from the copyright owner.

(b) A service provider cannot receive any financial benefit directly attributable to the infringing activity (as opposed to charging a flat fee for a subscription) if it has the right and ability to exercise control over the infringing activity.

4. Searching and Location Tools

This safe harbor applies under the following conditions:

(a) A service provider must remove or disable access to material if it :

(i) has actual knowledge of infringement, or

(ii) is aware of facts and circumstances that would make infringement apparent, or

(iii) receives a notification of claimed infringement from the copyright owner.

(b) A service provider cannot receive any financial benefit directly attributable to the infringing activity (such as compensation from the infringing site based on the number of referrals fiom the service provider) if it has the right and ability to exercise control over the infringing activity.

Note : These descriptions do not capture all of the detail of the statute. You should analyze pertinent sections of the Act before deciding whether your business falls into particular categories.

How Do I Appoint An Agent?

The Copyright Office has established an online registry of service provider agents at http.//lscweb. loc.gov/copyright/onlinesp. To see the Copyright Office's home page, go to http://lcweb.loc.gov/copyright. On the home page, there is a suggested form for designation of agents—to get to it directly, go to http.//lcweb.loc.gov/copyright/onlinesp/#agent. You will need to send a $20 check with your designation, and you will have to provide your agent's contact information on your website.

What Do Copyright Holders Need To Do?

Copyright holders need to be active in looking for infringements and should develop a form that complies with the Act for notifying service providers of suspected infringements. That form should:

- Identify the copyright holder;
- Provide contact information;
- Identify the allegedly infringing works;
- Identify the online location of the allegedly infringing works; and
- Provide a statement under penalty of perjury that the person providing the notice has authority

to act on behalf of the copyright holder and has a good-faith belief that there is no legal basis for the use of the materials by the allegedly infringing party.

REFERENCES

1. "A European Initiative on Electronic Commerce". COM(97) 157 final, 16.04.97.
2. Amongst the most recent are the directives on the "regulatory transparency mechanism", the protection of personal data, the protection of consumers in respect of contracts negotiated at a distance; and the proposals on the legal protection of conditional access services, electronic signatures, copyright and related rights and electronic money.
3. European Parliament Resolution A4-0173/98 on the Communication from the Commission on "A European Initiative on Electronic Commerce", 14.05.98.
4. COM (97) 157 final, 16,4.1997. Chapter 3.
5. Resolution on the communication from the Commission to the Council, the European Parliament, the Economic and Social Committee and the Committee of the Regions on "A European initiative in electronic commerce". A4-0173/98.
6. Resolution of 14 April 1998, point 14.
7. Opinion of the Economic and Social Committee on the "Communication from the Commission to the Council, the European Parliament, the Economic and Social Committee and the Committee of the Regions : "A European initiative in electronic commerce", OJ C 19, 21.1.1998, p. 72.
8. See point IV(2).
9. This consists of a questionnaire distributed as an insert in the "Commercial Communications" newsletter sponsored by Directorate General XV which was answered by interested parties. To date some 80 responses have been received.
10. See Case C-43/95 *Data Delecta and Forsberg* [1996] ECR 1-4061.
11. See footnote 3, point 32.
12. OJ 204 of 21.7.98, p. 37 as amended by European Parliament and Council Directive 98/98/EC of 20.7.98 amending Directive

98/34-EC laying down a procedure for the provision of information in the field of technical standards and regulations. OJ 217 of 05.08.1998 p. 18.

13. Common position of the Council on the adoption of Directive 98/... of the European Parliament and of the Council concerning the legal protection of services based on, or consisting of, conditional access.

14. The definition of a service does not require a payment by the recipient. In accordance with the casclaw of the Court of Justice, the concept of a service "normally provided for remuneration" (Article 60 of the Treaty which sets out what is meant by a service) does not make reference to specific means of financing a particular service "Art. 60 does not require the service to be paid for by those for whom it is performed." - case C352/85 para 16) but to the existence of an activity having an "economic character" or of consideration (case C109/92 para 15)

15. It should be noted that the geographical siting of the technology used is not to be taken into account; (the definition of "establishment" does not use criteria related to technology but to economic activity). This information society services using technology in third countries, for example, hosting on a server, are covered if the service provider is established in the Community. Likewise, service providers established in a third country using a server in the Community are not covered by the Directive.

16. OJL 204, 21.7.1998, p. 37, as amended by Directive 98/48/EC; OJ L 217, 5.8.1998, p. 18.

17. Case C-221/89 [1991] ECR 1-3905, paragraph 20.

18. Case C-56/96, [1997] ECR 1-3143, paragraph 19.

19. COM(1998) 121 final, 4.3.1998.

20. Directive 97/13/EC of the European Parliament and of the council of 10 April 1997 on a common framework for general authorisations and individual licences in the field of telecommunications services OJ L 117, 07.05.1997 pp. 0015-0027.

21. OJL 144, 4.6.1997, pp. 19-27.

22. OJL 144, 4.6.1997, pp. 19-27.

23. Proposal for a European Parliament and Council Directive on a common framework for electronic signatures; Communication from the Commission to the European Parliament, the Council, the Economic and Social Committee and the Committee of the Regions; COM(98) 297 final, 13.5.1998.

24. Proposal for a European Parliament and Council Directive on a common framework for electronic signatures; Communication from the Commission to the European Parliament, the Council, the Economic and Social Committee and the Committee of the Regions; COM(98) 297 final, 13.5.1998.

25. *Communication from the Commission to the European Parliament, the Council, the Economic and Social Committee and the Committee of Regions on an Action Plan on promoting safe use of the Internet. Adopted by the Commission on 12 November 1997 (COM 97 (582)).*

    Council Recommendation 98/560 of 24 September 1998 on the development of the competitiveness of the European audio-visual and information services industry by promoting national frameworks aimed at achieving a comparable and effective level of protection of minors and human dignity. OJ L 270 from 7/10/98 pp. 48-55.

26. Recommendation on the development of the competitiveness of the European audio-visual and information services industry by promoting national frameworks aimed at achieving a comparable and effective level of protection of minors and human dignity.

27. OJ L 204, 21.7.1998, p. 37, as amended by Directive 98/48/EC, OJ L 217, 5.8.98 pp. 18-26....

28. OJL 115. 17.4.1998, p. 31.

29. COM(98) 198 final.

30. Some conflict could arise between this latter directive and the present directive on electronic commerce. Given that directive 95/46/EC already guarantees the free circulation of personal data between Member States, it's ambit is excluded from the scope of application of the present directive.

31. COM(1998) 374 final.

32.

33.

34.

35. Case C-56/96, VT4, ECR 1997, pt 19.

36. OJL 144, 04/06/1997 pp. 19-27.

37. OJL 213, 30.07.1998, pp. 0009-0012. E-Commerce : Proposed Legal Framework.

38. OJL 144, 4.6.1997, p. 19.

39. OJL24 of 30.01.1998, pp. 1-8.

40. OJL 19, 24.1.1989, p. 16.

41. Proposal for a European Parliament and Council Directive on a common framework for electronic signatures : Communication from the Commission to the European Parliament, the Council, the Economic and Social Committee and the Committee of regions; COM(1998) 297 final of 13.05.98.
42. OJL 95, 21.4.1993, pp. 29-34.
43. OJL 144, 04/06/1997 pp. 19-27.
44. OJL 80, 18.3.1998, p. 27.
45. OJL 250, 19.9.1984.
46. OJL 158, 23.6.1998, p. 59.
47. OJ L 42, 12.2.1998 as modified by directives 90/88/EEC of 22.2.1990, OJ L 61 10.3.1990 and 98/7/EC of 16.2.1998, OJL 101 1.4.1998.
48. OJL 213, 30.7.1998.
49. OJL 115, 17.4.1998, p. 31.
50. COM (98) 50, 4.2.1998.
51. OJC 188, 22.7.1995, p. 1.
52. COM (95) 162 final.
53. Directive 97/13/EC of the European Parliament and of the Council of 10 April 1997 on a common framework for general authorisations and individual licences in the field of telecommunications services OJ L 117, 07.05.1997 pp. 0015-0027.
54. OJL 166, 11.6.1998, pp. 51-55.
55. Directive of the European Parliament and of the Council of 24.10.1995 on the protection of individuals with regard to the processing of personal data and on the free movement of such data; OJ L28I, 23.11.1995 pp. 31-50.

11 UNCITRAL MODEL LAW ON ELECTRONIC COMMERCE

Resolution adopted by the General Assembly *[on the report of the Sixth Committee (A/51/628)] 51/162 Model Law on Electronic Commerce adopted by the United Nations Commission on International Trade Law*

The General Assembly,

Recalling its resolution 2205 (XXI) of 17 December 1966, by which it created the United Nations Commission on International Trade Law, with a mandate to further the progressive harmonization and unification of the law of international trade and in the respect to bear in mind the interests of all peoples, in particular those of developing countries, in the extensive development of international trade,

Noting that an increasing number of transactions in international trade are carried out by means of electronic data interchange and other means of communication, commonly referred to as "electronic commerce", which involve the use of alternatives to paper-based methods of communication and storage of information,

Recalling the recommendation on the legal value of computer records adopted by the Commission at its eighteenth session, in 1985[1], and paragraph 5(b) of General Assembly resolution 40/71 of 11 December, 1985, in which the Assembly called upon Governments and international organizations to take action, where appropriate, in conformity with the recommendation of the Commission, so as to ensure legal security in the context of the widest possible use of automated data processing in international trade,

Convinced that the establishment of a model law facilitating the use of electronic commerce that is acceptable to States with different legal, social and economic systems, could contribute significantly to the development of harmonious international economic relations,

Noting that the Model Law on Electronic Commerce was adopted by the Commission at its twenty-ninth session after consideration of the observations of Governments and interested organizations,

Believing that the adoption of the Model Law on Electronic Commerce by the Commission will assist all States significantly in enhancing their legislation governing the use of alternatives to paper-based methods of communication and storage of information and in formulating such legislation where none currently exists.

1. *Expresses* its appreciation to the United Nations Commission on International Trade Law for completing and adopting the Model Law on Electronic Commerce contained in the annex to the present resolution and for preparing the Guide to Enactment of the Model Law;

2. *Recommends* that all States give favourable consideration to the Model Law when they enact or revise their laws, in view of the need for uniformity of the law applicable to alternatives to paper-based methods of communication and storage of information;

3. *Recommends* also that all efforts be made to ensure that the Model Law, together with the Guide, become generally known and available. *(85th plenary meeting, 16th December 1996).*

UNCITRAL MODEL LAW ON ELECTRONIC COMMERCE

PART ONE : ELECTRONIC COMMERCE IN GENERAL

CHAPTER I: GENERAL PROVISIONS

Article 1: Sphere of Application[a]

This Law[b] applies to any kind of information in the form of a data message used in the context[c] of commercial[d] activities.

(a) The Commission suggests the following text for States that might wish to limit the applicability of this Law to international data messages:
"This Law applies to a data message as defined in paragraph (1) of article 2 where the data message relates to international commerce."

(b) This Law does not override any rule of law intended for the protection of consumers.

(c) The Commission suggests the following text for States that might wish to extend the applicability of this Law: "This Law applies to any kind of information in the form of a data message, except in the following situations : [***]"

(d) The term "commercial" should be given a wide interpretation so as to cover matters arising from all relationships of a commercial nature, whether contractual or not. Relationships of a commercial nature include, but are not limited to, the following transactions : any trade transaction for the supply or exchange of goods or services; distribution agreement; commercial representation or agency; factoring; leasing; construction of works; consulting; engineering; licensing; investment; financing; banking; insurance; exploitation agreement or concession; joint venture and other forms of industrial or business co-operation; carriage of goods or passengers by air, sea, rail or road.

Article 2: Definitions

For the purposes of this Law :

(a) "Data message" means information generated, sent, received or stored by electronic, optical or similar means including, but not limited to, electronic data interchange (EDI), electronic mail, telegram, telex or telecopy;

(b) "Electronic data interchange (EDI)" means the electronic transfer from computer to computer of information using an agreed standard to structure the information;

(c) "Originator" of a data message means a person by whom, or on whose behalf, the data message purports to have been sent or generated prior to storage, if any, but it does not include a person acting as an intermediary with respect to that data message;

(d) "Addressee" of a data message means a person who is intended by the originator to receive the data message, but does not include a person acting as an intermediary with respect to that data message;

(e) "Intermediary", with respect to a particular data message, means a person who, on behalf of another person, sends, receives or stores that data message or provides other services with respect to that data message;

(f) "Information system" means a system for generating, sending, receiving, storing or otherwise processing data messages.

Article 3: Interpretation

(1) In the interpretation of this Law, regard is to be had to its international origin and to the need to promote

uniformity in its application and the observance of good faith.

(2) Questions concerning matters governed by this Law which are not expressly settled in it are to be settled in conformity with the general principles on which this Law is based.

Article 4: Variation by Agreement

(1) As between parties involved in generating, sending, receiving, storing or otherwise processing data messages, and except as otherwise provided, the provisions of Chapter III may be varied by agreement.

(2) Paragraph (1) does not affect any right that may exist to modify by agreement any rule of law referred to in chapter II.

CHAPTER II: APPLICATION OF LEGAL REQUIREMENTS TO DATA MESSAGES

Article 5: Legal Recognition of Data Messages

Information shall not be denied legal effect, validity or enforceability solely on the grounds that it is in the form of a data message.

Article 5 Bis: Incorporation by Reference

(as adopted by the Commission at its thirty-first session, in June 1998)

Information shall not be denied legal effect, validity or enforceability solely on the grounds that it is not contained in the data message purporting to give rise to such legal effect, but is merely referred to in that data message.

Article 6: Writing

(1) Where the law requires information to be in writing, that requirement is met by a data message if the information contained therein is accessible so as to be usable for subsequent reference.

(2) Paragraph (1) applies whether the requirement therein is in the form of an obligation or whether the law simply provides consequences for the information not being in writing.

(3) The provisions of this article do not apply to the following : [....].

Article 7: Signature

(1) Where the law requires a signature of a person, that requirement is met in relation to a data message if:

(a) a method is used to identify that person and to indicate that person's approval of the information contained in the data message; and

(b) that method is as reliable as was appropriate for the purpose for which the data message was generated or communicated, in the light of all the circumstances, including any relevant agreement.

(2) Paragraph (1) applies whether the requirement therein is in the form of an obligation or whether the law simply provides consequences for the absence of a signature.

(3) The provisions of this article do not apply to the following : [....].

Article 8: Original

(1) Where the law requires information to be presented

or retained in its original form, that requirement is met by a data message if :

(a) there exists a reliable assurance as to the integrity of the information from the time when it was first generated in its final form, as a data message or otherwise; and

(b) where it is required that information be presented, that information is capable of being displayed to the person to whom it is to be presented.

(2) Paragraph (1) applies whether the requirement therein is in the form of an obligation or whether the law simply provides consequences for the information not being presented or retained in its original form.

(3) For the purposes of sub-paragraph *(a)* of paragraph (1) :

(a) the criteria for assessing integrity shall be whether the information has remained complete and unaltered, apart from the addition of any endorsement and any change which arises in the normal course of communication, storage and display; and

(b) the standard of reliability required shall be assessed in the light of the purpose for which the information was generated and in the light of all the relevant circumstances.

(4) The provisions of this articles do not apply to the following : [... .].

Article 9: Admissibility and Evidential Weight of Data Messages

(1) In any legal proceedings, nothing in the application

of the rules of evidence shall apply so as to deny the admissibility of a data message in evidence :

(a) on the sole ground that it is a data message; or,
(b) if it is the best evidence that the person adducing it could reasonably be expected to obtain, on the grounds that it is not in its original form.

(2) Information in the form of a data message shall be given due evidential weight. In assessing the evidential weight of a data message, regard shall be had to the reliability of the manner in which the data message was generated, stored or communicated, to the reliability of manner in which the integrity of the information was maintained, to the manner in which its originator was identified, and to any other relevant factor.

Article 10: Retention of Data Messages

(1) Where the law requires that certain documents, records or information be retained, that requirement is met by retaining data messages, provided that the following conditions satisfied :

(a) the information contained therein is accessible so as to be usable for subsequent reference; and
(b) the data message is retained in the format in which it was generated, sent or received, or in a format which can be demonstrated to represent accurately the information generated, sent or received; and
(c) such information, if any, is retained as enables the identification of the origin and destination of a data message and the date and time when it was sent or received.

(2) An obligation to retain documents, records or information in accordance with paragraph (1) does not extend to any information the sole purpose of which is to enable the message to be sent or received.

(3) A person may satisfy the requirement referred to in paragraph (1) by using the services of any other person, provided that the conditions set forth in sub-paragraphs *(a)*, *(b)*, and *(c)* of paragraph (1) are met.

CHAPTER III: COMMUNICATION OF DATA MESSAGES

Article 11: Formation and Validity of Contracts

(1) In the context of contract formation, unless otherwise agreed by the parties, an offer and the acceptance of an offer may be expressed by means of data messages. Where a data message is used in the formation of a contract, that contract shall not be denied validity or enforceability on the sole ground that a data message was used for that purpose.

(2) The provisions of this article do not apply to the following : [....].

Article 12: Recognition by Parties of Data Messages

(1) As between the originator and the addressee of a data message, a declaration of will or other statement shall not be denied legal effect, validity or enforceability solely, on the grounds that it is in the form of a data message.

(2) The provisions of this article do not apply to the following : [...].

Article 13: Attribution of Data Messages

(1) A data message is that of the originator if it was sent by the originator itself.

(2) As between the originator and the addressee, a data message is deemed to be that of the originator if it was sent:

(a) by a person who had the authority to act on behalf of the originator in respect of that data message; or

(b) by an information system programmed by, or on behalf of, the originator to operate automatically.

(3) As between the originator and the addressee, an addressee is entitled to regard a data message as being that of the originator, and to act on that assumption, if:

(a) in order to ascertain whether the data message was that of the originator, the addressee properly applied a procedure previously agreed to by the originator for that purpose; or

(b) the data message as received by the addressee resulted from the actions of a person whose relationship with the originator or with any agent of the originator enabled that person to gain access to a method used by the originator to identify data messages as its own.

(4) Paragraph (3) does not apply :

(a) as of the time when the addressee has both received notice from the originator that the data message is not that of the originator, and had reasonable time to act accordingly; or

(b) in a case within paragraph (3)(b), at any time when the addressee knew or should have known, had it exercised reasonable care or used any agreed procedure, that the data message was not that of the originator.

(5) Where a data message is that of the originator or is deemed to be that of the originator, or the addressee is entitled to act on that assumption, then, as between the originator and the addressee, the addressee is entitled to regard the data message as received as being what the originator intended to send, and to act on that assumption. The addressee is not so entitled when it knew or should have known, had it exercised reasonable care or used any agreed procedure, that the transmission resulted in any error in the data message as received.

(6) The addressee is entitled to regard each data message received as a separate data message and to act on that assumption, except to the extent that it duplicates another data message and the addressee knew or should have known, had it exercised reasonable care or used any agreed procedure, that the data message was a duplicate.

Article 14: Acknowledgement of Receipt

(1) Paragraphs (2) to (4) of this article apply where, on or before sending a data message, or by means of that data message, the originator has requested or has agreed with the addressee that receipt of the data message be acknowledged.

(2) Where the originator has not agreed with the addressee that the acknowledgement be given in a particular form or by a particular method, an acknowledgement may be given by

(a) any communication by the addressee, automated or otherwise, or

(b) any conduct of the addressee, sufficient to indicate to the originator that the data message has been received.

(3) Where the originator has stated that the data message is conditional on receipt of the acknowledgement, the data message is treated as though it has never been sent, until the acknowledgement is received.

(4) Where the originator has not stated that the data message is conditional on receipt of the acknowledgement, and the acknowledgement has not been received by the originator within the time specified or agreed or, if no time has been specified or agreed, within a reasonable time, the originator :

(a) may give notice to the addressee stating that no acknowledgement has been received and specifying a reasonable time by which the acknowledgement must be received; and

(b) if the acknowledgement is not received within the time specified in sub-paragraph fa), may, upon notice to the addressee, treat the data message as though it had never been sent, or exercise any other rights it may have.

(5) Where the originator receives the addressee's acknowledgement of receipt, it is presumed that the related data message was received by the addressee. That presumption does not imply that the data message corresponds to the message received.

(6) Where the received acknowledgement states that the related data message met technical requirements, either

agreed upon or set forth in applicable standards, it is presumed that those requirements have been met.

(7) Except in so far as it relates to the sending or receipt of the data message, this article is not intended to deal with the legal consequences that may flow either from that data message or from the acknowledgement of its receipt.

Article 15: Time and Place of Dispatch and Receipt of Data Messages

(1) Unless otherwise agreed between the originator and the addressee, the dispatch of a data message occurs when it enters an information system outside the control of the originator or of the person who sent the data message on behalf of the originator.

(2) Unless otherwise agreed between the originator and the addressee, the time of receipt of a data message is determined as follows :

(a) if the addressee has designated an information system for the purpose of receiving data messages, receipt occurs:

   (i) at the time when the data message enters the designated information system; or

   (ii) if the data message is sent to an information system of the addressee that is not the designated information system, at the time when the data message is retrieved by the addressee;

(b) if the addressee has not designated an information system, receipt occurs when the data message enters an information system of the addressee.

(3) Paragraph (2) applies notwithstanding that the place where the information system is located may be different from the place where the data message is deemed to be received under paragraph (4).

(4) Unless otherwise agreed between the originator and the addressee, a data message is deemed to be dispatched at the place where the originator has its place of business, and is deemed to be received at the place where the addressee has its place of business. For the purposes of this paragraph:

(a) if the originator or the addressee has more than one place of business, the place of business is that which has the closest relationship to the underlying transaction or, where there is no underlying transaction, the principal place of business;

(b) if the originator or the addressee does not have a place of business, reference is to be made to its habitual residence.

(5) The provisions of this article do not apply to the following : [. ...].

PART TWO : ELECTRONIC COMMERCE IN SPECIFIC AREAS

CHAPTER 1 : CARRIAGE OF GOODS

Article 16: Actions Related to Contracts of Carriage of Goods

Without derogating from the provisions of part one of this Law, this Chapter applies to any action in connection with, or in pursuance of, a contract of carriage of goods, including but not limited to :

(a) (i) furnishing the marks, number, quantity or weight of goods;
(ii) stating or declaring the nature or value of goods;
(iii) issuing a receipt for goods;
(iv) confirming that goods have been loaded;

(b) (i) notifying a person of terms and conditions of the contract;
(ii) giving instructions to a carrier;

(c) (i) claiming delivery of goods;
(ii) authorizing release of goods;
(iii) giving notice of loss of, or damage to, goods;

(d) giving any other notice or statement in connection with the performance of the contract;

(e) undertaking to deliver goods to a named person or a person authorized to claim delivery;

(f) granting, acquiring, renouncing, surrendering, transferring or negotiating rights in goods;

(g) acquiring or transferring rights and obligations under the contract.

Article 17: Transport Documents

(1) Subject to paragraph (3), where the law requires that any action referred to in article 16 be carried out in writing or by using a paper document, that requirement is met if the action is carried out by using one or more data messages.

(2) Paragraph (1) applies whether the requirement therein is in the form of an obligation or whether the law simply provides consequences for failing either to carry out the action in writing or to use a paper document.

(3) If a right is to be granted, or an obligation is to be acquired by, one person and no other person, and if the law requires that, in order to effect this, the right or obligation must be conveyed to that person by the transfer, or use of, a paper document, that requirement is met if the right or obligation is conveyed by using one or more data messages, provided that a reliable method is used to render such data message or messages unique.

(4) For the purposes of paragraph (3), the standard of reliability required shall be assessed in the light of the purpose for which the right or obligation was conveyed and in the light of all the circumstances, including any relevant agreement.

(5) Where one or more data messages are used to effect any action in sub-paragraphs (f) and (g) of article 16, no paper document used to effect any such action is valid unless the use of data messages has been terminated and replaced by the use of paper documents. A paper document issued in these circumstances shall contain a statement of such termination. The replacement of data messages by paper documents shall not affect the rights or obligations of the parties involved.

(6) If a rule of law is compulsorily applicable to a contract of carriage of goods which is in, or is evidenced by, a paper document, that rule shall not be inapplicable to such a contract of carriage of goods which is evidenced by one or more data messages by reason of the fact that the contract is evidenced by such data message or messages instead of by a paper document.

(7) The provisions of this article do not apply to the following :[....].

GUIDE TO ENACTMENT OF THE UNCITRA.L MODEL LAW ON ELECTRONIC COMMERCE (1996)

Purpose of this Guide

1. In preparing and adopting the UNCITRAL Model Law On Electronic Commerce (hereinafter referred to as "the Model Law"), the United Nations Commission on International Trade Law (UNCITRAL) was mindful that the Model Law would be a more effective tool for States modernizing their legislation if background and explanatory information would be provided to executive branches of Governments and legislators to assist them in using the Model Law. The Commission was also aware of the likelihood that the Model Law would be used in a number of States with limited familiarity with the type of communication techniques considered in the Model Law. This Guide, much of which is drawn from the trayaux preparatories of the Model Law is also intended to be helpful to users of electronic means 'of communication as well as to scholars in that area. In the preparation of the Model Law, it was assumed that the draft Model Law would be accompanied by such a guide. For example, it was decided in respect of a number of issues not to settle them in the draft Model Law but to address them in the Guide so as to provide guidance to States enacting the draft Model Law. The information presented in this Guide is intended to explain why the provisions in the Model Law have been included as essential basic features of a statutory device designed to achieve-the objectives of the Model Law. Such information might assist States also in considering which, if any, of the provisions of the Model Law might have to be varied to take into account particular national circumstances.

I. INTRODUCTION TO THE MODEL LAW

A. Objectives

2. The use of modern means of communication such as electronic mail and electronic data interchange (EDI) for the conduct of international trade transactions has been increasing rapidly and is expected to develop further as technical supports such as information highways and the INTERNET become more widely accessible. However, the communication of legally significant information in the form of paperless messages may be hindered by legal obstacles to the use of such messages, or by uncertainty as to their legal effect or validity. The purpose of the Model Law is to offer national legislators a set of internationally acceptable rules as to how a number of such legal obstacles may be removed, and how a more secure legal environment may be created for what has become known as "electronic commerce". The principles expressed in the Model Law are also intended to be of use to individual users of electronic commerce in the drafting of some of the contractual solutions that might be needed to overcome the legal obstacles to the increased use of the electronic commerce.

3. The decision by UNCITRAL to formulate model legislation on electronic commerce was taken in response to the fact that in a number of countries the existing legislation governing communication and storage of information is inadequate or outdated because it does not contemplate the use of electronic commerce. In certain cases, existing legislation imposes or implies restrictions on the use of modern means of communication, for example by prescribing the use of "written", "signed" or "original" documents. While a few countries have adopted specific provisions to deal with certain aspects of electronic commerce, there exists no legislation dealing with electronic commerce as a whole. This may result in uncertainty as to

the legal nature and validity of information presented in a form other than a traditional paper document. Moreover, while sound laws and practices are necessary in all countries where the use of EDI and electronic mail is becoming widespread, this need is also felt in many countries with respect to such communication techniques as telecopy and telex.

4. The Model Law may also help to remedy disadvantages that stem from the fact that inadequate legislation at the national level creates obstacles to international trade, a significant amount of which is linked to the use of modern communication techniques. Disparities among, and uncertainty about, national legal regimes governing the use of such communication techniques may contribute to limiting the extent to which businesses may access international markets.

5. Furthermore, at an international level, the Model Law may be useful in certain cases as a tool for interpreting existing international conventions and other international instruments that create legal obstacles to the use of electronic commerce, for example by prescribing that certain documents or contractual clauses be made in written form. As between those States parties to such international instruments, the adoption of the Model Law as a rule of Interpretation might provide the means to recognise the use of electronic commerce and obviate the need to negotiate a protocol to the international instrument involved.

6. The objectives of the Model Law, which include enabling or facilitating the use of electronic commerce and providing equal treatment to users of paper-based documentation and to users of computer-based information, are essential for fostering economy and efficiency in international trade. By incorporating the procedures

prescribed in the Model Law in its national legislation for those situations where parties opt to use electronic means of communication, an enacting State would create a media-neutral environment.

B. Scope

7. The title of the Model Law refers to "electronic commerce". While a definition of "electronic data interchange (EDI)" is provided in article 2, the Model Law, does not specify the meaning of "electronic commerce". In preparing the Model Law, the Commission decided that, in addressing the subject matter before it, it would have in mind a broad notion of EDI, covering a variety of trade-related uses of EDI that might be referred to broadly under the rubric of "electronic commerce" (see A/CN.9/360, paras 28-29), although other descriptive terms could also be used. Among the means of communication encompassed in the notion of "electronic commerce" are the following modes of transmission based on the use of electronic techniques : communication by means of EDI defined narrowly as the computer-to-computer transmission of data in a standardized format; transmission of electronic messages involving the use of either publicly available standards or proprietary standards; transmission of free-formatted text by electronic means, for example through the INTERNET. It was also noted that, in certain circumstances, the notion of "electronic commerce" might cover the use of techniques such as telex and telecopy.

8. It should be noted that, while the Model Law was drafted with constant reference to the more modem communication techniques, e.g., EDI and electronic mail, the principles on which the Model Law is based, as well as its provisions, are intended to apply also in the context of less advanced communication techniques, such as telecopy.

There may exist situations where digitalized information initially dispatched in the form of a standardized EDI message might, at some point in the communication chain between the sender and the recipient, be forwarded in the form of a computer-generated telex or in the form of a telecopy of a computer print-out. A data message may be initiated as an oral communication and end up in the form of a telecopy, or it may start as a telecopy and end up as an EDI message. A characteristic of electronic commerce is that it covers programmable messages, the computer programming of which is the essential difference between such messages and traditional paper based documents. Such situations are intended to be covered by the Model Law, based on a consideration of the users' need for a consistent set of rules to govern a variety of communication techniques that might be used interchangeably. More generally, it may be noted that, as a matter of principle, no communication technique is excluded from the scope of the Model Law since future technical developments need to be accommodated.

9. The objective of the Model Law are best served by the widest possible application of the Model Law. Thus, although there is provision made in the Model Law for exclusion of certain situations from the scope of the articles, 6, 7, 8, 11, 12, 15 and 17, an enacting State may well decide not to enact in its legislation substantial restrictions on the scope of application of the Model law.

10. The Model law should be regarded as a balanced and discrete set of rules, which are recommended to be enacted as a single statute. Depending on the situation in each enacting State, however, the Model Law could be implemented in various ways, either as a single statute or in several pieces of legislation (see below, para 143).

C. Structure

11. The Model Law is divided into two parts, one dealing with electronic commerce in general and the other one dealing with electronic commerce in specific areas. It should be noted that part two of the Model Law, which deals with electronic commerce in specific areas, is composed of a Chapter I only, dealing with electronic commerce as it applies to the carriage of goods. Other aspects of electronic commerce might need to be dealt with in the future, and the Model Law can be regarded as an open-ended instrument, to be complemented by future work.

12. UNCITRAL intends to continue monitoring the technical, legal and commercial developments that underline the Model Law. It might, should it regard it advisable, decide to add new model provisions to the Model Law or modify the existing ones.

D. A "Framework" Law to be Supplemented by Technical Regulations

13. The Model Law is intended to provide essential procedures and principles for facilitating the use of modern techniques for recording and communicating information in various types of circumstances. However, it is a "framework" law that does not itself set forth all the rules and regulations that may be necessary to implement those techniques in an enacting State. Moreover, the Model Law is not intended to cover every aspect of the use of electronic, commerce. Accordingly, an enacting State may wish to issue regulations to fill in the procedural details for procedures authorized by the Model Law and to take account of the specific, possibly changing, circumstances at play in the enacting State, without compromising the objectives of the Model Law. It is recommended that, should it decide to issue such regulation, an enacting State should give particular attention to the need to maintain

the beneficial flexibility of the provisions in the Model Law.

14. It should be noted that the techniques for recording and communicating information considered in the Model Law, beyond raising matters of procedure that may need to be addressed in the implementing technical regulations, may raise certain legal questions the answers to which will not necessarily be found in the Model Law, but rather in other bodies of law. Such other bodies of law may include, for example, the applicable administrative, contract, criminal and judicial-procedure law, which the Model Law is not intended to deal with.

E. The "Functional-Equivalent" Approach

15. The Model Law is based on the recognition that legal requirements prescribing the use of the traditional paper-based documentation constitute the main obstacle to the development of modern means of communication. In the preparation of the Model Law, consideration was given to the possibility of dealing with impediments to the use of the electronic commerce posed by such requirements in national laws by way of an extension of the scope of such notions as "writing", "signature" and "original", with a view to encompassing computer-based techniques. Such an approach is used in a number of existing legal instruments, e.g., article 7 of the UNCITRAL Model Law on International Commercial Arbitration and article 13 of the United

Nations Convention on Contracts for the International Sale of Goods. It was observed that the Model Law should permit States to adapt their domestic legislation to developments in communications, technology applicable to trade law without necessitating the wholesale removal of the paper-based requirements themselves or disturbing the legal concepts and approaches underlying those requirements. At the same time, it was said that the electronic fulfillment of writing requirements might in some cases necessitate the development of new rules. This was due to one of many distinctions between EDI messages and paper-based documents, namely, that the-latter were readable by the human eye, while the former were not so readable unless reduced to paper or displayed on a screen.

16. The Model Law, thus relies on a new approach, sometimes referred to as the "functional equivalent approach", which is based on an analysis of the purposes and functions of the traditional paper-based requirement with a view to determining how those purposes or functions could be fulfilled through electronic-commerce techniques. For example, among the functions served by a paper document are the following : to provide that a document would be legible by all; to provide that a document would remain unaltered over time; to allow for the reproduction of a document so that each party would hold a copy of the same data; to allow for the authentication of data by means of a signature; and to provide that a document would be in a form acceptable to public authorities and courts. It should be noted that in respect of all the above-mentioned functions of a paper, electronic records can provide the same level of security as paper and, in most cases, a much higher degree of reliability and speed, especially with respect to the identification of the source and content of the data, provided that a number of technical and legal requirements are met. However, the adoption of the functional-equivalent approach should not result in imposing on users of electronic commerce more stringent standards of security (and the related costs) than in a paper-based environment.

17. A data message, in and of itself, cannot be regarded as an equivalent of a paper document in that it is of a

different nature and does not necessarily perform all conceivable functions of a paper document. That is why the Model Law adopted a flexible standard, taking into account the various layers of existing requirements in a paper based environment : when adopting the "functional-equivalent" approach, attention was given to the existing hierarchy of form requirements, which provides distinct levels of reliability, traceability and unalterability with respect to paper-based documents. For example, the requirement that data be presented in written form (which constitutes a "threshold requirement") is not to be confused with more stringent requirements such as "signed writing", "signed original" or "authenticated legal act".

18. The Model Law does not attempt to define a computer-based equivalent to any kind of paper document. Instead, it singles out basic functions of paper-based form requirements, with a view to providing criteria which, once they are met by data messages, enable such data messages to enjoy the same level of legal recognition as corresponding paper documents performing the same function. It should be noted that the functional-equivalent approach has been taken in articles 6 to 8 of the Model law with respect to the concepts of "writing", "signature" and "original" but not with respect to other legal concepts dealt with in the Model Law. For example, article 10 does not attempt to create a functional equivalent of existing storage requirements.

F. Default Rules and Mandatory Law

19. The decision to undertake the preparation of the Model Law was based on the recognition that, in practice, solutions to most of the legal difficulties raised by the use of modern means of communication are sought within contracts. The Model Law embodies the principle of party autonomy in article 4 with respect to the provisions contained

in Chapter III of part one. Chapter III of part one contains a set of rules of the kind that would typically be found in agreements between parties, e.g., interchange agreements or "system rules". It should be noted that the notion of "system rules" might cover two different categories of rules, namely, general terms provided by communication networks and specific rules that might be included in those general terms to deal with bilateral relationships between originators and addresses of data messages. Article 4 (and the notion of "agreement" therein) is intended to encompass both categories of "system rules".

20. The rules contained in Chapter III of part one may be used by parties as a basis for concluding such agreements. They may also be used to supplement the terms of agreements in cases of gaps or omissions in contractual stipulations. In addition, they may be regarded as setting a basic standard for situations where data messages are exchanged without a previous agreement being entered into by the communicating parties, e.g., in the context of open-networks communications.

21. The provisions contained in Chapter II of part one are of a different nature. One of the main purposes of the Model Law is to facilitate the use of modern communication techniques and to provide certainty with the use of such techniques where obstacles or uncertainty resulting from statutory provisions could not be avoided by contractual stipulations. The provisions contained in Chapter II, may, to some extent, be regarded as a collection of exceptions to well-established rules regarding the form of legal transactions. Such well-established rules are normally of a mandatory nature since they generally reflect decisions of public policy. The provisions contained in Chapter II should be regarded as stating the minimum acceptable form requirement and are, for that reason, of a mandatory mature,

unless expressly stated otherwise in those provisions. The indication that such form requirements are to be regarded as the "minimum acceptable" should not, however, be construed as inviting States to establish requirements stricter than those contained in the Model Law.

G. Assistance from UNCITRAL Secretariat

22. In line with its training and assistance activities, the UNCITRAL secretariat may provide technical consultations for Governments preparing legislation based on the UNCITRAL Model Law on Electronic Commerce, as it may for Governments considering legislation based on other UNCITRAL model laws, or considering adhesion to one of the international trade law conventions prepared by UNCITRAL.

23. Further information concerning the Model Law as well as the Guide and other model laws and conventions developed by UNCITRAL, may be obtained from the secretariat. The secretariat welcomes comments concerning the Model Law and the Guide, as well as information concerning enactment of legislation based on the Model Law.

II. ARTICLE-BY-ARTICLE REMARKS PART ONE : ELECTRONIC COMMERCE IN GENERAL

CHAPTER I. GENERAL PROVISIONS

Article 1: Sphere of Application

24. The purpose of article 1, which is to be read in conjunction with the definition of "data message" in article 2(a), is to delineate the scope of application of the Model Law. The approach used in the Model Law is to provide in principal for the coverage of all factual situations where information is generated, stored or communicated,

irrespective of the medium on which such information may be affixed. It was felt during the preparation of the Model Law that exclusion of any form or medium by way of a limitation in the scope of the Model Law might result in practical difficulties and would run counter to the purpose of providing truly "media-neutral" rules. However, the focus of the Model Law is on "paperless" means of communication and, except to the extent expressly provided by the Model Law, the is not intended to alter traditional rules on paper-based communications.

25. Moreover, it was felt that the Model Law should contain an indication that its focus was on the types of situations encountered in the commercial area and that it had been prepared against the background of trade relationships. For that reason, article 1 refers to "commercial activities" and provides, in footnote***, indications as to what is meant thereby. Such indications, which may be particularly useful for those countries where there docs not exist a discrete body of commercial law, are modelled, for reasons of consistency, on the footnote to article 1 of the UNCITRAL Model Law on International Commercial Arbitration. In certain countries, the use of footnotes in a statutory text would not be regarded as acceptable legislative practice. National authorities enacting the Model Law might thus consider the possible inclusion of the text of footnotes, in the body of the Law itself.

26. The Model Law applies to all kinds of data messages that might be generated, stored or communicated, and nothing in the Model Law should prevent an enacting State from extending the scope of the Model Law to cover uses of electronic commerce outside the commercial sphere. For example, while the focus of the Model Law is not on the relationships between users of electronic commerce and public authorities, the Model Law is not intended to be inapplicable to such relationships. Footnote*** provides

for alternative wordings, for possible use by enacting States that would consider it appropriate to extend the scope of, the Model Law beyond the commercial sphere.

27. Some countries have special consumer protection laws that may govern certain aspects of the use of information systems. With respect to such consumer legislation, as was the case with previous UNCITRAL instruments (e.g., the UNCITRAL Model Law on Internationals Credit Transfers), it was felt that an indication should be given that the Model Law had been drafted without special attention being given to issues that might arise in the context of consumer protection. At the same time, it was felt that there was no reason why situations involving consumers should be excluded from the scope of the Model Law by way of a general provision particularly since the provisions of the Model Law might be found appropriate for consumer protection, depending on legislation in each enacting State. Footnote** thus recognizes that any such consumer protection law may take precedence over the provisions in the Model Legislators may wish to consider whether the piece of legislation enacting the Model Law should apply to consumers. The question of which individuals or corporate bodies would be regarded as "consumers" is left to applicable law outside the Model Law.

28. Another possible limitation of the scope of the Model Law is contained in the first footnote! In principal, the Model Law applies to both international and domestic uses of the data messages. Footnote* is intended for use by enacting States that might wish to limit applicability of the Model Law to international cases. It indicates a possible test internationality for use by those States as possible criterion for distinguishing international cases from domestic ones. It should be noted, however, that in some jurisdictions particularly in federal States, considerable difficulties might

arise in distinguishing international trade from domestic trade. The Model Law should not be interpreted as encouraging enacting States to limit its applicability to international cases.

29. It is recommended that application of the Model Law be made as wide as possible. Particular caution should be used in excluding the application of the Model Law by way of limitation of its scope of international uses of data messages, since such a limitation may be seen as not fully achieving the objectives of the Model Law. Furthermore, the variety of procedures available under the Mode Law (particularly articles 6 to 8) to limit the use of data messages if necessary (e.g., for purposes of public policy) may make it less necessary to limit the scope of the Model Law. As the Model Law contains a number of articles (articles 6, 7, 8, 11, 12, 15 and 17) that allow a degree of flexibility to enacting States to limit the scope of application of specific aspects of the Model Law, a narrowing of the scope of application of the text to international trade should not be necessary. Moreover, dividing communications in international trade into purely domestic and international parts might be difficult in practice. The legal certainty to be provided by the Model Law is necessary for both domestic and international trade, and a duality of regimes governing the use of electronic means of recording and communication of data might create a serious obstacle to the use of such means.

References[2]

A/50/17, paras 213-219;

A/CN. 9/407, paras 3 7-40;

A/CN.9/406, paras 80-85; A/CN.9/WG.IV/WP.62, article 1;

A/CN.9/390, paras 21-43; A/CN.9/WG.IV/WP.60, article 1;

A/CN.9/387, paras 15-28; A/CN.9/WG.IV/WP.57, article 1;

A/CN.9/373, paras 21-25 and 29-3; A/CN.9/WG.IV/WP.55, paras 15-20.

Article 2: Definitions

"Data Message"

30. The notion of "data message" is not limited to communication but is also intended to incompass computer-generated records that are not intended for communication. Thus, the notion of "message" includes the notion of "record". However, a definition of "record" in line with the characteristic elements of "writing" in article 6 may be added in jurisdictions where that ; would appear to be necessary.

31. The reference to "similar means" is intended to reflect the fact that the Model Law was not intended only for application in the context of existing communication techniques but also to accommodate foreseeable technical developments. The aim of the definition of "data message" is to encompass all types of messages that are generated, stored, or communicated in essentially paperless form. For that purpose, all means of communication and storage of information that might be used to perform functions parallel to the functions performed by the means listed in the definition are intended to be covered by the reference to "similar means", although for example, "electronic" and "optical" means of communication might not be, strictly speaking, similar. For the purposes of the Model Law, the word "similar" connotes "functionally equivalent".

32. The definition of "data message" is also intended to cover the case of revocation or amendment. A data message is presumed to have a fixed information content but it may be revoked or amended by another data message.

"Electronic Data Interchange (EDI)"

The definition of EDI is drawn from the definition adopted by the Working Party on Facilitation of International Trade Procedures (WP.4) of the Economic Commission for

Europe which is the United Nations body responsible for the development of UN/EDIFACT technical standards.

34. The Model Law does not settle the question whether the definition of EDI necessarily implies that EDI messages are communicated electronically from computer to computer, of an whether that definition, while primarily covering situations where data messages are communicated through a telecommunications system, would also cover exceptional or incidental types of situation where data structured in the form of an EDI message would be communicated by means that do not involve telecommunications systems, for example, the case where magnetic disks containing EDI messages would be delivered to the addressee by courier. However, irrespective of whether digital data transferred manually is covered by the definition of "EDI", it should be regarded as covered by the definition of "data message" under the Model Law.

"Originator" and "Addressee"

35. In most legal systems, the notion of "person" is used to designate the subjects of rights and obligations and should be interpreted as covering both natural persons and corporate bodies or other legal entities. Data messages that are generated automatically by computers without direct human intervention are intended to be covered by sub-paragraph *(c)*. However, the Model should not be misinterpreted as allowing for a computer to be made the subject of rights obligations. Data messages that are generated automatically by computers without direct human intervention should be regarded as "originating" from the legal entity on behalf of which computer is operated. Questions relevant to agency that might arise in that context are to settled under rules outside the Model Law.

36. The "addressee" under the Model Law is the person with whom th originator intends to communicate by

transmitting the data message, as opposed to any person who might receive, forward or copy the data message in the course of transmission. The "originator" is the person who generated the data message even if that message was transmitted by another person. The definition of "addressee" contrasts with the definition of "originator" which is not focused on intent. It should be noted that, under the definitions of "originator" and "addressee" in the Model Law, the originator and the addressee of a given data message could be the same person, for example in the case where the data message was intended for storage by its author. However, the addressee who stores a message transmitted by an originator is not itself intended to be covered by the definition of "originator".

37. The definition of "originator" should cover not only the situation where information is generated and communicated, but also the situation where such information is generated and stored without being communicated. However, the definition of "originator" is intended to eliminate the possibility that a recipient who merely stores a data message might be regarded as an originator.

"Intermediary"

38. The focus of the Model Law is on the relationship between the originator and the addressee, and not on the relationship between either the originator or the addressee and any intermediary. However, the Model Law does not ignore the paramount importance of intermediaries in the field of electronic communications. In addition; the notion of "intermediary" is needed in the Model Law to establish the necessary distinction between originators or addressees and third parties.

39. The definition of "intermediary" is intended to cover both professional and non-professional intermediaries, *i.e.*, any person (other than the originator and the addressee)

who performs any of the functions of an intermediary. The main functions of an intermediary are listed in subparagraph *(e)*, namely receiving, transmitting or storing data messages on behalf of another person. Additional "value-added services" may be performed by network operators and other intermediaries, such as formatting, translating, recording, authenticating, certifying and preserving data messages and providing security services for electronic transactions. "Intermediary" under the Model Law is defined not as a generic category but with respect to each data message, thus recognizing that the same person could be the originator or addressee of one data message and an intermediary with respect to another data message. The Model Law, which is focused on the relationships between originators and addressees, does not, in general, deal with the rights and obligations of intermediaries.

"Information System"

40. The definition of "information system" is intended to cover the entire range of technical means used for transmitting, receiving and storing information. For example, depending on the factual situation, the notion of "information system" could be indicating a communications network, and in other instances could include an electronic mailbox or even a telecopier. The Model Law does not address the question of whether the information system is located on the premises of the addressee or on other premises, since location of information systems is not an operative criterion under the Model Law.

References

A/51/17, paras. 116-138;

A/CN.9/407, paras. 41-52;

A/CN.9/406, paras. 132-156; A/CN.9/WG.IV/WP.62, article 2;

A/CN.9/390, paras. 44-65; A/CN.9/WG.IV/WP.60, article 2;

A/CN.9/387, paras. 29-52; A/CN.9/WG.IV/WP.57, article 2;

A/CN.9/373, paras. 11-20, 26-28 and 35-36; A/CN.9/WG.IV/WP.55, paras. 23-26;

A/CN.9/360, paras. 29-31; A/CN.9/WG.IV/WP.53, paras. 25-33.

Article 3: Interpretation

41. Article 3 is inspired by article 7 of the Contract for the International Sale of Goods. It is intended to provide guidance for interpretation of the Model Law by courts and other national or local authorities. The expected effect of article 3 is to limit the extent to which a uniform text, once incorporated in local legislation, would be interpreted only by reference to the concepts of local law.

42. The purpose of paragraph (1) is to draw the attention of courts and other national authorities to the fact that the provisions of the Model Law (or the provisions of the instrument implementing the Model Law), while enacted as part of domestic legislation and therefore domestic in character, should be interpreted with reference to its international origin in order to ensure uniformity in the interpretation of the Model Law in various countries.

43. As to the general principles on which the Model Law is based, the following non-exhaustive list may be considered : (1) to facilitate electronic commerce among and within nations; (2) to validate transactions entered into by means of new information technologies; (3) to promote and encourage the implementation of new information technologies; (4) to promote the uniformity of law; and (5) to support commercial practice. While the general purpose of the Model Law is 10 facilitate the use of electronic means of communication, it should not be construed in any way as imposing their use.

References

A/50/17, paras. 220-224;

A/CN.9/407, paras. 53-54;
A/CN.9/406, paras. 86-87; A/CN.9/WG.IV/WP.62, article 3;
A/CN.9/390, paras. 66-73; A/CN.9/WG.IV/WP.60, article 3;
A/CN.9/387, paras. 53-58; A/CN.9/WG.IV/WP.57, article 3;
A/CN.9/373, paras. 38-42; A/CN.9/WG.IV/WP.55, paras. 30-31.

Article 4: Variation by Agreement

44. The decision to undertake the preparation of the Model Law was based on the recognition that, in practice, solutions to the legal difficulties raised by the use of modern means of communication are mostly sought within contracts. The Model Law is thus intended to support the principle of party autonomy. However, that principle is embodied only with respect to the provisions of the Model Law contained in Chapter III of part one. The reason for such a limitation is that the provisions contained in Chapter IJ of part one may, to some extent, be regarded as a collection of exceptions to well-established rules regarding the form of legal transactions. Such well-established rules are normally of a mandatory nature since they generally reflect decisions of public policy. An unqualified statement regarding the freedom of parties to derogate from the Model Law might thus be misinterpreted as allowing parties, through a derogation to the Model Law, to derogate from mandatory rules adopted for reasons of public policy. The provisions contained in Chapter IJ of part one should be regarded as stating the minimum acceptable form requirement and are, for that reason, to be regarded as mandatory, unless expressly stated otherwise. The indication that such form requirements are to be regarded as the "minimum acceptable" should not, however, be construed as inviting States to establish requirements stricter than those contained in the Model Law.

45. Article 4 is intended to apply not only in the

context of relationships between originators and addressees of data messages but also in the context of relationships involving intermediaries. Thus, the provisions of Chapter III of part one could be varied either by bilateral or multilateral agreements between the parties, or by system rules agreed to by the parties. However, the text expressly limits party autonomy to rights and obligations arising as between parties so as not to suggest any implication as to the rights and obligations of third parties.

References

A/51/17, paras. 68, 90 to 93, 110, 137, 188 and 207 (article 10);

A.50/17, paras. 271-274 (article 10);

A/CN.9/407, para. 85;

A/CN.9/406, paras. 88-89; A/CN.9/WG.IV/WP.62, article 5;

A/CN.9/390, paras. 74-78; A/CN.9/WG.IV/WP.60, article 5;

A/CN.9/387, paras. 62-65; A/CN.9/WG.IV/WP.57, article 5;

A/CN.9/373, para. 37; A/CN.9/WG.IV/WP.55, paras. 27-29.

CHAPTER II. APPLICATION OF LEGAL REQUIREMENTS TO DATA MESSAGES

Article 5: Legal Recognition of Data Messages

46. Article 5 embodies the fundamental principle that data messages should not be discriminated against, i.e., that there should be no disparity of treatment between data messages and paper departments. It is intended to apply notwithstanding any statutory requirements for a "writing" or original. That fundamental principle is intended to find general application and its scope would not be limited to evidence or other matters covered in Chapter II. It should be noted, however, that such a principle is not intended to override any of the requirements contained in Articles 6 to 10. By stating that "information shall not be denied legal effectiveness, validity or errceability solely on

the grounds that it is in the foorm of data message, article 5 merely indicates that the form in which certain information is presented or retained cannot be used as the only reason for which that information would be denied legal effectiveness, validity or errceability. However, article 5 should not be misinterpreted as establishing the legal validity of any given data message or of any information contained therein.

References

A/51/17, paras. 92 to 97 (article 4);

A.50/17, paras. 225-227 (article 4);

A/CN.9/407, para. 55;

A/CN.9/406, paras. 91-94; A/CN.9/WG.IV/WP.62, article 5; *bis;*

A/CN.9/390, paras. 79-87;

A/CN.9/387, paras. 93-94.

Article 5 Bis.: Incorporation by Reference

46.1 Article 5 *bis* was adopted by the Commission at its thirty-first session, in June 1998. It is tended to provide guidance as to how legislation aimed at facilitating the use of electronic commerce might deal with the situation where certain terms and conditions, although not stated in full but merely referred to in a data message, might need to be recognised as having the same degree of legal effectiveness as if they had been fully stated in the text of that data message. Such recognition is acceptable under the laws of many States with respect to conventional paper communications, usually with some rules of law providing safeguards, for example rules on consumer protection. The expression "incorporation by reference" is of then used as a concise means of describing situations where a document refers generically to provisions which are detailed elsewhere, rather than reproducing them in full.

46.2 In an electronic environment, incorporation by reference is often regarded as essential to widespread use of electronic data interchange (EDI), electronic mail, digital certificates and other foorm of electronic commerce. For example, electronic communications are typically structured in such a way that large numbers of messages are exchanged, with each message containing brief information, and relying much more frequently than paper document on reference to information accessible elsewhere. In electronic communications, practitioners should not have imposed upon them an obligation to overload their data messages with quantities of free text when they can take advantage of extrinsic sources of information, such as databases, code lists or glossaries, by making use of abbreviations, codes and other references to such information.

46.3 Standards for incorporating data messages by reference into other data messages may also be be essential to the use of public key certificates, because these certificates are generally brief records with rigidly prescribed contents that are finite in size. The trusted third party which issues the certificate, however, is likely to require the inclusion of relevant contractual terms limiting its liability. The scope, purpose and effect of a certificate in commercial practice, therefore, would be ambiguous and uncertain without external terms being incorporated by reference. This is the case especially in the context of international communications involving diverse parties who follow varied trade practices and customs.

46.4 The establishment of standards for incorporating data messages by reference into other data messages is critical to the growth of a computer-based trade infrastructure. Without the legal certainty fostered by such standards, there might be a significant risk that the application of traditional tests for determining the enforceability of terms that seek to be incorporated by reference might be ineffective when applied to corresponding electronic commerce terms because of the differences between traditional and electronic commerce mechanisms.

46.5 While electronic commerce relics heavily on the mechanism of incorporation by reference, the accessibility of the full, text of the information being referred to may be considerably improved by the use of electronic communications. For example, a message may have embedded in it uniform resource locators (URLs), which direct the reader to the referenced document. Such URLs can provide "hypertext links" allowing the reader to use a pointing device (such as a mouse) to select a key word associated with a URL. The referenced text would then be displayed. In assessing the accessibility of the referenced text, factors to be considered may include : availability (hours of operation of the repository and ease of access); cost of access; integrity (verification of content, authentication of sender, and mechanism for communication error correction); and the extent to which that term is subject to later amendment (notice of updates; notice of policy of amendment).

46.6 One aim of article *5 bis* is to facilitate incorporation by reference in an electronic context by removing the uncertainty prevailing in many jurisdictions as to whether the provisions dealing with traditional incorporation by reference are applicable to incorporation by reference in an electronic environment. However, in enacting article 5 *bis,* attention should be given to avoid introducing more restrictive requirements with respect to incorporation by reference in electronic commerce than might already apply in paper-based trade.

46.7 Another aim of the provision is to recognize that consumer-protection or other national or international law of a mandatory nature (e.g., rules protecting weaker parties in the context of contracts of adhesion) should not be interfered with. That result could also be achieved by validating incorporation by reference in an electronic environment "to the extent permitted by law", or by listing the rules of law that remain unaffected by article 5 *bis*. Article 5 *bis* is not to be interpreted as creating a specific legal regime for incorporation by reference in an electronic environment. Rather, by establishing a principle of non-discrimination, it is to be construed as making the domestic rules applicable to incorporation by reference in a paper-based environment equally applicable to incorporation by reference for the purposes of electronic commerce. For example, in a number of jurisdictions, existing rules of mandatory law only validate incorporation by reference provided that the following three conditions are met: (*a*) the reference clause should be inserted in the data message; (*b*) the document being referred to, e.g., general terms and conditions, should actually be known to the party against whom the reference document might be relied upon; and (*c*) the reference document should be accepted, in addition to being known, by that party.

References

A/53/17, paras. 212-221;

A/CN.9/450;

A/CN.9/446, paras. 14-24;

A/CN.9 AVG.IV/WP.74;

A/52/17, paras. 248-250;

A/CN.9/437, paras. 151-155;

A/CN.9/WG.IV/WP. 71, paras. 77-93;

A/51/17, paras. 222-223;

A/CN.9/421, paras. 109 and 114;

A/CN.9/WG.IV/WP.69, paras. 30, 53, 59-60 and 91;

A/CN.9/407, paras. 100-105 and 117;

A/CN.9/WG.IV/WP.66;
A/CN.9/WG.IV/WP.65;
A/CN.9/406, paras. 90 and 178-179;
A/CN.9/WG.IV/WP.55, paras. 109-113;
A/CN.9/360, paras. 90-95;
A/CN.9/WG.IV/WP.53, paras. 77-78;
A/CN.9/350, paras. 95-96;
A/CN.9/333, paras. 66-68.

Article 6: Writing

47. Article 6 is intended to define the basic standard to be met by a data message in order to be considered as meeting a requirement (which may result from statute, regulation or judge-made law) that information be retained or presented "in writing" (or that the information be contained in a "document" or other paper-based instrument). It may be noted that article 6 is part of a set: of three articles (articles 6, 7 and 8), which share the same structure and should be read together.

48. In the preparation of the Model Law, particular attention was paid to the functions traditionally performed by various kinds of "writings" in a paper-based environment. For example, the following non-exhaustive list indicates reasons why national laws required the use of "writings" : (1) to ensure that there would be tangible evidence of the existence and nature of the intent of the parties to bind themselves; (2) to help the parties be aware of the consequences of their entering into a contract; (3) to provide that a document would be legible by all; (4) to provide that a document would remain unaltered over time and provide a permanent record of a transaction; (5) to allow for the reproduction of a document so that each party would hold a copy of the same data; (6) to allow for the authentication of data by means of a signature (7) provide

that a document would be in a form acceptable to public authorities and courts; (8) to finalise the intent of the author of the "writing" and provide a record of that intent; (9) to allow for the easy storage of data in a tangible form: (10) to facilitate control and subsequent audit for accounting, tax or regulatory purposes; and (11) to bring legal rights and obligations into existence in those cases where a "writing" was required for validity purposes.

49. However, in the preparation of the Model Law, it was found that it would be inappropriate to adopt an overly comprehensive notion of the functions performed by writing. Existing requirements that data be presented in written form often combine the requirement of a "writing" with concepts distinct from writing, such as signature and original. Thus, when adopting a functional approach, attention should be given to the fact that the requirement of a "writing" should be considered as the lowest layer in a hierarchy of form requirements, which provide distinct levels of reliability, traceability and unalterability with respect to paper documents. The requirement that data be presented in written form (which can be described as a "threshold requirement") should thus not be confused with more stringent requirements such as "signed writing", "signed original" or "authenticated legal act". For example, under certain national law a written document that is neither dated nor signed, and the author of which either is not identified in the written document or is identified by a mere letterhead, would be regarded as a "writing" although it might be of little evidential weight in the absence of other evidence (e.g testimony) regarding the authorship of the document. In addition, the notion of unalterability should not be considered as built into the concept of writing as an absolute requirement since a "writing" in pencil might still be considered a "writing" under certain existing legal definitions. Taking into account the way in which

such issues as integrity of the data and protection against fraud are dealt with in a paper-based environment, a fraudulent document would nonetheless be regarded as a "writing". In general, notions such as "evidence" and "intent of the parties to bind themselves" are to be tied to the more general issues of reliability and authentication of the data and should not be included in the definition of a "writing".

50. The purpose of article 6 is not to establish a requirement that, in all instances, data messages should fulfil all conceivable functions of a writing. Rather than focusing upon specific functions of a "writing", for example, its evidentiary function in the context of tax law or its warning function in the context of civil law, article 6 focuses upon the basis notion of the information being reproduced and read. That notion is expressed in article 6 in terms that were found to provide an objective criterion, namely that the information in a data message must be accessible so as to be usable for subsequent reference. The use of the word "accessible" is meant to imply that information in the form of computer data should be readable and interpretable, and that the software that might be necessary to render such information readable should be retained. The word "usable" is not intended to cover only human use but also computer processing. As to the notion of "subsequent reference", it was preferred to such notions as "durability" or "non-alterability", which would have established too harsh standards, and to such notions as "readability" or "intelligibility", which might constitute too subjective criteria.

51. The principle embodied in paragraph (3) of articles 6 and 7, and in paragraph (4) of article 8, is that an enacting State may exclude from the application of those articles certain situations to be specified in the legislation enacting

the Model Law. An enacting State may wish to exclude specifically certain types of situations, depending in particular on the purpose of the formal requirement in question. One such type of situation may be the case of writing requirements intended to provide notice or warning of specific factual or legal risks, for example, requirements for warnings to be placed on certain types of products. Another specific exclusion might be considered, for example, in the context of formalities required pursuant to international treaty obligations of the enacting State (e.g., the requirement that a cheque be in writing pursuant to the Convention providing a Uniform Law for Cheques, Geneva, 1931) and other kinds of situations and areas of law that are beyond the power of the enacting State to change by means of a statute.

52. Paragraph (3) was included with a view to enhancing the acceptability of the Model Law. It recognizes that the matter of specifying exclusions should be left to enacting States, an approach that would take better account of differences in national circumstances. However, it should be noted that the objectives of the Model Law would not be achieved if paragraph (3) were used to establish blanket exceptions, and the opportunity provided by paragraph (3) in that respect should be avoided. Numerous exclusions from the scope of articles 6 to 8 would raise needless obstacles to the development of modern communication techniques, since what the Model Law contains are very fundamental principles and approaches that are expected to find general application.

References

A/51/17, paras. 180-181 and 185-187 (article 5);

A/50/17, paras. 228-241 (article 5);

A/CN.9/407, paras. 56-63;

A/CN.9/406, paras. 95-101; A/CN.9/WG.IV/WP.62, article 6;

A/CN.9/390, paras. 88-96; A/CN.9/WG.IV/WP.60, article 6;

A/CN.9/387, paras. 66-80, A/CN.9/WG.IV/WP.57, article 6; A/CN.9/WG.IV/WP.58, annex;

A/CN.9/373, paras. 45-62; A/CN.9/WG.IV/WP.55, paras. 36-49;

A/CN.9/360, paras. 32-43; A/CN.9/WG.IV/WP.53, paras. 37-45;

A/CN.9/350, paras. 68-78;

A/CN.9/333, paras. 20 28;

A/CN.9/265, paras. 59-72.

Article 7: Signature

53. Article 7 is based on the recognition of the functions of a signature in a paper-based environment. In the preparation of the Model Law, the following functions of a signature were considered : to identify a person; to provide certainty as to the personal involvement of that person in the act of signing; to associate that person with the content of a document. It was noted that, in addition, a signature could perform a variety of functions, depending on the nature of the document that was signed. For example, a signature might attest to the intent of a party to be bound by the content of a signed contract; the intent of a person to endorse authorship of a text; the intent of a person to associate itself with the content of a document written by someone else; the fact that, and the time when, a person had been at a given place.

54. It may be noted that, alongside the traditional handwritten signature, there exist various types of procedures (e.g., stamping, perforation), sometimes also referred to as "signatures", which provide various levels of certainty. For example, in some countries, there exists a general requirement that contracts for the sale of goods above a certain amount should be "signed" in order to be enforceable. However, the concept of a signature adopted in that context is such that a stamp, perforation or even a

typewritten signature or a printed letterhead might be regarded as sufficient to fulfil the signature requirement. At the other end of the spectrum, there exist requirements that combine the traditional handwritten signature with additional security procedures such as the confirmation of the signature by witnesses.

55. It might be desirable to develop functional equivalents for the various types and levels of signature requirements in existence. Such an approach would increase the levrl of certainty as to the degree of legal recognition that could be expected from the use of the various means of authentication used in electronic commerce practice as substitutes for "signatures". However, the notion of signature is intimately linked to the use of paper. Furthermore, any attempt to develop rules on standards and procedures to be used as substitutes for specific instances of "signatures" might create the risk of tying the legal framework provided by the Model Law to a given state of technical development.

56. With a view to ensuring that a message that was required to be authenticated should not be denied legal value for the sole reason that it was not authenticated in a manner peculiar to paper documents, article 7 adopts a comprehensive approach. It establishes the general conditions under which data messages would be regarded as authenticated with sufficient credibility and would be enforceable in the face of signature requirements which currently present barriers to electronic commerce. Article 7 focuses on the two basic functions of a signature, namely to identify the author of a document and to confirm that the author approved the content of that document. Paragraph (l)(a) establishes the principle that, in an electronic environment, the bask legal functions of a signature are performed by way of a method that identifies the originator

of a data message and confirms that the originator approved the content of that data message.

57. Paragraph (1)(b) establishes a flexible approach to the level of security to be achieved by the method of identification used under paragraph (l)(a). The method used under paragraph (1) (a) should be as reliable as is appropriate for the purpose for which the data message is generated or communicated, in the light of all the circumstances, including any agreement between the originator and the addressee of the data message.

58. In determining whether the method used under paragraph (1) is appropriate, legal, technical and commercial factors that may be taken into account include the following : (1) the sophistication of the equipment used by each of the parties; (2) the nature of their trade activity; (3) the frequency at which commercial transactions take place between the parties; (4) the kind and size of the transaction; (5) the function of signature requirements in a given statutory and regulatory environment; (6) the capability of communication systems; (7) compliance with authentication procedures set forth by intermediaries; (8) the range of authentication procedures made available by any intermediary; (9) compliance with trade customs and practice; (10) the existence of insurance coverage mechanisms against unauthorized messages; (11) the importance and the value of the information contained in the data message; (12) the availability of alternative methods of identification and the cost of implementation; (13) the degree of acceptance or non-acceptance of the method of identification in the relevant industry or field both at the time the method was agreed upon and the time when the data message was communicated; and (14) any other relevant factor.

59. Article 7 does not introduce a distinction between the situation in which users of electronic commerce are

linked by a communication agreement and the situation in which parties had no prior contractual relationship regarding the use of electronic commerce. Thus, article 7 may be regarded as establishing a basic standard of authentication for data messages that might be exchanged in the absence of a prior contractual relationship and, at the same time, to provide guidance as to what might constitute an appropriate substitute for a signature if the parties used electronic communications in the context of a communication agreement. The Model Law is thus intended to provide useful guidance both in a context where national laws would leave the question of authentication of data messages entirely to the discretion of the parties and in a context where requirements for signature, which were usually set by mandatory provisions of national law, should not be made subject to alteration by agreement of the parties.

60. The notion of an "agreement between the originator and the addressee of a data message" is to be interpreted as covering not only bilateral or multilateral agreements concluded between parties exchanging directly data messages (e.g., "trading partners agreements", "communication agreements" or "interchange agreements") but also agreements involving intermediaries such as networks (e.g., "third-party service agreements"). Agreements concluded between users of electronic commerce and networks may incorporate "system rules", *i.e.*, administrative and technical rules and procedures to be applied when communicating data messages. However, a possible agreement between originators and addressees of data messages as to the use of a method of authentication is not conclusive evidence of whether that method is reliable or not

61. It should be noted that, under the Model Law, the mere signing of a data message by means of a functional

equivalent of a handwritten signature is not intended, in and of itself, to confer legal validity on the data message. Whether a data message that fulfilled the requirement of a signature has legal validity is to be settled under the law applicable outside the Model Law.

References

A/51/17, paras. 180-181 and 185-187 (article 6);

A/50/17, paras. 242-248 (article 6);

A/CN.9/407, paras. 64-70;

A/CN.9/406, paras. 102-105; A/CN.9/WG.IV/WP.62, article 7;

A/CN.9/390, paras. 97-109; A/CN.9/WG.IV/WP.60, article 7;

A/CN.9/387, paras. 81-90; A/CN.9/WG.IV/WP.57, article 7;
A/CN.9/WG.IV/WP.58, annex;

A/CN.9/373, paras. 63-76; A/CN.9/WG.IV/WP.55, paras. 50-63;

A/CN.9/360, paras. 71-75; A/CN.9/WG.IV/WP. 53, paras. 61-66;

A/CN.9/350, paras. 86-89;

A/CN.9/333, paras. 50-59;

A/CN.9/265, paras. 49-58 and 79-80.

Article 8: Original

62. If "original" were defined as a medium on which information was fixed for the first time, it would be impossible to speak of "original" data messages, since the addressee of a data message would always receive a copy thereof. However, article 8 should be put in a different context. The notion of "original" in article 8 is useful since in practice many disputes relate to the question of originality of documents, and in electronic commerce the requirement for presentation of originals constitutes one of the main obstacles that the Model Law attempts to remove. Although in some jurisdictions the concepts of "writing", "original" and "signature" may overlap, the Model Law approaches

them as three separate and distinct concepts. Article 8 is also useful in clarifying the notions of "writing" and "original", in particular in view of their importance far purposes of evidence.

63. Article 8 is pertinent to documents of title and negotiable instruments, in which the notion of uniqueness of an original is particularly relevant. However, attention is drawn to the fact that the Model Law is not intended only to apply to documents of title and negotiable instruments, or to such areas of law where special requirements exist with respect to registration or notarization of "writings", e.g., family matters or the sale of real estate. Examples of documents that might require an "original" are trade documents such as weight certificates, agricultural certificates, quality or quantity certificates, inspection reports, insurance certificates, etc. While such documents are not negotiable or used to transfer rights or title, it is essential that they be transmitted unchanged, that is in their "original" form, so that other parties in international commerce may have confidence in their contents. In a paper-based environment, these types of document are usually only accepted if they are "original" to lessen the chance that they be altered, which would be difficult to detect in copies. Various technical means are available to certify the contents of a data message to confirm its "originality". Without this functional equivalent of originality, the sale of goods using electronic commerce would be hampered since the issuers of such documents would be required to retransmit their data message each and every time the goods are sold, or the parties would be forced to use paper documents to supplement the electronic commerce transaction.

64. Article 8 should be regarded as stating the minimum acceptable form requirement to be met by a data message for it to be regarded as the functional equivalent of an original. The provisions of article 8 should be regarded as mandatory, to the same extent that existing provisions regarding the use of paper-based original documents would be regarded as mandatory. The indication that the form requirements stated in article 8 are to be regarded as the "minimum acceptable" should not, however, be construed as inviting States to establish requirements stricter than those contained in the Model Law.

65. Article 8 emphasizes the importance of the integrity of the information for its originality and sets out criteria to be taken into account when assessing integrity by reference to systematic recording of the information, assurance that the information was recorded without lacunae and protection of the data against alteration. It links the concept of originality to a method of authentication and puts the focus on the method of authentication to be followed in order to meet the requirement. It is based on the following elements : a simple criterion as to "integrity" of the data; a description of the elements to be taken into account in assessing the integrity; and an element of flexibility, *i.e.*, a reference to circumstances.

66. As regards the words "the time when it was first generated in its final form" in paragraph (l)(a), it should be noted that the provision is intended to encompass the situation where information was first composed as a paper document and subsequently transferred on to a computer. In such a situation, paragraph (l)(a) is to be interpreted as requiring assurances that the information has remained complete and unaltered from the time when it was composed as a paper document onwards, and not only as from the time when it was translated into electronic form. However,

where several drafts were created and stored before the final message was composed, paragraph (l)(a) should not be misinterpreted as requiring assurance as to the integrity of the drafts.

67. Paragraph (3)(a) sets forth the criteria for assessing integrity, taking care to except necessary additions to the first (or "original") data message such as endorsements, certifications, notarizations, etc. from other alterations. As long as the contents of a data message remain complete and unaltered, necessary additions to that data message would not affect its "originality". Thus when an electronic certificate is added to the end of an "original" data message to attest to the "originality" of that data message, or when data is automatically added by computer systems at the start and the finish of a data message in order to transmit it, such additions would be considered as if they were a supplemental piece of paper with an "original" piece of paper, or the envelope and stamp used to send that "original" piece of paper.

68. As in other articles of Chapter II of part one, the words "the law" in the opening phrase of article 8 are to be understood as encompassing not only statutory or regulatory law but also judicially created law and other procedural law. In certain common law countries, where the words "the law" would normally be interpreted as referring to common law rules, as opposed to statutory requirements, it should be noted that, in the context of the Model Law, the words "the law" are intended to encompass those various sources of law. However, "the law", as used in the Model Law, is not meant to include areas of law that have not become part of the law of a State and are sometimes, somewhat imprecisely, referred to by expressions such as "lex mercatoria" or "law merchant".

69. Paragraph (4), as was the case with similar provisions in articles 6 and 7, was included with a view to enhancing the acceptability of the Model Law. It recognizes that the matter of specifying exclusion should be left to enacting States, an approach that would take better account of differences in national circumstances. However, it should be noted that the objectives of the Model Law would not be achieved if paragraph (4) were used to establish blanket exceptions. Numerous exclusions from the scope of articles 6 to 8 would raise needless obstacles to the development of modern communication techniques, since what the Model Law contains are very fundamental principles and approaches that are expected to find general application.

References

A/51/17, paras. 180-181 and 185-187 (article 7);

A/50/17, paras. 249-255 (article 7);

A/CN.9/407, paras. 71-79;

A/CN.9/406, paras. 106-110; A/CN.9/WG.IV/WP.62, article 8;

A/CN.9/390, paras. 110-133; A/CN.9/WG.IV/WP.60, article 8;

A/CN.9/387, paras. 91,97; A/CN.9/WG.IV/WP.57, article 8;

A/CN.9/WG.IV/WP.58, annex;

A/CN.9/373. paras. 77-96;

A/CN.9/WG.IV/WP.55 naras. 64-70;

A/CN.9/360, paras. 60-70; A/CN.9/WG.IV/WP.53, paras. 56-60;

A/CN.9/350, paras. 84.85;

A/CN.9/265, paras. 43-48;

Article 9: Admissibility and Evidential Weight of Data Messages

70. The purpose of article 9 is to establish both the admissibility of data, messages as evidence in legal proceedings and their evidential value. With respect to admissibility, paragraph (1), establishing that data messages

should not be denied admissibility as evidence in legal proceedings on the sole ground that they are in electronic form, puts emphasis on the general principle stated in article 4 and is needed to make it expressly applicable to admissibility of evidence, an area in which particularly complex issues might arise in certain jurisdictions. The term "best evidence" is a term understood in, and necessary for, certain common law jurisdictions. However, the notion of "best evidence" could raise a great deal of uncertainty in legal systems in which such a rule is unknown. States in which the term would be regarded as meaningless and potentially misleading may wish to enact the Model Law without the reference to the "best evidence" rule contained in paragraph (1).

71. As regards the assessment of the evidential weight of a data message, paragraph (2) provides useful guidance as to how the evidential value of data messages should be assessed *(e.g.,* depending on whether they were generated, stored or communicated in a reliable manner).

References

A/50/17, paras. 256-263 (article 8);

A/CN.9/407, paras. 80-81;

A/CN.9/406, paras. 111-113; A/CN.9/WG.IV/WP.62, article 9;

A/CN.9/390, paras. 139-143; A/CN.9/WG.IV/WP.60, article 9;

A/CN.9/387, paras. 98-109; A/CN.9/WG.IV/WP.57, article 9;

A/CN.9/ WG.IV/WP.58, annex;

A/CN.9/373, paras. 97-108; A/CN.9/WG.IV/WP.55, paras. 71-81;

A/CN.9/360, paras. 44-59; A/CN.9/WG.IV/WP.53, paras. 46-55;

A/CN.9/350, paras. 79-83 and 90-91;

A/CN.9/333, paras. 29-41;

A/CN.9/265, paras. 27-48.

Article 10: Retention of Data Messages

72. Article 10 establishes a set of alternative rules for existing requirements regarding the storage of information (*e.g.*, for accounting or tax purposes) that may constitute obstacles to the development of modern trade.

73. Paragraph (1) is intended to set out the conditions under which the obligation to store data messages that might exist under the applicable law would be met. Sub-paragraph (a) reproduces the conditions established under article 6 for a data message to satisfy a rule which prescribes the presentation of a "writing". Sub-paragraph *(b)* emphasizes that the message does not need to be retained unaltered as long as the information stored accurately reflects the data message as it was sent. It would not be appropriate to require that information should be stored unaltered, since usually messages are decoded, compressed or converted in order to be stored.

74. Sub-paragraph (c) is intended to cover all the information that may need to be stored, which includes, apart from the message itself, certain transmittal information that may be necessary for the identification of the message. Sub-paragraph *(c)*, by imposing the retention of the transmittal information associated with the data message, is creating a standard that is higher than most standards existing under national laws as to the storage of paper-based communications. However, it should not be understood as imposing an obligation to retain transmittal information additional to the information contained in the data message when it was generated, stored or transmitted, or information contained in a separate data message, such as an acknowledgement of receipt. Moreover, while some transmittal information is important and has to be stored, other transmittal information can be exempted without the integrity of the data message being compromised.

That is the reason why sub-paragraph *(c)* establishes distinction between those elements of transmittal information that are important for the identification of the message and the very few elements of transmittal information covered in paragraph (2) *(e.g.,* communication protocols), which are of no value with regard to the data message and which, typically, would automatically be stripped out of an incoming data message by the receiving computer before the data message actually entered the information system of the addressee.

75. In practice, storage of information, and especially storage of transmittal information, may often be carried out by someone other than the originator or the addressee, such as an intermediary.

Nevertheless, it is intended that the person obligated to retain certain transmittal information cannot escape meeting that obligation simply because, for example, the communications system operated by that other person does not retain the required information. This is intended to discourage bad practice or wilful misconduct. Paragraph (3) provides that in meeting its obligations under paragraph (1), an addressee or originator may use the services of any third party, not just an intermediary.

References

A/51/17, paras. 185-187 (article 9);

A/50/17, paras. 264-270 (article 9);

A/CN.9/407, paras. 82-84;

A/CN.9/406, paras. 59-72; A/CN.9/WG.IV/WP.60, article 14;

A/CN.9/387, paras. 164-168;

A/CN.9/WG.IV/WP.57, article 14;

A/CN.9/373, paras, 123-125; A/CN.9/WG.IV/WP.55, para. 94;

CHAPTER III. COMMUNICATION OF DATA MESSAGES

Article 11: Formation and Validity of Contracts

76. Article 11 is not intended to interfere with the law on formation of contracts but rather to promote international trade by providing increased legal certainty as to the conclusion of contracts by electronic means. It deals not only with the issue of contract formation but also with the form in which an offer and an acceptance may be expressed. In certain countries, a provision along the lines of paragraph (1) might be regarded as merely stating the obvious, namely that an offer and an acceptance, as any other expression of will, can be communicated by any means, including data messages. However, the provision is needed in view of the remaining uncertainties in a considerable number of countries as to whether contracts can validly be concluded by electronic means. Such uncertainties may stem from the fact that, in certain cases the data messages expressing offer and acceptance are generated by computers without immediate human intervention, thus raising doubts as to the expression of intent by the parties. Another reason for such uncertainties is inherent in the mode of communication and results from the absence of a paper document.

77. It may also be noted that paragraph (1) reinforces, in the context of contract formation, a principle already embodied in other articles of the Model Law, such as articles 5, 9 and 13, all of which establish the legal effectiveness of data messages. However, paragraph (1) is needed since the fact that electronic messages may have legal value as evidence and produce a number of effects, including those provided in articles 9 and 13, does not necessarily mean that they can be used for the purpose of concluding valid contracts.

78. Paragraph (1) covers not merely the cases in which both the offer and the acceptance are communicated by electronic means but also cases in which only the offer or only the acceptance is communicated electronically. As to the time and place of formation of contracts in cases where an offer or the acceptance of an offer is expressed by means of a data message, no specific rule has been included in the Model Law in order not to interfere with national law applicable to contract formation. It was felt that such a provision might exceed the aim of the Model Law, which should be limited to providing that electronic communications would achieve the same degree of legal certainty as paper-based communications. The combination of existing rules on the formation of contracts with the provisions contained in article 15 is designed to dispel uncertainty as to the time and place of formation of contracts in cases where the offer or the acceptance are exchanged electronically.

79. The words "unless otherwise stated by the parties", which merely restate, in the context of contract formation, the recognition of party autonomy expressed in article 4, are intended to make it clear that the purpose of the Model Law is not to impose the use of electronic means of communication on parties who rely on the use of paper-based communication to conclude contracts. Thus, article 11 should not be interpreted as restricting in any way party autonomy with respect to parties not involved in the use of electronic communication.

80. During the preparation of paragraph (1), it was felt that the provision might have the harmful effect of overruling otherwise applicable provisions of national law, which might prescribe specific formalities for the formation of certain contracts. Such forms include notarization and other requirements for "writings", and might respond to

considerations of public policy, such as the need to protect certain parties or to warn them against specific risks. For that reason, paragraph (2) provides that an enacting State can exclude the application of paragraph (1) in certain instances to be specified in the legislation enacting the Model Law.

References

A/51/17, paras. 89-94 (article 13);

A/CN.9/407, para. 93;

A/CN.9/406, paras. 34-41; A/CN.9/WG.IV/WP.60, article 12;

A/CN.9/387, paras. 145-151; A/CN.9/WG.IV/WP.57, article 12;

A/CN.9/373, paras. 126-133; A/CN.9/WG.IV/WP.55, paras. 95-102;

A/CN.9/360, paras. 76-86;

A/CN.9/WG.IV/WP.53, paras. 67-73; A/CN.9/350, paras. 93-96;

A/CN.9/333, paras. 60-68.

Article 12: Recognition by Parties of Data Messages

81. Article 12 was added at a late stage in the preparation of the Model Law, in recognition of the fact that article 11 was limited to dealing with data messages that were geared to the conclusion of a contract, but that the draft Model Law did not contain specific provisions on data messages that related not to the conclusion of contracts but to the performance of contractual obligations (*e.g.*, notice of defective goods, an offer to pay, notice of place where a contract would be performed, recognition of debt). Since modern means of communication are used in a context of legal uncertainty, in the absence of specific legislation in most countries, it was felt appropriate for the Model Law not only to establish the general principle that the use of electronic communication should not be discriminated against, as expressed in article 5, but also to include specific illustrations of that principle. Contract formation is but one of the areas where such an illustration is useful and

the legal validity of unilateral expressions of will, as well as other notices or statements that may be issued in the form of data messages, also needs to be mentioned.

82. As is the case with article 11, article 12 is not to impose the use of electronic means of communication but to validate such use, subject to contrary agreement by the parties. Thus, article 12 should not be used as a basis to impose on the addressee the legal consequences of a message, if the use of a non-paper-based method for its transmission comes as a surprise to the addressee.

References

A/51/17, paras. 95-99 (new article 13 *bis.)*.

Article 13 : Attribution of Data Messages

83. Article 13 has its origin in article 5 of the UNCITRAL Model Law on International Credit Transfers, which defines the obligations of the sender of a payment order. Article 13 is intended to apply where there is a question as to whether a data message was really sent by the person who is indicated as being the originator. In the case of a paper-based communication the problem would arise as the result of an alleged forged signature of the purported originator. In an electronic environment, an unauthorized person may have sent the massage but the authentication by code, encryption or the like would be accurate. The purpose of article 13 is not to assign responsibility. It deals rather with attribution of data messages by establishing a presumption that under certain circumstances a data massage would be considered as a massage of the originator, and goes on to qualify that presumption in case the addressee knew or ought to have known that the data message was not that of the originator.

84. Paragraph (1) recalls the principle that an originator

is bound by a data message if it has effectively sent that message. Paragraph (2) refers to the situation where the message was sent by a person other than the originator who had the authority to act on behalf of the originator.

Paragraph (2) is not intended to displace the domestic law of agency, and the question as to whether the other person did in fact and in law have the authority to act on behalf of the originator is left to the appropriate legal rules outside the Model Law.

85. Paragraph (3) deals with two kinds of situations, in which the addressee could rely on a data message as being that of the originator : firstly, situations in which the addressee properly applied an authentication procedure previously agreed to by the originator; and secondly, situations in which the data message resulted from the actions of a person who, by virtue of its relationship with the originator, had access to the originator's authentication procedures. By stating that the addressee "is entitled to regard a data as being that of the originator", paragraph (3) read in conjunction with paragraph (4)(a) is intended to indicate that the addressee could act on the assumption that the data message is that of the originator up to the point in time it received notice from the originator that the data message was not that of the originator, or up to the point in time when it knew or should have known that the data message was not that of the originator.

86. Under paragraph (3)(a), if the addressee applies any authentication procedures previously agreed to by the originator and such application results in the proper verification of the originator as the source of the message, the message is presumed to be that of the originator. That covers not only the situation where an authentication procedure has been agreed upon by the originator and the addressee but also situations where an originator,

unilaterally or as a result of an agreement with an intermediary, identified a procedure and agreed to be bound by a data message that met the requirements corresponding to that procedure. Thus, agreements that became effective not through direct agreement between the originator and the addressee but through the participation of third-party service providers are intended to be covered by paragraph (3)(a). However, it should be noted that paragraph (3)(a) applies only when the communication between the originator and the addressee is based on a previous agreement, but that it does not apply in an open environment.

87. The effect of paragraph (3)(b), read in conjunction with paragraph (4)(b), is that the originator or the addressee, as the case may be, is responsible for any unauthorized data message that can be shown to have been sent as a result of negligence of that party.

88. Paragraph (4)(a) should not be misinterpreted as relieving the originator from the consequences of sending data message, with retroactive effect, irrespective of whether the addressee had acted on the assumption that the data message was that of the originator. Paragraph (4) is not intended to provide that receipt of a notice under sub-paragraph (a) would nullify the original message retroactively. Under sub-paragraph *(a)*, the originator is released from the binding effect of the message after the time notice is received and not before that time. Moreover, paragraph (4) should not be read as allowing the originator to avoid being bound by the data message by sending notice to the addressee under sub-paragraph (a), in a case where the message had, in fact, been sent by the originator and the addressee properly applied agreed or reasonable authentication procedures. If the addressee can prove that the message is that of the originator, paragraph (1) would

apply and not paragraph (4)(a). As to the meaning of"reasonable time", the notice should be such as to give the addressee sufficient time to react. For example, in the case of just-in-time supply, the addressee should be given time to adjust its production chain.

89. With respect to paragraph (4)(b), it should be noted that the Model Law could lead to the result that the addressee would be entitled to rely on a data message under paragraph (3)(a) if it had properly applied the agreed authentication procedures, even if it knew that the data message was not that of the originator. It was generally felt when preparing the Model Law that the risk that such a situation could arise should be accepted, in view of the need for preserving the reliability of agreed authentication procedures.

90. Paragraph (5) is intended to preclude the originator from disavowing the message once it was sent, unless the addressee knew, or should have known, that the data message was not that of the originator. In addition, paragraph (5) is intended to deal with errors in the content of the message arising from errors in transmission.

91. Paragraph (6) deals with the issue of erroneous duplication of data messages, an issue of considerable practical importance. It establishes the standard of care to be applied by the addressee to distinguish an erroneous duplicate of a data message from a separate data message.

92. Early drafts of article 13 contained an additional paragraph, expressing the principle that the attribution of authorship of a data message to the originator should not interfere with the legal consequences of that message, which should be determined by other applicable rules of national law. It was later felt that it was not necessary to express that principle in the Model Law but that it should be mentioned in this Guide.

References

A/51/17, paras. 189-194 (article 11);

A/50/17, paras. 275-303 (article 11);

A/CN.9/407, paras. 86-89;

A/CN.9/406, paras. 114-131; A/CN.9/WG.IV/WP.62, article 10;

A/CN.9/390, paras. 144-153; A/CN.9/WG.IV/WP.60, article 10;

A/CN.9/387, paras. 110-132; A/CN.9/WG.IV/WP.57, article 10;

A/CN.9/373, paras. 109-115; A/CN.9/WG.IV/WP.55, paras. 82-86.

Article 14 : Acknowledgement of Receipt

93. The use of functional acknowledgements is a business decisions to be made by users of electronic commerce; the Model Law does not intend to impose the use of any such procedure. However, taking into account the commercial value of a system of acknowledgement of receipt and the widespread use of such systems in the context of electronic commerce, it was felt that the Model Law should address a number of legal issues arising from the use of acknowledgement procedures. It should be noted that the notion of "acknowledgement" is sometimes used to cover a variety of procedures, ranging from a mere acknowledgement of receipt of an unspecified message to an expression of agreement with the content of a specific data message. In many instances, the procedure of "acknowledgement" would parallel the system known as "return receipt requested" in postal systems. Acknowledgements of receipt may be required in a variety of instruments, *e.g.*, in the data message itself, in bilateral or multilateral communication agreements, or in "system rules". It should be borne in mind that variety among acknowledgement procedures implies variety of the related costs. The provisions of article 14 are based on the assumption that acknowledgement procedures are to be used at the discretion of the originator. Article 14 is not intended to deal with the legal consequences that may

flow from sending an acknowledgement of receipt, apart from establishing receipt of the data message. For example, where an originator sends an offer in a data message and requests acknowledgement of receipt, the acknowledgement of receipt simply evidences that the offer has been received. Whether or not sending that acknowledgement amounted to accepting the offer is not dealt with by the Model Law but by contract law outside the Model Law.

94. The purpose of paragraph (2) is to validate acknowledgement by any communication or conduct of the addressee (e.g., the shipment of the goods as an acknowledgement or receipt of a purchase order) where the originator has not agreed with the addressee that the acknowledgement should be in a particular form. The situation where an acknowledgement has been unilaterally requested by the originator to be given in a specific form is not expressly addressed by article 14, which may entail as a possible consequence that a unilateral requirement by the originator as to the form of acknowledgements would not affect the right of the addressee to acknowledge receipt by any communication or conduct sufficient to indicate to the originator that the message had been received. Such a possible interpretation of paragraph (2) makes it particularly necessary to emphasize in the Model Law the distinction to be drawn between the effects of an acknowledgement of receipt of a data message and any communication in response to the content of that data message, a reason why paragraph (7) is needed.

95. Paragraph (3), which deals with the situation where the originator has stated that the data message is conditional on receipt of an acknowledgement, applies whether or not the originator has specified that the acknowledgement should be received by a certain time.

96. The purpose of paragraph (4) is to deal with the more common situation where an acknowledgement is requested, without any statement being made by the originator that the data message is of no effect until an acknowledgement has been received. Such a provision is needed to establish the point in time when the originator of a data message who has requested an acknowledgement of receipt is relieved from any legal implication of sending that data message if the requested acknowledgement has not been received. An example of a factual situation where a provision along the lines of paragraph (4) would be particularly useful would be that the originator of an offer to contract who has not received the requested acknowledgement from the addressee of the offer may need to know the point in time after which it is free to transfer the offer to another party. It may be noted that the provision does not create any obligation binding on the originator, but merely establishes means by which the originator, if it so wishes, can clarify its status in cases where it has not received the requested acknowledgement. It may also be noted that the provision does not create any obligation binding on the addressee of the data message, who would, in most circumstances, be free to rely or not to rely on any given data message, provided that it would bear the risk of the data message being unreliable for lack of an acknowledgement of receipt. The addressee, however, is protected since the originator who does not receive a requested acknowledgement may not automatically treat the data message as though it had never been transmitted, without giving further notice to the addressee. The procedure described under paragraph (4) is purely at the discretion of the originator. For example, where the originator sent a data message which under the agreement between the parties had to be received by a certain time, and the originator requested an acknowledgement of receipt, the addressee

could not deny the legal effectiveness of the message simply by withholding the requested acknowledgement.

97. The rebuttable presumption established in paragraph (5) is needed to create certainty and would be particularly useful in the context of electronic communication between parties that are not linked by a trading-partners agreement. The second sentence of paragraph (5) should be read in conjunction with paragraph (5) of article 13, which establishes the conditions under which, in case of an inconsistency between the text of the data message as sent and the text as received, the text as received prevails.

98. Paragraph (6) corresponds to a certain type of acknowledgement, for example, an EDIFACT message establishing that the data message received is syntactically correct, *i.e.,* that it can be processed by the receiving computer. The reference to technical requirements, which is to be construed primarily as a reference to "data syntax" in the context of EDI communications, may be less relevant in the context of the use of other means of communication, such as telegram or telex. In addition to mere consistency with the rules of "data syntax", technical requirements set forth in applicable standards may include, for example, the use of procedures verifying the integrity of the contents of data messages.

99. Paragraph (7) is intended to dispel uncertainties that might exist as to the legal effect of an acknowledgement of receipt. For example, paragraph (7) indicates that an acknowledgement of receipt should not be confused with any communication related to the contents of the acknowledged message.

References

A/5/17, paras. 63-88 (article 12);

A/CN.9/407, paras. 90-92;

A/CN.9/406, paras. 15-33; A/CN.9/WG.IV/WP.60, article 11; A/CN.9/387, paras. 133-144; A/CN.9/WG.IV/WP.57, article 11; A/CN.9/373, paras. 116-122; A/CN.9/WG.IV/WP.55, paras. 87-93; A/CN.9/360, para. 125; A/CN.9/WG.IV/WP.53, paras. 80-81; A/CN.9/350, para. 92; A/CN.9/333, paras. 48-49.

Article 15 : Time and Place of Dispatch and Receipt of Data Messages

100. Article 15 results from the recognition that, for the operation of many existing rules of law, it is important to ascertain the time and place of receipt of information. The use of electronic communication techniques makes those difficult to ascertain. It is not uncommon for users of electronic commerce to communicate from one State to another without knowing the location of information systems through which communication is operated. In addition, the location of certain communication systems may change without either of the parties being aware of the change. The Model Law is thus intended to reflect the fact that the location of information systems is irrelevant and sets forth a more objective criterion, namely, the place of business of the parties. In that connection, it should be noted that article 15 is not intended to establish a conflict-of-laws rule.

101. Paragraph (1) define the time of dispatch of a data message as the time when the data message enters an information system outside the control of the originator, which may be the information system of an intermediary or an information system of the addressee. The concept of "dispatch" refers to the commencement of the electronic transmission of the data message. Where "dispatch" already has an established meaning, article 15 is intended to supplement national rules on dispatch and not to displace them. If dispatch occurs when the data message reaches

an information system of the addressee, dispatch under paragraph (1) and receipt under paragraph (2) are simultaneous, except where the data message is sent to an information system of the addressee that is not the information system designated by the addressee under paragraph

102. Paragraph (2), the purpose of which is to define the time of receipt of a data message, addresses the situation where the addressee unilaterally designates a specific information system for the receipt of a message (in which case the designated system may or may not be an information system of the addressee), and the data message reaches an information system of the addressee that is not the designated system. In such a situation, receipt is deemed to occur when the data message is retrieved by the addressee. By "designated information system", the Model Law is intended to cover a system that has been specifically designated by a party, for instance in the case where an offer expressly specifies the address to which acceptance should be sent. The mere indication of an electronic mail or telecopy address on a letterhead or other document should not be regarded as express designation of one or more information systems.

103. Attention is drawn to the notion of "entry" into an information system, which is used for both the definition of dispatch and that of receipt of a data message. A data message enters an information system at the time when it becomes available for processing within that information system. Whether a data message which enters an information system is intelligible or usable by the addressee is outside the purview of the Model Law. The Model Law does not intend to overrule provisions of national law under which receipt of a message may occur at the time when the message enters the sphere of the addressee, irrespective of

whether the message is intelligible or usable by the addressee. Nor is the Model Law intended to run counter to trade usages, under which certain encoded messages are deemed to be received even before they are usable by, or intelligible for, the addressee. It was felt that the Model Law should not create a more stringent requirement than currently exists in a paper-based environment, where a message can be considered to be received even if it is not intelligible for the addressee or not intended to be intelligible to the addressee *(e.g.,* where encrypted data is transmitted to a depository for the sole purpose of retention in the context of intellectual property rights protection).

104. A data message should not be considered to be dispatched if it merely reached the information system of the addressee but failed to enter it. It may be noted that the Model Law does not expressly address the question of possible malfunctioning of information systems as a basis for liability. In particular, where the information system of the addressee does not function at all or functions improperly or, while functioning properly, cannot be entered into by the data message *(e.g.,* in the case of a telecopier that is constantly occupied), dispatch under the Model Law does not occur. It was felt during the preparation of the Model Law that the addressee should not be placed under the burdensome obligation to maintain its information system functioning at all times by way of a general provision.

105. The purpose of paragraph (4) is to deal with the place of receipt of a data message. The principal reason for including a rule on the place of receipt of a data message is to address a circumstance characteristic of electronic commerce that might not be treated adequately under existing law, namely, that very often the information system of the addressee where the data message is received, or from which the data message is retrieved, is located in a

jurisdiction other than that in which the addressee itself is located. Thus, the rationale behind the provision is to ensure that the location of an information system is not the determinant element, and that there is some reasonably connection between the addressee and what is deemed to be the place of receipt, and that that place can be readily ascertained by the originator. The Model Law does not contain specific provisions as to how the designation of an information system should be made, or whether a change could be made after such a designation by the addressee.

106. Paragraph (4), which contains a reference to the "underlying transaction", is intended to refer to both actual and contemplated underlying transactions. References to "place of business", "principal place of business" and "place of habitual residence" were adopted to bring the text in line with article 10 of the United Nations Convention on Contracts for the International Sale of Goods.

107. The effect of paragraph (4) is to introduce a distinction between the deemed place of receipt and the place actually reached by a data message at the time of its receipt under paragraph *(2).* That distinction is not to be interpreted as apportioning risks between the originator and the addressee in case of damage or loss of a data message between the time of its receipt under paragraph (2) and the time when it reached its place of receipt under paragraph *(4).* Paragraph (4) merely establishes an irrebuttable presumption regarding a legal fact, to be used where another body of law *(e.g.,* on formation of contracts or conflict of laws) require determination of the place of receipt of a data message. However, it was felt during the preparation of the Model Law that introducing a deemed place of receipt, as distinct from the place actually readied by that data message at the time of its receipt, would be inappropriate outside the context of computerized

transmissions (*e.g.*, in the context of telegram or telex). The provision was thus limited in scope to cover only computerized transmissions of data messages. A further limitation is contained in paragraph (5), which reproduces a provision already included in articles 6, 7, 8, 11 and 12 (see above, para. 69).

References

A/51/17, paras. 100-115 (article 14);

A/CN.9/407, paras. 94-99;

A/CN.9/406, paras. 42-58; A/CN.9/WG.1V/WP.60, article 13;

A/CN.9/387, paras. 152-163; A/CN.9/WG.IV/WP.57, article 13;

A/CN.9/373, paras. 134-146; A/CN.9/WG.IV/WP.55, paras. 103-108;

A/CN.9/360, paras. 87-89; A/CN.9/WG.IV/WP.53, paras. 74-76;

A/CN.9/350, paras. 97-100;

A/CN.9/333, paras. 69-75;

PART TWO : ELECTRONIC COMMERCE IN SPECIFIC AREAS

108. As distinct from the basic rules applicable to electronic commerce in general, which appear as part one of the Model Law, part two contains rules of a more specific nature. In preparing the Model Law, the Commission agreed that such rules dealing with specific uses of electronic commerce should appear in the Model Law in a way that reflected both the specific nature of the provisions and their legal status, which should be the same as that of the general provisions contained in part one of the Model Law. While the Commission, when ădopting the Model Law, only considered such specific provisions in the context of transport documents, it was agreed that such provisions should appear as Chapter I of part two of the Model Law. It was felt that adopting such an open-ended structure would make it easier to add further specific provisions to

the Model Law, as the need might arise, in the form of additional chapters in part two.

109. The adoption of a specific set of rules dealing with specific uses of electronic commerce, such as the use of EDI messages as substitutes for transport documents does not imply that the other provisions of the Model Law are not applicable to such documents. In particular, the provisions of part two, such as articles 16 and 17 concerning transfer of rights in goods, presuppose that the guarantees of reliability and authenticity contained in articles 6 to 8 of the Model Law are also applicable to electronic equivalents to transport documents. Part two of the Model Law does not in any way limit or restrict the field of application of the general provisions of the Model Law.

CHAPTER I. CARRIAGE OF GOODS

110. In preparing the Model Law, the Commission noted that the carriage of goods was the context in which electronic communications were most likely to be used and in which a legal framework facilitating the use of such communications was most urgently needed. Articles 16 and 17 contain provisions that apply equally to non-negotiable transport documents and to transfer of rights in goods by way of transferable bills of lading. The principles embodied articles 16 and 17 are applicable not only to maritime transport but also to transport of goods by other means, such as road, railroad and air transport.

Article 16: Actions Related to Contracts of Carriage of Goods

111. Article 16, which establishes the scope of Chapter I of part two of the Model Law, is broadly drafted. It would encompass a wide variety of documents used in the context of the carriage of goods, including, for example,

charter-parties. In the preparation of the Model Law, the Commission found that, by dealing comprehensively with contracts of carriage of goods, article 16 was consistent with the need to cover all transport documents, whether negotiable or non-negotiable, without excluding any specific document such as charter-parties. It was pointed out that, if an enacting State did not wish Chapter I of part two to apply to a particular kind of document or contract, for example if the inclusion of such documents as charter-parties in the scope of that chapter was regarded as inappropriate under the legislation of an enacting State, that State could make use of the exclusion clause contained in paragraph (7) of article 17.

112. Article 16 is of an illustrative nature and, although the actions mentioned therein are more common in maritime trade, they are not exclusive to such type of trade and could be performed in connection with air transport or multimodal carriage of goods.

References

A/51/17, paras. 139-172 and 198-204 (draft article x);

A/CN.9/421, paras. 53-103; A/CN.9/WG.IV/WP.69, paras. 82-95;

A/50/17, paras. 307-309;

A/CN.9/407, paras. 106-118; A/CN.9/WG.IV/WP.67, annex; A/CN.9/WG.IV/WP.66, annex II;

A/49/17, paras. 198, 199 and 201;

A/CN.9/390, para. 155-158.

Article 17: Transport Documents

113. Paragraphs (1) and (2) are derived from article 6. In the context of transport documents, it is necessary to establish not only functional equivalents of written information about the actions referred to in article 16, but also functional equivalents of the performance of such actions through the use of paper documents. Functional

equivalents are particularly needed for the transfer of rights and obligations by transfer of written documents. For example, paragraphs (1) and (2) are intended to replace both the requirement for a written contract of carriage and the requirements for endorsement and transfer of possession of a bill of lading. It was felt in the preparation of the Model Law that the focus of the provision on the actions referred to in article 16 should be expressed clearly, particularly in view of the difficulties that might exist, in certain countries, for recognizing the transmission of a data message as functionally equivalent to the physical transfer of goods, or to the transfer of a document of title representing the goods.

114. The reference to "one or more data messages" in paragraphs (1), (3) and (6) is not intended to be interpreted differently from the reference to "a data message" in the other provisions of the Model Law, which should also be understood as covering equally the situation where only one data message is generated and the situation where more than one data message is generated as support of a given piece of information. A more detailed wording was adopted in article 17 merely to reflect the fact that, in the context of transfer of rights through data messages, some of the functions traditionally performed through the single transmission of a paper bill of lading would necessarily imply the transmission of more than one data message and that such a fact, in itself, should entail no negative consequently as to the acceptability of electronic commerce in that area.

115. Paragraph (3), in combination with paragraph (4), is intended to ensure that a right can be conveyed to one person only, and that it would not be possible for more than one person at any point in time to lay claim to it. The effect of the two paragraphs is to introduce a requirement

which may be referred to as the "guarantee of singularity". If procedures are made available to enable a right or obligation to be conveyed by electronic methods instead of by using a paper document, it is necessary that the guarantee of singularity be one of the essential features of such procedures. Technical security devices providing such a guarantee of singularity would almost necessarily be built into any communication system offered to the trading communities and would need to demonstrate their reliability. However, there is also a need to overcome requirements of law that the guarantee of singularity be demonstrated, for example in the case where paper documents such as bills of lading are traditionally used. A provision along the lines of paragraph (3) is thus necessary to permit the use of electronic communication instead of paper documents.

116. The words "one person and no other person" should not be interpreted as excluding situations where more than one person might jointly hold title to the goods. For example, the reference to "one person" is not intended to exclude joint ownership of rights in the goods or other rights embodied in a bill of lading.

117. The notion that a data message should be "unique" may need to be further clarified, since it may lend itself to misinterpretation. On the one hand, all data messages are necessarily unique, even if they duplicate an earlier data message, since each data message is sent at a different time from any earlier data message sent to the same person. If a data message is sent to a different person, it is even more obviously unique, even though it might be transferring the same right or obligation. Yet, all but the first transfer might be fraudulent. On the other hand, if "unique" is interpreted as referring to a data message of a unique kind, or a transfer of a unique kind, then in that sense no data message is unique, and no transfer by means of a

data message is unique. Having considered the risk of such misinterpretation, the Commission decided to retain the reference to the concepts of uniqueness of the data message and uniqueness of the transfer for the purposes of article 17, in view of the fact that the notions of "uniqueness" or "singularity" of transport documents were not unknown to practitioners of transport law and users of transport documents. It was decided, however, that this Guide should clarify that the words "a reliable method is used to render such data message or messages unique" should be interpreted as referring to the use of a reliable method to secure that data messages purporting to convey any right or obligation of a person might riot be used by, or on behalf of, that person inconsistently with any other data messages by which the right or obligation was conveyed by or on behalf of that person.

118. Paragraph (5) is a necessary complement to the guarantee of singularity contained in paragraph (3). The need for security is an overriding consideration and it is essential to ensure not only that a method is used that gives reasonable assurance that the same data message is not multiplied, but also that no two media can be simultaneously used for the same purpose. Paragraph (5) addresses the fundamental need to avoid the risk of duplicate transport documents. The use of multiple forms of communication for different purposes, *e.g.*, paper-based communications for ancillary messages and electronic communications for bills of lading, does not pose a problem. However, it is essential for the operation of any system relying on electronic equivalents of bills of lading to avoid the possibility that the same rights could at any given time be embodied both in data messages and in a paper document. Paragraph (5) also envisages the situation where a party having initially agreed to engage in electronic communications has to switch to paper communications

where it later becomes unable to sustain electronic communications.

119. The reference to "terminating" the use of data messages is open to interpretation. In particular, the Model Law does not provide information as to who would effect the termination. Should an enacting state decide to provide additional information in that respect, it might wish to indicate, for example, that, since electronic commerce is usually based on the agreement of the parties, a decision to "drop down" to paper communications should also be subject to the agreement of all interested parties. Otherwise, the originator would be given the power to choose unilaterally the means of communication. Alternatively, an enacting State might wish to provide that, since paragraph (5) would have to be applied by the bearer of a bill of lading, it should be up to the bearer to decide whether it preferred to exercise its rights on the basis of a paper bill of lading or on the basis of the electronic equivalent of such a document, and to bear the costs for its decision.

120. Paragraph (5), while expressly dealing with the situation where the use of data messages is replaced by the. use of a paper document, is not intended to exclude the reverse situation. The switch from data message to a paper document should not affect any right that might exist to surrender the paper document to the issuer and start again using data messages.

121. The purpose of paragraph (6) is to deal directly with the application of certain laws to contracts for the carriage of goods by sea. For example, under the Hague and Hague-Visby Rules, a contract of carriage means a contract that is covered by a bill of lading. Use of a bill of lading or similar document of title results in the Hague and Hague-Visby Rules applying compulsorily to a contract of carriage. Those rules would not automatically apply to

contracts effected by one or more data message. Thus, a provision such as paragraph (6) is needed to ensure that the application of those rules is not excluded by the mere fact that data messages are used instead of a bill of a lading in paper form. While paragraph (1) ensures that data messages are effective means for carrying out any of the actions listed in article 16; that provision does not deal with the substantive rules of law that might apply to a contract contained in, or evidenced by, data messages.

122. As to the meaning of the phrase "that rule shall not be inapplicable" in paragraph (6) a simpler way of expressing the same idea might have been to provide that rules applicable to contracts of carriage evidenced by paper documents should also apply to contracts of carriage evidenced by data messages. However, given the broad scope of application of article 17, which covers not only bills of lading but also a variety of other transport documents, such a simplified provision might have had the undesirable effect of extending the applicability of rules such as the Hamburg Rules and the Hague Visby Rules to contracts to which such rules were never intended to apply. The Commission felt that the adopted wording was more suited to overcome the obstacle resulting from the fact that the Hague Visby Rules and other rules compulsorily applicable to bills of lading would not automatically apply to contracts of carriage evidenced by data messages, without inadvertently extending the application of such rules to other types of contracts.

References

A/51/17, paras. 139-172 and 198-204 (draft article x);

A/CN.9/421, paras. 53-103; A/CN.9/WG.IV/WP.69, paras 82-95;

A/50/17, paras. 307-309;

A/CN.9/407, paras. 106-118; A/CN.9/WG.IV/WP.67, annex; A/CN.9/WG.IV/WP.66, annex II;

A/49/17, paras. 198, 199 and 201;
A/CN.9/390, para. 155-158.

III. HISTORY AND BACKGROUND OF THE MODEL LAW

123. The UNCITRAL Model Law on Electronic Commerce was adopted by the United Nations Commission on International Trade Law (UNCITRAL) in 1996 in furtherance of its mandate to promote the harmonization and unification of international trade law, so as to remove unnecessary obstacles to international trade caused by inadequacies and divergences in the law affecting trade. Over the past quarter of a century, UNCITRAL, whose membership consists of States from all regions and of all levels of economic development, has implemented its mandate by formulating international conventions (the United Nations Conventions on Contracts for the International Sale of Goods, on the Limitation Period in the International Sale of Goods, on the Carriage of Goods by Sea, 1978 ("Hamburg Rules"), on the Liability of Operators of Transport Terminals in International Trade, on International Bills of Exchange and International Promissory Notes, and on Independent Guarantees and Stand-by Letters of Credit), model laws (the UNCITRAL Model Laws on International Commercial Arbitration, on International Credit Transfers and on Procurement of Goods, Construction and Services), the UNCITRAL Arbitration Rules, the UNCITRAL Conciliation Rules, and legal guides (on construction contracts, counter trade transactions and electronic funds transfers).

124. The Model Law was prepared in response to a major change in the means by communications are made between parties using computerized or other modern techniques in doing business (sometimes referred to as "trading partners"). The Model Law is intended serve as a

model to countries for the evaluation and modernization of certain aspects of their laws and practices in the field of commercial relationships involving the use of computerized or other modem communication techniques, and for the establishment of relevant legislation where none presently exists. The text of the Model Law, as reproduced above, is set forth in annex I to the report of UNCITRAL on the work of its twenty-ninth session[3].

125. The Commission, at its seventeenth session (1984), considered a report of the Secretary General entitled "Legal aspects of automatic data processing" (A/CN.9/254), which identified several legal issues relating to the legal value of computer records, the requirement of a "writing", authentication, general conditions, liability and bills of lading. The Commission took note of a report of the Working Party on Facilitation of International Trade Procedures (WP.4), which is jointly sponsored by the Economic Commission for Europe and the United Nations Conference on Trade and Development, and is responsible for the development of UN/EDIFACT standard messages. That report suggested that, since the legal problems arising in this field were essentially those of international trade law, the Commission as the core legal body in the field of international trade law appeared to be the appropriate central forum to undertake and coordinate the necessary action.[4] The Commission decided to place the subject of the legal implications of automatic data processing to the flow of international trade on its programme of work as a priority item.[5]

126. At its eighteenth session (1985), the Commission had before it a report by the Secretariat entitled "Legal value of computer records" (A/CN.9/265). That report came to the conclusion that, on a local level, there were fewer problems in the use of data stored in computers is

evidence in litigation than might have been expected. It noted that a more serious legal obstacle to the use of computers and computer-to-computer telecommunications in international trace arose out of requirements that documents had to be signed or be in paper form. After discussion of the report, the Commission adopted the following recommendation, which expresses some of the principles on which the Model Law is based :

> "The United Nations Commission on International Trade Law,
>
> "*Noting* that the use of automatic data processing (ADP) is about to become firmly established throughout the world in many phases of domestic and international trade as well as in administrative services,"
>
> "*Noting* also that legal rules based upon pre-ADP paper based means of documenting international trade may create an obstacle to such use of ADP in that they lead to legal insecurity or impede the efficient use of ADP when its use is otherwise justified,"
>
> "*Noting* further with appreciation the efforts of the Council of Europe, the Customs Co-operation Council and the United Nations Economic Commission for Europe to overcome obstacles to the use of ADP in international trade arising out of these legal rules,"
>
> "*Considering* at the same time that there is no need for a unification of the rules of evidence regarding the use of computer records in international trade, in view of the experience showing that substantial difference; in the ruler

of evidence as they apply to the paper-based system of documentation have caused so far no noticeable harm to the development of international trade,"

"*Considering* also that the developments in the use of ADP are creating a desirability in a number of legal systems for an adaptation of existing legal rules to these developments, having due regard, however, to the need to encourage the employment of such ADP means that would provide the same or greater reliability as paper-based documentation,

"1. *Recommends* to Governments :

(a) to review the legal rules affecting the use of computer records as evidence in litigation in order to eliminate unnecessary obstacles to their admission, to be assured that the rules are consistent with developments in technology, and to provide appropriate means for a court to evaluate the credibility of the data contained in those records;

(b) to review legal requirements that certain trade transactions or trade related documents be in writing, whether the written form is a condition to the enforceability or to the validity of the transaction or document, with a view to permitting, where appropriate, the transaction or document to be recorded and transmitted in computer-readable form;

(c) to review legal requirements of a handwritten signature or other paper-based method of authentication on trade related documents with a view to permitting, where appropriate, the use of electronic means of authentication;

(d) to receive legal requirements that documents for submission to Governments be in writing and manually signed with a view to permitting, where appropriate, such documents to be submitted in computer-readable form to those administrative services which have acquired the necessary equipment and established the necessary procedures;

2. *Recommends* to international organizations elaborating legal texts related to trade to take account of the present Recommendation in adopting such texts and, where appropriate, to consider modifying existing legal texts is line with the present Recommendation."[6]

127. That recommendation (hereinafter referred to as the "1985 UNCITRAL Recommendation") was endorsed by the General Assembly in resolution 40/71, paragraph 5(b), of 11 December, 1985 as follows :

"The General Assembly,

"...Calls upon Governments and international organizations to take action, where appropriate, in conformity with the Commission's recommendation so as to ensure legal security in the context of the widest possible use of automated data processing in international trade;...".[7]

128. As was pointed out in several documents and meetings involving the international electronic commerce community, *e.g.* in meetings of WP.4, there was a general

feeling that, in spite of the efforts made through the 1985 UNCITRAL Recommendation, little progress had been made to achieve the removal of the mandatory requirements in national legislation regarding the use of paper and handwritten signatures. It has been suggested by the Norwegian Committee on Trade Procedures (NORPRO) in a letter to the Secretariat that "one reason for this could be that the 1985 UNCITRAL Recommendation advises on the need for legal update but does not give any indication of how it could be done". In this vein, the Commission considered what follow-up action to the 1985 UNCITRAL Recommendation could usefully be taken so as to enhance the needed modernization of legislation. The decision by UNCITRAL to formulate model legislation on legal issues of electronic data interchange and related means of communication may be regarded as a consequence of the process that led to the adoption by the Commission of the 1985 UNCITRAL Recommendation.

129. At its twenty-first session (1988), the Commission considered a proposal to examine the need to provide for the legal principles that would apply to the formation of international commercial contracts by electronic means. It was noted that there existed no refined legal structure for the important and rapidly growing field of formation of contracts by electronic means and that future work in that area could help to fill a legal vacuum and to reduce uncertainties and difficulties encountered in practice. The Commission requested the Secretariat to prepare a preliminary study on the topic[8].

130. At its twenty-third session (1990), the Commission had before it a report entitled "Preliminary study of legal issues related to the formation of contracts by electronic means" (A/CN.9/333). The report summarized work that had been undertaken in the European Communities and

in the United States of America on the requirement of a "writing" as well as other issues that had been identified as arising in the formation of contracts by electronic means. The efforts to overcome some of those problems by the use of model communication agreements were also discussed[9].

131. At its twenty-fourth session (1991), the Commission had before it a report entitled "Electronic Data Interchange" (A/CN.9/350). The report described the current activities in the various organizations involved in the legal issues of electronic data interchange (EDI) and analysed the contents of a number of standard interchange agreements already developed or then being developed. It pointed put that such documents varied considerably according to the various needs of the different categories of users they were intended to serve and that the variety of contractual arrangements had sometimes been described as hindering the development of a satisfactory legal framework for the business use of electronic commerce. It suggested thai there was a need for a general framework that would identify the issues and provide a set of legal principles and basic legal rules governing communication through electronic commerce. It concluded that such a basic framework could, to a certain extent, be created by contractual arrangements between parties to an electronic commerce relationship and that the existing contractual frame works that were proposed to the community of users of electronic commerce were often incomplete, mutually incompatible, and inappropriate for international rise since they relied to a large extent upon the structures of local law.

* * * *

134. After deliberation, the Commission decided that a session of the Working Group of International Payments would be devoted to identifying the legal issues involved and to considering possible statutory provisions, and that

the Working Group would report to the Commission on the desirability and feasibility of undertaking further work such as the preparation of a standard communication agreement[10-11].

135. The Working Group on International Payments, at its twenty-fourth session, recommended that the Commission should undertake work towards establishing uniform legal rules on electronic commerce. It was agreed that the goals of such work should be to facilitate the increased use of electronic commerce and to meet the need for statutory provisions to be developed in the field of electronic commerce, particularly with respect to such issue as formation of contracts; risk and liability of commercial partners and third-party service providers involved in electronic commerce relationships; extended definitions of "writing" and "original" to be used in an electronic commerce environment; and issues of negotiability and documents of title (A/CN.9/360).

136. While it was generally felt that it was desirable to seek the high degree of legal certainty and harmonization provided by the detailed provisions of a uniform law, it was also felt that care should be taken to preserve a flexible approach to some issues where legislative action might be premature or inappropriate. As an example of such an issue, it was stated that it might be fruitless to attempt to provide legislative unification of the rules on evidence that may apply to electronic commerce messaging (*ibid.-*, para. 130). It was agreed that no decision should be taken at that early stage as to the final form or the final content of the legal rules to be prepared. In line with the flexible approach to be taken, it was noted that situations might arise where the preparation of model contractual clauses would be regarded as an appropriate way of addressing specific issues (*ibid.*, para. 132).

137. The Commission, at its twenty-fifth session (1992), endorsed the recommendation contained in the report of the Working Group (*ibid.*, paras. 129-133) and entrusted the preparation of legal rules on electronic commerce (which was then referred to as "electronic data interchange" or "EDI") to the Working Group on International Payments, which it renamed the Working Group on Electronic Data Interchange.[12]

138. The Working Group devoted its twenty-fifth to twenty-eighth sessions to the preparation of legal rules applicable to "electronic data interchange (EDI) and other modern means of communication" (reports of those sessions are found in documents A/CN.9/373, 387, 390 and 406).[13]

139. The Working Group carried out its task on the basis of background working papers prepared by the Secretariat on possible issues to be included in the Model Law. Those background papers included A/CN.9/WG.IV/WP.53 (Possible issues to be included in the programme of future work on the legal aspects of EDI) and A/CN.9/WG.IV/WP.55 (Outline of possible uniform rules on the legal aspects of electronic data interchange). The draft articles of the Model Law were submitted by the Secretariat in documents A/CN.9/WG.IV/WP.57, 60 and 62. The Working Group also had before it a proposal by the United Kingdom of Great Britain and Northern Ireland relating to the possible contents of the draft Model Law (A/CN.9/WG.IV/WP.58).

140. The Working Group noted that, while practical solutions to the legal difficulties raised by the use of electronic commerce were often sought within contracts (A/CN.9/WG.IV/WP.53 paras. 35-36), the contractual approach to electronic commerce was developed not only because of its intrinsic advantages such as its flexibility,

but also for lack of specific provisions of statutory or case law. The contractual approach was found to be limited in that it could not overcome any of the legal obstacles to the use of electronic commerce that might result from mandatory provisions of applicable statutory or case law. In that respect, one difficulty inherent in the use of communication agreements resulted from uncertainty as to the weight that would be carried by some contractual stipulations in case of litigation. Another limitation to the contractual approach resulted from the fact that parties to a contract could not effectively regulate the rights and obligations of third parties. At least for those parties not participating in the contractual arrangement, statutory law based on a model law or an international convention seemed to be needed (*see* A/CN.9/350, para 107).

141. The Working Group considered preparing uniform rules with the aim of eliminating the legal obstacles to, and uncertainties in, the use of modern communication techniques, where effective removal of such obstacles and uncertainties could only be achieved by statutory provisions. One purpose of the uniform rules was to enable potential electronic commerce users to establish a legally secure electronic commerce relationship by way of a communication agreement within a closed network. The second purpose of the uniform rules was to support the use of electronic commerce outside such a closed network, *i.e.*, in an open environment. However, the aim of the uniform rules was to enable, and not to impose, the use of EDI and related means of communication. Moreover, the aim of the uniform rules was not to deal with electronic commerce relationships from a technical perspective but rather to create a legal environment that would be as secure as possible, so as to facilitate the use of electronic commerce between communicating parties.

142. As to the form of the uniform rules, the Working Group was agreed that it should proceed with its work on the assumption that the uniform rules should be prepared in the form of statutory provisions. While it was agreed that the form of the text should be that of a "model law", it was felt, at first, that, owing to the special nature of the legal text being prepared, a more flexible term than "model law" needed to be found. It was observed that the title should reflect that the text contained a variety of provisions relating to existing rules scattered throughout various parts of the national laws in an enacting State. It was thus a possibility that enacting States would not incorporate the text as a whole and that the provisions of such a "model law" might not appear together in any one particular place in the national law. The text could be described, in the parlance of one legal system, as a "miscellaneous statute amendment act". The Working Group agreed that this special nature of the text would be better reflected by the use of the term "model statutory provisions". The view was also expressed that the nature and purpose of the "model statutory provisions" could be explained in an introduction of guidelines accompanying the text.

143. At its twenty-eighth session, however, the Working Group reviewed its earlier decision to formulate a legal text in the form of "model statutory provisions" (A/CN.9/390, para, 16). It was widely felt that the use of the term "model statutory provisions" might raise uncertainties as to the legal nature of the instrument. While some support was expressed for the retention of the term "model statutory provisions", the widely prevailing view was that the term "model law" should be preferred. It was widely felt that, as a result of the course taken by the Working Group as its work progressed towards the completion of the text, the model statutory provisions could be regarded as a balanced

and discrete set of rules, which could also be implemented as a whole in a single instrument (A/CN.9/406, para. 75). Depending on the situation in each enacting State, however, the Model Law could be implemented in various ways, either as a single statute or in various pieces of legislation.

144. The text of the draft Model Law as approved by the Working Group at its twenty-eighth session was sent to all Governments and to interested international organizations for comment. The comments received were reproduced in document A/CN.9/409 and Add. 1-4. The text of the draft articles of the Model Law as presented to the Commission by the Working Group was contained in the annex to document A/CN.9/406.

145. At its twenty-eighth session (1995), the Commission adopted the text of articles 1 and 3 to 11 of the draft Model Law and, for lack of sufficient time, did not complete its review of the draft Model Law, which was placed on the agenda of the twenty-ninth session of the commission.[14]

146. The Commission,at its twenty-eighth session,[15] recalled that, at its twenty-seventh session (1994), general support had been expressed in favour of a recommendation made by the Working Group that preliminary work should be undertaken on the issue of negotiability and transferability of rights in goods in a computer-based environment as soon as the preparation of the Model Law had been completed.[16] It was noted that, on that basis, a preliminary debate with respect to future work to be undertaken in the field of electronic data interchange had been held in the context of the twenty-ninth session of the Working Group (for the report on that debate. *see* A/CN.9/407, paras. 106-118). At that session, the Working Group also considered proposals by the International Chamber of Commerce (A/CN.9/WG.IVAVP.65) and the United Kingdom of Great Britain and Northern Ireland (A/CN.9/WG.IV/WP.66)

relating to the possible inclusion in the draft Model Law of additional provisions to the effect of ensuring that certain terms and conditions that might be incorporated in a data message by means of a mere reference would be recognized as having the same degree of legal effectiveness as if they had been fully stated in the text of the data message (for the report on the discussion, *see* A/CN.9/407, paras. 100-105). It was agreed that the issue of incorporation by reference might need to be considered in the context of future work on negotiability and transferability of rights in goods (A/CN.9/407. para-103). The Commission endorsed the recommendation made by the Working Group that the Secretariat should be entrusted with the preparation of a background study on negotiability and transferability of EDI transport documents, with particular emphasis on EDI maritime transport documents, taking into account the views expressed and the suggestions made at the twenty-ninth session of the Working Group.[17]

47. On, the basis of the study prepared by the Secretariat (A/CN.9/WG.IV/WP.69) Working Group, at its thirtieth session, discussed the issues of transferability of rights in the context of transport documents and approved the text of draft statutory provisions dealing with the specific issues of contracts of carriage of goods involving the use of data messages (for the report on that session, *see* A/CN.9/421). The test of those draft provisions as presented to the Commission by the Working Group for final review and possible addition as part II of the Model Law was contained in the annex to document A/CN.9/421.

148. In preparing the Model Law, the Working Group noted that it would be useful to provide in a commentary additional information concerning the Model Law. In particular, at the twenty-eighth session of the Working Group, during which the text of the draft Model Law was

finalized for submission to the Commission, there was general support for a suggestion that the draft Model Law should be accompanied by a guide to assist States in enacting and applying the draft Model Law. The guide, much of which could be drawn from the *travaux preparatoires* of the draft Model Law, would also be helpful to users of electronic means of communication as well as to scholars in that area. The Working Group noted that, during its deliberations at that session, it had proceeded on the assumption that the draft Model Law would be accompanied by a guide. For example, the Working Group had decided in respect of a number of issues not to settle them in the draft Model Law but to address them in the guide so as to provide guidance to States enacting the draft Model Law. The Secretariat was requested to prepare a draft and submit it to the Working Group for consideration at its twenty-ninth session (A/CN.9/406, para. 177).

149. At its twenty-ninth session, the Working Group discussed the draft Guide to Enactment of the Model Law (hereinafter referred to as "the draft Guide") as set forth in a note prepared by the Secretariat (A/CN.9/WG.IV/WP.64). The Secretariat was requested to prepare a revised version of the draft Guide reflecting the decisions made by the Working Group and taking into account the various views, suggestions and concerns that had been expressed at that session. At its twenty-eighth session, the Commission placed the draft Guide to Enactment of the Model Law on the agenda of its twenty-ninth session.[18]

150. At its twenty-ninth session (1996), the Commission, after consideration of the text of the draft Model Law as revised by the drafting group, adopted the following decision at its 605th meeting, on 12 June, 1996 :

> ***"The United Nations Commission on International Trade Law;***

Recalling its mandate under General Assembly resolution 2205 (XXI) of 17 December, 1966 to further the progressive harmonization and unification of the law of international trade, and in that respect to bear in mind the interests of all peoples, and in particular those of developing countries, in the extensive development of international trade,

Noting that an increasing number of transactions in international trade are carried out by means of electronic data interchange and other means of communication commonly referred to as 'electronic commerce', which involve the use of alternatives to paper-based forms of communication and storage of information,

Recalling the recommendation on the legal value of computer records adopted by the Commission at its eighteenth session, in 1985, and paragraph 5(b) of General Assembly resolution 40/71 of 11 December, 1985 calling upon Governments and international organisations to take action, where appropriate, in conformity with the recommendation of the Commission[19] so as to ensure legal security in the context of the widest possible use of automated data processing in international trade,

Being of the opinion that the establishment of a model law facilitating the use of electronic commerce, and acceptable to States with different legal, social and economic systems, contributes to the development of harmonious international economic relations,

Being convinced that the UNCITRAL Model Law on electronic Commerce will significantly assist all States in enhancing their legislation governing the use of alternatives to paper-based forms of communication and storage of information, and in formulating such legislation where none currently exists,

1. *Adopts the* UNCITRAL Model Law on Electronic Commerce as it appears in annex I to the report on the current session;

2. *Requests* the Secretary-General to transmit the text of the UNCITRAL Model Law on Electronic Commerce, together with the Guide to Enactment of the Model Law prepared by the Secretariat, to Governments and other interested bodies;

3. *Recommends* that all States give favourable consideration to the UNCITRAL Model Law on Electronic Commerce when they enact or revise their laws, in view of the need for uniformity of the law applicable to alternatives to paper-based forms of communication and storage of information.[20]

REFERENCES

1. *See Official Records of the General Assembly, Fortieth Session Supplement No. 17* (A/ 40/ 17) Chap. VI, sec. B.
2. Reference materials listed by symbols in this Guide belong to the following three categories of documents :

   A/50/17 and A/51/17 are the reports of UNCITRAL to the General Assembly on the work of its twenty-eighth and twenty-ninth sessions, held in 1995 and 1996, respectively;

   A/CN.9/... documents are reports and notes discussed by UNCITRAL in the context of its annual session, including reports presented by the Working Group to the Commission;

   A/CN.9/WG.IV/... documents are working papers considered by the UNCITRAL Working Group on Electronic Commerce (formerly known as the UNCITRAL Working Group on Electronic Data Interchange) in the preparation of the Model Law.
3. *Official records of the General Assembly, Fifty-first Session, Supplement No. 17* (A/5 1/17), Annex I.
4. *"Legal aspects of automatic trade data interchange"* (TRADE/WP.4R. 185/Rev. 1). The report submitted to the Working Party is reproduced in A/CN.9/238, annex.

5. *Official Records of the General Assembly Thirty-ninth Session Supplement No.* 77(A/39/ 17), para 136.
6. *Official Records of the General Assembly Fortieth Session, Supplement No.* 17(A/40/ 17), para 360.
7. Resolution 40/71 was reproduced in *United Nations Commission on International Trade Law Yearbook,* 1985. vol. XVI, Part One, D. (United Nations publications, Sales No. E87.V.4).
8. *Official Records of the General Assembly, Forty-third Session, Supplement No.* 17(A/43/ 17). para 46 and 47, and *ibid., Forty-fourth Session. Supplement No.* 17(A/44/17), para 289.
9. *Ibid., Forty-fifth Session, Supplement No.* 17 (A/45/17), paras 38 to 40.

10-11. *Official Records of the General Assembly, Forty-sixth Session, Supplement No. 17* (A/ 46 / 17), paras to 317.

12. *Ibid., Forty-seventh Session, Supplement No.* /7(A/47/17), paras 141 to 148.
13. The notion of "EDI and related means of communication" as used by the Working Group is not to be construed as a reference to narrowly defined EDI under article 2(b) of the Model Law but to a variety of trade-related uses of modern communication techniques that was later referred to broadly under the rubric of "electronic commerce". The Model Law is not intended only for application in the context of existing communication techniques but rather as a set of flexible rules that should accommodate foreseeable technical developments. It should also be emphasized that the purpose of the Model Law is not only to establish rules for the movement of information communicated by means of data message but equally to deal with the storage of information in data message that are not intended for communication.
14. *Official Records of the General Assembly, Fiftieth Session. Supplement No.* /7(A/50/17), para 306.
15. *Ibid., para* 307.
16. *Ibid., Forty-ninth Session, Supplement No.* 17(A/49/17), para 201.
17. *Ibid.. Fortieth Session, Supplement No.* 17(A/50/17), para 309.
18. *Ibid., para* 306.
19. *Ibid., Fortieth Session, Supplement No.* 17(A/40/17), paras 354-360.
20. *Ibid., Fifty-first Session, Supplement No.* 17(A/51/17), para 209.

12 CYBER CRIME IN INDIA

- *Indian Airlines was defrauded of several lakh rupees when open-ended tickets for shorter sectors were issued in fictitious names by some staff members. Computer records were tampered with to show longer sectors and refunds obtained.*
- *In the Purulia arms drop case, the main players used the Internet extensively for international communication, planning and logistics.*
- *Post-Pokhran, hackers gained access to the Bhabha Atomic Research Centre computer system and pulled out vital data.*
- *Computer professionals who prepared the software in an MBBS examination were found responsible for altering data by manipulating the computer's corrector reader. They had been giving an upward revision of scores to students in return for a hefty fee.*

Cyber crime has now become reality in India. Difficult to detect, seldom reported and even more difficult to prove, computer-related crime lacks a traditional paper audit trail, is away from conventional policing and requires specialists with a sound understanding of computer technology.

With the country poised to enter the information superhighway—over three million computers in place—

and industry and banks networked, the realisation of the dangers and threats is finally sinking in. "The biggest challenge is jurisdiction. Technology has eroded the concept of state boundaries and created a borderless world," says N.R. Wasan, deputy director, CBI, who is credited with computerising the investigating agency in 1992. In the age of automation, computer applications are likely targets for theft, fraud, vandalism, extortion, and even espionage, which can be termed the darker side of the computer revolution.

In the West, hackers have managed to sabotage data and computer networks of key defence organisations, acting on "behalf of foreign intelligence operatives, steal and sell cellular phone numbers, and use the Internet for banking frauds, whereby encrypted messages can be decrypted and used fraudulently.

It was the securities scam of 1992 that woke up enforcement agencies in India to the potential threat of more banks and financial institutions being targeted by professional white-collar criminals. "It was scary and it has taken a long time before we are deciding to act," says Dr. K.P.C. Gandhi, director of Hyderabad's Forensic Laboratory.

Software professionals, specialists from FBI, Interpol, IBM, and London's Computer Forensic Limited recently conducted a brainstorming session with officials from banks, insurance companies as well as Central and state police organisations, on India's vulnerability to computer-related crime. "India is virgin territory, if hackers or computer cartels break into computers and telecommunications systems, they can create havoc," says Keiron Sharp of Interpol. Recent studies show that the real threat is mostly from insiders, with employees having access to computer systems and external threats are also on the rise.

Technology has integrated the financial markets, access to the electronic market is open to all— including the criminal. The probable hacker could well be an insider looking for quick financial returns. "We know that computer crime could emerge as a major problem area for the law-enforcement agencies in India—that is why an ounce of prevention is better than a pound of cure," says R.K. Raghavan, the CBI director. The techno-savvy Raghavan has been focussing his attention on computerising cases handled by the agency so far and has also started a CBI homepage.

Most system penetrations go unreported, say forensic and CBI officials, even though there has been adequate publicity in recent years about system risks and attacks. Corporations and government agencies are often hesitant to report and prosecute computer break-ins because of the risk of adverse publicity, loss of public confidence and the possible charge of managerial incompetence. Further, organisations such as "banks fear lawsuits based on the emerging 'standards of care.' These sentiments are echoed by Kevin Griffin, special agent in the Federal Bureau of Investigation (FBI) who finds the same situation prevalent in America. He says, "Companies don't come forward to report these incidents because they don't want negative publicity. They also fear that proprietary information may become public".

Sample a few of the cases that were brought to the attention of investigators almost a year *after* the incidents. Punjab National Bank suffered a loss of close to Rs. 1.39 crore when the computer records were manipulated to create false debits and credits. In the Bank of Baroda, Rs 2.5 lakh was misappropriated through the computerised creation of false bank accounts. We want bank managers and other officials of financial institutions to come forward and report such crimes to us straightaway, but they are reluctant.

A more well-known case is that of Mahanagar Telephone Nigam Limited (MTNL) in Delhi. A junior telecom official was charged for reversing electronic telephone meter systems, thereby allowing some commercial export houses to make overseas calls without the charges being directed to their telephone numbers—again by manipulating MTNL's computer terminals.

In the absence of sufficient checks, the behemoth Indian Railways has also fallen victim to computer crime. The computerised reservation records in Mumbai were manipulated to accommodate favoured persons; money was siphoned out through false accounting by recategorising upper class monthly tickets as second class seasonal tickets; the computer system in a metropolitan city was turned off, ostensibly because it needed repairs, but in reality so that one group could issue manual tickets to customers in return for bribes.

1998 : WHAT HAPPENED?	
Virus contamination	27.0%
Notebook theft	24.0%
Insider abuse of net access	12.8%
Telecom fraud	6.9%
Unauthorised access by insiders	6.7%
Theft of property info	5.8%
Financial fraud	5.3%
Sabotage	4.5%
System penetration by outsiders	3.5%
Spoofing	1.0%
Active wiretapping	1.4%
Telecom eavesdropping	1.1%

The computer as an instrument to aid crime is on the rise in a broad spectrum of areas, from business espionage to stealing cellular time. It's a cause for worry for mobile telephone operators such as Airtel and Essar, particularly with regard to the growing problem of individuals using cellular phones and electronically billing charges to other customers. In these cases, offenders obtain cellular billing identification codes by using scanning devices, which are small parabolic antennae connected to portable computers or laptops. When activated, these scanners capture and store account numbers transmitted by cellular, phones. No case till date has come to light in India, though.

"The offenders operate nearby net connections on highways, because motorists frequently make calls from their cars," says a revenue intelligence officer. Once they capture the computerised billing codes, they programme these codes into other cellular phones simply by hooking up the phone to a personal computer. Then, using software originally developed by programmers in London, they reprogramme the signal chip in the cellular phone. The use of this software, which is easy to copy and use, is spreading across the United States and Canada.

Without effective cyberlaws in place, Indian companies are already permitting the use of' credit cards for transactions through the Internet. None of these transactions are secure as the card numbers are not encrypted and checked. "So if someone else knows your credit card number, he may punch it in and leave you holding a fat bill," says a CBI officer. There is also no efficient way to verify an address given on the phone as belonging to the person whose account number is stated. Merchants who take verbal orders for merchandise on credit are facing mounting losses from rip-offs.

Even the Personal Identification Number (PIN) of a credit card, derived solely by an algorithmic conversion of customer data, is not secure. PIN pads do not guarantee secrecy since too many people have access to the secret number, which is generated by a computer and written on a letter handled by computer staff, mailmen and the customer's family and associates.

"Some time ago a 15-year-old schoolboy withdrew huge amounts of money from Citibank's ATM in Delhi's commercial hub. He was subsequently caught and it was later discovered that his sister worked in the bank," says Wasan.

1998 : WHO BROKE IN?

Human error	55%
Disgruntled employee	9%
Dishonest employee	10%
Computer Virus	4%
Outsiders	2%
Physical threat	20%

Clearly, it's time for a cyber police force to come to the rescue. And strategies to combat cyber crime and introduce legal measures are on the anvil.* A draft for a proposed Information and Technology Act, drawn up jointly by the Department of Electronics and the CBI, shall combat cyber crime before the cabinet. The Act provides for penalties for offences such as tampering of computer source documents, committing electronic forgery and cheating, unauthorised access to computer networks and databases and making available obscene material on the Internet. The National Computer Crime Resource Centre, a body comprising

*An Act will now deal with this grey area of law : defining a computer crime, fixing suitable penalties.

experts and professionals, is also likely to be set up in order to establish rules, regulations and standards of authentication of electronic records.

What's is of utmost importance about the proposed Act is that it provides for a comprehensive legislation defining a computer crime. This would entail amendments in the Indian Evidence Act, the Indian Penal Code, the Bankers Book of Evidence and the Companies Act. "A floppy now is not admissible in the court. Instead, huge bank ledgers are accepted. This will change when the Act becomes law," says a CBI official. Putting penal offences and banking secrecy laws on an equal footing, feel officials, will go a long way in tackling computer crimes.

COMUTERSPEAK

Term	*Definition*
Hackers	Use illegal methods of accessing a computer resource
Crackers	Program to extract information
Cyber-crime	Activity via the computer network that crosses the legal parameters
Stealers	Beg/borrow/steal passwords/steal serial numbers

Technocrats feel that the CBI should also have a central computer crime response wing to act as a nodal agency to advise the state and other investigative agencies to guide and coordinate in computer crime investigations. Says an official, "The CBI and state police agencies should immediately set up an exclusive computer investigation centre to train, supervise and investigate such crimes."

India's passion for software stocks and professionals is compounding the problem of computer crime in the country. Investor confidence in this sector has caught the fancy of foreign institutional investors, prompting many companies to raise the ceiling on foreign institutional ownership to 30 per cent from 24 per cent. India's most successful software firms earn over 70 per cent of their revenue from exporting services, mainly to the United States.

Says Kevin Griffin of the FBI, who investigates computer crimes : "India has some of the best computer programmers in the world. Surely you'll also have the best hackers." And the highly skilled inventory of computer professionals has caught the attention of global enforcement agencies.

"It is just a matter of time before computer programmers realise that there is more money to be made by hacking than by working in the United States," remarks Sanjay Dhawan, director, information risk management at KPMG Peat Marwick.

With trading on the country's stock exchanges going online, the RBI insisting on 70 per cent of banking functions to be computerised by 2001 and the Central Vigilance Commission wanting to introduce electronic payments by all listed companies, it could be an opportune time for the hackers to strike. The incidence of frauds, above Rs 1 crore, in the central bank in the past three years has already increased. Says RBI's deputy governor S.P. Talwar : "With computerisation progressing at its present pace, there is a crying need for safeguarding access controls and security checks".

In the words of Cosmos, the character in the motion picture, *Sneakers* : "The world is not run by weapons anymore or energy or money. It's run by ones and zeros—little bits of data. It's all electrons... and there's a war there."

Bank Robbers Become Cyber Savvy

In the era of Web, the very definition of robbery is undergoing a change. Conventional methods of looting are passe. Thieves have gone hi-tech. No more do you require hardcore weapons or goondas. Computers will do it for you now. Modems offer ready points of entry for spies, thieves, disgruntled employees or bored teens. And the weapon is just a keystroke away.

Believe it or not, a large public sector bank in India was electronically molested recently by hackers who allegedly transferred cash to the tune of Rs 60 lakh by invading the bank's network. "This is just the tip of the iceberg. A majority of companies and people are not aware that somewhere, someone is spying on them," says Vineet Nayar, president, HCL Comnet. He points out that there is every possibility of an organisation losing trade secrets or having their operations sabotaged if it is not secured properly.

HCL Comnet offers security solutions across the globe by providing customised network security and specialises in the banking sector, high-tech software and Internet Service Providers. One time hobbyists, the present-day hackers are the blue-eyed boys handling all forms of professional white-collar crime, especially corporate espionage. And they leave no trail!

Indian companies don't seem to bother even after computer hackers created havoc at the Citibank causing an estimated loss of $500 million and teenage hackers from Germany vandalised the Bhabha Atomic Research Centre (BARC) mail server by accessing sensitive e-mail in the wake of the Pokhran explosions. "It is like building a house without locks. Your home can never be safe. This applies to computer networks too," says Nayar, whose company has launched a comprehensive safety system through E-secure, a division of HCL Comnet. Once the hacker steps inside the front door there is is no stopping him. Nobody locks the doors between the kitchen, dining and drawing rooms. It is similar story once a prankster enters a network.

In collaboration with Checkpoint, Security Dynamics, NetPartners and WebTrends, E-Secure provides a watchdog policy for safe networking. E-Secure is currently providing security solutions to the National Stock Exchange, the home ministry, the ministry of defence, the Indian Navy, the Stock Holding Corporation and a couple of private banks in India.

If money in banks cannot be protected, how safe is your e-mail correspondence? "Zero," says Hanif Zohrab, product manager (data security and Internet services), HCL Comnet, "If there is no safety system such as encryption software or authentication policy." That's not all. In white-collar crime, enemies come as friends. For example, the latest dread is a Happy-99 e-mail doing the rounds, as sniffers. If you have received this mail and your network is unsafe, you're finished. These are programmes planted in a computer which is connected to a network and act as hidden recorders. "They inject worms through which you can get inside information on anything and everything flowing through your company," explains Zohrab.

Despite these horror stories, a majority of the companies have not installed rudimentary defences. They insist that employees use hard-to-guess passwords. A step-by-step guide on hacking through various Websites has already opened up avenues for software savvy Indians, making their profession exotic. With a dozen ways to steal passwords—Trojan horses password cracker and file scavengers cyberpranksters, the cyber-police are having a tough time protecting security on the Net.

Improving Vigilance Administration in Banks

The Central Vigilance Commission Ordinance 1998 under Section 8(l)(h) directs that the power and function of the CVC will be the following :

> "exercise superintendence over the vigilance administration of the various Ministries of the Central Government or corporations established by or under any Central Act, Government companies, societies and local authorities owned or controlled by that Government".

2. Improving vigilance administration is possible only if system improvements are made to prevent the possibilities of corruption and also encourage a culture of honesty. In exercise of the powers conferred on the CVC by Section 8(l)(h), the following instructions are issued for compliance:

2.1 Electronics Clearance System

2.1.1 All the banking companies, financial institutions under the purview of the CVC will have to compulsorily offer electronic clearance services to their customers with immediate effect. This step is visualised as a method of checking fraud because a significant part of the frauds in the banks are related to the remittances and collection in the payment system.

2.1.2 The Reserve Bank of India will put up a network of 438 VSATs linked with their hub so that the Wide Area Network (WAN) becomes operational, within one year. The CVC will take up the matter with concerned authorities to see that requisite transponder capacity is made available to RBI. RBI may examine whether the spare capacity of earth stations in the software technology parks of the

Department of Electronics can be utilised by them to quickly set up a WAN so that the electronic clearance system becomes operational at the earliest. RBI must be able to have its VSAT network in place latest before 1-1-2000.

2.2 *Computerisation of the Branches of the Banks*

2.2.1 All the banks must ensure that 70% of their business is captured through computerisaion before 1-1-2001. As this issue is directly related to improving the vigilance administration in the banks, this will not be an issue to be negotiated by the bank management with the unions. This principle will be applicable mutatis mutandis to all concerned with the computerisation of the clearing houses.

2:2.2 In order to achieve this goal, the banks will need technical manpower both at entry level and at supervisory levels. Within the present framework they can fill up posts up to 25% through direct recruitment. This flexibility must be used for inducting both at entry level and senior levels, competent technical manpower so that lack of availability of skilled manpower does not become a negative factor in slowing the pace of computerisation of the banks in achieving their target of computerising the banks by 1 -1 -2001.

2.2.3 One of the difficulties expressed by the banks was that the hardware and software was not available and more important even after sale service were not satisfactory. In the context of achieving the goal of computerisation before 1-1-2001, MAIT and NASSCOM must be asked to gear up their services and interact closely with the Indian Banks Association as well as the individual banks to resolve the issue. They could give a schedule of how these difficulties can be overcome.

2.2.4 At the time of computerisation, we should also take care of the need for encryption as well as safety in the banking operations so that computer frauds are not encouraged, for which the DRDO may be consulted.

2.3 Lack of Communication between Banks

2.3.1 All cases of wilful default of Rs. 25 lakhs and above will be reported by al! banks to RBI as and when they occur or are detected.

2.3.2 Whether a matter is a case of wilful default will be decided in each bank by a Committee of Officers.

2.3.3 The RBI will circulate the information received from the banks of wilful default, every three months. The data with the RBI will also be accessible directly by the banks concerned after the WAN is installed in position.

2.3.4 There should be greater intra bank communication about wilful default, frauds, cheating cases etc. so that the same bank does not get exploited in different branches by the same defaulting parties.

TECHNOLOGY TOMORROW

Thumbnail-Sized Displays, Internet in Your Car, Wristwatch PCs

Vision of the Future

Bulky displays and eyestrain are commonly associated with computing, but that could soon be the thing of the past.

Companies have begun addressing this need with what arc called micro displays. As the name implies, micro displays are small displays about the size of a semiconductor chip or a thumbnail. However, the picture projected by a micro display is anything but small. Built-in optics enlarge the image from 10 to 1,000 time. The result is a miniature device that can create the same image as a bulky TV set or monitor but consumes only 400 milliwatts of power-about a tenth of what's used in a standard laptop display. The implementation can come in the form of a pair of glasses, with two micro displays built in. The image produced by this is equivalent to that of a 19" display at 2.5 feel.

Among the three major technologies popular today, the most promising one —LCOS or Liquid Crystal on Silicon—works by switching liquid-crystal material from transparent to opaque and back by altering the voltage applied to it. In many ways LCOS like a magnified miniature LCD.

However, there are problems to be solved before these products can be picked off the shelf-such as the unwanted magnification of screen defects.

Further information on it is available at: www.inviso.com, www.kopin.com, www.mcgweb.com. www.microdisplay.com, www.ti.com.

e-Picture Frame

The front end of this new device looks pretty much the same as your wood-and-glass picture frame. Routed to its back are some power and phone connections. Users plug in the cords, set up a photo account at the Ceiva Website—www.ceiva.com—and the appliance dials into the account overnight to download and display digital images. The whole unit is powered by an internal processor with an embedded proprietary operating system and 1 MB of memory. A V34 modem handles the nightly dial-up. The cost of the frame is $250, and Ceiva also charges a monthly $3 for Web space.

A Really Big Game of Tetris

What would you do if you were stranded on Rhode Island alone? You sure won't get bored if you happen to be a Tetris addict. Brown University, on the Rhode Island, sports a towering 14-storey video display that allows passers by to play a game of Tetris, which can be seen for several kilometers. The project, called " La Bastille", is currently the world's largest fully-functional Tetris game. It contains 11 custom built circuit boards, a 12-storey data network, a PC running Linux, and over 10,000 Christmas lights.

Information on Your Wrists

Casio has unveiled a series of three watches that can act as your, PC or camera. He pleaded guilty last month to 12 counts and now is serving six months in jail. Says Dyson : "He's fortunate the law got there first.

Online, trout was malicious. In jail, Jason Mewhiney is clean-cut and "very shy—until you put him in front of a computer," says Corporal Alain Chabot, one of the arresting officers. "Sometimes these kids are Einsteins in front of their screens, but drop them off downtown without a bus map, and they're helpless."

Dyson's other nemesis, u4ea, is still at large. Word in the hacker underground is that u4ea is a mole, but an FBI spokeswoman denies it and says an investigation continues. Dyson believes he has traced u4ea's identity to that of a young man in the Washington area, but he isn't handing that information to the FBI. Dyson wants to exact his own revenge. "I have no intention of dragging u4ea to the authorities," he says, fingering his .45. "This is strictly between him and me. I will do whatever it takes to see this end come about."

INDEX

K

L